Missouri's
Confederate

MISSOURI BIOGRAPHY SERIES

WILLIAM E. FOLEY, EDITOR

Missouri's Confederate

CLAIBORNE FOX JACKSON

and the Creation of Southern Identity in the Border West

Christopher Phillips

University of Missouri Press
Columbia and London

Copyright ©2000 by
The Curators of the University of Missouri
University of Missouri Press, Columbia, Missouri 65201
Printed and bound in the United States of America
All rights reserved
5 4 3 2 1   04 03 02 01 00

Library of Congress Cataloging-in-Publication Data

Phillips, Christopher, 1959–
    Missouri's Confederate : Claiborne Fox Jackson and the creation of
southern identity in the border West / Christopher Phillips.
        p.   cm.—(Missouri biography series)
    Includes bibliographical references and index.
    ISBN 0-8262-1272-7 (alk. paper)
    1. Jackson, Claiborne Fox, 1806-1862.   Missouri—Politics and
government—1861–1865.   3. Governors—Missouri—Biography.
I. Title.   II. Series.

    E469.J33 P47   2000
    977.8'03–dc21   00-021061

©™ This paper meets the requirements of the
American National Standard for Permanence of Paper
for Printed Library Materials, Z39.48, 1984.

Text design: Elizabeth K. Young
Jacket design: Susan Ferber
Typesetter: Bookcomp, Inc.
Printer and binder: Edwards Brothers, Inc.
Typefaces: Galliard, Helvetica Neue Light Condensed, Meridien Medium

For Jill,
and for Bill Parrish,

a southerner who went west, and a westerner who went south.
Both found Missouri in their passings.

CONTENTS

PREFACE

THIS BOOK IS not so much about a man as it is about a man's world. For a study of Claiborne Fox Jackson, I feel this is only proper. Yet because biographers are by nature Ptolemaists, constructing universes in which their subjects are centers, any biography that adopts a heliocentric model cuts decidedly against the grain. Call me Copernicus, for I did not write this book as a traditional biography, if even such a thing exists.

When William Foley, editor of the Missouri Biography Series for the University of Missouri Press, first approached me about writing this book, I was, in a word, reluctant. Heeding biographer Paul Murray Kendall's mantra that life-writers bear the burden of making their subjects significant, I found myself unable initially to legitimate Jackson as the subject of an entire biography. Having already published one book in the series (on Nathaniel Lyon, the leading federal protagonist in Missouri's secession crisis), I was well aware of Claib Jackson. Elected Missouri's governor in 1860 after a career as a state legislator and Democratic party chief, Jackson served as focal point for a movement for the neutral state's secession before a federal sortie exiled him from office. Replaced with a provisional government that maintained allegiance to the Union, Jackson gathered and led a rump assembly that drafted an ordinance of secession in October 1861. He then spearheaded the acceptance of that ordinance by the Confederate Congress, with Missouri becoming the Confederacy's twelfth state the following month despite the largest portion of his home state's populace refusing to recognize the act. Just over a year later, in December 1862, after struggling in vain for military support to liberate Missouri, Jackson died in Arkansas, an apparent footnote to the war that engulfed his region and that consumed him.[1]

Neither bit character nor leading man, Claib Jackson nonetheless stole what was arguably the most important scene of Missouri's historical tableau, earning him lasting acclaim—or scorn—for his brief yet showstopping performance. Yet his star streaked across Missouri's darkening sky so quickly that I could not envision writing a study of him that did not perforce devote itself largely either to the intricacies of Missouri's prewar politics or to the explosive few months of Jackson's gubernatorial career and wartime service.

1. Paul Murray Kendall, *The Art of Biography,* 12–18.

With so many good books and articles already published on each, I could not perceive the importance of writing yet another on either.

Yet as I contemplated Jackson, I began to realize that he was a player in a drama much larger than his own life. Moreover, in my opinion, the tale has not yet been adapted adequately. The circumstance of Missouri's Civil War—one that formally began with the establishment of and violence in Kansas, well before the riot in St. Louis in May 1861 and the ensuing four years of bitter partisan warfare—allowed historians for many years to neglect, even negate, the ideology of nineteenth-century, proslavery Missourians. The unwillingness of historians to legitimate the worldview of these Missourians caused a frustrated Floyd Shoemaker, longtime director of the State Historical Society of Missouri, in 1954 to complain (singling out the topic of the Kansas struggle, for which those Missourians are known most notoriously) that

> it has been by-passed by Missouri historians almost in inverse ratio to its heavily volumed treatment by Kansas and Northern writers. . . . Whereas a score of such works favorable to the free-soil settlers of Kansas are still preserved in the research libraries of historical societies, universities, and other public collections, I have not found a single contemporary volume favorable to Missouri. . . . It is one of the few examples I know of of one side being simon-pure and the other side being simply poor, of one side having all the proof and the other side getting all the punishment, of one side receiving the bravos and the other side, the Bronx cheers.[2]

While recent works on the Kansas struggle by such authors as Gunja SenGupta and the late Bill Cecil-Fronsman have lent depth to proslavery Missourians, I could not help but feel that an important aspect of Missouri's story remained unexplored. While the institution of slavery might have ended in this country in 1865 after the four bloodiest years of our history, its legacy haunts us still in the creation and sustenance of regional identity. Living and teaching in Kansas since moving from Georgia has exposed me for the first time to the conflict over identity that still prevails on traditional American regional borderlands. While modern Kansans debate whether they are midwesterners or westerners, they easily brand Missourians as southerners, conjuring historic images when gearing for their modern collegiate football incarnation of the "border war" that once plagued residents on both sides of the state line. Modern Missourians, who, too, carry a "two-ness" as midwesterners and—distinct from Kansans—as southerners, easily invoke the

---

2. Floyd C. Shoemaker, "Missouri's Proslavery Fight for Kansas," 221 (quote). For a similar criticism of the delegitimation of antebellum southern conservatism, see Eugene D. Genovese, *The Southern Tradition: The Achievement and Limitations of an American Conservatism*, ix–9 and passim.

ghosts of the past when considering Kansas, as I learned when I approached a tobacco farmer in his barn near Weston, Missouri. I asked to purchase a stick of the tobacco he was curing, to use as a teaching aid for my courses on early America and the American South at Emporia State University. Telling him that I lived in Lawrence, his reply was simple and direct: "f_cking Jayhawker town," he growled as he gave me the tobacco, refusing payment, either from generosity or disdain. Clearly, to this Missouri resident, Lawrence, Kansas— no mere place of Jayhawks but a *Jayhawker* town—represented far more than the home of Mizzou's leading sports rival.

In pondering Claib Jackson and his world, I found myself intrigued by the identities of the border region that I for the last seven years have called home. I received full introduction to the debate over identity while in graduate school at the University of Georgia, where as a native, rural Illinoisan I encountered the often heated debate among my southern mates about the character and evolution of southern culture. After observation and eventual participation, and as I absorbed the South and its literature, historical and otherwise, I misplaced southern identity within a perceptible and seemingly timeless matrix of the modern southern culture in which I was living and which was distinct from that in which I was raised. Only upon leaving Georgia for Kansas, and thus teaching and living on the geocultural border between North, South, and West, did I begin to place regional identity within a political, rather than a cultural, realm. Indeed, historian Lawrence Levine has reminded us that "culture is not a fixed condition but a process: the product of interaction between the past and the present. Its toughness and resiliency are determined not by a culture's ability to withstand change, which indeed may be a sign of stagnation not life, but by its ability to react creatively and responsively to the realities of a new situation." As with culture, identity is mutable, as much a response to shifting conditions as a product of them. As a response, regional identity is in itself intrinsically political, especially in the historical context of the American South, where it developed as a defense against the North's political threat to the institution of slavery and the federal government's direct attacks on slaveholding residents in the ensuing war. In the postwar period, southern identity became a means by which residents of former slave states sought to reestablish hegemony in defiance of federal authority during and after Reconstruction. Southern identity, then, was not born, it was created, in C. Vann Woodward's time-honored argument, more from a postwar culture of "frustration, failure, and defeat" than from any prewar culture of abundance and mastery. Quite naturally, the bitter fruit that became these southerners' newfound identification, their raison d'être, was the construction of an ideology that interpreted to their best advantage the new political relation with the federal government as well as the new social relation with northerners, whom southerners heaped scorn upon for being purveyors of sectional strife and destructive war.[3]

As thousands of contemporary Missourians celebrate their southern heritage, whether through family genealogy, as Confederate reenactors, or by touring the state's antebellum homes they associate with a genteel, slaveholding past, they effectively deconstruct the identity of the early national Missourians who uniformly regarded themselves as westerners. In countless ways, and from French Creoles to Anglo frontier people to the leonine Thomas Hart Benton, Missouri's residents celebrated their status as vanguard of the westward expansion of America. As I contemplated this lost patriarchy, I realized that the process by which these Missouri westerners became and remain Missouri southerners centered—and still centers—upon the events surrounding the American Civil War. In an evening conversation with one Missouri Confederate over Kentucky bourbon (what else would an unreconstructed Confederate drink?), I was intrigued by his wishful comment on Claiborne Jackson's role in the state's secession crisis in 1861—one that told me as much about his concept of the present as it did of his understanding of the past—that "*we* [Missouri] would have made it out if *he* had been stronger." Only then did I see Claib Jackson's life and deeds as significant, for he has served as both protagonist and symbol of two Missouris: one lost and one found, one western and one southern.

When discussing my ideas with the acquisitions editor at the University of Missouri Press, Clair Willcox, he suggested that I actually wanted to write two books. I pondered his pointed observation, but realized that what I wanted was not, in truth, two books, but one, albeit with two stories. As such, I have constructed the book to reflect this desire. While most chapters offer Jackson as central character, three chapters—two, five, and eight—along with a sizable portion of the epilogue are largely interpretive, dealing with issues and events for which Jackson is but tangent. Though not "traditional" biographic form, I believe this to be in keeping with a heliocentric universe.

Finally, a word on sources, or more accurately, on one source. In 1962, Walter Morrow Burks completed his dissertation on Claiborne Fox Jackson at the University of Kansas City (now the University of Missouri–Kansas City). Professor Burks's work has offered much assistance in my own study of Jackson and his world, and I am indebted to him for it as well as for a useful conversation on Jackson. In his dissertation, as well as in his master's thesis, Professor Burks cited numerous manuscripts held in private collections,

3. Lawrence W. Levine, *Black Culture and Black Consciousness: Afro-American Folk Thought from Slavery to Freedom*, 5 (first quote); Paul M. Gaston, *The New South Creed: A Study in Southern Mythmaking*, 4–13; C. Vann Woodward, *The Burden of Southern History*, 27 (second quote).

including his own, to which he directed me. Despite lengthy efforts, I was unable to locate any of these primary sources or evidence of their existence. Moreover, while perusing both his thesis and especially his dissertation, I found discrepancies in cited sources available in public repositories. Consequently, I have not used those unverifiable sources, whether private or public, in my own work. Thus any errors, whether of source or interpretation, are purely my own.[4]

CHRISTOPHER PHILLIPS
CRITTENDEN, KENTUCKY
NOVEMBER 1999

4. Walter Morrow Burks, "Thunder on the Right"; Burks, "Missouri Medicine Man."

ABBREVIATIONS

Duke	Special Collections, Perkins Library, Duke University, Durham, North Carolina
Huntington	Henry E. Huntington Library and Art Gallery, San Marino, California
IndHS	Indiana Historical Society Library, Indianapolis
KDLA	Kentucky Department of Libraries and Archives, Frankfort
KSHS	Kansas State Historical Society, Topeka
LC	Library of Congress, Washington, D.C.
MHR	*Missouri Historical Review*
MHS	Missouri Historical Society, St. Louis
MSA	Missouri State Archives, Jefferson City
NA	National Archives, Washington, D.C.
ORR	*The War of the Rebellion: A Compilation of the Official Records of the Union and Confederate Armies.* 4 ser., 128 vols. Washington, D.C., 1881–1901.
SHSM	Western Historical Manuscripts Collection, Joint Collection—State Historical Society of Missouri/University of Missouri, Ellis Library, The University of Missouri, Columbia
UK	Special Collections and Archives, Margaret I. King Library, University of Kentucky, Lexington

Missouri's
Confederate

It is a strange desire to seek power and to lose liberty.

—Francis Bacon, *Of Great Place*

The people never give up their liberties but under some delusion.

—Edmund Burke, Speech at County Meeting of Buckinghamshire, 1784

THE ROOTLESS

AND TO IGNORE the frontier and time in setting up a conception of the social state of the Old South is to abandon reality. For the history of this South throughout a very great part of the period from the opening of the nineteenth century to the Civil War (in the South beyond the Mississippi until long after that war) is mainly the history of the roll of frontier upon frontier—and on to the frontier beyond.

WILBUR J. CASH, *THE MIND OF THE SOUTH*

Dempsey Jackson's world was one of margins. Born in April 1763, in Goochland County, Virginia, a sprawling near-Northside piedmont county located squarely between the tidewater and the eastern edge of the Blue Ridge, Jackson spent his childhood on the frontier of the Old Dominion, the oldest of the British American colonies. Correspondingly, his early life bore witness to the painful human struggle of transition, caught between "savagism and civility," neither evolving completely from one nor creating totally the other. The men of the West lived on the periphery, in a world in which they not only imposed the European myth of primal condition upon the noble savages, the Indians, but also found themselves regarded similarly by those living in the center, the more established areas of the East. His entire life was spent in a forested purgatory, forever struggling to become something—or someone— else. The same would be true for his sons.[1]

Dempsey's grandfather, Joseph Jackson, had himself proven the embodiment of marginality. One of seven brothers, Joseph had served as an apprentice in a wool factory in England, combing and racking raw wool prior to its being spun into thread. According to family legend, Joseph was "an uncommon stout man," and soon grew bored with his trade, longing to work as a house joiner "on account of his strength." His master, however, refused to allow the young man out of his labor contract. Desperate, Joseph ran away, finding his way to London. A fugitive without prospects, he indentured

1. Burks, "Thunder on the Right," 22; Bernard Sheehan, *Savagism and Civility: Indians and Englishmen in Colonial Virginia*, 1–8 (quote, p. 1); Jack P. Greene, *Peripheries and Center: Constitutional Development in the Extended Polities of the British Empire and the United States, 1607–1788*, ix–xii. For an illuminating discussion of the continuous and varied evolution of antebellum southern culture, see Christopher Morris, *Becoming Southern: The Evolution of a Way of Life, Warren County and Vicksburg, Mississippi, 1770–1860*.

himself once again, this time to the captain of a ship bound for America. Arriving in Virginia about 1724, Joseph Jackson served a man named Hews for four years, apparently as a carpenter, then struck out on his own with little more than trade skills, perhaps freedom dues, and unbounded determination. He found his way to Goochland County, the first Virginia county established entirely in the colony's piedmont.[2]

Joseph Jackson escaped the tragic fate of so many indentured servants in the early Chesapeake. Not only did he live long enough to receive his freedom, but he quickly married Ann Jarvis, a former servant, and acquired Northside land with water access to the James River, four hundred acres in 1731 and another four hundred in 1744. Between 1728 and 1742, the couple had at least five children, three sons followed by two daughters. Moreover, as early as 1741 he had acquired the terms of at least two indentured servants to assist him in his carpentry business as well as on his farm. Neither Joseph Jackson's own servitude nor church membership appear to have left any discernible mark of moral distinction upon him insofar as treatment of his own laborers was concerned. In 1741, he received orders from the county court to cease his "immoderate correction of his servant," John McGuire. The same year, one other servant, Major Bollings, absconded for twenty-five days.[3]

Joseph Jackson and his three sons, Jarvis, Joseph, Jr., and John, appear to have remained for some time in their home county. In 1750, Joseph, Sr., deeded two hundred acres "on Bolling Creek . . . being part of the track that I now live on" to his eldest son, Jarvis, and seven years later gave land to his second son, Joseph, Jr. All three of the sons married, joined their father's church, had children, and bought and sold land in the area. Yet by the late 1760s, perhaps in the glow of confidence following the end of the Seven Years' War, two of the brothers, Jarvis and John, sold their Goochland property and moved southwestward to Bedford and Pittsylvania Counties, respectively, Southside frontier counties that the colony had partitioned recently from Lunenburg County. Their father and brother followed shortly, and in 1772 Joseph, Sr., and his two eldest sons were listed as members of the Peaks of Otter Presbyterian Church, located near the source of the

2. Jarvis Jackson to Dear Nephew, July 5, 1882, quoted in Lyle Keith Williams, "Joseph Jackson (1705–1774) of Bedford and Goochland Counties, Virginia, and Descendants," 154–55; Writer's Program, *Virginia; a Guide to the Old Dominion*, 620. Goochland County was formed from Henrico County in 1727.

3. M[ilo] S. Hadlock, "Our Early Virginia Ancestor," in Williams, "Joseph Jackson," 156; Allan Kulikoff, *Tobacco and Slaves: The Development of Southern Cultures in the Chesapeake*, 141–44.

Otter River in the Blue Ridge highlands. Two years later, on the eve of the Revolution, Joseph, Sr., died and was buried there.[4]

The move established a pattern that would characterize the Jackson family. At precisely the time that the Jacksons left Goochland, its society was engaged in the tangled process of ordering itself along the lines of the tidewater counties. Its economy was becoming integrated into that of the tobacco economy of the colony as a whole, and the resultant cultural and political alignments reflected the timeworn hegemony of the tidewater gentry. Indications suggest that the Jackson men fled rather than led the charge toward societal maturity. As the frontier gave way to civilization, these men appear to have continued to inhabit the county's cultural frontier. Their religious affiliation—a means of ordering their world and thus a litmus of their social standing—reflected their position as the county's retinue; as Presbyterians, they fell between the Anglicans, the traditional cultural elite whom they emulated, and the insurgent Baptists, the leveling "enthusiasts" who influenced them as well. Rather than confront the changes of society around them, to embrace and struggle to ascend the rungs of the tobacco hierarchy, the Jackson men withdrew, retreating to the frontier. They sought a margin in which they were neither defined nor hemmed, a place where they were safe in their self-determination and thus expected to be who they were not, a place where they could continually be becoming something. The frontier offered safety to the Jackson men, for there they did not have to confront the reality of having achieved neither social leadership nor independence of will. These "venturous conservatives," as one historian has termed westering Americans, sought the margin in order to buffer themselves from the sobering fact that they themselves were now marginal.[5]

Ironically, though the Jacksons left a place that they considered to be overpopulated, they moved to a Southside county which itself was developing rapidly. Thus, by the time of their arrival, opportunities for success were already minimized. Large landholders, both resident and not, had taken up the best tobacco land in the Southside and brought slaves to work the fields. Forty percent of landholders in Lunenburg in 1769 owned three hundred acres or more; nearly 20 percent owned more than five hundred acres. In fact, one-fifth of the slaveholders in Lunenburg County as early as 1750—

---

4. Milo S. Hadlock, "Jackson Chronology," in Williams, *Joseph Jackson,* 159–60; Richard R. Beeman, *The Evolution of the Southern Backcountry: A Case Study of Lunenburg County, Virginia, 1746–1832,* 60–61.

5. Beeman, *Evolution of the Southern Backcountry,* 61–62, 99–113; Rhys Isaac, *The Transformation of Virginia, 1740–1790,* 345–68; Marvin Meyers, *The Jacksonian Persuasion: Politics and Belief,* 42.

only four years after the county was organized and which included the later-organized Bedford County—had not resided there at all, but merely held land for future sons or speculation. The Jackson men managed only to find land that was literally pressed to the edge of the mountains, with small parcels of thin soil squeezed between hillsides. They probably paid dearly for it; land in newly established Pittsylvania County, Bedford's neighbor to the south, between 1767 and 1769 cost twice as much as land in Amelia County—near where the Jacksons had moved from initially—had cost in 1735.[6]

At the onset of the Revolution, family tradition holds that all three sons enlisted in the Virginia militia and served in the war. A multitude of reasons induced many Virginia men to do so: genuine patriotic fervor, a desire for social and political elevation, a fear of Indian attack, or perhaps an interest in overturning their county's social hierarchy by overthrowing the loyalist elite. Family genealogists have claimed that Jarvis and Joseph, Jr., enlisted as soldiers in unnamed units during the war, while in the fall or winter of 1777 John enlisted in a special force that served under George Rogers Clark in his expedition through the Cumberland Gap into Kentucky and beyond the falls of the Ohio. The story continues that John remained in the West after his term of service, acquiring land in Lincoln County, Kentucky, and enlisting in a local company of light cavalry later in the war. Such claims are likely products of hagiography; no evidence corroborates any such claims other than an 1874 obituary for one of Joseph, Jr.'s sons, Dempsey, which holds that he, rather than his father, had served with Daniel Morgan in Virginia and the Carolinas, despite his having been twelve at the outset of the war. Family tradition holds that Dempsey Jackson celebrated his seventeenth birthday by enlisting with Morgan and saw action at Cowpens. The evidence, or rather the lack of it, suggests that the Jacksons of Bedford County saw the war as did many in their frontier region: as a fight for home rule, rather than for who should rule at home.[7]

---

6. Kulikoff, *Tobacco and Slaves,* 152–55; Beeman, *Evolution of the Southern Backcountry,* 174–75.

7. Williams, "Joseph Jackson," 1–3, 159–60; Robert Middlekauff, *The Glorious Cause: The American Revolution, 1763–1789,* 469–78; Rachel L. Klein, "Frontier Planters and the American Revolution: The South Carolina Backcountry, 1775–1782," 54–58; Chester Raymond Young, ed., *Westward into Kentucky: The Narrative of Daniel Trabue,* 44; Obituary of Dempsey Pickett Jackson, undated [1874], John Sappington Collection, Mss. 1036, folder 4: Sappington Miscellany, SHSM; Burks, "Thunder on the Right," 22; Virgil D. White, ed., *Index to Revolutionary War Service Records,* vol. 2, 1425–29; Samuel M. Wilson, ed., *Catalogue of Revolutionary Soldiers and Sailors of the Commonwealth of Virginia to whom Land Bounty Warrants were Granted by Virginia for Military Services in the War of Independence,* 46–47; John H. Gwathmey, ed., *Historical Register of Virginians in the Revolution: Soldiers—Sailors—Marines, 1775–1783,* 411–12. One John Jackson is listed in Lincoln County, Kentucky, in 1787, but whether it is the same John Jackson

Yet one piece of evidence connects Joseph Jackson, Jr., to the war, if circumstantially. While his brothers continue to show up in the postwar records in Bedford County, the last evidence of Joseph, Jr., in the Southside was in October 1774, when he sold to one John Phillpot of Goochland County the final two hundred acres of land he acquired by grant deed from his father. At some point thereafter, he appears to have migrated (as did thousands of war veterans) to yet another frontier, Fauquier County, in sight of the Blue Ridge in the new state's northernmost portion. That no record exists of any land grant offered to Joseph Jackson, Jr., in Virginia's northern frontier as a result of military service leaves his veteran status in doubt. Any such migration from the Southside must have been an especially difficult choice for Joseph, Jr., for at war's end he was no rootless young man with a surfeit of life energy brought on by a wartime brush with mortality. Any move from the Southside at this point in his life came only with risk, for Joseph Jackson already had a family for which to provide.[8]

Well before the war, Joseph Jackson, Jr., had begun to acquire secular stock by the most cardinal of means: he had started a family. On August 27, 1760, he had married Susannah Carter, a distant cousin to the powerful tidewater family. Within three years, three sons—George, Joseph III, and Dempsey Carroll—were born to the Jacksons, followed two years later by another son, William. With this growing brood Jackson moved to Fauquier and watched his sons grow to manhood. Their hard work contributed to the growth of the family farm as well, and census records from the summer of 1787 (when the Virginia legislature authorized and conducted its first state census) not only indicate Joseph's presence in the county, but reveal that by the age of fifty-seven he had attained at least a modest amount of property and standing. Just as Virginia's "demigods" in distant Philadelphia were directing the construction of a new republic, Joseph Jackson of Fauquier County had managed to build a middling place in local society, reflected in his property acquisitions. An owner of eight slaves—three over and five under the age of sixteen—as well as seven horses or mules and fifteen cattle, Joseph Jackson was far from being a member of the gentry, but was just as far from languishing in social and political insignificance.[9]

---

is unclear. See Netti Schreiner Yantis and Florene Speakman Love, eds., *1787 Census of Virginia*, vol. 1, 196, 310.

8. Williams, "Joseph Jackson," 1–2, 21, 157, 159–60; Yantis and Love, eds., *1787 Census of Virginia*, vol. 1, 196; Gertrude E. Gray, ed., *Virginia Northern Neck Land Grants*, vols. 2 and 3, passim. In 1787, Jarvis Jackson of Bedford County held one slave, six horses or mules, and thirty-six cattle, indicating that he did not enter into the ranks of the planter gentry in his home county.

9. Williams, "Joseph Jackson," 1–2, 21, 157, 159–60; Yantis and Love, eds., *1787 Census of Virginia*, vol. 1, 294, also 267–301 passim.

As little remains of young Dempsey Jackson's formative years in Fauquier as of his father's life and labors there. He was certainly no child when he arrived in the county, but neither was he a man. As late as 1787, Dempsey Jackson appears not to have held land, but neither did he live in his father's household, suggesting that he hired himself out either as a farm laborer or in some sort of trade. Unlike his older brothers, he as yet had no taxable wealth, whether livestock or slaves, and thus it was unlikely that he yet rented land to farm for himself. However, just four days after Christmas of that year, at age twenty-five, Dempsey made a significant life change. He married Mary Pickett, or "Molly," as she was called, five years his junior and seventh child and third daughter of a prosperous local planter, William Sanford Pickett, a captain of the Fauquier County militia during the Revolution. Similarly, Molly's eldest brother, John, also was an officer in the war, and the two men's commissions indicate as much about the Picketts' social standing as any military involvement or expertise. The Reverend John Monroe, a local Baptist minister, performed the service, offering Dempsey an aperture into the faith that not only had swept the piedmont during the egalitarian fervor of the Revolutionary era but also now ironically helped to stratify the region's social landscape. Thus, such a step also offered Dempsey Jackson discernible social advancement. His father-in-law was a significant property holder, with more than 750 acres of land, cattle, horses, and twenty-two slaves in his possession. No struggling tobacco farmer, his house was filled with furniture and beds and he provided for his ten children upon their marriages, either through inheritances or dowries. By "marrying up" with Molly Pickett, Dempsey Jackson had forced a wedge into the upper reaches of the social hierarchy that both his father and his father's father had never accomplished.[10]

While living in Fauquier, Dempsey and Molly Jackson witnessed the births of five of their eventual thirteen children: two sons, Craven and George, and three daughters, Ann, Betsey, and Octavia.[11] However little we might know

10. Gwathmey, ed., *Historical Register of Virginians in the Revolution*, 624; John K. Gott, ed., *Fauquier County, Virginia, Marriage Bonds: 1759–1854, and Marriage Returns, 1785–1848*, 105; Yantis and Love, eds., *1787 Census of Virginia*, 285, and 267–301 passim; Gray, ed., *Virginia Northern Neck Land Grants*, vol. 2, 108–9, 111; J. Estelle Stewart King, ed., *Abstracts of Wills, Administrations, and Marriages of Fauquier County, Virginia, 1759–1800*, 35; Karen C. Boggs and Louise M. Coutts, eds., *Howard County [Missouri] Cemetery Records*, 192; Rhys Isaac, "Evangelical Revolt: The Nature of the Baptists' Challenge to the Traditional Order in Virginia, 1765–1775," 345–68. For an excellent study of the household furnishings on tobacco farms in the colonial era, see Lois Green Carr, Russell R. Menard, and Lorena S. Walsh, *Robert Cole's World: Agriculture and Society in Early Maryland*, 102–7.

11. Kulikoff, *Tobacco and Slaves*, 145–48; Williams, "Joseph Jackson," 22; Obituary of Dempsey Pickett Jackson, undated [1874], John Sappington Collection, Mss. 1036, folder 4: Sappington Miscellany, SHSM; Seventh U.S. Census, 1850, Population Sched-

of the young couple in the early years of their marriage, one thing is certain. In 1792, Dempsey Jackson, like his father and grandfather before him, uprooted his young family for the uncertainties of the frontier. The brutal pair—ambition and a late birth (and thus lower inheritable position as the third son in his family)—had conspired to drive yet another Jackson man to the margin of society. In this case, however, the periphery that drew him so inexorably lay across the high mountains that had succeeded in hemming his rootless fore-bears. Dempsey Jackson's frontier was the wilderness known as Kentucky.[12]

That Dempsey Jackson selected 1792 for the date of his family's sojourn into the western wilderness was probably not mere happenstance. Settlers who had arrived in the 1770s and into the subsequent decade, such as Daniel Boone and James Harrod, suffered regularly from Indian raids from above and below the Ohio, of the Mingos, Shawnees, and especially the powerful Wyandottes. These assaults, which aimed to drive the nuclei of intruders from the then Virginia county, succeeded largely if temporarily in that they disrupted the flow of white settlers into the region whose name in Cherokee meant "the land where we will live." The 1782 battle at Blue Licks, arguably "the last battle of the American Revolution," represented the high tide of Indian hostility in Kentucky. Violence continued sporadically for another decade, but increasingly it offered less concern to potential emigrants, and cleared the way toward an accelerated white migration into the western region. Frontier "stations" (two-story, windowless log cabins erected within a few yards of one another, linked by palisades and thus serving as forts) offered the primary loci for settlement and early pioneers gravitated to them, settling nearby and clearing fields in view of or a short trip from the protective stations. These stations, themselves crude yet democratic throwbacks to feudalism, offered a means by which safe settlement could occur during the uneasy period prior to statehood. The Indian menace, while still very real, gradually minimized if not disappeared in the public imagination. By the time of Dempsey Jackson's arrival, Kentucky had the reputation in the East as being a secure place to live, yet another wilderness Zion.[13]

---

ule, Howard County, Missouri, NA. In 1773, John Jackson sold land along Hurricane Creek, a tributary of the Otter River; he and his wife, Elizabeth, sold land in Lincoln County, Kentucky, as early as 1785, and died there on September 10, 1821. Hadlock, "Jackson Chronology," 159–60.

12. Mason County [Kentucky] Tax Assessment Books, 1790–1797, 1799–1809, microfilm reel 008140, KDLA; Burks, "Thunder on the Right," 21n2. The names and birth dates of the Jackson children were: Craven (1788–89), Ann (1790), George (1791), Betsey (1792), Octavia (1793–94), Malinda (1795), Dempsey Pickett (1796), Wade Moseby (1797), Thomas (1799), William Pickett (1800), Eldridge (1801), Claiborne Fox (1806), Susan (1809).

13. Steven A. Channing, *Kentucky: A Bicentennial History,* 4 (quote), 29–35; Stephen Aron, *How the West Was Lost: The Transformation of Kentucky from Daniel Boone to Henry*

Dempsey Jackson was a western man. He was born and grew to sturdy manhood in Virginia's Near West, and staked his claim to the new nation's Far West. His figurative rebirth in Kentucky in the late spring of 1792, following the melting of the winter snows, coincided exactly with the state's own nativity. On February 4, 1791, the first U.S. Congress had passed an act admitting Kentucky for statehood. Yet because the territorial convention offered a petition requesting admission to the Union that set June 1, 1792, as the official date of admittance, Kentucky became the new nation's fifteenth state only on that day, preceded by Vermont because of a technicality. Kentucky was the first state with an umbilical scar, the first state carved out of the massive trans-Appalachian forest, the first state of the Great West. Yet the country was hardly a virgin wilderness at the time of Dempsey Jackson's arrival. In the years during and following the Revolution, thousands of settlers from the seaboard states had floated their flatboats down the Ohio or trudged by foot through the Cumberland Gap and up the mountain valleys along the Wilderness Road into the Bluegrass region, where they found natural clearings of fertile soil, nourished by limestone springs and freshwater streams. In 1777, with local governance emplaced, five thousand settlers lived in the hardwoods of Kentucky County; within a decade that number had grown to fifty thousand, and by the time of Dempsey Jackson's arrival, more than seventy-five thousand had laid claim to Kentucky land as their future homes. Moses Austin recalled of a conversation with one of a sea of travelers to the West in 1796: "Ask these Pilgrims what they expect when they git to Kentuckey the Answer is Land. have you any. No, but I expect I can git it. have you any thing to pay for land, No." So many came to the land they regarded generally as "the garden of the West" that the greatest of Kentuckians, Daniel Boone, had already left the territory years before, allegedly claiming that he was "unable to call a single acre his own."[14]

Well after Boone had left Kentucky to find land at "some point beyond the bounds of civilization," Dempsey Jackson arrived, but too late. His was

---

Clay, 29–57; Nicky Hughes, "Battle of Blue Licks," in John E. Kleber, ed., *The Kentucky Encyclopedia*, 92–93; Marion Tinling and Godfrey Davies, eds., *The Western Country in 1793: Reports on Kentucky and Virginia by Harry Toulmin*, 64; Malcolm J. Rohrbough, *The Trans-Appalachian Frontier: People, Societies, and Institutions, 1775–1850*, 18.

14. Figures drawn from Rohrbough, *Trans-Appalachian Frontier*, 16; Thomas D. Clark, ed., *The Voice of the Frontier: John Bradford's Notes on Kentucky*, 145–46; "A Memorandum of M. Austin's Journey from Virginia to Louisiana," 525–26 (first quote); Arthur K. Moore, *The Frontier Mind: A Cultural Analysis of the Kentucky Frontiersmen*, 23 (second quote); John Mack Faragher, *Daniel Boone: The Life and Legend of an American Pioneer*, 235, 262–63 (third quote). Virginia extended county government to Kentucky in 1776, the first official government in the trans-Appalachian frontier. The first county court met at Harrodsburg in September 1777. See Rohrbough, *Trans-Appalachian Frontier*, 34–35.

the sin of his father. Land-hungry speculators and settlers had preceded him, following well-worn buffalo traces and Indian paths into the interior of the territory, redeeming Virginia land warrants and carving notches, blazes, and crude designations into trees to mark the boundaries of their oft-disputed claims to the prime Bluegrass tracts. As early as 1780, the Virginia Land Court reported entries and surveys in Kentucky amounting to nearly 3.5 million acres, over one-eighth of the area of the then-county's entire mother state. In subsequent years, immigrants filled up the rolling landscape too rapidly as Virginia governors issued land warrants with aplomb, war veterans applied for and received military warrants for their services in the Revolution, settlers who brought immigrants received warrants based upon "importation rights," other less affluent settlers cleared land and made improvements and thus received "preemption" warrants, and squatters often obtained warrants on credit. Various historians have estimated that from three to ten claimants existed for every acre of land in Kentucky, resulting in innumerable accounts of land parcels being "shingled over" by overlapping claims. A labyrinthine patchwork of conflicting land claims—only made worse by poor surveyors such as Daniel Boone—soon forced the establishment of a land court to sort out this legal monstrosity. Its decisions plagued these frontier people for decades and dispossessed thousands of land they believed—in many cases rightly—was theirs and which in many cases they had occupied for years. Indeed, one early historian claimed that Kentucky lands "were all given out by 1790."[15] Moses Austin would write grimly as early as 1796 that

> Kentuckey [is] not the Promis.d land its not the goodly inheratence the Land of Milk and Honey. and when arriv.d at this Heaven in Idea what do they find? a goodly land I will allow but to them a forbiden Land. exausted and worn down with distress and disappointment they are at last Oblig.d to become hewers of wood and Drawers of water.[16]

Like his father before him, upon his escape to the margin, Dempsey Jackson found himself already marginalized.

The land thus claimed and much of it quickly and crudely settled, Kentucky's frontier society rapidly gave way to an aggressive, acquisitive, agrarian capitalism that transformed the new state into a place in which material possession and family name measured a man's worth. Whether rugged individualists or frontier democrats, these men of the West sought to establish

15. Faragher, *Daniel Boone*, 262 (first quote); Aron, *How the West Was Lost*, 58–81; Lewis C. Gray, *History of Agriculture in the Southern United States to 1860*, vol. 2, 623–24; Mary K. Bonsteel Tachau, "Land Claims, Early," in Kleber, ed., *The Kentucky Encyclopedia*, 535 (second, third, and fourth quotes); Ivan E. McDougle, *Slavery in Kentucky, 1792–1865*, 4 (fifth quote).

16. "A Memorandum of M. Austin's Journey," quoted in Moore, *The Frontier Mind*, 26.

in Kentucky an order to their lives that at once rejected and embraced the hierarchy of their fathers' world. Yet these "men at the center," as writer W. J. Cash has termed the agrarian frontiersmen, possessed a far more complex social and economic comportment and worldview than their christener avowed them to have. By the 1790s, once the eastern promoters proclaimed Kentucky open to vigorous settlement, the settlers of the new state reflected a mixture of piedmont gentry as well as yeomen, with the latter dominating numerically and the former fashioning an unmistakable imprint upon the complexion of their burgeoning society. Indeed, one historian of the state has termed this complex environment a "deferential democracy."[17]

No mere replication of the Chesapeake low country's oligarchy, Kentucky's early society nonetheless bore the stamp of aristocracy on its frontier democracy. Those of aristocratic gentility, such as the Breckinridges, Todds, and Marshalls, brought to the West privileged educations from William and Mary, law training and practices along with recommendations from respected tidewater and piedmont lawyer-planters, experience in government drawn from terms in the House of Burgesses, and military commissions, as well as ample capital and laborers afforded by their gentry families. They settled on large tracts of land also acquired by wealthy family members. They intermarried with gentryfolk who came later, such as the Prestons, the Johnstons, and the Morgans, to create powerful kin networks that together formed the warp of the nascent social fabric of Kentucky, and their presence helped to establish Transylvania University, the first such center of higher learning west of the Appalachians, to which many would send their sons for training in the gentlemen's professions of law and medicine. These First Families served collectively as bellwether of the social maturation in the territory and state, a process that caused men such as Daniel Boone and Simon Kenton to lose all that they had worked for prior to leaving Kentucky in utter disgust.[18]

And those First Families laid an equally unmistakable claim to the Kentucky region as a future slave state. Of those some seventy-five thousand inhabitants at the time of Dempsey Jackson's immigration, nearly twelve thousand were black (only 114 of whom were free), meaning that prior to statehood virtually one-sixth of the pioneer population was composed

17. Wilbur J. Cash, *The Mind of the South*, 30–35 (first quote, p. 35); Frederick Jackson Turner, "The Significance of the Frontier in American History," 199–227; Channing, *Kentucky*, 47 (second quote).

18. Channing, *Kentucky*, 43–48; William C. Davis, *Breckenridge: Statesman Soldier Symbol*, 4–6; James C. Klotter, *The Breckinridges of Kentucky*, 1–9. Betty B. Ellison, "John Todd," 887; Charles C. Hay III, "William Preston," 738–39; Charles P. Roland, "Albert Sidney Johnston," 476–77; James A. Ramage, "John Hunt Morgan," 650–51; John D. Wright, Jr., and Eric H. Christianson, "Transylvania University," 894–96; Jean W. Calvert, "Simon Kenton," 488; all in Kleber, ed., *The Kentucky Encyclopedia*.

of bound African Americans. Indeed, black and white pioneers crossed the mountains together. In 1751, a black servant accompanied Christopher Gist on the first foray into the region, only to discover another black man living with Indians on the Scioto River. A slave guided Daniel Boone into Kentucky in 1760, and African Americans helped to defend Boone and his settlers against Indian attacks on more than one occasion prior to the Revolution. Indeed, slaves and those few free blacks who lived in the region were integral components of the system of wartime defense on the frontier. In 1777, John Cowan's census of the inhabitants at Harrod's Fort listed nineteen slaves in a total population of 198; John Filson's estimate of settlers seven years later included four thousand black Kentuckians. By the time of Dempsey Jackson's arrival, that number had tripled.[19]

As settlers streamed into the Bluegrass, claiming the richest soils in Kentucky and sustaining their Chesapeake slaveholding birthright, they introduced into the region another of Virginia's heritable commodities, its cash crop, tobacco. The "stinking weed" soon thrived in the loamy soil, created from the decay of deciduous leaves and bluegrasses for hundreds of centuries. As early as 1783, the Virginia General Assembly provided for tobacco inspection on the "western waters," and Kentuckians sent petitions for additional warehouses from 1787 to 1790. Kentucky's tobacco market flourished similarly once the Spanish opened the port of New Orleans in 1789, and soon hogsheads of Kentucky tobacco crowded flatboats on their way down the Ohio and Mississippi Rivers before being loaded onto sailing vessels bound for eastern and European markets. Indeed, as early as July of that year, James Wilkinson, former Revolutionary War general turned entrepreneur and founder of the town (and later state capital) of Frankfort, advertised in Lexington's *Kentucky Gazette* for Kentucky tobacco for his New Orleans warehouse.[20]

When one of three tax assessors canvassed Mason County, Kentucky, in September 1792, among the new residents he found who possessed taxable wealth was twenty-nine-year-old Dempsey Jackson. He and his young family had likely traveled in a group with other Fauquier families (possibly brothers or cousins, for several men of that name—including William, Samuel, James, and Thomas Jackson, all names that would appear in later generations of the Jackson family—arrived in Mason County simultaneous with Dempsey's arrival) along a route well worn by thousands before them: northwestward

19. Marion B. Lucas, *A History of Blacks in Kentucky—Volume 1: From Slavery to Segregation, 1760–1891*, xi–xvi.

20. Channing, *Kentucky*, 51; Gray, *History of Agriculture in the Southern United States*, 2:754–55; Jeffrey Scott Suchanek, "James Wilkinson," in Kleber, ed., *The Kentucky Encyclopedia*, 955–56.

by wagon from Fauquier County through the Blue Ridge gaps to the lower Shenandoah Valley, crossing the Potomac into Maryland, then heading westward over to the valley town of Cumberland, then picking up Braddock's infamous and well-used road through the Allegheny mountain passes to the Monongahela River, following the river then fifty more miles to Fort Pitt, or Pittsburgh, as the town which had grown up around the fort was now called. With well over two hundred tortuous miles behind them, the Jackson clan probably sold their wagons and purchased a flatboat or barge—which cost them as much as a dollar a foot—and provisions and floated themselves, their families, and their precious household cargoes down the gradually slowing current of the mighty Ohio for nearly four hundred final miles. After nearly two months of arduous travel, the weary group arrived at Limestone, as the locals called the ramshackle string of buildings and wharves, between which were wedged a few log houses, a tobacco warehouse, and the Boone Tavern, a "house of entertainment" owned by the son of the famed frontiersman. There, boastful "half-horse, half-alligator" riverboatmen drank, gambled, and fought in their lusty insignificance. Together this motley collection of nondescript structures—many built of dismantled flatboats and which housed more than two hundred families—and raucous inhabitants constituted one of the most important early American ports along the Ohio. In the midst of this crudity, Dempsey Jackson and his family disembarked.[21]

In 1792, sprawling Mason County—which stretched from the Sandy River on the east to the Licking River on the west and south, 160 miles from end to end—was the northernmost county in Kentucky. Limestone, which in terms of river travel lay in the virtual center of the expanse, sat just west of the Knobs, the breaking point where the piedmont gave way to the ineffably fertile Bluegrass. Nearly three-fourths of Mason County's inhabitants lived within eight miles of the county seat, Washington, described in 1788 by resident Daniel Drake as "something of a Village" consisting of some fifty families and located atop a high hill four miles inland from Limestone on the arterial entryway to the state's interior, the Limestone Trace. Drake further recalled of the Mayslick area that "within six years . . . the number of settlers had increased to such an extent that one could not wander a mile in any

21. Tinling and Davies, eds., *The Western Country in 1793*, 116; Faragher, *Daniel Boone*, 235–36 (first quote); Channing, *Kentucky*, 51 (second quote); Moore, *The Frontier Mind*, 107–9; Mason County [Kentucky] Tax Assessment Books, 1790–1797, 1799–1809, microfilm reel 008140, KDLA; Fifth U.S. Census, 1830, Population Schedule, Howard County, Missouri, NA; James Rood Robertson, ed., *Petitions of the Early Inhabitants of Kentucky to the General Assembly of Virginia 1769 to 1792*, 117–19. Limestone was in 1787 officially named Maysville, though locals continued for some time to call it by its original designation. See Richard C. Smoot, "Maysville," in Kleber, ed., *The Kentucky Encyclopedia*, 621–22.

direction, without meeting with a clearing of two to ten acres, often enclosed with a brush fence, and designated as a human residence by a one story unhewed log cabin, with the latch string always out."[22]

Most likely, the Jacksons, too, moved inland and took up such residence, living on land described by Unitarian minister Harry Toulmin, who arrived in Mason County from Lancashire, England, shortly after Dempsey Jackson, as "broken . . . [or] *waving,* neither dead flat nor hilly." The family's trip to Kentucky had been expensive, for Jackson and his family arrived in their new home landless and without capital enough to acquire it immediately. Such a condition was far from uncommon in Mason County. Toulmin, a keen observer, wrote to his family in Virginia that "the surest way [to gain employment] is for a man to rent a few acres of land, sufficient to maintain a few cows, hogs, and sheep, so as not to be entirely dependent upon the exercise of their trade." Jackson appears to have followed this custom of the country, for in 1792 the county assessed him taxes on four cattle and three horses or mules; four years later, he owned ten cattle, along with four horses or mules. Moreover, he brought with him a trait that had characterized Americans nearly since the founding of his own birth state: an indomitable will to own his own farm and to prosper.[23]

As Kentucky became the lodestar for settlement of the Great West, the state's economic landscape soon took on a decidedly different character from that of its parent state. Unlike in Virginia, transportation difficulties plagued the marketing of tobacco; the nearly five-hundred-mile trip from Louisville to New Orleans took a month and could cost more than one hundred dollars (depending upon whether the boat hands required wages or worked for passage), not including the cost of transportation from the farm to Limestone. Such ventures also depended upon the caprice of the Spanish government (which had periodically closed the right of passage and thus deprived western farmers of their sole outlet for export), the fickle prices of tobacco at New Orleans (which were often lower than those in the East), and of course the great danger involved in traveling so great a distance, whether guiding the heavy and cumbersome flatboat down the volatile river or the return trip on horseback or on foot along the Natchez Trace, referred to

22. Moore, *The Frontier Mind,* 11; Daniel Drake, *Pioneer Life in Kentucky, 1785–1800,* 43–44, 10 (first and second quotes); Federal Writers' Project, *Kentucky,* 366; Thomas D. Clark, *Kentucky: A Students' Guide to Localized History,* 8. The Virginia legislature incorporated Washington as a town in 1787. See Robertson, ed., *Petitions of the Early Inhabitants of Kentucky,* 91–92.

23. Tinling and Davies, eds., *The Western Country in 1793,* 71 (first quote), 65 (second quote); Wilford A. Bladen and Gyula Pauer, *Geography of Kentucky: A Topical-Regional Overview,* 75; Mason County [Kentucky] Tax Assessment Books, 1790–1797, 1799–1809, microfilm reel 008140, KDLA.

as "the Devil's backbone" as a result of the constant robberies and murders of unsuspecting travelers. Small farmers could afford neither the expense nor the time lost, and thus they were forced to store their leaf at the local warehouse and sell to agents for prices invariably below market value.[24]

Facing such conditions, farmers in Mason County, like those in large sections of Kentucky as a whole, diversified their crop mix. They raised livestock—cattle, hogs, sheep, and especially horses, to be driven over the mountains to the East—and grew a variety of crops such as corn, oats, flax, wheat, rye, barley, and hemp. One county resident wrote that "estates are appropriated chiefly to grain, . . . Indian corn forever, except what is appropriated to hemp." Another observer reported in 1798 that "within the last three years the exportation of tobacco has diminished and flour seems to take its place." By 1839, Kentucky was the second-leading corn-growing state in the nation, behind only Tennessee. Grain fields and pastures dominated the landscape, interspersed with tobacco patches (rather than large fields of the crop) that dotted the rolling countryside. In fact, farmers often grew tobacco to reduce the soil's fertility, which was necessary for a good wheat crop. Indeed, Kentucky flour, meal, and pork far outstripped tobacco exports down the Mississippi for the first three decades of the nineteenth century. Such crop diversification continued to characterize the region, which came to be known collectively as "the border." By the late antebellum years, the border states produced nearly 80 percent of all grain crops grown in the slave states other than corn (and even then they grew more than 60 percent of that staple food crop), largely for export to the cotton-producing states farther to the south.[25]

As residents from all over the Chesapeake settled in the region, so did many from farther north, rendering a demographic mix that contributed to the diversification of the economy of the West as much as it did the population. One resident of Mason County wrote of his neighbors in 1794 as being largely those "who have emigrated from New England, New York, Jersey, and Pennsylvania," rather than from Virginia. Decidedly unfamiliar with staple crop production, these immigrants introduced economic ways dissimilar from those of the tobacco-dominated regions of the tidewater and piedmont. Though tobacco and slavery offered a well-worn path to economic

24. Donald R. Adams, Jr., "Prices and Wages in Maryland," 625–45; Jonathan Daniels, *The Devil's Backbone: The Story of the Natchez Trace*, passim; Tinling and Davies, eds., *The Western Country in 1793*, 116, 121; Gray, *History of Agriculture in the Southern United States*, 2:810–22; Channing, *Kentucky*, 50–51.

25. Tinling and Davies, eds., *The Western Country in 1793*, 82 (first quote), 116, 121; Douglass C. North, *The Economic Growth of the United States, 1790–1860*, 135; Thomas S. Berry, *Western Prices before 1861: A Study of the Cincinnati Market*, 156 (second quote); Gray, *History of Agriculture in the Southern United States*, 2:765–66, 876; Channing, *Kentucky*, 50–51.

respectability in Kentucky, Yankee pioneers soon cleared other avenues to success in the once-impenetrable western wilderness. Commercial and man-ufacturing interests of all sorts sprang up in the region, processing raw and agricultural materials such as tobacco, hemp, salt, maple sap, hardwoods, and grains into salable goods such as tobacco plugs, rope, cotton bagging, sugar, paper, lumber, gunpowder, and bourbon whiskey. Kentucky, shaped by a mixture of influences, soon reflected a social, economic, and political outlook decidedly unique from its progenitor.[26]

Dempsey Jackson brought with him to Kentucky one of his Virginia birthrights, which he and the society he sought alternately to escape and to embrace all deemed most crucial to social and economic advancement. Accompanying the family on the long trip and helping to guide the flatboat were three slaves, two of whom were over the age of sixteen, all presumably men. Most likely, they were deed gifts from his father-in-law as part of a dowry offered to Jackson with his daughter's hand. With this largesse, Jackson and his laborers managed to hack a farm out of the rolling expanse of oaks, hickories, dogwoods, locusts, pawpaws, and sweetgums. Indeed, possession of such laborers had value beyond his own fields; Jackson may have traded his slaves' labor for rent. Harry Toulmin noted that one land-rich resident of Mason County, Capt. Thomas Marshall, allowed tenants to live rent-free for four years (precisely the tenure of Jackson's tenancy) in return for clearing as much as four-fifths of the land. In terms of monetary value, Toulmin estimated that "a good healthy Negro will earn £30 [$50] a year in clearing land." This sort of arrangement magnified the importance of slave labor in the region, for even if the owner was not engaged immediately in tobacco production—even if he did not possess any land or cash at all—his chances for survival increased exponentially on the rough-and-tumble frontier. Labor, not land, in essence dictated the terms of success.[27]

Jackson's ownership of three slave laborers thrust him immediately not only into a distinct minority in Mason County but also potentially into its small cadre of political leadership. The demographic mix of the county alone offered him a distinct advantage. Harry Toulmin wrote that the county

---

26. Tinling and Davies, eds., *The Western Country in 1793,* 68 (quote); Gray, *History of Agriculture in the Southern United States,* 2:875–78; Channing, *Kentucky,* 50–51.

27. Mason County [Kentucky] Tax Assessment Books, 1790–1797, 1799–1809, microfilm reel 008140, KDLA; Tinling and Davies, eds., *The Western Country in 1793,* 65 (quote), 68, 71–74, 76–77; Adams, "Prices and Wages in Maryland," 625–45. William Pickett's will, registered in Fauquier County, Virginia, on January 10, 1798, and patented six weeks later, fails to provide any sort of property for four of Pickett's six daughters—all married, including Molly Jackson—suggesting that their dowries offered personal property which, if the bequeathments to Pickett's other legatees provide any indication, included slaves. King, ed., *Abstracts of Wills, Administrations, and Marriages of Fauquier County,* 35.

"has hitherto been settled principally by the poorest class of people . . . and whose finances were too low to enable them to proceed any farther into the country." Largely Baptists, steeped in the leveling traditions of the faith, nearly all found land and worked it as did Jackson. Toulmin estimated that tenants manned three-quarters of the five to eight hundred farms settled in the county. Mason's 1,660 inhabitants owned just 160 slaves and, lacking indentured servants, they served as the county's singular source of labor. No indentured servants resided in Mason County, and one resident recalled that "it is peculiarly difficult for a man of property to hire a laborer." By 1798, when the state carved Fleming County from Mason, Jackson was one of 372 propertied white men in the county and owned three of the fifty-four slaves who labored there. No tidewater aristocrat, Dempsey Jackson nonetheless sought more than simple respectability on the edge of the Bluegrass.[28]

Slaveholding in Kentucky may have owed its birth to its mother state, but its practice in the West mirrored the organic nature of a westward-marching society. In sum, as the social institutions of Virginia evolved into those reflecting a self-conscious Kentucky populace, so did that institution which would fast define—and ultimately divide—America as a whole: slavery. Unlike the Old Dominion, Kentucky was preeminently a land of small slaveholders. In terms of percentage, slaves never made up as much as a quarter of the state's population; as late as 1860, Kentucky's 38,645 slave owners represented 22.8 percent of its white population, which ranked at that time above all other border slave states, but below those of the Upper and Deep South and a far cry from the Old Southwest's nearly 50 percent. Yet with the exception of Virginia, Kentucky in 1860 had numerically more slaveholders owning from one to seven slaves than any other state, and with the exception of Virginia and Georgia, it boasted in raw numbers a greater number of slaveholders than any other state. Moreover, slavery seemed a far more egalitarian institution in terms of white participation than in states farther south; on the eve of the Civil War, no Kentuckian owned more than three hundred slaves while only seven owned more than one hundred and but seventy held fifty or more. Characteristic of the upcountry portions of what was fast becoming the lower South, planters did not enjoy hegemony in Kentucky; the yeomanry made up the backbone of the state's leadership even compared with other border slave states, a distinction which antebellum newspaper titles reflect. While southern Marylanders boasted the *Planter's Advocate*, bluegrass Kentuckians read the *Kentucky Yeoman*.[29]

28. Tinling and Davies, eds., *The Western Country in 1793*, 68 (first quote), 78–79 (second quote, p. 79); Mason County [Kentucky] Tax Assessment Books, 1790–1797, 1799–1809, microfilm reel 008140, KDLA; Drake, *Pioneer Life in Kentucky*, 29.

29. Gray, *History of Agriculture in the Southern United States*, vol. 2, 482. E. Merton Coulter, *The Civil War and Readjustment in Kentucky*, 7–8. For an excellent discussion of

Most white residents of Kentucky measured the value of slaves not on an economic scale, but on one of liberty. No mere constitutional right (residents of Virginia's former Kentucky County had rejected the document), their dead reckoning drew upon values more uniquely western. Slaveholding, widely dispersed over the new state, was imbued within the largest portion of Kentuckians as an ideological construct of their inherent commitment to personal liberties. One Kentuckian, Leeland Hathaway, recalled that

> Slavery came to Kentucky as heritage & Kentuckians accepted & held to it as part of their birth right The negro came with our Virginia blood & we would as soon have questioned our right to one as to the other—We no more thought of wrong doing in holding & using slaves than in Eating our hog & hominy or in breathing the air which swept across the Blue Ridge & the Alleghenies—We owned the negro.[30]

Yet unlike the later cotton states, where the tie between slavery and economic fortune would hone a much sharper edge to its populace's commitment to personal freedoms, Kentucky's people as yet had every reason to believe—indeed, no reason to disbelieve—that they could discern the simultaneous maintenance of slavery and a commitment to the union of states sparked by the circumstances of its own birth and deepened by the West's spectacular growth. Such was no romantic unionism, for no sense of nostalgia yet motivated this burgeoning people. Kentuckians inherited their views of slaveholding as an inheritance of the Revolution, a right that victory actuated and natural law decreed. Slavery in a sense became part of the same universalist conception of freedom that guaranteed the right of expansion. By 1830, Kentucky's slaves had reached their zenith at 24.7 percent of the overall population, and Kentuckians such as Dempsey Jackson saw no reason why westernness should not include slaveholding. Only to the north and west did such considerations have any bearing (the Northwest Ordinance having barred the institution from that region), their extended liberty placing slaveholding Kentuckians, at least as they perceived themselves, on a plane above those living north of the Ohio. Unrestricted in their personal liberties, products of the birthplace of presidents, flush in the knowledge that they were physically detached from the established and jaded East and thus were fresh, utopian offshoots of the cradle of civilization, Kentuckians considered themselves as haut monde. Neither southern nor northern—the concepts were as embryonic as was the debate over slavery and the West; in fact, the two were merged—Kentuckians would have believed themselves better than either. Slavery, that pilaster of societal advancement, was as much a part of the

yeoman hegemony, or "country Whig" ideology, see Lacy K. Ford, *The Roots of Southern Radicalism: The South Carolina Upcountry, 1800–1865*, passim.

30. Civil War Reminiscences of Leeland Hathaway, 1893–94, Hathaway Papers, microfilm file M-20, UK.

region as the hog and hominy that formed its residents' diet. Kentuckians' seed may have been sown in the East, but their crop, of which they were the cream, ripened only in the West.[31]

In 1796, after four years of working land that was not his with slave laborers who were, Dempsey Jackson purchased 150 acres of second-rate land near Johnson Creek, a tributary of the Licking River some twenty miles southwest of Maysville. This portion of the county was its most densely settled outside Limestone and Washington; as many as seventeen farms lined the road between Mayslick and Blue Licks, most of which lay in the three-mile stretch north of Johnson Creek where the farms nearly abutted one another. The land here was hillier, the soil less black and loamy than that deemed first-rate, yet it was rich and level enough to grow all the crops that the first-rate land could sustain. Jackson's tract was, however, far from prime tobacco land. In fact, few of the settlers—even Thomas Marshall, who owned upwards of a thousand acres and twenty-two slaves—appear to have grown tobacco as their major crop. Within a few miles sat a newly completed station occupied by fellow Virginian and militia colonel John Fleming, a sober reflection of the settlers' awareness of their vulnerability to Indian attack, despite the present détente. More ominously, Jackson's tract sat just five miles from the "dark and bloody ground" of white Kentuckians, the Blue Licks battle site, a chilling reminder that no doubt encouraged Fleming to build not just one, but three stations in the area. Daniel Drake remembered as a child near Mayslick that prior to Anthony Wayne's victory at Fallen Timbers in 1794, "the danger from Indians still continued; . . . I well remember that Indian wars, midnight butcheries, captivities and horse stealings, were the daily topics of conversation. Volunteering to pursue marauding parties occasionally took place and sometimes men were drafted." Dempsey Jackson's new world involved not only risk, but danger.[32]

Staking claim to the rich soil of the Kentucky interior could offer men such as Dempsey Jackson the chance for entrance into the area's social aristocracy. Yet like his father and grandfather before him, he too would fail to enter the ranks of the state's planter gentry. While he would eventually achieve a level of prosperity surpassing his Virginia family, Jackson lived in the outer

31. Lucas, *History of Blacks in Kentucky,* vol. 1, xvi.

32. Thomas D. Clark, ed., *Historical Maps of Kentucky,* 76; Mason County [Kentucky] Tax Assessment Books, 1790–1797, 1799–1809, microfilm reel 008140, KDLA; Tinling and Davies, eds., *The Western Country in 1793,* 71–74, 79; "John Fleming," and "Fleming County," both in Kleber, ed., *The Kentucky Encyclopedia,* 324–25; Drake, *Pioneer Life in Kentucky,* 28–29. Historians dispute the origin of the term "dark and bloody ground," but refer to it most commonly as a moniker for the violent history of the region prior to the arrival of white settlers. See "Dark and Bloody Ground," in Kleber, ed., *The Kentucky Encyclopedia,* 253.

Bluegrass, a ring of counties that surround the fertile soils and high-priced lands of the heart of the agricultural region. While the soils of the Bluegrass's outer lip were relatively productive—certainly more so than in the Knobs or the mountains to the east or even the steep ridges to the north—the region remained on the new state's geographic, cultural, and political cusp. The inner Bluegrass, called by some the "Great Kentucky Prairie," an elliptical hub with Lexington as its nucleus, was settled by tidewater gentry who held title not only to Kentucky's best land but also to some degree its social franchise. Dempsey Jackson's existence stood in sharp silhouette to the reality of life for most western migrants; despite the West's democratic promise, power and standing proved to be as inherited as the slave laborers the migrants brought to the transmontane.[33]

In Fleming County, Dempsey Jackson built a log cabin and attended the local Baptist church, a log structure located a quarter mile south of Mayslick on the Limestone Trace and attended by a minister from Washington. Daniel Drake recalled "all the people being either professors of religion in, or adherents to, the Baptist Church." Jackson's family continued to grow, supplementing the labor provided by his three slave laborers in the fields and woods of his burgeoning farm. By 1810, the federal census lists the family as having eleven children, three daughters and eight sons. The eldest child, Craven, born in Virginia, was followed by three daughters, including Ann and Octavia, and seven successive sons, including Dempsey Pickett, Wade Moseby, William, and Thomas, all born in Kentucky in the decade following their arrival in the state. On April 4, 1806, the family's youngest son was born; the couple named him Claiborne Fox.[34]

By the time of Claib Jackson's birth, Dempsey Jackson had managed to acquire another hundred acres, bringing his total to 250, but he still possessed only three slaves. The expense of such a large family no doubt interrupted any further purchases of slaves, had he even desired them, for the prospect of eight young sons as farmhands might well have quelled any great need for them. Indeed, it would appear that Dempsey required his sons and daughters to work on the farm; the census in 1820 lists eight persons engaged

33. Bladen and Pauer, *Geography of Kentucky*, 71–74; Clark, *Kentucky*, 89 (quote); Aron, *How the West Was Lost*, 125–33.

34. Drake, *Pioneer Life in Kentucky*, 29 (quote); Aron, *How the West Was Lost*, 130–33; Williams, *Joseph Jackson*, 22; Third U.S. Census, 1810, Population Schedule, Fleming County, Kentucky, NA; Seventh and Eighth U.S. Censuses, 1850 and 1860, Population Schedule, Howard County, Missouri, NA. I was unable to determine the origin of Claiborne Fox Jackson's middle name. Conceivably, his parents named him for the Fox Springs, a well-known natural sulfur spring in east-central Fleming County that soon would become a popular spa. See "Fleming County" in Kleber, ed., *Kentucky Encyclopedia*, 324–25.

in agriculture, accounting largely for the Jackson sons, while three were engaged in manufacturing, most likely his wife and daughters who produced domestically for the farm and for local sale. Dempsey appears to have been a demanding taskmaster, insisting upon his children's labor, especially once they had come of age. In 1811, just a year after the Jackson's final child, Susan, was born, the Jackson house divided as a result of the struggle for autonomy that maturation brings inevitably. The eldest of Jackson's sons—Craven and Dempsey Pickett—left the farm bound for Nashville, Tennessee, after separate disputes with the family patriarch. While the exact nature of Craven's departure is unknown, Dempsey claimed later to have left after his father forbade him from attending school, in order that he manage the farm labor. If the story is correct, such schooling—offered by a Baptist minister—must have been of a practical curriculum, for Daniel Drake recalled that as late as 1817 not one schoolmaster offered classical or mathematical instruction in Fleming, Mason, or Bracken Counties. No Transylvania University existed for yeomen's sons on the Bluegrass rim.[35]

Claib Jackson grew to young manhood with his father, mother, brothers, and sisters in a Fleming County that witnessed years of alternately unparalleled prosperity and great economic disruption in the West. Kentucky farmers worked their fields not for mere self-sufficiency, but with an eye for export. The continental wars in Europe had raged nearly since the end of the Revolution, and the demand for American grain caused the interior to become a breadbasket for the world. As the prices for corn, wheat, oats, and rye soared, Kentuckians—including hundreds of thousands more who resettled over the mountains to take advantage of the boom—enjoyed flush times. Even the Embargo of 1808—Jefferson's infamous "damn-bargo"—only mildly deflated prices and but for a couple of years. Three subsequent years of war seem not to have interrupted a quarter century of steady demand for American agricultural products; if anything, they increased it. Flour prices began rising in 1812 and peaked at nine dollars a barrel in late 1814. The following year, the Jackson farm was valued at more than six thousand dollars, with its 250 acres of land assessed at ten dollars per acre and fifteen horses and ten slaves (four of whom were over sixteen)

35. Fourth U.S. Census, 1820, Population Schedule, Fleming County, Kentucky, NA; Obituary of Dempsey Pickett Jackson, undated [1874], John Sappington Collection, Mss. 1036, folder 4: Sappington Miscellany, SHSM; Fourth U.S. Census, 1820, Population Schedule, Davidson County, Tennessee, NA; Seventh U.S. Census, 1850, Population Schedule, Howard County, Missouri, NA; Drake, *Pioneer Life in Kentucky*, 33–34, 142; Federal Writer's Project, *Kentucky*, 205. The census for 1820 lists a Graven [likely Craven] Jackson in Davidson County, Tennessee, though he shows up in no other census. He practiced the plastering trade and owned no slaves.

included in its property assessment. Claib's father appeared on the doorstep of untrammeled success.[36]

Any such euphoria would have proved short-lived for the Jackson family. The end of the War of 1812—the first year of peace in a generation—brought great economic hardships to the West. Though prices remained high for several years, agricultural production in Europe gradually rebounded after the defeat of Napoleon, triggering a reduction in demand for western grain. Land prices (and sales) followed suit, and the availability of credit spurred thousands to go into debt in order to purchase land and to capitalize on the economy's breakneck pace. The bubble burst in 1818, followed the next year by the nation's first great "panic." Punitive British industrialists sought "to stifle in the cradle" those infant American manufacturers they considered their hereditary inferiors, and began to find other suppliers of raw materials for their factories. Cotton prices began to fall, followed by tobacco, wheat, corn, and hemp. Tobacco cultivation, which had expanded greatly after 1815 as a result of high prices, collapsed disastrously in 1819, and with the exception of one short period of higher prices in the early 1830s, remained low for more than a decade. In 1833, Kentucky reported that its farmers had exported only four thousand hogsheads of tobacco. From 1816 to 1825, wheat sold for less than 60 percent of its normal price (it continued low until as late as 1834); from 1821 to 1825, corn—which held out a bit longer before dropping dramatically—sold for just more than half its average price. Wheat exports from 1820 to 1829 declined by more than 96 percent from just thirty years before, a time that coincided precisely with Dempsey Jackson's arrival in the West. Dependent upon the dwindling European markets and also on the expanding cotton states, Kentucky farmers struggled to avoid foreclosure on bank loans they took during the flush years while their legislators cleaved over the implementation of relief measures. Indeed, in October 1822, the *Louisville Public Advertiser* noted that the $2.3 million of Kentucky paper currency in circulation had depreciated by half, forcing merchants to resort to a hard-money system and reduce all prices at the same rate as the currency's depreciation.[37]

The Jackson family appears to have weathered the storm, but not without considerable buffeting. Between 1815 and 1820, Jackson acquired no land but his slaveholdings (which doubtless included females, as well as males)

36. Channing, *Kentucky,* 76–78; North, *Economic Growth of the United States,* 53–58; Berry, *Western Prices before 1861,* 157–60; Mason County [Kentucky] Tax Assessment Books, 1790–1797, 1799–1809, microfilm reel 008140, KDLA.

37. Channing, *Kentucky,* 78 (quote); Berry, *Western Prices before 1861,* 183, 400–405; Gray, *History of Agriculture in the Southern United States,* 2:876–77.

increased from ten to twelve, the new acquisitions all children and thus presumably offspring of those he owned already. He acquired neither land nor even horses during the period, and though his property's assessed value increased by 15 percent, such an increase was largely attributable to the increased level of taxation attendant with wartime and the economic depression that ensued for years afterward. By 1825, although Dempsey Jackson had managed to acquire 125 more acres, all second-rate (quite possibly through a dispossession auction, given the wide speculation of the previous decade and the resultant widespread bankruptcies later), and possessed two more slave children, he owned no more horses than he had a decade earlier. The 1820s were lean indeed for many western farmers, and the Jacksons were not excluded.[38]

At the quarter point of the nineteenth century, Dempsey Jackson had reached the apex of his social advancement. He had achieved respectability, but not great respect. He occupied a social position perhaps comparable to his father's, but nowhere near that commanded by his father-in-law. His farm was of at best a middling size, achieved only after he had reached the age of sixty, in the last decade of his life. By the time of his death on June 22, 1833, Dempsey Jackson possessed an estate of 377 acres, ten slaves (seven of whom were under the age of sixteen), and eleven horses, which together was assessed at less than half of what it had been assessed a decade earlier. The farm offered little opportunity for eight sons, and by 1831 just one remained at home. In the decade prior to his death, beginning at the height of the postwar depression, an exodus of sorts occurred in the Jackson clan. Between 1823 and 1826, four more of Dempsey Jackson's sons—Thomas, William, Wade, and Claib, the latter the sole bachelor—as well as seven adult male Jackson cousins followed the path of their ancestors. These sons of rootless ambition moved to the new frontier of Missouri.[39]

38. Fleming County [Kentucky] Tax Assessment Books, 1822, 1824–1829, 1831, 1833–1834, 1837–1841, microfilm reel 007970, KDLA.

39. Fleming County [Kentucky] Tax Assessment Books, 1822, 1824–1829, 1831, 1833–1834, 1837–1841, microfilm reel 007970, KDLA; Fifth U.S. Census, 1830, Population Schedule, Fleming County, Kentucky, Howard County, Missouri, NA; Howard County [Missouri] Tax Lists, vols. 1–2 (1816–1841), microfilm reel S244, MSA. Dempsey Jackson died intestate. Fleming County [Kentucky] Will Books, General Index, 1798–1962, microfilm reel 344037, KDLA; Burks, "Thunder on the Right," 26n16.

A SLAVEHOLDERS' DEMOCRACY

POLITICALLY KENTUCKY PRIDED itself on its fierce defense of democracy, but its democracy was a matter of definition depending on whether the citizen was a slaveholding planter in the Bluegrass or a rifleman in the clearings on the border of the Indian country.

LOUIS B. WRIGHT, *CULTURE ON THE MOVING FRONTIER*

Claib Jackson and his older brothers were no pioneers in the nation's newest state. Dempsey Jackson's sons arrived in Missouri in the 1820s as had their father in the nation's then vernal state, Kentucky, three decades earlier—driven by ambition yet too late to become planter parvenus in this slave-holders' frontier. As early as 1816, Missouri land fever had gripped Virginians and Kentuckians, so much so that no less than the Virginia state treasurer, John Preston, wrote to his brother-in-law in that year that "with every intelligent person I have met, and many others, Missouri has been the subject of conversation. I find *all* have their minds turned that way. I have no doubt but it will be *all the rage* in two or three years, just like the Ohio was ten years ago or less." Anticipating the imminent flood of migrants, Preston urged his cautious relative to travel to the country's newest frontier without delay as their land company's agent: "Every year and day will make it worse for us. . . . I want to be beforehand; get good choices [of land] and at low prices; and this I fear cannot be done unless we set about the work seriously this fall and winter."[1]

Preston was right about the impending exodus to Missouri. Within four years, the territory had become the nation's twenty-fourth state, brought into the union amid the young Republic's greatest political controversy. This was a young men's flood tide, and five of the Jackson brothers emigrated while in their early twenties. One of the early arrivals was older sibling Dempsey Pickett Jackson, who had left Nashville in 1816 and emigrated first to St. Louis, and by 1821 to near Natchez, Mississippi. In 1823, two of the younger Jackson brothers—Thomas and William—settled in the interior of the new state. At their urging, Wade Moseby joined his siblings three years later and within another year twenty-one-year-old Claib arrived in the region he would call home for nearly the next four decades. Without mountains to cross, the brothers' trips proved less strenuous than had been their parents'

1. Quoted in Ulrich B. Phillips, *Life and Labor in the Old South*, 86.

three decades earlier; these young westerners each traveled the Ohio and Mississippi Rivers by steamer to St. Louis, then up the state's main artery, the Missouri River, to Franklin, a thriving river town and seat of Howard County. Steamboats had begun plying the turbid waters of the Missouri to Franklin in 1819, complementing the "Boon's Lick Trace" that connected St. Charles with Franklin. Howard County, with Franklin as its centerpiece, was the heart of Missouri's current lodestone of immigration—the Boon's Lick country.[2]

The Boon's Lick—a belt of rolling hills, fertile valleys, and broad prairies some sixty miles wide and seventy-five miles long, lying on each side of the Missouri and encompassing its great northward bends—had already replaced the counties immediately surrounding St. Louis as the state's fastest growing. Ten years before the Jackson brothers' arrival, just over a thousand residents had lived along the Missouri River between the Osage and the western Indian boundary, organized in 1816 by the territorial legislature as Howard County. By the time of statehood in 1821, more than twenty thousand white settlers and three thousand black slaves lived in Missouri's central river counties, the new state's geographic, and soon economic, heart. One New England missionary recalled of the public imagination toward the Boon's Lick region that "the whole current of immigration set towards this country, Boon's Lick . . . Ask one of them whither he was moving, and the answer was, 'To Boon's Lick to be sure.' " By the time Claib Jackson set foot in Franklin, the claim had become axiomatic. Howard County, named for territorial governor Benjamin Howard, boasted 10,860 residents despite having been reduced dramatically in size after the legislature had carved Chariton, Saline, Cooper, Cole, Ray, and Lillard Counties from its original demarcation just three years earlier. Four of these newcomers were Jackson brothers; another was a slave owned by Thomas Jackson.[3]

In 1827, Franklin was central Missouri's boomtown. Situated on the floodplain known as "Cooper's Bottom" on the north bank of the Missouri River, Franklin was a decade old and the seat of Howard County. The town sprawled well past its original fifty-acre site, and its principal streets were

2. Howard County [Missouri] Tax Lists, vols. 1–2 (1819–1841), microfilm reel S244, MSA; *Missouri Intelligencer* [Franklin], May 12, 1826; *Missouri Intelligencer and Boon's Lick Advertiser* [Fayette], July 12, 1827; *History of Howard and Chariton Counties, Missouri, Written and Compiled from the Most Official Authentic and Private Sources, Including a History of Its Townships, Towns and Villages,* 167–68; Donald H. Welch, "Travel by Stage on the Boonslick Road," 335; Burks, "Thunder on the Right," 30.

3. Malcolm J. Rohrbough, *The Trans-Appalachian Frontier: People, Societies, and Institutions, 1775–1850,* 135–36 (quote), 137–38; William E. Foley, *The Genesis of Missouri: From Wilderness Outpost to Statehood,* 238–41, 262–63; Fifth U.S. Census, Population Schedule, Howard County, Missouri, NA; Howard County [Missouri] Tax Lists, vols. 1–2 (1819–1841), microfilm reel S244, MSA.

nearly thirty yards wide. Within three years the river had offered both feast and famine. Though it had brought more than a thousand new people to the mid-Missouri town, the unpredictable Missouri's recurring floods had forced Franklin's relocation to the low bluffs nearly two miles to the northeast. The town boasted a thriving business climate, enough to spur the construction of hundreds of homes (at least two of brick), a two-acre public square, more than twenty stores and businesses including two mills, a post office, a printing office and newspaper, the *Missouri Intelligencer* (the first published west of St. Louis), four taverns, a two-story log jail filled with drunks and disputants who took the law into their own hands (especially those laws involving land), and a brick courthouse and federal land office that together attempted to mediate against such violent conflicts. By the time of the last Jackson's arrival, Franklin boasted a population of more than fifteen hundred, the largest among the state's interior towns and the third largest in the state, behind only St. Louis and Ste. Genevieve. Though dwarfed by limestone bluffs that lined the wide Missouri, Franklin now towered above a myriad of such river towns, all of whose founders both believed and touted that theirs would soon supplant St. Louis as the West's leviathan.[4]

The Jackson brothers joined in a sanguine migration that first brought thousands of individuals from largely the middle portions of the nation to the great trans-Mississippi frontier. Though the expanse far surpassed that which their father had confronted, by the time of the sons' migration the West was anything but dark and foreboding. American vistas had changed dramatically since Dempsey Jackson's transmontane trek. The opening of the Louisiana Territory (and especially Lewis and Clark's adventures beyond) had offered the nation's restless imagination yet another seemingly endless and often exotic expanse of land at a time when its people had only begun to fill the forests recently won from England. American Romanticism completed the erasure of the frightful image of the frontier as exile, replacing it with a West (whether Kentucky or Missouri) as new Eden, an Earthly paradise where buckskin-clad heroes communed with nature in virtuous harmony and pushed the increasingly marginalized Indians out of their path. The acquisition of this prairied landscape—the first territory acquired from a

---

4. Foley, *Genesis of Missouri*, 241; William F. Switzler, *History of Missouri*, 193; Burks, "Thunder on the Right," 32; *History of Howard and Chariton Counties*, 166, 169; Federal Writers' Project, *Missouri*, 350, 352; Jonas Viles, "Old Franklin: A Frontier Town of the Twenties," 271–74; Alma Merle West, "The Earlier Political Career of Claiborne Fox Jackson, 1836–1851," 4; Perry McCandless, *A History of Missouri: Volume II—1820–1860*, 34. In 1820, St. Louis had just over ten thousand residents, while Ste. Genevieve had a population of between fifteen hundred and two thousand. Four other Missouri towns boasted populations of more than five hundred: Cape Girardeau, Jackson, Potosi, and St. Charles.

completely foreign nation and thus the embodiment of bloodless triumph, of manifest destiny—only augmented the hopes that the nation placed on the West of its own imagination. New England minister Timothy Flint only sparked such castle-building with a widely read book in 1825, in which he wrote of the countryside in the Missouri River counties that one needed not "be very young or very romantic, in order to have dreams steal over the mind, of spending an Arcadian life in these remote plains, which just begin to be vexed with the plough, far removed from the haunts of wealth and fashion, in the midst of rustic plenty, and of this beautiful nature."[5]

As Americans pushed westward, they brought civilization and democratic order to the West, and this progressive, frontier ideal became in effect the American ideal. The removal of Daniel Boone, the archetypal frontiersman, from Kentucky—the first West—to Missouri only legitimized the state as the land of nature's noblemen. The conquest of the West had become synonymous with democratic ascendancy and for many potential emigrants, Missouri—like its own birth state nearly three decades earlier—became the newest lodestar of America's rising fortunes, of national greatness and, as important, of the realization of personal ambition. One recent emigrant, William B. Napton, placed "confidence in the intelligence and virtue of the great mass of the people, more especially the honest and independent yeomanry of the country—the man who eats his own bread and meat and is not affected by the downfall of one politician and the elevation of another. It is here that the last footholds of liberty will be found—their wish is only for the welfare of the country and though they may be misled by artful demagogues, they ultimately get right and pursue honestly that policy they think best calculated to promote the interest of their country." No less than the nation's greatest orator, Daniel Webster, proclaimed Missouri an infant Hercules, soon to lift the nation on its mighty back. As the Jacksonians would soon trumpet, the West had become America.[6]

And the Boon's Lick was nature's miracle, a "farmer's paradise." Pro-moters touted its deep, yellow loess soil, abundant woodlands, and rolling terrain as the "Canaan of America," the nation's promised land. Moreover, its wondrous river system, with deep creeks such as the Bonne Femme, Salt, Moniteau, Cedar, and Roche Perche, and navigable rivers such as the Osage,

5. Moore, *The Frontier Mind*, 106–8; Timothy Flint, *Recollections of the Last Ten Years*, 122 (quote); Thomas D. Clark, *Frontier America: The Story of the Westward Movement*, 238–48.

6. John William Ward, *Andrew Jackson—Symbol for an Age*, 39–41; Diary of William B. Napton, Typescripts, folder 1, p. 46, William B. Napton Papers, MHS (first quote), hereafter cited as Napton Diary; Paul C. Nagel, *Missouri: A Bicentennial History*, 50 (second quote).

Chariton, Grand, Black (or Blackwater), and Lamine, all feeding directly or indirectly into the mighty thoroughfare of the West, the Missouri, offered both transportation and trade to settlers seeking such connections with St. Louis and New Orleans, and thus the rest of the nation and even the world. Yet the Boon's Lick was removed from the established, settled areas around St. Louis, and therefore beckoned to those who sought personal freedoms betokened by its physical distance from civilization. Finally, the chance for economic independence attendant with cheap land and bountiful, profitable harvests lured settlers past the French influences of St. Louis and St. Charles, which they regarded with disdain, and to the open countryside of the Boon's Lick, broken by lush valleys filled with oaks, sycamores, black walnuts, and hickories.[7]

Missouri—especially the central river counties—was the avowed progeny of Kentucky, the heart of the West. The largest segment of its people traced their bloodline proudly not only to the Bluegrass, but to their ancestral home, the Old Dominion, a migratory entail that bound the three states into a socio-political-cultural trinity. In 1829 the young luminary Edward Everett proclaimed in Lexington, Kentucky, that "beyond the Wabash— beyond the Mississippi—there are now large communities, who look to these their native fields with the same feeling with which your fathers looked back to their native homes in Virginia." Indeed, at the time of the Jacksons' arrival in Howard County, former Kentuckians had virtually populated the interior river counties of the state; by 1860, one hundred thousand Kentuckians called Missouri their home—more than three times those from any other state. More still came from the piedmont areas of Virginia and the Carolinas and from the Nashville basin, as well as many earlier transplants from the state's Bootheel, driven panic-stricken to the Boon's Lick following the catastrophic New Madrid earthquake of 1811. Together they established a second generation, upcountry patrimony that prompted Baptist minister John Mason Peck to note in 1816 that it appeared to him "as though Kentucky and Tennessee were breaking up and moving to the 'Far West.'" At the time of Missouri's statehood, perhaps two-thirds of those living in the central river counties had been born in either Kentucky, Tennessee, or Virginia; as late as 1850 (when the census enumerated birth states for the first time), 36 percent of its residents still claimed those states as the places of birth, with Kentuckians forming the highest percentage in five of the seven counties. Indeed, a full third of all Kentucky-born who left their birth state for any other destination ended their journey in Missouri. Prideful of

7. Federal Writers' Project, *Missouri*, 359; R. Douglas Hurt, *Agriculture and Slavery in Missouri's Little Dixie*, 51 (first quote), 79 (second quote); Nagel, *Missouri*, 75.

his state's role as progenitor, one senator boasted that Kentucky's middle western offspring "are bone of our bone and flesh of our flesh."[8]

As much as the immigrants to the Boon's Lick were by birthright children of Kentucky, they owed their political heritage to a Virginia grandfather of sorts. The preponderance of these immigrants were simple yeomen seeking frontier freeholds, espousing Jeffersonian democratic notions that they attributed to their greatest spokesman. So dogged was their devotion to the Sage of Monticello that when in 1821 the first state legislature sited its future capital fifty miles downriver from Franklin, local settlers exultantly named the hamlet City of Jefferson, thus offering a living memorial to the demigod. These plain husbandmen held out high hopes for the establishment of an agrarian utopia west of the Mississippi where these "labor[ers] in the earth," as their champion had written, would claim their divine right as the "chosen people of God, if ever He had a chosen people." Kentuckian John Breckinridge noted as early as 1797 that it appeared to him that "the poorer Class of people" was headed for that part of the Spanish territory that eventually became Missouri. These earliest settlers to the Boon's Lick country brought with them the base elements of a subsistence economy, as reflected by an 1819 editorial in Franklin's *Missouri Intelligencer:* "Boon's Lick—two years since, a wilderness; now, rich in corn and cattle."[9]

By the time of the Jacksons' emigration, however, residents of the Boon's Lick offered decidedly different descriptions of the "mountain torrent" of humanity raging into the region. No longer the offscourings of the piedmont or Cumberland Plateau, these settlers brought with them a relative amount of wealth and property—a distinction that set the Boon's Lick apart from other areas of settlement farther to the east. As late as 1830, young William B. Sappington, son of one of the Boon's Lick's most prominent

8. Russell L. Gerlach, "Population Origins in Rural Missouri," 5–15; *Orations and Speeches on Various Occasions by Edward Everett* (Boston, 1850), 2d ed., vol. 1, 205, in Coulter, *Civil War and Readjustment in Kentucky,* 13 (first quote), 14 (fourth quote); Robert M. Crisler, "Missouri's Little Dixie," 131 (second quote); Seventh U.S. Census, 1850, Population Schedule, Boone, Callaway, Clay, Cooper, Howard, Lafayette, and Saline Counties, Missouri, NA; Rufus Babcock, ed., *Forty Years of Pioneer Life: Memoir of John Mason Peck, D. D.,* 146 (third quote). According to the 1860 census, 25 percent of residents of the region claimed to have been born in one of the three states; assuming an approximate 10 percent increase in each decade (slightly less than the amount of decrease between 1850 and 1860), I derived the two-thirds figure in 1820.

9. Foley, *Genesis of Missouri,* 238–39; Federal Writers' Project, *Missouri,* 226–27; Hurt, *Agriculture and Slavery in Little Dixie,* 8; Merrill D. Peterson, *Thomas Jefferson and the New Nation,* 256 (first and second quotes); John Breckinridge to James Breckinridge, May 9, 1797, quoted in Faragher, *Daniel Boone,* 274 (third quote); *Missouri Intelligencer* [Franklin], June 11, 1819, quoted in Rohrbaugh, *Trans-Appalachian Frontier,* 136 (fourth quote). Jefferson City was situated a few miles from a former French trading village, Côte sans Dessein.

residents, physician John Sappington, wrote from Cumberland College in Princeton, Kentucky, to his brother, Erasmus, living near Jonesborough in Saline County, that he was "glad to hear of Missourie filling up more, and aspecilly of our near neighbours as they are quite respectable, and also will keep out other of a quite low standing for I assure you there is a vast number of that kind pass here going to missouri and Illinois but the most of them to the latter place, and the most from Tennessee—Ford that keeps the ferry on the Ohio river is getting very wealthy by keeping the ferry." Another observer noted a year earlier that the newest arrivals "appear generally to be persons of considerable property and respectability—having with them slaves and considerable money."[10]

In keeping with their upland roots, Missouri farmers lived largely in simple two-story, Federal-style wooden farmhouses. Often unadorned and set back from the road or on the peaks of rolling hills, these farmhouses looked far more like those in the lower parts of the Old Northwest than any of the genteel plantation homes characteristic of southern aristocrats. A life consumed by hard farm work with a diversity of crops and other commercial endeavors—even with the advantage of slave labor—offered precious little time and even less surplus capital for decadent construction. Rare indeed were brick mansions such as Alfred Morrison's "Lilac Hill," Abiel Leonard's "Oakwood," both located on the outskirts of Fayette, William Sappington's "Prairie Park" west of Arrow Rock, and William O. Anderson's magnificent home just outside Lexington. Indeed, what few such brick structures existed in the region tended to be located in or near the region's towns, rather than secluded in the country. Only sixty brick homes existed in the entire region in 1840—as compared with 556 wooden houses and innumerable log cabins. Rather, most slaveholding farmers built simple frame dwellings with whitewashed clapboard siding which themselves indicated respectability over the various progressions of hand-hewn log houses that dotted the countryside. Saline County luminary Dr. John Sappington, with fifty slaves, lived his entire life in a two-story dogtrot log home and decried his son William's project as "a monument to damned fools" when in 1843 William built his magnificent brick home a mile from the Sappington homestead.[11]

10. Hurt, *Agriculture and Slavery in Little Dixie*, 24 (first quote), 51 (third quote); William B. Sappington to Erasmus D. Sappington, November 14, 1830, John S. Sappington Papers, Mss. 1027, box 1, folder 18, SHSM (second quote); Sappington family details, ibid., box 1, folder 1.

11. Hurt, *Agriculture and Slavery in Little Dixie*, 188; Richard Pyle Power, *Planting Corn Belt Culture: The Impress of the Upland Southerner and Yankee in the Old Northwest*, 102–5; Nicole Etcheson, *The Emerging Midwest: Upland Southerners and the Political Culture of the Old Northwest, 1787–1861*, 1–14; Federal Writers' Project, *Missouri*, 375; Marcia Joy Prouse, ed., *Arrow Rock: 20th-Century Frontier Town*, 185; J. C. Sappington

The arrival of these "substantial farmers, and enterprising merchants and mechanics" altered the nature of agriculture, trade, and cultural mores of the Boon's Lick. While the lure of a better life drew nearly all to the region, these people of property sought more than mere subsistence; they pursued profit through commercial ventures, whether agricultural or trade, and enough to achieve the social ascendance that drove them from their homes to Missouri. Upon his arrival in 1829, one resident noted the egalitarian capitalism of

> the people of the west generally . . . [and] their eager pursuit of money and restless enterprise and unceasing activity by which alone their favourite object can be attained. This is obvious to every one and the Kentuckian yields not a whit to the yankee in resorting to every means, however contemptible they might be thought in old Virginia, to amass wealth, knowing well that once attained, nobody cares to enquire how or in what crooked way he came by it. As an evidence of this, horse trading, negro-trading, hog-driving, shaving an exorbitant interest, trading on flat-boats or (as they are sometimes called) broadhorns to New Orleans, constitute the pursuit of almost every money-making man in the community.[12]

Because most of these entrepreneurs had moved to central Missouri from areas that had sustained various types of cash crops—tobacco, hemp, and cotton—they naturally brought with them aspirations for success with these timeworn staples. Planting familiar crops and raising livestock offered psychological sustenance beyond its economic practicality; the familiarity of the soil and even the climate (though the latter proved somewhat harsher than that of their piedmont or Bluegrass homes) only cemented their faith in the new land. While Alabamians née Georgians and Carolinians moved to Mississippi, Virginians and Kentuckians moved to Missouri and brought the distinguishing features of their culture with them. The emplacement of such upcountry "mental furniture," as one historian has called the transference of familiar social-cultural-economic norms to the frontier, and the immediate success they derived from them quickly caused land in the Boon's Lick to appreciate in value. Settlers who sought choice lands to grow their crops paid far more than the $1.25 per acre minimum price for available public lands; by 1827 the best land in Howard County often cost five times that and more. Prices only continued to rise during the subsequent decade. Those like the Jacksons who arrived during the mid to late 1820s would pay dearly

to Charles Van Ravenswaay, January 20, 1937, Charles Van Ravenswaay Collection, Mss. 2668, folder 7, SHSM. William O. Anderson's mansion appears never to have had a distinctive name. One can find a number of frame farmhouses standing along Missouri Route 124 east of Fayette in Howard and Boone Counties.

12. *Missouri Intelligencer and Boon's Lick Advertiser* [Fayette], November 2, 1826, quoted in Hurt, *Agriculture and Slavery in Little Dixie,* 52 (first quote); Napton Diary, folder 1, pp. 44–45, MHS (second quote).

for the most facile access to economic, and thus cultural, hegemony, in an elite class that proved far different in Missouri from that of their predecessors in Kentucky and Virginia.[13]

THAT THE JACKSON brothers' arrival in the nation's newest state coincided with the year Thomas Jefferson drew his last anointed breath proved prophetic. The Eden that these latecomers lay claim to in the Boon's Lick region had as one of its cornerstones the ownership of bound laborers. The strand of counties lying along the Missouri would soon become the epicenter of slave ownership in the entire state, with Howard as the crown jewel. At the very founding of the state, a full 13 percent of the overall populations of Howard and Cooper Counties were bondpeople. The numbers climbed steadily during the ensuing decades, so that by 1850 eight of the Boon's Lick counties had slave populations that constituted a quarter or more of their overall populations. In that year, those counties formed eight of the ten largest slave owning counties in the entire state. A decade later, Howard County's 5,886 slaves made up 37 percent of its overall population, eclipsed only in raw numbers—but not percentage—by Lafayette, and only then in the final antebellum years, with its 6,374 bondpeople accounting for just less than 32 percent of its residents in 1860. In that year, slaveholding in the state as a whole averaged just 10 percent. Clearly, the democracy that evolved in the Boon's Lick was one in which slaveholding figured conspicuously into the social equation.[14]

The deep adherence of Missouri's upcountry yeomanry to Jefferson as their ideological standard bearer offers a decided irony given the Sage of Monticello's paradoxical connection to the issue of slavery in the political creation and ultimate settlement patterns of the Middle West. These newest Missourians had completely disregarded—if they ever had any notion—that Jefferson had been the architect of the Northwest Ordinance, including in his plan for the entire British cession a provision that forbade slavery in any territories and states carved from the West. The plan as accepted by the Confederation Congress ultimately applied only to the territories north of the Ohio River and east of the Mississippi, thus excluding what would become Missouri. Yet Jefferson's stance as early as 1784 held unmistakably that, at least in his mind, slavery in the West was of national importance and

---

13. Frank L. Owsley, "The Pattern of Migration and Settlement on the Southern Frontier," 147 (first quote); Thomas D. Clark and John D. W. Guice, *Frontiers in Conflict: The Old Southwest, 1795–1830,* 16–18, 100–101, 166–67, 258–59; Hurt, *Agriculture and Slavery in Little Dixie,* 52, 56, 64–65.

14. Hurt, *Agriculture and Slavery in Little Dixie,* 217–18, 220. For the most complete discussion of slavery and slaveholding in the nonplantation South, see James Oakes, *The Ruling Race: A History of American Slaveholders.*

overrode all local autonomy. More telling, Jefferson's response to Missouri's controversial entrance into the union of states only punctuated the concern he felt for the future of the West—of the nation—with regard to slavery. Pronouncing the debate over slavery and the Louisiana Purchase an "act of suicide upon themselves, and of treason against the hopes of the world," Jefferson offered bitterly that "I regret that I am now to die in the belief, that the useless sacrifice of themselves by the generation of 1776, to acquire self-government and happiness to their country, is to be thrown away by unwise and unworthy passions of their sons." He claimed that "this momentous question, like a fire-bell in the night, awakened and filled me with terror" and portended that the Missouri issue or, more broadly, slavery in the West, would be "the knell of the Union." The Jefferson who envisioned Missouri was wholly unlike the Jefferson who post-statehood Missourians invented when they hoisted the framing timbers of their new society.[15]

As these new Missourians fanned out into the Boon's Lick interior, they introduced profit-driven agricultural endeavors that were the legacy of their upcountry origins. The staple crops introduced into the region—tobacco, hemp, and cotton—offered a commercial vehicle for accumulating profits, and farmers hastily cleared land enough to begin production. In 1822, farmers from Tennessee introduced and raised cotton successfully enough for reports to reach St. Louis the following spring that the Boon's Lick had produced a full twenty-five thousand pounds. Prices of as much as $140 per ton for dew-rotted hemp in 1832 stimulated local farmers to plant large fields of the labor-intensive crop, used largely for rope and bagging for cotton bales. Commission buyers solicited hemp throughout the region, buying farmers' entire crops and offering on occasion free shipping to St. Louis and even direct shipping to New York, bypassing the penultimate market at New Orleans in pursuit of the highest price. One farmer boasted that he had planted 60 of his 258 acres in hemp, and river watchers noted the hemp bales that regularly lined the cargo decks of the riverboats that plied the Missouri.[16]

While hemp and cotton quickly spread into the Boon's Lick country, tobacco—as in Kentucky and Virginia before—became the lifeblood of the region's staple economy. An inheritance of their fathers, tobacco culture defined the very culture of the settlers themselves, and the pattern of life enjoyed by them derived from its rhythms. The rich soil and moist summer heat of the region encouraged widespread production of the hearty plant, whose growing season was shorter than cotton's and its harvest well ahead of

---

15. Peterson, *Thomas Jefferson*, 282–83; Thomas Jefferson to John Holmes, April 22, 1820, in Merrill D. Peterson, ed., *The Portable Thomas Jefferson*, 567–69.

16. Hurt, *Agriculture and Slavery in Little Dixie*, 65, 115; Miles W. Eaton, "The Development and Later Decline of the Hemp Industry in Missouri," 351.

any killing frost. With water access to the New Orleans market, with the best-quality tobacco fetching as much as seven cents a pound in New Orleans and second-rate leaf going for nearly as much, and with land capable of producing a thousand pounds of tobacco per acre in the 1820s, many farmers saw great opportunity in the "sure crop," tobacco. By 1840, central Missourians produced nearly 37 percent of all the tobacco gathered in the state and tobacco merchants opened warehouses in river towns such as Franklin, Chariton, and Glasgow, offering cash advances to compete with the buyers from St. Louis who increasingly scoured the burgeoning countryside.[17]

While profit impulses entrenched tobacco cultivation in central Missouri, its proliferation came as more than a mere economic inheritance—the construction of these Missourians' *mentalité* caused them intrinsically to associate tobacco production with social and even cultural progress. Such social ordering was a legacy of their earliest tidewater ancestors. Colonial Virginians derived their local status in part from the quality of the leaf they produced and, if expert in its mysteries, their resultant success assured them a distinct advantage in future dealings with and prices from English buyers. As they continued to receive consistently higher prices based upon reputation and access to deep waterways, these business dealings became a self-fulfilling prophesy that translated into a social prestige which often endured for the entirety of planters' lives. Planted eight generations deep in this cultural loam was the psychology of tobacco uplift, a worldview which held that the successful cultivation of the "stinking weed" was more than a means of simple economic advancement. Tobacco was respectability.[18]

Yet staple crops never came to dominate the new region's economy as they would the south Atlantic states and the later Old Southwest. Other than tobacco, the amount of the crops produced in the mid-Missouri counties nowhere reflected their having yet achieved preeminence in the region during these developmental years. The vagaries of nature soon extinguished any hopes for successful long-term cotton cultivation, and by 1840 area farmers produced just 837 pounds of it—less than the weight of two pressed bales—a far cry from the nearly ten thousand pounds produced in Cape Girardeau County; the small yield represented less than 1 percent of the state's total. Quickly and painfully, central Missouri proved itself simply too far north and west to avoid early or late frosts brought by cold fronts from the Plains that proved catastrophic to a fragile cotton crop requiring a minimum of 180 frost-free growing days. Hemp, a Kentucky legacy that grew well in the

---

17. Hurt, *Agriculture and Slavery in Little Dixie,* 80–81, 90–91 (quote, p. 90), 94–95, 101.

18. T[imothy] H. Breen, *Tobacco Culture: The Mentality of the Great Tidewater Planters on the Eve of Revolution,* 58–75.

climate (some judged Missouri hemp of better quality even than the mother state's), expanded slowly after its introduction in 1820, so slowly that a full two decades later the river counties produced just 1,265 tons of the crop, constituting just 7 percent of the state's harvest. Hemp production would expand with the price of cotton during the late 1840s and into the 1850s, but its importance to the period of settlement of central Missouri was minimal. Farmers grew no rice or sugarcane, both staples of the Atlantic sea islands and Louisiana—regions of which the Boon's Lick, at least judging by its economy, was as yet not a part.[19]

And even if the residents of the Boon's Lick had been committed to staple-crop agriculture, the primary products that flourished in the region were in no way associated solely with the southern plantation states once established. Farmers as far north as Lower Canada and the Connecticut River Valley cultivated tobacco, and the crop contributed greatly to each regions' local economy. Even more pronounced, tobacco enjoyed heavy production throughout the Middle West, with many of the lower counties of Ohio producing as many pounds annually as Kentucky counties south of the Ohio River. Kentuckians, Marylanders, and Virginians, who grew tobacco nearly as their own dominion, hardly considered themselves southerners or their crop plantation stock. And hemp, if one New York buying house's assessment is accurate, was an avowed "Staple of the West." MacGregor and Wise printed flyers for their "Western friends" in Missouri, Kentucky, Illinois, Indiana, and Ohio touting the potential success of hemp production in their region, the quality of which was *"intrinsically* superior to the Russian, or *any* foreign production," and the inevitable monopoly of home consumption supplied largely to the "Southern market . . . in the manufacture of rope and bagging." Neither tobacco nor hemp carried any stigma as being southern staples; their success in Missouri derived from decidedly more nationalistic impulses.[20]

If climate provides any indication, the culture of the Boon's Lick was as dissimilar to the southern states as was its residents' commitment to staple crop production. Such incongruence was not lost on the earliest of the modern American historians. The first words of the most well-known book of the eminent historian of the Old South, Ulrich B. Phillips, read: "Let us

19. Phillips, *Life and Labor in the Old South,* 104n3; Harrison A. Trexler, *Slavery in Missouri 1804–1865,* 23–28; *Compendium of the Enumeration of the Inhabitants and Statistics of the United States in 1840,* 310–14. Statistics in this and subsequent paragraphs derive from the following Missouri counties: Boone, Callaway, Chariton, Clay, Cooper, Howard, Lafayette, and Saline. The average weight of a pressed bale of cotton was five hundred pounds.

20. "American Hemp," Broadside, December 1843, John Sappington Family Papers, box 1, MHS; Sixth U.S. Census, 1840, Agriculture, NA.

begin by discussing the weather, for that has been the chief agency in making the South distinctive." Similarly, the great historian of the Great Plains, Walter Prescott Webb, opens his tour de force with a quote from the explorer John Wesley Powell: "The physical conditions which exist in that land . . . inexorably control the operations of men." Such sage pronouncements only echo the father of western history, Frederick Jackson Turner, whose forceful argument that environmental determinants have played the largest part in shaping American culture has directed the canon of western historiography for a full century. If one follows these similar yet divergent dicta, the climate in Missouri alone created a culture distinctive of the Old South or the Great Plains.[21]

Straddling the thirty-ninth parallel, central Missouri lay six latitudinal degrees (or four hundred miles) and more north of what would become the Cotton (or "Black") Belt. As a result, the region had at best but 170 to 180 frost-free growing days per year, while the Cotton Belt boasted 40 or 50 more than that each year, allowing the southern states an extra six growing weeks between the last killing frosts in spring and first killing frosts in the fall. Its location on the edge of the Plains resulted in the Boon's Lick's growing season being 10 to 20 days shorter even than the piedmont of Virginia, which the Appalachians sheltered from the driving cold fronts that chilled the Middle West. The average minimum temperature in the region was as much as thirty degrees colder than in much of the Black Belt, allowing for nearly twenty more inches of frost penetration into the soil. One resident of Saline County wrote in January 1831 that "the Ground has not been clear of snow for 5 or 6 weeks, . . . I believe they have been driving loaded Waggons across the Missouri for weeks." While the Boon's Lick received nearly the same amount of rainfall—twenty-four inches—as the Cotton Belt during the summer months, only four to eight inches of moisture (largely snow) fell during the winter months, a far cry from the fourteen to sixteen inches of rain received throughout much of the southern states during those months. All told, central Missouri received between ten and fifteen inches less rain, so vital to most staple crops, than did many of the southern states. While the emigrants to the Boon's Lick may have envisioned a society which replicated or even bettered that of their upcountry homes, the distinctive climate of the region forced upon the social landscape adaptations commensurate with this new physical landscape.[22]

21. Phillips, *Life and Labor in the Old South,* 3; Walter Prescott Webb, *The Great Plains,* 2; Turner, "Significance of the Frontier in American History," 199–227.

22. O. E. Baker, ed., *Atlas of American Agriculture,* 30–31, 38–40, 43, 46–47, 50–51, 58–59; Charles B. Hunt, *Physiography of the United States,* 59; Lavinia Marmaduke to William B. Sappington, January 8, 1831, John Sappington Family Papers, box 1, MHS (quote).

The true legacy of these Missourians' upcountry ancestors was a diversified economy and society, one that had set apart the residents of the border from those in the south Atlantic states since colonial times. Starting in the middle of the seventeenth century, tobacco had been a notoriously fickle crop, with regular downturns of the international market depressing prices and minimizing profits for struggling planters. Diversification proved necessary for planters (a term that in the northern Chesapeake denoted occupation rather than economic status and in Missouri, well into the nineteenth century and unlike the rice-, sugar-, and cotton-growing states, was applied nearly interchangeably with the terms *farmers* and *yeomen*) to weather the tempests of the south Atlantic tobacco market and protect their fragile position as freeholders. Even the great planters of Maryland and Virginia engaged in commercial endeavors beyond tobacco cultivation, such as land speculation, tenancy, manufacturing, merchandising, loan making, the practice of law and medicine, and especially commercial livestock raising and cereal grain production. Indeed, the offspring of these resourceful entrepreneurs carried their fathers' wide economic spectrum across the Appalachians into the Bluegrass of Kentucky, and theirs brought such notions into central Missouri. If anything, Missouri's frontier resembled that of the Old Southwest before the intrusion of cotton culture. Yet even the term "plantation" was foreign to the region, having given way long before to the more appropriate "farm," an appellation that Dr. John Sappington (Claib Jackson's future father-in-law and owner of twenty-five slaves in 1830) applied self-consciously to his thirteen-hundred-acre Saline County homestead, "Pilot Hickory Farm." While tobacco may have symbolized progress, it was but one of many avenues that river county residents traveled toward autonomy.[23]

Though tobacco, hemp, and cotton were the only staple crops grown in central Missouri by 1840 (a small amount of rice was grown in the state's Bootheel), they were by no means the only sources of commercial agriculture. Central Missourians grew a number of grain crops specifically for profit, selling them to local and St. Louis millers. In 1837, one Saline Countian proclaimed that his home county was "great wheat country" that produced yields of as much as thirty bushels an acre and sold for a dollar a bushel. Similarly, corn brought upwards of fifty cents a bushel downriver in St. Louis, and with a good crop averaging twenty bushels an acre, farmers stood to make well over a hundred dollars from just fifteen acres of corn—

23. Allan Kulikoff, *The Agrarian Origins of American Capitalism*, 66–71; Clark and Guice, *Frontiers in Conflict*, 14–18; Christopher Phillips, *Freedom's Port: The African American Community of Baltimore, 1790–1860,* 10; Aubrey C. Land, "Economic Base and Social Structure: The Northern Chesapeake in the Eighteenth Century," 645–54; Fifth U.S. Census, 1830, Population Schedule, Saline County, Missouri, NA; Lynn Morrow, "Dr. John Sappington: Southern Patriarch in the New West," 58.

an acreage that two men could handle easily. In 1854, one farmer near Lexington grossed $3,850 from sales of his corn, wheat, and oats alone. Many of his neighbors produced even more of such crops, along with hay, flax, buckwheat, barley, rye, hops, and potatoes, their motives clearly more than simple home consumption. Though small producers, these farmers were clearly committed to commercial agriculture.[24]

Livestock production also assumed an early importance in the economic life of Missouri. Farmers took advantage of the ample grasslands of the Boon's Lick to raise hogs, cattle, sheep, and mules for far more than self-sufficiency or local consumption; they sought out national and even international markets for their animal husbandry. As early as 1820, cattle buyers from the Ohio Valley circulated regularly through the region, offering more than twenty dollars per head and driving long trains back across the Mississippi to Ohio, where they fattened on lush grass before being sold in the East. Some cattlemen looked to improve their herds by breeding, importing purebred Shorthorns from Kentucky. In 1823, merchants in Franklin offered merchandise and dry goods as payment for "corn-fed" pork, while local firms paid cash for shipment and sale downriver. Farmers packed their butchered and salted hog meat or drove their swine to towns with local markets or buyers, and wool manufacturers from as far away as Columbia sent commission men to Fayette monthly to acquire local wool and to deliver finished cloth to merchants. Others sold sheep that had been raised for mutton to buyers from St. Louis for slaughter. Missouri mules had difficulty competing in price with those exported from Kentucky, but became and remained important enough to southern agriculture that one Mississippian wrote that "thousands and tens of thousands of dollars are annually paid to Tennessee, Kentucky, Ohio, Missouri, Indiana and other States" for their beasts of burden. So widespread was the practice of mule raising that during the 1820s farmers often leased pasture—getting between $1.60 and $1.75 per head during the spring and $2.20 during the winter—to mule breeders who sent soliciting agents southward in pursuit of buyers. In all, a quarter of the mules, horses, and sheep, more than 18 percent of the swine and cattle, and 21 percent of the poultry raised in Missouri came from eight of the central river counties.[25]

The commercial farm economy of the central Missouri river counties also drew strength from a remarkable array of industries. Both through home industry and mass consumer manufacturing, the region bore witness to a

24. Hurt, *Agriculture and Slavery in Little Dixie,* 68–70 (quote, p. 68).
25. Ibid., 126, 127–28 (first quote, p. 28), 138–39, 146–47, 150; John Ashton, "History of Hogs and Pork Production in Missouri," 42; Renner, "The Mule in Missouri Agriculture, 1821–1950," 439–42; John Hebron Moore, *The Emergence of the Cotton Kingdom in the Old Southwest: Mississippi, 1770–1860,* 55 (second quote).

flurry of industrial endeavors that regularly accounted for proportionately more of the state's production than its populace—which constituted just 16 percent of the state's white population as a whole—led one to expect. Some of these industries related directly to the agricultural bounty that the Boon's Lick provided its residents. Not surprisingly, nearly 27 percent of the tobacco manufactured in Missouri—largely into chewing plugs and twists—came from the central river counties, while more than a third of those employed in the industry were employed there and nearly half of the capital invested in the industry was spent there as well. The sixty-nine distilleries that manufactured the area's surplus corn into more than 128,000 gallons of whiskey represented nearly a quarter of the state's total, both in number of such establishments and output, while ten ropewalks (nearly half those in the state) produced nearly two-thirds of the state's rope from the hemp grown there. Twenty-eight flour mills—nearly half those in the state—ground more than 15,500 barrels of flour, or nearly a third of that ground in Missouri, while more than a quarter of the state's grist mills, 21 percent of its sawmills, and more than half of its oil mills churned along the streams of the Boon's Lick. More than four-tenths of the dairy products produced in the state in 1840 came from the central river counties, while the region produced a third of the value of Missouri's orchard products. The thirty-two hundred bushels of domestic salt refined in the Boon's Lick represented more than half of the state's total, and a quarter of the leather manufactured in Missouri was tanned and processed in the region. More than half of the glass and earthenware and nearly a third of the small arms and cannon manufactured in Missouri originated in the river counties. In addition to all of the entrepreneurial activity generated above the state average, other less numerous establishments in the region produced hats, caps, bricks, lime, lumber and other forest products, extracted precious metals and coal, printed newspapers and other materials, and made chocolate and other confections.[26]

By 1840, slightly less than 15 percent of the region's residents held avocations outside agriculture, concentrated in manufacturing, trades, and commerce; in Lafayette and Chariton Counties the figure was as high as 22 and 19 percent, respectively. The figure proves especially significant when compared with the 10 percent witnessed in the Bootheel counties, where agriculture most closely resembled that of the maturing southern plantation states. Far from emulating one-crop, staple production as in those southern states, central Missourians exhibited an acute capacity for diversifying their commercial efforts, setting the region apart at least economically from that

---

26. *Compendium of the Inhabitants of the United States in 1840*, 310–21. The eight counties enumerated were Boone, Callaway, Chariton, Clay, Cooper, Howard, Lafayette, and Saline.

to which others later connected it. Moreover, residents of the Boon's Lick—even those who were wealthy and prominent—readily acceded to the lower per capita wealth than in areas with more lucrative economic bases, plantation or otherwise. William B. Napton, a prominent lawyer, editor, and future state supreme court justice from Saline County, wrote to his wife, Melinda, in 1839 from Potosi, Missouri, in the southeastern portion of the state, that "every body is here seized with the mineral mania—they talk of nothing else—They think of millions here, with as much non chalance as we Boons Lickers do of hundreds."[27]

What connected the society in the Boon's Lick with those farther south was its degree of dependence upon the institution of chattel bondage. Already by 1819, Howard Countian George Tompkins lamented that his "political career is ended: for . . . I had declared my sentiments against slavery. . . . I believe no man will be elected from these counties unless he declare himself for slavery, & perhaps it will require a property in slaves to qualify him in the eyes of the people. . . . I believe that nine tenths of the people of Howard & Cooper are in favor of slavery." Yet slavery was a practice exclusive neither to the nineteenth century nor to the central river counties; as early as the late seventeenth century, the French *coureurs de bois* and later *habitants*, the first explorers and residents of Upper Louisiana, brought black servants to the river valleys that fed into the Mississippi and those few cities lying along or near the great river, such as Ste. Genevieve, St. Louis, St. Charles, and Cape Girardeau. After 1720, French residents, new and old, imported enough black servants for French authorities to enact the *Code Noir* to regulate the conduct of slaves and free blacks who labored in the territory's fields, lead mines, and private homes. According to the 1772 Spanish census, nearly 38 percent of the region's roughly one thousand inhabitants were of African ancestry. The slave population only increased after 1790 once Anglo-Americans began entering Missouri in large numbers, so much so that in 1804, after the United States had purchased the entirety of Louisiana from the French, 15 percent of the 10,350 residents—still clustered along the Mississippi—were bondpeople.[28]

By 1821, when Missouri had achieved statehood, slaves and slavery had moved well into the interior. Of 67,000 newly christened Missourians, more than 10,000 were black servants. Immediately, the central river counties saw denser numbers of slaves than anywhere else in the state; Howard and Cooper counties, together encompassing the whole of the Boon's Lick in 1820,

27. Ibid., 89; William B. Napton to Melinda Napton, May 1839, William B. Napton Papers, box 1, MHS (quote).

28. George Tompkins to George C. Sibley, July 30, 1819, Sibley Papers, MHS (quote); Foley, *History of Missouri*, 46–50; Foley, *Genesis of Missouri*, 80, 84, 114–15.

boasted 15,033 inhabitants, 2,726 (or 18 percent) of them slaves. Howard County's total was higher; its 2,089 slaves represented only slightly less than a quarter of its population. During the next two decades, the number of residents of African descent only increased and at a strikingly higher rate than that of those of European ancestry. In 1830, the number of slaves in the river counties had nearly tripled to 7,379, while the white population more than doubled. The spread of slavery into the region became especially noticeable during the 1830s; while the white populations of the river counties increased by 41 percent, the slave population of those counties grew by more than 120 percent to 16,297. The number of slaves in Lafayette County exploded, growing by 364 percent from 1830 to 1840. During the same period, the white population of Howard County had increased by 21 percent; its slave population nearly doubled again. The Boon's Lick may have captured the imagination of a restless white population, but the paradise that these settlers envisioned—and ultimately created—was by no means a land for white men and women only.[29]

Undeniably, slaves and slavery formed an essential component in the social construct of the central river counties of Missouri. Curiously, however, until 1840, the density of slaveholding in the individual counties of the region stood in nearly inverse relationship to the amount of staple crops grown in those counties themselves. None of the top five slaveholding counties—Howard, Callaway, Boone, Clay, and Cooper, in order from top to bottom—produced comparatively as much tobacco and hemp as their slaveholdings would suggest. Boone County, its 3,008 slaves the third-largest such population among the counties, ranked first in tobacco production, but only sixth in hemp production. Clay County, with 2,875 bondpeople, ranked third in tobacco grown, but sixth in hemp production. Cooper County's 2,157 slaves ranked it fifth-largest in slave population, but it ranked only fourth in tobacco production, and its dismal seventy tons of dew-rotted hemp ranked it next to last. By contrast, among counties with the sparsest number of slaves, Chariton County produced the second-largest crop of tobacco while Lafayette produced the largest crop of hemp of any of the counties. Saline, ranked next to last in slaves, produced the fourth-largest crop of hemp. In only one county—Callaway—did slaveholding relatively equal its residents' production of tobacco and hemp.[30]

Nowhere was this anomalous disparity between slaveholding and staple crop agriculture more apparent than in Howard County. Though Howard

29. *Census for 1820*, 38–40; *Fifth Census; or, Enumeration of the Inhabitants of the United States, 1830*, 150–51; *Compendium of the United States in 1840*, 88–89; Hurt, *Agriculture and Slavery in Little Dixie*, 218.

30. *Compendium of the Inhabitants of the United States in 1840*, 310–14.

boasted the densest population of slaves in the state (more than three and a half times that of Chariton and approximately double that of either Saline or Lafayette), the county produced no better than the fifth-greatest amounts of tobacco and hemp of the central river counties. More striking, the level of production of either of these crops paled when compared to the region's leaders. Howard Countians grew less than one-seventeenth the amount of tobacco that Boone Countians produced, and well less than a third of the bales of dew-rotted hemp marketed from Lafayette County, all while holding more slaves than any other county in Missouri. Judging at least by staple crop production, slave ownership as it existed in the Boon's Lick during its formative years grew disproportionately to any devotion its populace might have had to traditional plantation-based commercial agriculture. As one contemporary recalled appropriately, "slavery in western Missouri was like slavery in northern Kentucky—much more a domestic than a commercial institution." So independent were Missouri's slaveholding farmers of their slaves' labor that bondpeople customarily received a full five weeks of freedom at Christmastide, with masters allowing them, as one former slave recalled, "to come and go as much as we pleased and go for miles as far as we wanted to, but we had better be back by de first of February."[31]

By all accounts, slaves performed the bulk of the region's labor. Few white men were available or reliable enough for fieldwork of any kind, prompting one prominent resident to complain, "I want to get along this season without a white man, there are none to be had worth having." Thus farmers came to depend on slave labor for the cultivation of many types of crops and for other farm chores. One farmer near Lexington used a slave force of fifteen men and six women to produce eight hundred bushels of wheat and fifteen hundred barrels of corn, as well as a large crop of oats, while cultivating two hundred acres of hemp and breeding mules for sale. Another farmer in Saline County used eight slaves to cultivate his 240 acres, a fourth of which were planted in hemp. Slave children as young as eight served on farms as water haulers and weed pullers, while in towns such as Fayette and Columbia slave men and women worked in homes, mills, shops, and taverns. Farmers regularly hired slaves to provide farm labor as needed, and the great diversity of production on central Missouri farms allowed flexibility enough to secure hired bondpeople even during such peak times as spring planting and fall harvest, when in southern plantation society the need for slave labor was so great that few were either available or affordable. So prevalent was the practice of hiring slaves that one slaveholding widow commented that hiring out her bondpeople was "better business" than farming.[32]

As in the piedmont of Virginia and the Bluegrass of Kentucky, central Missouri was a land of numerous, but small, slaveholders. The decades immediately after statehood brought expansion in a number of forms to the Boon's Lick, slave ownership being only one of them. In 1830, as many as 16 percent of the adult population as a whole held slaves, while as many as a quarter of white men (the most likely to own land and slaves) held bondpeople. Nearly three in ten white men in Howard and Boone Counties—which boasted the highest concentration of slave owners both numerically and per capita of the region—owned slaves. Indeed, central Missouri's single largest slaveholder, Eli Bass, possessor of thirty-eight slaves, grew tobacco and other crops on his Boone County farm. By 1840, slave owning had grown even more widespread among the residents of the Boon's Lick and was especially prolific in the westernmost counties such as Lafayette and Saline, the latter of which boasted the region's then largest slaveholder, Rice G. Harlow, with sixty-two bondpeople. In all, nearly 18 percent of the population held slaves, while as many as 27 percent of white men were slave owners, a figure remarkably uniform in all of the river counties save one. In Callaway County, as many as a third of white men owned black chattel servants.[33]

Masters in central Missouri, however, were far from being planters, a term that historians have interpreted somewhat too rigidly as individuals who owned exceptionally large plantations, and one that these farmers would not have associated implicitly with the ownership of twenty slaves or more during the antebellum period. Because of the limited spatial dimensions still prevalent in early-nineteenth-century rural America, local conditions were cardinal determinants of status, and central Missouri's preponderance of small to middling farms and numerous businesses and manufactories did

32. Nathaniel Leonard to Abiel Leonard, February 22, 1841, Abiel Leonard Collection, Mss. 1013, folder 50, SHSM (first quote); William C. Boon to William Carson, Esq., August 12, 1841, William C. Boon Letter, Mss. 2209, SHSM; Bill from C. L. Lewis to C. F. Jackson, July–November 1857, John S. Sappington Papers, Mss. 1027, box 3, folder 65, SHSM; Hurt, *Agriculture and Slavery in Little Dixie*, 69, 238–40, 241–43 (second quote, p. 241), 262.

33. Hurt, *Agriculture and Slavery in Little Dixie*, 219–20, 307–8; *Compendium of the Inhabitants of the United States in 1840*, 88–89; Fifth and Sixth U.S. Censuses, 1830 and 1840, Population Schedules, Boone, Callaway, Chariton, Clay, Cooper, Howard, Lafayette, and Saline Counties, Missouri, NA. I have used R. Douglas Hurt's data for slaveholders in the above counties. To figure white male slave ownership percentages, I separated male and female slaveholders in the manuscript censuses above, and divided the raw number of male slaveholders into the number of adult male residents (twenty years of age and older) as a whole.

not create a need for large workforces. Slaveholding was thus limited as well; slave owners in the river counties held an average of 6.1 slaves, somewhat less than the 7.7 bondpeople owned by other border slave state slaveholders and considerably less than the 12.7 held by typical southern masters. Indeed, the region's twenty-seven "planters" in 1830 constituted just 1.3 percent of slaveholders; just two owned as many as thirty. A decade later, the sixty-four owners of twenty slaves or more made up just 1.8 percent of slaveholders; fifteen owned thirty or more. In 1860, the region's slaveholding height, just 4 percent owned twenty slaves or more, a third of the number who held planter status in the Deep South. Conversely, two-thirds of the Boon's Lick's slaveholders owned fewer than five slaves in 1830, and in 1840 only a slightly smaller percentage (63.4 percent) did so. In all, nearly nine of ten slaveholders in the region owned fewer than ten slaves prior to 1840.[34]

This tendency, a legacy of the upcountry, contrasts remarkably with the South, where as many as 12 percent of owners were considered planters. Consistent with their border heritage, most masters in central Missouri had few designs on achieving planter status for the sake of social prestige, as was generally associated with slaveholding in the southern plantation states. These were small-scale farmers who sought labor beyond their personal or family capacity in order to farm commercially on that most valuable of commodities—land—in this yeoman-bred culture. This distinction was not lost on those central Missourians who traveled to the South, for they could not help but notice the dissimilarity of their cultures. In 1835, Nathaniel Leonard wrote home to his brother, Abiel, while on a mule trading foray to Alabama that "this is fine country to make cotton and money, but when you have said that you have said all. A planter here worth $10,000 don't live half so well as a Missouri farmer worth $5,000. All they want here is a large cotton field and plenty of Negroes and they have no other use for money but to buy more Negroes."[35]

SLAVERY IN THE West indeed represented far more than mere status. While "Old Republicans" in the East, even as they debated Missouri's creation, could rationalize the institution's existence by abstraction, first as necessary evil then as positive good, westerners largely dispensed with theory. For them, the introduction and maintenance of slavery were purely pragmatic. Missourians in the 1820s would have found far more than rhetorical British writer Samuel Johnson's sarcastic challenge to colonial patriots, "How is it that we hear the loudest yelps for liberty among the drivers of Negroes?"

34. Hurt, *Agriculture and Slavery in Little Dixie,* 219.
35. Ibid., 219–22, 307–8; Frederic A. Culmer, "Selling Mules Down South in 1835," 540 (quote).

framing in one brief, if biting, query perhaps the fundamental incongruity of the early American experience. Historians of the border slave states, in many ways parroting later nostalgic residents of central Missouri, have commonly allowed the existence of slavery in the region to subsume the incontrovertible fact that the institution—no matter how important to those who either engaged in the practice or wished to—was in these westerners' collective psyches merely one component, albeit an important one, of their paramount life quest. Any discussion that might have occurred among the residents of the Boon's Lick of the actual economic viability of slave labor was overshadowed by the deafeningly silent canon that slavery was integral to the West's staff of life: a commitment to individual liberty.[36]

Westerner Abraham Lincoln certainly recognized the overriding commitment to liberty practiced by Americans when he offered in a later speech, "We all declare for liberty; but in using the same *word* we do not all mean the same *thing*. With some the word liberty may mean for each man to do as he pleases with himself, and the product of his labor; while with others the same word may mean for some men to do as they please with other men, and the product of other men's labor. Here are two, not only different, but incompatible things, called by the same name—liberty." Lincoln's observation offers two important insights: one, the conflicting definitions in the nation's border region—and by that time the country as a whole—of just what that liberty entailed, and two, the essentiality of labor ideology in various Americans' construction of liberty.[37]

Lincoln was decidedly not alone in his observations of Americans' passion for liberty, however distinct. Unlike the Illinoisan, Alexis de Tocqueville, America's greatest nineteenth-century observer, claimed that the freedom of spirit, of hope, unified rather than divided the nation's people. In his sweeping interpretation of national character, Tocqueville argued that "in America, even more than in Europe, there is only one society," thus offering at once the most illuminating sophism made for the pattern of middle-period American development. While claiming that the American people's character was far more one-dimensional than it was stratified either by region or by geography, the Frenchman acceded that the glaring anomaly of chattel slavery within the democratic order allowed the South alone to maintain a unique society in the American conglomerate. The West offered some variants to national character, particularly in that its residents were looser or rougher in

36. Samuel Johnson, *Taxation No Tyranny,* in Johnson, *Works,* vol. 6, 262 (first quote); Robert E. Shalhope, *John Taylor of Caroline: Pastoral Republican,* 142–51; Norman K. Risjord, *The Old Republicans: Southern Conservatism in the Age of Jefferson,* 215–16 (second quote), 217–27.

37. Roy F. Basler, ed., *The Collected Works of Abraham Lincoln,* vol. 7, 301–2 (quote).

manners than those in the East, but even they fell basically within the "plane of a uniform civilization" in their celebration of the democratic order. Slavery, Tocqueville claimed, was simply out of step with American democratic notions and the march of progress would ultimately cause it to collapse, not so much from any conflict of labor, but from its incompatibility with democratic principles. Yet in setting up his argument, Tocqueville ignored one fundamental fact; millions of westerners, from Kentucky to the Boon's Lick, most decidedly did not reject slavery as incongruent with democratic ascendance, but rather embraced the institution as perfectly consistent with the egalitarian social progress they associated implicitly with national growth. While free-labor ideologues, eschewing moral pronouncements, would condemn the nation's slave-based society as socially stagnant, economically irrational, and thoroughly undemocratic, early slaveholding westerners beat them to the proverbial punch. For them, slavery was a perfectly democratic institution, consistent with the promise of western expansion.[38]

The celebration of democratic ideals set loose a peculiarly American psychosis of liberty—particularly within the *mentalité* of westerners, who brandished a particularly strong fervor for democratic disorder—in the form of an inherent dialectic in which the drive for equality created both independence and dependence of will. Clearly, Jacksonian Americans no longer held forth their revolutionary forebears' dialectic between liberty and democracy; rather, they now had fused the two concepts into a new, if convenient, hybrid. As the unleashed mass of social peers at once freed individuals from the constraints of established deference, a new authority of merit had emplaced individual talent, accomplishment, or simply diligence as the litmus by which Americans would measure social elevation. In effect, Tocqueville argued that capitalistic acquisitiveness, rather than any political standard, would serve as the vehicle for this democratic ascendance, for "between poverty and themselves there is nothing but a scanty fortune, upon which they immediately fix their apprehensions and their hopes." Yet the leavening of the social classes offered a new, complex, and pervasive fear, that of failure, of social stagnation, which a fixed, hierarchical society served to suppress by stifling all possibility of advancement but which the new environment allowed to flourish. As Tocqueville observed,

> When the inhabitant of a democratic country compares himself individually with all those about him, he feels with pride that he is the equal of any one of them; but when he comes to survey the totality of his fellows and to place

38. Alexis de Tocqueville, *Democracy in America,* vol. 1, 356–81, 392–95; vol. 2, 236–37 (quotes); Meyers, *Jacksonian Persuasion,* 49–50. For a full discussion of the free labor ideology, see Eric Foner, *Free Soil, Free Labor, Free Men: The Ideology of the Republican Party before the Civil War,* 11–72.

himself in contrast with so huge a body, he is instantly overwhelmed by the sense of his own insignificance and weakness. The same equality that renders him independent of each of his fellow citizens, taken severally, exposes him alone and unprotected to the influence of a greater number. The public, therefore, among a democratic people, has a singular power, which aristocratic nations cannot conceive; for it does not persuade others to its beliefs, but it imposes them and makes them permeate the thinking of everyone by a sort of enormous pressure of the mind of all upon the individual intelligence.[39]

Indeed, William B. Napton, a New Jersey native and Princeton graduate who had tutored on a Virginia plantation and had been educated at and by a direct Jeffersonian legacy—the state university—before emigrating to Missouri in 1829, noted immediately that this psychosis manifested itself most clearly in the new state's politics. He could not refrain from contrasting Missouri's mayhem of party politics to that in his adopted Virginia home, which he considered "more nearly the standard of what is just and open and honourable . . . moderate and dignified . . . than the party warfare of any other state." "I wish I could say the same in relation to the politics of this state," Napton lamented, "to witness one struggle of party warfare here, is sufficient to lower one's estimate of human nature—it is calculated to make converts to the doctrine of universal human depravity. The mixed nature of our population is no doubt the cause of it—consisting of individuals thrown together—from various quarters, possessing more than an ordinary spirit of intelligence and enterprise, bent upon personal aggrandizement, in the pursuit of wealth or fame or ready (with some honorable exceptions) according to the western phrase, to take all advantages." Another transplanted Boon's Licker, artist George Caleb Bingham, would soon immortalize the common man's politics he witnessed in Jacksonian Missouri in an even more visible medium.[40]

To suppress this deep-seated insecurity, aside from yet part of politics and economics, many democratic-minded westerners such as those in Missouri considered slavery as more than simply consistent with democratic principles; the institution was as essential to democracy as liberty itself. For most middle Missourians, neither nationalistic fervor nor labor concerns alone dictated the terms of slavery's support in the West; rather, these far westerners operated from a hunger even more consuming, one that had existed since the first move from the tidewater into the piedmont as much as from the Bay

39. Tocqueville, *Democracy in America,* vol. 2, 253 (first quote), 10 (second quote); Meyers, *Jacksonian Persuasion,* 52–53; David Brion Davis, "Some Themes of Counter-Subversion: An Anatasis of Anti-Masonic, Anti-Catholic, and Anti-Mormon Literature," 208–12; Richard Hofstadter, "The Pseudo-Conservative Revolt," in Daniel Bell, ed., *The Radical Right,* 88–90.

40. Napton Diary, folder 1, pp. 44–46, MHS (quotes); Federal Writers' Project, *Missouri,* 170–71; McCandless, *History of Missouri,* 184–85.

to the Narragansett country and from Manhattan to the Mohawk. Their urgency derived from the simultaneous insecurity and intoxication of the frontier. By putting distance between their often dominating fathers (who characteristically often resisted their leaving) and thus the authority that once held their "manly independence" in check, these frontier pioneers severed those constraints from family tyranny. Physically removed from the checks that societal maturation had emplaced, the West offered welcome relief from such impediments. Freedom as these pioneers envisioned it needed space and perhaps a certain degree of anonymity, both from domineering families and from the society that controlled them.

On a grander scale, the move to the frontier represented a retreat from the imposition of government presence, a relaxation of restrictive codes of enforceable behavior. The West became the bastion of democracy in that in this protean region, this new Eden, away from the corruptive influence of society, the individual free exercise of "natural rights" offered those sagacious individuals who migrated the chance to mold a society in which people could govern themselves with as little hindrance as possible. With classic liberal thought, these new pioneers believed that the individual was more important than institutions, especially the state. Personal freedom involved an inherent intolerance, or at best distrust, of governmental or any other intrusion. More than anywhere in the nation, these westerners suffered through the Lockean conundrum of supporting limited government—but only so far as it protected individual rights—while considering governmental power as the greatest threat to those same rights. Such logic moved Howard County politico Duff Green in 1819 to offer a biting toast, ironically just as he called for an unrestricted statehood for Missouri: "The Union—It is dear to us, but liberty is dearer."[41]

Yet, as central Missouri's sanguine settlers found, the frontier was no paradise. When the grandchildren of the Chesapeake weighed anchor and left the confining safety of their homes—as often from the lack of inheritable land, the least arduous vehicle for advancement, as from any willful rejection of a landed birthright—they found dangers and challenges they might have anticipated, but for which they had precious little preparation. Success without direction or, more important, advantage came only with great emotional and physical cost. As revealed by the two-century migration that had taken women and men from the tidewater of Virginia across the mountains to Kentucky and eventually to central Missouri, environmental factors forced

---

41. For a discussion of the conflict between planter fathers and sons over southwestern migration, see Joan E. Cashin, *A Family Venture: Men and Women on the Southern Frontier,* 32–44; James Oakes, *Slavery and Freedom: An Interpretation of the Old South,* 63; McCandless, *History of Missouri,* 6 (quote).

settlers to adapt their known behaviors to the unknown challenges of their new homes. With classic human frailty, western migration offered psychological insecurity as pioneers confronted that which they feared most—their own fallibility. The test of nerves engendered by the proverbial cutting of the apron strings often steeled men in their dealings with other men, the climate of fear turning personal confrontations regularly into quick and violent affairs. Domination of other men, physically, economically, or legally, either separately or in combination, became a sign of ascendance in this land of disestablished social mores. More important, this oppression offered the opportunity to establish supremacy in the leveled atmosphere of democratic egalitarianism. For many westerners, slavery, in effect, *was* democracy.[42]

In fact, slavery's intrinsic consistency with the West's legacy of conquest (the warp of the region's history) actuated westerners—whether in the Northwest or Southwest—in their daily lives on the nation's frontier. However inaccurate, the bar of history has held up the cultural heritage of white slave ownership among these people of the western border—along with those of the southwestern frontier—to mark them as distinct from those who moved into the northwestern frontier in their exploitive nature and capacity. Historians Frederick Jackson Turner, Walter Prescott Webb, and others established a lasting and romantic image of a virgin West settled by independent white pioneers who created out of the wilderness and plains a free and democratic society. Clearly, this rendition of the western past—conjured from post-emancipation influences—not only ignored the prolonged existence of slavery in the largest geographic portion of the western American territories but also largely discounts two centuries of wanton destruction of Indian life and tribal integrity at the hands of puritans, cavaliers, *encomienderos,* or *habitants,* and virtually every European immigrant group who had settled in the New World whether North or South, Spanish, French, English, Dutch, or Russian. All of these peoples had enslaved others and reveled in the proliferation of forced or bound labor well before the Missouri migration. Violent exploitation was not reserved for English-speaking people who had moved to the southern seaboard of the North American continent. The abundance of frontier land that stimulated American capitalism might have encouraged individualism and even democracy, but in no way did it secure the birth of freedom in its fullest sense. In fact, the scramble for frontier land encouraged the extinguishment of others' freedoms in pursuit of individual gain. As one Dutch scholar observed, "slavery will generally occur where

42. James A. Henretta, "Families and Farms: *Mentalité* in Pre-Industrial America," 3–32; Elliot Gorn, "Gouge and Bite, Pull Hair and Scratch: The Significance of Fighting in the Southern Backcountry," 18–32; Michael A. Morrison, *Slavery and the American West: The Eclipse of Manifest Destiny and the Coming of the Civil War,* 61–63.

there is still some free land available, . . . [for] where there are still open resources, no one is dependent on another for his earning, and it is necessary to use force if others are to be made to work for an individual."[43]

The Old Northwest, where slavery was apparently a forbidden fruit, proved no exception. Just across the Mississippi from Missouri, in the state of Illinois, flourished a de facto form of chattel slavery, thinly veiled under the legal fiction known as contract apprenticeship, the state's black code harsher and wider in scope than those of the slave states. Within three years of Missouri's statehood, Illinoisans—supposedly never soiled by the stain of slavery—narrowly defeated a movement to abolish the antislavery clause of its 1818 constitution, which would have nearly nullified the hallmark of Thomas Jefferson's vision for the entire Old Northwest. Not that these Illinois westerners' desire for slavery was at all tempered by the constitutional prohibition, either immediately or much later in the century. As late as 1863, native Kentuckian Jane Phillips, living near Atlanta, in McLean County, Illinois, wrote home to her sister in Lexington, Kentucky, that her husband, Cellie, "has been cutting wheat ten days, and I have had all the cooking to do for 6 men, besides the family and he will not get through in less than ten more. Whether I shall keep up or not I think doubtful, if you had that to do, dont you think you'd like to have a darkie[?] I would, God knows I would. . . . I think they are much needed here[.]"[44]

In their quest for personal freedom, these uplanders legitimized slavery as embodying not just western, but American progress. Early national Americans from both North and South looked to the West as the region that would legitimize the triumphant Republic, that would assure its march toward world power. For many, conquest of other peoples, whether in the West or wherever the American advance should ultimately go, would only verify the notions of cultural superiority that America's recent victory over the British had sparked. Built upon a proslavery defense that had emerged during the immediate postrevolutionary period (articulated most strongly, ironically, by New Englanders, not southerners), this new nationalism included an innate belief in racial hierarchy that assumed a prerogative in which Caucasians—particularly those of English extract—would ultimately triumph in the race

43. Patricia Nelson Limerick, *The Legacy of Conquest: The Unbroken Past of the American West*, 17–32 and passim; David Brion Davis, *Slavery and Human Progress*, 154–68 and passim; Walter Prescott Webb, *The Great Frontier*, passim; H. J. Nieboer quoted in Howard R. Lamar, "From Bondage to Contract: Ethnic Labor in the American West, 1600–1890," 295 and passim.

44. N. Dwight Harris, *The History of Negro Servitude in Illinois and the Slavery Agitation in That State*, 6–49; Robert P. Howard, *Illinois: A History of the Prairie State*, 103–4, 129–33; Jane Phillips to Annie M. Cooper, July 21, 1863, and April 5, 1862, Cooper-Phillips Family Papers, Mss. 66M37, UK (quote).

of life. From science to literature, Americans embraced the broad divisions within humankind, and with laissez-faire certainty trumpeted American distinctiveness, even over those of other white cultures. No less than Missouri's Thomas Hart Benton recognized this American prepotence when in a speech he referred proudly to the "Celtic-Anglo-Saxon division" of the white race. Westward expansion assumed racial-cultural superiority, of which for many, slavery was but a logical extension.[45]

Jefferson's visionary attempt to block slavery's extension into the Northwest originated from a keen sense of those he knew best: namely, Virginians. He recognized cultural and ideological differences between his piedmont neighbors, who had as their cultural genesis the rapacious gentleman capitalists of Jamestown, and those in the tight communities of New England who had as their progenitors the idealistic puritan architects of cities upon hills. Having toured New England on holiday just as he unveiled his plan for the West, he noted the cursory distinctions between these northerners and southerners, that New Englanders were "cool sober laborious persevering [and] independent," and that Virginians were "fiery voluptuary indolent unsteady [and] independent." Jefferson, the writer of the world's most famous declaration, naturally connected these peoples in their love of independence. However, the observer then offered what he perceived as the telling connection between these seemingly distinct yet related peoples—their attitudes toward liberty. "In the North," wrote Jefferson, "they are jealous of their own liberties, and just to those of others"; conversely, "in the South they are zealous for their own liberties, but trampling on those of others." Jefferson nearly replicated the observations of Scottish minister Andrew Burnaby, written nearly a quarter century earlier. "The[ir] public or political character," Burnaby declared of Virginians in 1760, "corresponds with their private one: they are haughty and jealous of their liberties, impatient of restraint, and can scarcely bear the thought of being controuled by any superior power."[46]

By linking them under one devotion—liberty—the Sage of Monticello adroitly measured perhaps these westerners' greatest difference. Jefferson knew well that as those Virginians moved westward across the mountains into

45. Larry E. Tise, *Pro-Slavery: A History of the Defense of Slavery in America, 1701–1840*, 41–74; Reginald Horsman, *Race and Manifest Destiny: The Origins of American Racial Anglo-Saxonism*, 158–64 (quote), 165–86, and passim.

46. Peterson, *Thomas Jefferson*, 278–86, 293–94 (first and second quotes); Rev. Andrew Burnaby, *Travels through the Middle Settlements in North America, in the Years 1759 and 1760; With Observations upon the State of the Colonies*, in John Pinkerton, ed., *A General Collection of the Best and Most Interesting Voyages and Travels in All Parts of the World* (London, 1812), quoted in Timothy H. Breen, "The Culture of Agriculture: The Symbolic World of the Tidewater Planter, 1760–1790," 254.

lands he had helped to acquire, with lockstep cadence these zealots would systematically stampede the rights of any people in their way while extending the hegemony they already enjoyed over hundreds of thousands of African American slaves. Jefferson may have anticipated the hegemonic inertia that the transmontane West would create, even in those Yankees who the Sage had deemed "just to the rights of others." Indeed, at the time of Missouri's entrance into the Union, slavery was but two decades away from its legal abolition in all of the northeastern states, and more than that amount of time from its complete disappearance in those states. Two of the Boon's Lick's most prominent slaveholders, Nathaniel and Abiel Leonard, were natives of the frontier state of Vermont—ironically the first American state to outlaw the practice of chattel bondage and the only one to do so immediately, by constitutional amendment—while another, William B. Napton, hailed from New Jersey—just as ironically the last of the northern states to give up the practice completely.[47]

Slavery was thus no privilege in the West. Farmers on the western border saw the peculiar institution not so much as a constitutional right, the dais from which some of its leaders would later deliver their dissevering sermons, but as a natural, *democratic* right. While planting, weeding, and harvesting crops, felling trees, processing hemp or tobacco, hauling water, and other forms of labor that needed to be performed on farms and in manufacturing establishments might have been the traditional services for which middle Missourians sought slaves, labor needs did not prove the sole reasons for their ardent support of the institution. Slaves were a means to an end, rather than an end in themselves, and that end was true democratic ascendance as much as any antislavery ideologue in the East claimed the opposite. Just as democracy unleashed a psychological storm among free white men, anxious at their own vulnerability, so did slavery fill an appetite among those who practiced it by offering the advantage they needed to legitimize their advancement, whether economically, socially, or masculinely. On the nation's western frontier, particularly, slavery filled a powerful psychological need in that it allowed white settlers to dominate other human beings in a social and legal arena in which these inferior people (as they deemed them) could not easily fight back. Dominance of others filled the void created by the insecurity of distance that the West naturally forced upon its frightened inhabitants. In the holding of slaves, Pennsylvanian Charles Jared Ingersoll augmented Jefferson's private observations when he wrote in 1810 that "the haughtiness

47. Ira Berlin, *Many Thousands Gone: The First Two Centuries of Slavery in North America,* 229; Nathaniel Leonard to Abiel Leonard, February 5, 1837, Abiel Leonard Collection, Mss. 1013, folder 44, SHSM; Abiel Leonard to Nathaniel Leonard, August 15, 1854, ibid., folder 123, SHSM; *History of Howard and Chariton Counties,* 252–53.

of domination combines with the spirit of freedom, fortifies it, and renders it invincible." To be masters of a small world counteracted the stark reality that these new westerners were no longer, if they ever had been, masters of all worlds. The right of conquest which was the western experience extended first to those who most traditionally would and could be oppressed, and only from that starting point could they conquer the entire region and beyond. Far from being insouciant about the institution of slavery, middle Missourians—westerners—considered chattel bondage the marrow of freedom itself and Missouri, as one observer hailed, was "the strongest pillar in the temple of Democracy on the Western Continent."[48]

Into this world, Claib Jackson stepped, determined to become master of whatever he encountered, and willing to trample on the rights of those who sought to impede his ascendance. Jackson would become a conquistador, a man of the West.

---

48. Tise, *Pro-Slavery*, 43–44 (first quote); Stephanie McCurry, *Masters of Small Worlds: Yeoman Households, Gender Relations, and the Political Culture of the Antebellum South Carolina Low Country*, vii–ix and passim; *Jefferson Inquirer*, April 29, 1848 (second quote).

3

"A MOST ENLIGHTENED MAN OF BUSINESS"

THE WESTERN MERCHANT who perseveres in the single appropriate line of his business, is absolutely sure of succeeding in his object. . . . C. F. J[ackson was] . . . a most enlightened man of business, . . . It is no wonder that when he retired with an ample fortune, an unusual degree of popularity should keep him constantly in the councils of the state, and elevate him to the chair of the Assembly.

JOHN BEAUCHAMP JONES, *THE WESTERN MERCHANT*

Hungry with ambition, in late June 1826, Claib Jackson stepped down the gangplank from the Missouri River steamer that had carried him from St. Louis to bustling Franklin. The scene that greeted him might well have dissuaded anyone with less resolve to succeed from settling in this place. After a trip of nearly three weeks—probably the only and unquestionably the longest journey of his young life—aboard a rickety paddle wheeler that snags and sand bars forced to stop regularly in its languid ascent, Jackson disembarked into not one but two towns, Old and New Franklin, both decidedly in disarray. A series of catastrophic floods beginning in 1826 had washed away nearly half of Old Franklin's 150 city blocks, and commenced a gradual relocation of the remaining structures on the river bottom to New Franklin, situated on the low bluffs two miles away from the river. Neither locale was impressive, whether to displaced residents or newcomers. As one recent arrival noted, the town's residents "were removing the buildings themselves (most frame) back to the hills; and the new village in the woods presented the grotesque appearance of a new town built in a measure of old materials." Many more simply moved away, especially to the new county seat, Fayette, a dozen miles north of New Franklin. Within a couple of years, one observer passing by on a riverboat would remark that "Old Franklin was once considered as the most flourishing town on the Missouri, it is now quite deserted . . . [and] rapidly washing away."[1]

1. John Beauchamp Jones, *The Western Merchant, A Narrative Containing useful instruction for the Western man of business who makes his purchases in the east; also, Information for the eastern man whose customers are in the west; Likewise, Hints for those who design emigrating to the west. Deduced from actual experience by Luke Shortfield*, 40; Certificate of Hickman and Lamme to John S. Sappington (signed by C. F. Jackson),

While the peripatetic village of Franklin was certainly not visually impressive to the first-time observer, its newest resident undoubtedly was. Standing more than six feet tall, slender but well proportioned, Claib Jackson looked every bit the part of a conquistador. He cut a handsome figure with a high forehead, coal-dark auburn hair worn long and flowing, and hazel eyes. Such a robust appearance belied the fact that he had been a sickly child who had spent a great many of his earliest years with his mother learning to work a hand loom. Bookish young Claib had acquired a great propensity for learning during his Kentucky childhood, and demonstrated an early mastery of the common school subjects of reading, writing, and ciphering. He was exacting in all things, acquiring a hand far surpassing mere legibility (so much so that one acquaintance later commented that the mature Jackson was "the most accomplished chirographer [he] ever met with"), an aptitude for mathematics well beyond his limited educational opportunities, and a commitment to personal appearance consistent with his lofty aspirations. The insistent demands of his father for farm labor in the absence of his eldest sons (who had left the farm when Claib was just five) forced the boy to shed his childhood frailties and interrupted what little formal wintertime education the Baptist ministers in the Mayslick district could afford him. Farm work may have nourished his body enough to sculpt a 170-pound frame, but Claib's quick mind craved far more sustenance than any Bluegrass soil, however fertile, could offer. Following his brothers to their Howard County farms may have afforded a convenient means of leaving his father's seigniory, but Claib Jackson harbored no intention of entering another form of servility by tilling any Missouri earth. He had resolved to become a merchant.[2]

Jackson's decision to enter the trade of merchandising reveals far more than any unwillingness to accept the mundane and plodding advance of life offered by commercial agriculture. Moreover, his vocational choice in no way suggests any rejection of the means by which central Missourians ordered their society around such husbandry. If anything, his later life would indicate that he embraced and even championed the social order. Rather,

July 6, 1826, Sappington Family Papers, box 1, MHS; *History of Howard and Chariton Counties*, 168–69; Notes on a trip to Boonville from St. Louis, n.d. [1830s], Howard County Papers, MHS (quote). Fayette replaced Franklin as the Howard County seat in 1823.

2. Paintings in the Arrow Rock Tavern, National Society of the Colonial Dames in the State of Missouri Papers, 1968–1974, Mss. 3584, folder 1, SHSM; *History of Saline County, Missouri, Carefully Written and Compiled from the Most Authentic Official and Private Sources, Including a History of its Townships, Cities, Towns and Villages*, 403, 406; *Jefferson Inquirer*, April 29, 1848; William B. Napton, *Past and Present of Saline County, Missouri*, 325; West, "Earlier Political Career of Jackson," 3–4, 7–8; Jones, *Western Merchant*, 154–55 (quote); Howard County [Missouri] Tax Lists, microfilm reel S244, vol. 1 (1816–1827), MSA.

Jackson's pursuit of the mercantile class suggests an ambitious nature, one that might have opted for advance by means more swift than agriculture, but one that still centered around the needs of the farmers who constituted the largest percentage of the local population. Wealth seemed nearly inevitable; one local merchant, John Beauchamp Jones, recalled of his peers that "every one of them, so far as I am informed, who pursued the legitimate business of a merchant, without being enticed aside into other channels of ill-considered speculation, met with certain success, and reaped a rich reward for all their toils and privations." Jackson gauged accurately that merchants both profited and wielded great weight in the Boon's Lick. Merchandising offered operative capital with which to invest in other enterprises. Indeed, Jones—the first merchant to set up shop in nearby New Philadelphia, some twelve miles upriver from Franklin—wrote that "the merchant was an important individual in society. His standing took precedent even of that of the professional gentleman, who, at that day, at least, were rarely in affluent circumstances. Indeed, the merchants in a manner monopolized all the wealth in the country, and wielded the popular influence."[3]

However embellished, Jones's portrayal captures the singularity of western merchants to the local economy. Apart from their obvious role as buyers of local produce, these merchants acted in vital capacity as agents for local farmers in marketing their goods—staple or otherwise—to commission houses in St. Louis and beyond. Thus they bought those products that farmers labored to produce during the year, offering incentive to continued production and boosting the area's economy as a whole. As important, these merchants imported goods from downriver, providing farmers the opportunity to acquire essential products in their farming operations such as agricultural implements, hand tools, fertilizer, and seed. More alluring, the merchants imported a number of household goods and products to relieve the tedium of life on the frontier, including bulk dry goods such as tea, coffee, sugar, and flour, as well as liquor, medicines, and candies. Merchants also offered such manufactured items as hardware, leather goods, kettles and pots, nails, dishes, paints, glass, and books.[4]

Many merchants offered even more enticing fineries, from which they often made smarter profits. The firm of Kyle and McCausland in Franklin advertised in 1826 a raft of fabrics and clothing items "just received, by late arrivals," including

> Super Prince Regent's extra blue Cloths; Extra Super and Superfine do.
> Superior Saxony Blue Cassimeres; A case of superior Irish Linens, in half

3. Robert E. Shalhope, *Sterling Price: Portrait of a Southerner,* 17; Jones, *Western Merchant,* 155 (first quote), 41 (second quote).

4. Lewis E. Atherton, *The Frontier Merchant in Mid-America,* 17–19.

pieces; Superior rich figured gros de Naples Robes; Black figured Silks and Satins; Colored do do [Silks and Satins]. Mandarine Crape robes, all colors; Figured and plain Canton Crapes; Black, white, pink and blue Italian Crapes; Black Silk Laces, white do do [silk laces]; Gauze Ribbons, Dress handkerchiefs, Gauze Handkerchiefs, Hair Nets; Elegantly worked Swiss Jaconet and Book Muslins; Jaconet & Mull Muslins; 4–4 and 6–4 Cambrics, very cheap; Pink, blue and black Cambrics; Figured and plain Book Muslins; Furniture and Cambric Dimities; Chintz Calicoes, new style; 4–4 Furniture Checks; 3–4 and 4–4 Checks, very fine quality; 3–4 and 4–4 Plaid Cottons; 3–4 and 4–4 Shirtings; 4–4 and 6–4 Waltham Sheetings; Bleached do do [sheetings]; Carls waist Buckles; Long white Kid Gloves; Insertion Trimmings, a fine assortment; Cotton Cords and Wadding, a new article; Linen Diapers and Lawns; Fine white and black cotton Hose; Half do do [white and black cotton Hose]; White and black Superfine Silk do [Hose]. White and Prunella and Kid Shoes; Children's Boots; Oil Cloths and Paper Hanging; A superior assortment of Satinetts. 130 pieces Blue Stroud; 30 do. Scarlet Cloth; 2 & 2 1/2 point Mackina Blankets. With a variety of other articles.

"All of which," the proprietors claimed, "we will sell at our usual low prices."[5]

In addition to facilitating trade, merchants in the West served the vital purpose of establishing or augmenting towns. These frontier towns served as entrepôts for the import and export trade, created markets for local produce, collected and held mail, and stimulated the economy of the entire region by expanding the land market both in town and out. New towns attracted a variety of professionals and entrepreneurs, who in turn offered services to local residents generally unavailable in the countryside. Moreover, such activity encouraged the settlement of legal and governmental offices, and bustling centers of commerce often lured seats of government away from those county seats that the legislature had platted at the counties' incorporation. Mercantile activity, carried on by retail and wholesale merchants, determined the stature of the community and created the connection between not only the rural farmers and townspeople but also the area's inhabitants and the rest of the country. The connections made and kept by merchants in St. Louis and Franklin allowed the latter town to continue to be a locus of immigration as well as guaranteeing that it would continue to be a regular site for the embarkation and debarkation of steamboats plying the Missouri River.[6]

While the retailing of goods was the most obvious of a merchant's activities to benefit the local community, perhaps the most vital role that traders performed locally was their extension of monetary and exchange services. Cash was often scarce in this western region, and banks to provide currency were nonexistent beyond St. Louis. Under these conditions, the marketing of local goods and services operated to some degree upon bartering, but

5. Ibid., 51–52; *Missouri Intelligencer* [Franklin], June 16, 1826 (quotes).
6. Atherton, *Frontier Merchant in Mid-America*, 16–17.

merchants found such practices disadvantageous, if not outright untenable. In the absence of a more regularized system of exchange, merchants assumed the additional role of bankers and creditors. At its most basic level, the system allowed farmers to trade their produce for goods at the merchant's store, with a ledger book recording the exchanges, credits, and debits. In many cases, however, the system was far more complex. Customers actually deposited currency with merchants, either in kind or in cash, and withdrew as needed, with the merchants offering circulating notes in trade for goods at their store. With access to St. Louis capital, merchants often were the only locals who possessed specie, and they offered loans to strapped farmers in time of need, with interest ranging as high as 6 to 10 percent. Often the merchants advanced currency so that farmers could ready their cash crops for market— generally those that the merchant could sell to commission houses—and would charge interest on the loan as well as a commission on the sales, which the merchants would consign, although they often would not handle the actual produce. Because they often made great profit from their variety of monetary services, merchants in Franklin stymied efforts at state banking legislation, preserving and extending their influence for nearly a decade after Jackson's arrival in Franklin. As John Beauchamp Jones wrote, the merchant "is a general locum tenens, the agent of everybody! And familiar with every transaction in his neighborhood."[7]

The importance of merchants to the local economy of Franklin often served as segue to their participation in local politics. Those who were regarded as dealing fairly with farmers often enjoyed the personal benefits that their profitable relationship afforded. Merchants were not educated men; one historian found that just 15 percent of those he studied in the Middle West had attended school past the age of fifteen. This decided lack of formal education, when coupled with a strong business sense, actually worked to their advantage when dealing with largely uneducated farmers who preferred fair dealers to slick, schooled profiteers. Stores served as more than places of business; they were meeting places, centers of socialization and gossip, and regularly offered their establishments, however humble, as sites of political debate and even organization. Merchants were often partisan in their politics, and used their positions to entice customers who supported their party affiliation. They considered this practice good business; holding the prevailing local political sentiment would attract a wide clientele, and if the merchant was competitive enough in price, he could afford such public party loyalty even among opponents—many customers could overlook any difference of political opinion in search of the best buy. If an area boasted but one merchant, political posture of course meant little in the way of business,

7. Ibid., 17–18, 123–27; Jones, *Western Merchant,* v (quote).

that is of course until individuals became endebted to that merchant, who in the era of public balloting could easily pressure debtors into voting for his party of choice. The store as a center of local activity offered those individuals a signal opportunity to influence and regulate the local political landscape, in part through the uniquely American form of debt peonage. Not surprisingly, nearly a quarter of merchants in the West entered politics.[8]

Without capital enough to start his own business, Claib had secured a position as early as the first week of July 1826 as a clerk in the New Franklin mercantile establishment of Hickman and Lamme. William Lamme and James Hickman had formed a trading partnership in 1823, establishing branches in Franklin, Richmond, and Liberty. The Lamme brothers—William, Samuel, and David—were the most prominent traders in the Boon's Lick, having operated stores since 1820 in those towns, as well as in Columbia and Independence. William Lamme had formed an initial partnership in that year with R. S. Barr, offering goods from as far away as Philadelphia. The two men conducted business in Franklin for two years when Hickman purchased Barr's shares and entered the largest mercantile house in town, which included a tobacco manufactory that offered receipts for goods from the company's trading enterprise in exchange for good leaf tobacco. Lamme and Hickman accepted as payment other farm goods as well, charging interest and commission on the latter. Lamme routinely traveled to the East to acquire manufactured goods, and was away from the store frequently and for long periods of time. By the time of Hickman's death in June 1827, Claib Jackson had not only secured employment with the firm but also stood tall enough in the eyes of both the surviving proprietor and the deceased's executor to offer the young clerk the responsibility of collecting the firm's debts. A public advertisement announced his new position.[9]

Young Claib Jackson's appealing personality only complemented his exacting nature and burning ambition for success, the traits conjoining in Lamme's and Hickman's estimation to signal great potential as a businessman. Others corroborated the assessment. Described by observers as "extremely affable" and "naturaly [*sic*] very cheerful," Jackson appeared to have cultivated "an unusual degree of popularity," in part by swapping stories and jokes happily with others in his company. Commonly referred to by the shortened version of his given name—a sign of acceptance—one of his friends recalled that he loved "tall fish stories," was an inveterate card player, and that he had

8. Atherton, *Frontier Merchant in Mid-America*, 27–30, 32.

9. Certificate of Hickman and Lamme to John S. Sappington (signed by C. F. Jackson), July 6, 1826, Sappington Family Papers, box 1, MHS; *Missouri Intelligencer* [Franklin], July 16, 1821; *Missouri Intelligencer and Boon's Lick Advertiser* [Fayette], July 12, 1827; *History of Howard and Chariton Counties*, 168–69; Atherton, *Frontier Merchant in Mid-America*, 16, 21, 127–28, 143, 156.

a penchant for practical jokes, while another related that he was a "happy lover of humor in others, and affording a constant fund of it himself." His upcountry dialect reflected his Kentucky roots, no doubt enhancing his appeal to customers and acquaintances in Franklin.[10]

Despite a strong grasp of the written language, throughout his life Jackson demonstrated perfection only in the decidedly imperfect, self-styled western vernacular. Ridiculed by easterners, the dialect was so distinct that the editor of the *Missouri Intelligencer* thought it necessary to publish a "PROVINCIAL DICTIONARY, *For the convenience of Emigrants.*" As Jackson said it, he "had came" to the courthouse and on his way "thar" he "seen a heap" (quantity) of folks "patering" (ambling along) to get there. He "reckoned" (supposed) that the year's "crap" (crop) of tobacco would be "tolerable" (decent), expected many "powers" (quantities) of it to be traded in town, and he was "up and a doing" his job when "toting" (carrying) sacks of flour and meal to "whar" the customers' wagons were parked. If he saw a friend who hadn't frequented the store in a long time, he asked "couldn't a body hear from you once in a while?" When business was good, profits were "right smart," and he "let on" (divulged) to the customers that he occasionally splashed an extra "drap" (drop) or two into their whiskey jugs before he "cyphered" (calculated) their bill so as to secure their repeat business. He never "disremembered" (forgot) to lock up the owners' store, and after he "done so" he saddled up his "marr" (mare) and went "coon" and "barr" (bear) hunting on the forested bluffs on the "fanent" (opposite) side of the Missouri from New Franklin.[11]

Yet Jackson's genial nature masked an intense determination not only to succeed, but to dominate. He was not above fisticuffs or even more serious violence in his dealings with other men he viewed as competitors. As early as May 1827, Rice Challes, a Franklin merchant, brought suit against Jackson and J. C. Gordon, both clerks for Hickman and Lamme,

10. Jones, *Western Merchant,* 154–55 (first, third, and fifth quotes); *Jefferson Inquirer,* April 29, 1848 (second quote); Thomas Claiborne Rainey, *Along the Old Trail,* 38 (fourth quote).

11. Interview with Mary Sappington Price, undated, cited in Burks, "Thunder on the Right," 54*n*76; *Missouri Intelligencer* [Franklin], March 4, 1823 (first, fourth through ninth, eleventh, fourteenth through sixteenth, eighteenth, twentieth, twenty-second and twenty-third quotes); *Missouri Statesman* [Columbia], May 14, 1852 (second quote); "Old Time Politics—How Campaigns Went in Benton's Day," newspaper clipping, cited in Burks, "Thunder on the Right," 465 (third and twelfth quotes); C. F. Jackson to M. M. Marmaduke, August 7, 1840, Sappington Family Papers, box 3, MHS (tenth quote); C. F. Jackson to Thomas Reynolds, January 6, 1841, Governors' Papers, Record Group 3: Thomas Reynolds Papers, Correspondence, box 2, folder 57, MSA (thirteenth, seventeenth, and nineteenth quotes); Daniel M. Grissom, "Personal Recollections of Distinguished Missourians: Claiborne F. Jackson," 505 (twenty-first quote).

for assault and trespass, charging that on April 7 they had come to Challes's place of business, which adjoined their employers', and "with force and arms &c, made an assault upon him . . . and then & there with certain sticks, stones, pot-metal & lead, and with their fists, gave and struck [him] a great many violent blows and strokes on and about his head, face, breast, back, shoulders, arms, legs and divers other parts of his body." Challes claimed that the beating was so severe and that he had been "bruised and wounded, and became and was sick, sore, lame and disordered," and "was hindered and prevented from performing and transacting his . . . business" for six full weeks. Faced with damages of five hundred dollars, Jackson and Gordon retained Fayette attorney Abiel Leonard to defend them for the fee of fifteen dollars. Leonard disputed before the court not the assault, but its severity. Though acting on behalf of his employer, the incident—as with so many such legal entanglements—derived from a previous personal altercation between Challes and Jackson. By all indications, the affray only further endeared the young Kentucky hotspur to his employers.[12]

Sibling rivalry probably enhanced the clearly headstrong and ambitious Claib Jackson's drive to succeed. By 1828, brother Wade had attained social prominence enough to gain appointment as a justice of the peace in Howard's Moniteau Township, and both Wade and brother Thomas would soon serve as representatives from Howard County in the state legislature. Yet Claib was too independent simply to follow the prevailing winds in choosing his bailiwick. His decision not to follow his brothers into farming— an occupation that allowed them to bring as many as fifteen slaves from their father's Kentucky farm to till their collective fields, many of whom followed the family matriarch, who emigrated to Howard County after Dempsey Jackson's death and lived with son Thomas—forced the youngest Jackson, not offered such largesse, to accelerate any plans for advancement he might already have held. Jackson would find other means of personal ascendance.[13]

Young Claib held out for even loftier ambitions than did his brothers and initiated his climb early, with an eye to local persuasions that would assist his ascent. He participated with the Howard County militia in several "wars" with the region's Indians—especially the Osage, Shawnee, and Delaware.

12. *Rice Challes v. Claiborne F. Jackson and John S. Gordon*, Circuit Court Cases, 1827, Howard County [Missouri], box 6, folder 105, MSA (quotes); Abiel Leonard, Private Account Book No. 31, January 1825, to November 1827, Abiel Leonard Papers, Mss. 1013, folder 582, SHSM. No record of the outcome of the case exists.

13. Fifth U.S. Census, 1830, Population Schedule, Howard County, Missouri, NA; Burks, "Thunder on the Right," 35*n*46, 50–51; *History of Saline County*, 402; Shalhope, *Sterling Price*, 33; *Missouri Democrat*, March 16, 1846. Mary Pickett Jackson died on March 7, 1846, and is buried in the Fayette City Cemetery. Boggs and Coutts, eds., *Howard County Cemetery Records*, 192.

After being voted unanimously a first lieutenant in a local "Ranger" company nearly immediately upon his arrival in Franklin, he exhibited enough skill and fortitude over the next decade to be voted to the rank of major, a title he continued to use—and others used of him—late in his political life. The rank reflected his social bearing among men as much as any exceptional martial aptitude, though his remarkable skill with a gun (rumored to allow him to "kill a bird on the wing eight times out of ten shots, with a rifle and a single bullet") caused his peers to regard him as "the best shot in Missouri." He maintained a peripheral affiliation with the Baptist church (perhaps in deference to the strongly Methodist leanings of the region and the family he would ultimately marry into), and unlike many other merchants he eschewed any connection with the Masons, considering them undemocratic elitists. Impetuous, young Claib Jackson could not remain in another person's employment for long. Within two years, in the late fall of 1828, while still employed by William Lamme, he applied to the Howard County clerk for vendor's licenses to sell both merchandise and liquor, preparatory to opening his own store. Paying a sum of twenty dollars for the two licenses, and using the title "C. F. Jackson & Co.," he was one of fifteen who received such permission that year to engage in local mercantile trading.[14]

By the summer of 1829, Jackson and Company, in partnership with Lamme and Brothers, was offering goods for sale in his small New Franklin store. Yet despite his firm resolution and aptitude as a merchant, such small operations—with little venture capital with which to stock the store, especially with the variety of services provided by large establishments such as those operated by his former employer—rendered any business at best extremely fragile. His business was small enough for him not to advertise in the Franklin newspaper, not unusual for tiny operations but a decided disadvantage in competing with the larger houses doing business in the growing town. Yet by all indications, Jackson and Company did well in its first months of operation, well enough for Jackson to obtain a second vendor's license in May 1829. The license, with an ad valorem fee dependent upon the amount of business done in the previous year, cost him $59.41, nearly three times what he had paid the previous fall and the most paid for such a license in the entire county.[15]

14. *Missouri Statesman*, June 1, 1849; *Jefferson Inquirer*, April 29, 1848 (quotes); John McElroy, *The Struggle for Missouri*, 75; McCandless, *History of Missouri*, 55–57; *Missouri Intelligencer and Boon's Lick Advertiser*, December 12, 1828. McElroy claims that Jackson served in the Black Hawk War.

15. *Missouri Intelligencer and Boon's Lick Advertiser*, June 5, 1829, December 4, 11, 25, 1829; Atherton, *Frontier Merchant in Mid-America*, 156–57. Of the 140 merchants he studied throughout the frontier Middle West, Atherton estimates that only about a third advertised their wares and services in local newspapers.

Yet by November of that year, the enterprising young Jackson was out of business, trying to collect debts to avoid bankruptcy. The Lamme brothers advertised his remaining merchandise for auction as part of the same sale as that of one of the brothers, Samuel C. Lamme, who had been killed on the return trip from Santa Fe in Spanish New Mexico. The young entrepreneur appears to have invested heavily in the risky Santa Fe trade. An undated "Memo: of Articles for Santa fe" in Jackson's hand includes a wide variety of goods, from expensive silks, satins, cassimeres, and cassinettes to needles, pins, buttons, combs, knives, tableware, candlesticks, spices, and eyeglasses. Most likely, he had stretched himself too thin, borrowed too much, and carried an overhead too high to survive any potential loss on the perilous trail. The coincidence of Jackson's failed business and Lamme's death on the Santa Fe Trail—and the fact that the Lammes handled the sale of his merchandise in conjunction with the deceased brother's goods—suggests strongly that the ambitious young man from Kentucky had ventured boldly but disastrously into the risky yet potentially lucrative overland trade with New Mexico.[16]

That Jackson and other central Missouri entrepreneurs were lured into high-stakes trading ventures with the Spanish borderlands was a natural extension of their commercial surroundings. Missouri—and particularly Franklin—had figured prominently in the earliest efforts at opening a line of commerce between Upper Mexico and the Mississippi Valley. The effort did not come without risk; if the venturesome traders managed to traverse the thousand-mile-long journey to Santa Fe over high plains, desert, and mountains through Indian country without harm, they faced Spain's rigid exclusion of all foreign merchants and traders. In 1817, two St. Louisans had managed to approach the city only to have soldiers arrest them and confiscate thirty thousand dollars' worth of their goods. Prospective traders drew hope from the knowledge that the welcoming local residents most often circumvented such laws in their desire for manufactured goods, as well as the New Mexican officials' notoriously lax enforcement of Spain's laws in their distant province. The trip back, of course, was just as long and perhaps riskier than the initial journey to the New Mexican capital, given that the traders

16. *Missouri Intelligencer and Boon's Lick Advertiser,* December 11, 1829; "Memo: of Articles for Santa fe," undated, John S. Sappington Papers, Mss. 1027, folder 3, SHSM. As late as 1833, Jackson continued to employ the court system to collect debts owed to Jackson and Company. See July 1, 1830, entry, "C. F. Jackson v. S. Brownejohn," Abiel Leonard Private Account Book No. 51, May 1830 to May 1832, Abiel Leonard Papers, Mss. 1013, folder 585, SHSM; also Abiel Leonard to Anonymous, March 16, 1831, ibid., box 3, folder 54, SHSM; C. F. Jackson to Abiel Leonard, October 3, 1833, ibid., box 3, folder 70, SHSM.

now carried specie. In the late summer of 1821, William Becknell organized an expedition from Franklin to capture wild horses and mules in the southern Rockies and while there learned of Mexican independence. Becknell hastened there, then returned to Franklin and advertised in the *Missouri Intelligencer* that he would leave Franklin that fall to trade with Santa Fe. With thirty men, three wagons, and five thousand dollars in merchandise, Becknell made the trip and reputedly, upon the caravan's return the following year, he dumped his glittering treasure on the town sidewalk for all the gawking townspeople to see. In 1823 and again in 1825 the Franklin newspaper published in serial form the journals Becknell kept on his trips to New Mexico. The "father of the Santa Fe trail" had inadvertently thrown the doors to the Southwest wide open, with Franklin at least temporarily its eastern terminus.[17]

Trading ventures with Santa Fe were expensive, and grew only more so. To guarantee safety, some traders resorted to large caravans, which raised the investment required of such enterprises steeply but succeeded in insuring their considerable stake. The potential profits were worth the risk to many entrepreneurs. Buoyed by Becknell's successes, Virginia-born Meredith Miles Marmaduke of Saline County, an engineer who had surveyed and laid out the town of New Philadelphia, served as a county court justice in Saline, and later became the state's governor and Jackson's brother-in-law, organized an expedition in the spring of 1824 from Franklin to Santa Fe that boasted 83 persons (two of them slaves), $30,000 in trade goods, 24 light wagons and carts, 200 horses and mules, and a small cannon. Marmaduke's gambit paid off handsomely; the caravan made its trip without incident and returned in the fall of 1825 with $180,000 in gold and silver and another $10,000 worth of furs. By 1830, one caravan numbered 120 men, 200 wagons, and carried goods worth $200,000. Few traders (apparently not Samuel C. Lamme and his partners) could afford such a high investment.[18]

The growing value of the Santa Fe trade to Missouri—as well as the continued Indian attacks on trading parties both without and within the borders of Missouri—induced a call for governmental intervention to stem

17. Ray Allen Billington, *The Far Western Frontier, 1830–1860*, 23–25; William E. Parrish, "William Becknell," in Howard R. Lamar, ed., *The New Encyclopedia of the American West*, 89; Isaac J. Cox, "Opening the Santa Fe Trail," 30–66; Sampson, ed., "The Journals of Capt. Thomas [William] Becknell from Boone's Lick to Santa Fe and from Santa Cruz to Green River," 65 (quote), 67; Hulbert, ed., *Southwest on the Turquoise Trail; The First Diaries on the Road to Santa Fe*, 56–68.

18. Burks, "Thunder on the Right," 42, 52; Certificate of appointment, Justice of County Court of Saline County, Missouri, John C. Miller to M. M. Marmaduke, January 20, 1831, Sappington Family Papers, box 1, MHS; F. A. Sampson, ed., "Journal of M. M. Marmaduke of a Trip from Franklin, Missouri to Santa Fe, New Mexico in 1824," 1–3, 9; Billington, *Far Western Frontier*, 26.

the continued losses of lives and investments. Visiting the Boon's Lick in the summer of 1824, Missouri Senator Thomas Hart Benton found ample sentiment among merchants and traders—decidedly out of western character—clearly solicitous of governmental intervention. That fall, Benton sponsored an appropriation bill to buy peace with the tribes along the trail and improve the thoroughfare to and from Santa Fe. Three official tribal negotiators and another thirty-three Boon's Lickers spent two years surveying the New Mexican territory and negotiating with both Indians and Mexicans, culminating in a report to Congress in 1827 that declared the Santa Fe Trail safe and prosperous. In reality, depredations continued for decades, to the extent that in 1830 the state legislature unanimously approved a resolution to Congress requesting a "corps of Rangers, to be kept in constant service, . . . for the protection of the Trade to Mexico, and the defence of the frontiers of this State, . . . against the Hordes of Barbarians, . . . at the expense of the United States." With the river's devastation of Franklin, the "cradle" of the trade moved farther west, first to New Philadelphia (soon called Arrow Rock), then to Lexington, and ultimately to Independence.[19]

While financial misfortune might have cost Jackson his infant business, it was a remarkably temporary setback. Just after Thanksgiving of 1829, a new partner, hatter Moss Prewitt, invested enough capital in the business to counteract Jackson's Santa Fe losses and save the entire stock of goods about to be auctioned, and within a week they were back in business. Prewitt invested five thousand dollars to Jackson's twenty-five hundred, with Jackson paying Prewitt 10 percent annually on his partner's extra investment, but Jackson could end the interest payments by buying back Prewitt's additional investment. Each shared equally in the store's profits with personal charges being at cost plus 6 percent interest. The contract the two signed was to run for two years unless terminated earlier by either partner, with three months' notice. In the same issue of the *Intelligencer* that advertised the sale of his defunct mercantile house, Jackson informed the public that he and Prewitt would offer those same goods "for sale in the same house [in New Franklin].

19. Missouri Legislature, "Select Committee . . . on protection for those who trade between Missouri and Mexico," December 21, 1830, Beinecke Library, Yale University, in *Western Americana,* microfilm reel 373, entry 3666, 1, 7–8 (first quote); Sampson, "Journal of M. M. Marmaduke," 2; Billington, *Far Western Frontier,* 27–28 (second quote); Atherton, *Frontier Merchant in Mid-America,* 106–14. The commissioners report, along with journals of the expedition, are in Kate L. Gregg, ed., *The Road to Santa Fe: The Journal and Diaries of George Champlin Sibley and others, pertaining to the surveying and marking of a road from the Missouri frontier to the settlements of New Mexico, 1825–1827,* passim. In 1833, New Philadelphia would become Arrow Rock, renamed for the nearby river-sculpted prominence called originally "Pierre à Flèche" by French traders from an Osage legend. Local settlers had called the town "Airy Rock" nearly from its founding. See Prouse, ed., *Arrow Rock,* 178, 180–81.

The very low terms upon which they purchased their goods, enables them to say that as good bargains may be had of them as at any store in this country. Their assortment is large & well selected." Fortune had indeed smiled upon Claib Jackson, and he would make the most of this timely largesse.[20]

Jackson and Prewitt had barely gotten the firm on its feet when the senior partner's appetite for advancement piqued again. As early as 1829, Jackson pursued an opportunity to expand beyond his business in Franklin. By December 1830, having repaid the debt to Prewitt for bailing out Jackson and Company, Jackson entered a business partnership with Caleb Jones, and together they opened a branch store in the growing town of New Philadelphia, situated on the west bank of the Missouri River in Saline County, twelve miles west of Franklin. During the painfully slow removal of Old Franklin to New Franklin, Jackson ran the branch store in New Philadelphia while Prewitt operated the store in New Franklin and Jones the one in Old Franklin. Jackson was the buyer for all three stores, thus minimizing costs, and by all indications he "had an uncanny ability to know what the people wanted and the prices they would be able to pay." Little competition and the promise of the new town's imminent growth prompted Jackson and Jones to relocate there, directly across the street from the large tavern and inn built earlier that year and in which Jackson would soon take residence. Though by 1830 New Philadelphia was only beginning to supplant Franklin as the locus of the Santa Fe trade, it was the sole trading center for Saline County, the fastest-growing part of the Boon's Lick. The venture was successful; within a year, the firm's monthly gross income from the three stores exceeded three thousand dollars.[21]

Though Jackson lived in Franklin through the winter of 1830 and 1831, he quickly found reason to relocate to Saline County only partially attributable to business interests. And as Jackson saw it, his newfound interest in Saline only facilitated his burning ambition. He had found a bride—and in her father, at last, a patron—who would assure his social ascent. As with his father before him, Jackson prepared to wed in hopes of an elevated social class. Unlike Dempsey Jackson, however, young Claib's union would actually signal this ascendance, but only after prolonged personal tragedy.

The family that Jackson set his sights upon entering was that of John Sappington, a man as close to nobility as this western frontier democracy would sustain. Born in Maryland in the year of independence, Sappington

20. Contract of Moss Prewitt and C. F. Jackson, December 1, 1829, John S. Sappington Papers, Mss. 1027, box 1, folder 17, SHSM; Atherton, *Frontier Merchant in Mid-America,* 121; *History of Howard and Chariton Counties,* 168; *Missouri Intelligencer,* December 1, 1829 (quote).

21. Prouse, ed., *Arrow Rock,* 178, 180–81; Burks, "Thunder on the Right," 37 (quote), 41–43.

came from a distinguished family of physicians, including his father and uncle, who were both trained at the Philadelphia College of Medicine. Raised in the Tennessee Basin south of Nashville and educated largely in Maryland, the younger Sappington learned from his father, Mark, the essential conjoining of medicine, business, and politics as a keen avenue to success on the emerging frontier by working in the family mercantile trade as well as assisting in his father's medical practice. Sappington practiced medicine while speculating in land south of Nashville, and there helped to establish the town of Franklin, Tennessee, where he was living in 1804 when he married Jane Breathitt of the powerful Kentucky family. He was a civic leader, successful planter and businessman, and a close friend of Franklin lawyer Thomas Hart Benton when, seeking professional credentials, in 1814 he returned to the East to study medicine at the University of Pennsylvania for a year. Two years later, at Benton's urging, Sappington decided to "lay the foundations of a great fortune" in the West and left middle Tennessee, following Benton to Missouri.[22]

Rather than settle in St. Louis, as had his friend Benton (who was now editor of the popular *St. Louis Enquirer)*, Sappington borrowed $950 from the lawyer-turned-editor and moved in 1817 to the Boon's Lick, acquiring land in Howard County and serving as chairman of Franklin's board of commissioners. In 1821 he fashioned the town's ordinance for slave patrols, a natural concern of Sappington's, having himself slaves by this time. Yet Sappington's time in Franklin would be short; in 1819, he had staked his claim on the nation's westernmost edge of settlement, Saline County. His investment was sound. Within a few years, Sappington owned at least seven thousand acres of land five miles southwest of New Philadelphia that formed the speculative core of an extensive network of trade and services. He was the only physician in Saline and one of but a handful west of St. Louis, and his patients ranged from Columbia to Independence.[23]

22. Eulogy for John S. Sappington, undated [1856], John S. Sappington Papers, Mss. 1027, box 1, folder 5, SHSM; Obituary of Jane B. Sappington, undated clipping [1852], Sappington Miscellany, John Sappington Collection, Mss. 1036, folder 4, SHSM; Thomas B. Hall, "John Sappington, M. D.—1776–1856," 177–83; Morrow, "Dr. John Sappington," 39n1, 39–42; Eula Gladys Riley, "John Sappington, Doctor and Philanthropist," 8–18; Burks, "Missouri Medicine Man," 41–42; Burks, "Thunder on the Right," 43–47; McCandless, *History of Missouri*, vol. 2, 216–17; T. H. Benton to John Sappington, July 2, 1817, John S. Sappington Papers, Mss. 1027, box 1, folder 12, SHSM. John Breathitt, Jane's older brother, later became governor of Kentucky from 1832–1834, dying of tuberculosis in office, while George Breathitt, another of Jane's brothers, served as Andrew Jackson's personal emissary during the nullification crisis. Breathitt County, Kentucky, is named for John Breathitt. See Lowell H. Harrison, "John Breathitt" and "Breathitt County," both in Kleber, ed., *The Kentucky Encyclopedia*, 115–16.

23. Morrow, "Dr. John Sappington," 42–44; Franklin [Missouri] Board of Commissioners, Slave Patrol Ordinance, n.d. [1821], Sappington Family Papers, box 1, MHS;

Yet Sappington did not limit himself to medicine; he had emulated his father well and traveled throughout the Boon's Lick selling meat, vegetables, grain, cider, and medicine as well as extending credit to area residents. Sappington employed agents—including prominent local attorney Abiel Leonard—to collect his payments. Later he and his sons-in-law—Alonzo Pearson, who married Sappington's eldest daughter, Eliza, and Meredith M. Marmaduke, who married daughter Lavinia—as well as his sons Erasmus and William together operated stores and mills in New Philadelphia and Jonesborough, a hamlet nine miles west of New Philadelphia. In addition to trade products and usury, by the 1820s Sappington was manufacturing salt, growing and ginning cotton (as much as a thousand pounds a day), and producing hemp and tobacco, all with the assistance of as many as twenty-five slaves. By 1830, Sappington was one of the largest slave owners in the Boon's Lick, a Democratic standard bearer and established as one of the region's social, economic, and political patriarchs. An avowed free thinker, Sappington's personal library—which Jackson estimated to contain some three thousand volumes—was the finest west of St. Louis.[24]

Claib Jackson recognized his chance for entrance into the Boon's Lick's haut monde when he met Mary Jane Breathitt Sappington, the third daughter of John and Jane Sappington. Tennessee-born, educated, vivacious, and beautiful, Jane (as she was called) was only days shy of eighteen on Christmas Eve of 1830 when she attended a holiday ball hosted by attorney Thomas Shackelford of the Arrow Rock district in southeast Saline County. Jane's older sister, Lavinia, who had married Meredith M. Marmaduke four years earlier, wrote to her husband of the "host of Gallants, too numerous to mention" from across the Boon's Lick that her younger sister attracted during a remarkable series of parties that lasted the entire holiday week, including one at her father's stately log home on Pilot Hickory Farm. The young people danced and played cards for eight of the next nine days, often until the early hours of morning. "Jane," her sister recalled, was "a great roast here," and by all indications was the center of attention. Jackson, seven years her senior, pursued her immediately and earnestly. The young woman responded nearly as quickly to the handsome merchant suitor; as her sister wrote a week later, she rejected "2 beaux lately, Mr. [Thomas] Conway & a Doct. Robinson of Boon County, and has the third one, Jackson

---

John Sappington to James Callaway, January 13, 1823, John S. Sappington Papers, Mss. 1027, box 1, folder 14, SHSM; Hurt, *Agriculture and Slavery in Little Dixie*, 61, 65, 219.

24. Morrow, "Dr. John Sappington," 42–44; Fifth U.S. Census, 1830, Population Schedule, Saline County, Missouri, NA; John Sappington to Charles M. Cravens, March 7, 1838, John S. Sappington Papers, Mss. 1027, box 2, folder 28, SHSM; Burks, "Thunder on the Right," 54, 46–47; *History of Saline County*, 402.

of Franklin, which I think she looks more pleasing at, and is this day at Father's." The courtship was whirlwind, and on February 17, 1831, before a small but stunned audience, Howard County Methodist minister Justin Williams married the couple at the Sappington home, the site of Jane's two older sisters' weddings. Eschewing the moral strictures of his more pious Methodist guests, Sappington threw a celebration for the newlyweds following the service, complete with music, dancing, and card playing. The setting for the union proved especially fitting given Jackson's fervent desire to cloak himself in Sappington robes.[25]

Within months, Jackson had buried his beautiful young wife. On July 21, 1831, just five months after their wedding day, Jane died, likely of the ague, a malarial fever that plagued frontier settlers in the West and South recurrently through the warm seasons of the year. Family tradition holds that she was pregnant, and apparently suffered for more than a month before the relapse that killed her, as indicated by a letter from Jackson dated June 10, in which he commented wishfully to Marmaduke that "Jane's health is much improved." Within six weeks she was dead, and the benumbed family laid her to rest in a creekside grove a half-mile northeast of the Sappington home, the first grave in what would become the family cemetery. The family was grief-stricken, none more so than its patriarch. In a letter to the girl's father requesting that the Sappington's sixteen-year-old daughter, Louisa, accompany his family on a trip to Virginia, friend, neighbor, and lawyer Nathaniel Beverly Tucker counseled that the girl's trip would "depend on your feelings. These I do not pretend to understand. 'The heart knoweth it's own bitterness,' and each man has within himself his own peculiar antidote to affliction. Let none then prescribe for another." Sappington's personal anguish was only deepened by the inconsolable fact that in this most exigent of cases, he was a healer who could not heal; his daughter had died of the very pestilence against which he had been experimenting for a decade.[26]

25. Elizabeth Prather Ellsberry, ed., *Cemetery Records of Saline County, Missouri,* vol. 2, 36; Morrow, "Dr. John Sappington," 45; Burks, "Missouri Medicine Man," 50n4; John S. Sappington to Alonzo Pearson, July 25, 1829, and Lavinia Marmaduke to William B. Sappington, January 8, 1831 (quotes), both in Sappington Family Papers, box 1, MHS; Burks, "Thunder on the Right," 48–51; *History of Howard and Chariton Counties,* 207; Deed Records, Saline County, Missouri, vol. A, 254, microfilm reel C6227, MSA; *History of Saline County,* 180. Jane Sappington was born on January 1, 1813.

26. Ellsberry, ed., *Cemetery Records of Saline County,* vol. 2, 36; Eleanora G. Park and Kate S. Morrow, *Women of the Mansion: Missouri, 1821–1936,* 121; Prouse, *Arrow Rock,* 188; Morrow, "Dr. John Sappington," 48–50; C. F. Jackson to M. M. Marmaduke, June 10 [1831], Sappington Family Papers, box 6, MHS; [Nathaniel] Beverly Tucker to John S. Sappington, undated [1831], John S. Sappington Papers, Mss. 1027, box 1, folder 3, SHSM.

Sappington's "hobby," as relatives referred to it, was the use of quinine sulfate in the treatment of malarial fevers. This newest "wonder drug," introduced in the 1820s, quickly supplanted Peruvian bark as the most common treatment of the widespread fevers that offered the frontier people their greatest health problem. Yet for a decade, quinine remained unperfected, with side effects nearly as dangerous to patients as the ailment the doctors sought to treat. Many country doctors offered quinine indiscriminately and in inconsistent dosages with disastrous results, causing many to refrain from further administrations of it. Sappington had become convinced of the potential effectiveness of quinine as soon as the powder became available in 1823, but was unable to determine correct dosages of the drug, experimenting even on himself with pure quinine while continuing to prescribe a combination of quinine and bark to his patients as late as 1830. Jane's death snapped Sappington out of his conservative approach; by 1832 he had extended his use of quinine to patients throughout the Boon's Lick as empirical studies of its effects. Three years later, using slaves who labored in a small factory behind the main house on Pilot Hickory Farm, Sappington began manufacturing and nationally marketing "Sappington's Anti-Fever Pills."[27]

While the antidote to Sappington's overwhelming grief proved a redoubling of exertions to perfect a quinine-based cure for malaria, Jackson's prescription lay in quick action, rather than in any written lamentations. Having gained ingress into the lofty social world offered by the Sappingtons, he was unwilling to relinquish it. While others might have allowed his powerful in-laws to introduce him to eligible daughters of social peers, secure in the knowledge that the prematurity of his—and their—personal tragedy ensured a deep bond with them, Jackson laid claim to far more than any convenience their affection or pity might have offered; only an immediate and lifelong ligature would guarantee the lineage he now asserted as his right. After enduring a requisite mourning period that Victorian standards of social decorum demanded, conveniently the precise amount of time necessary to allow his newfound love to reach, if barely, a marriageable age, Jackson married again. On September 12, 1833, just over two years after the death of his

---

27. Morrow, "Dr. John Sappington," 48*n21*, 48–50; John Duffy, "Medical Practice in the Ante Bellum South," 53–72; W. A. Strickland, Jr., "Quinine Pills Manufactured on the Missouri Frontier, 1832–1862," 62; Edwin H. Ackerknecht, *Malaria in the Upper Mississippi Valley, 1760–1900*, 103–5; Burks, "Thunder on the Right," 62*n92*. Burks cites the working formula for Sappington's pills, in the John S. Sappington Family Papers of the Missouri Historical Society, as follows: for 5,760 pills, "sulphate of quinine, two pounds; pulverized extract of licorice, one and a half pounds; pulverized gum of myrrh, one-half pound; oil of sassafras; acqua[*sic*] pura [distilled water]." Each pill was to contain one grain of quinine, but a chemical analysis done in 1958 revealed that each pill actually contained nearly one and one-half grains of quinine.

first young wife, Jackson took a second bride—Louisa Catherine Sappington, Jane's next-youngest sister, then, as was her sister when she and Jackson had married, just eighteen years old.[28]

The timing of Jackson's entrance and in particular his steadfast continuation in the Sappington clan was not purely coincidental. As Jackson married a Sappington daughter for the first time, the marriage of the eldest daughter, Elizabeth (or Eliza, as the family called her) was ending in a most public way. Eliza's first husband, Alonzo Pearson, a native Georgian, moved to the Boon's Lick in 1821 and briefly taught in a local academy. The couple wed that September and during the next eight years Eliza bore five children while Alonzo formed a successful business partnership with his new brother-in-law, Erasmus, and became chief manager of his father-in-law's mercantile and financial operations in Saline. In 1830, the family discovered that Pearson had a wife in Alabama, whom he had married in Georgia in 1820 and had deserted while pregnant "and in a state of absolute want" after taking her father's dowry of nearly two thousand dollars. He had never divorced his wife, and covered up the entire affair by escaping to Missouri, assuming a new name from his given name of Augustine Parsons before "beguiling" Eliza into marrying him. The scandal broke when the jilted first wife learned of Pearson's, or Parsons's, whereabouts and filed for support; the shamed Pearson admitted the grave infelicity to his business partner, Erasmus Sappington, who commented sympathetically that "Pearson looks more like a dead man than like a living one," yet sustained his father's response on behalf of the family. Despite Eliza's plaintive remonstrances as she lay in bed after delivering the couple's fifth child, the elder Sappington banished Pearson from the family rather than endure the shame of bigamy, recovered from the Georgian the dowry he had granted to the couple upon their "pretended marriage," dissolved the Pearson and Sappington Company, and petitioned the legislature for an annulment of the marriage, which it granted by one vote in 1831, precisely as Jackson entered the Sappington fold for the first time.[29]

28. Ellsberry, ed., *Cemetery Records of Saline County, Missouri*, vol. 2, 36; Park and Morrow, *Women of the Mansion*, 122.

29. Morrow, "Dr. John Sappington," 44, 46; Carolyn M. Barteis, ed., *Howard County Marriages*, 36; Accounts to Doctor John Sappington from Alonzo Pearson, October 20, 1826, and June 19, 1828, John S. Sappington Papers, Mss. 1027, box 1, folders 15 and 18, SHSM; Edward Bates to M. M. Marmaduke, January 4, 1831, Sappington Family Papers, box 1, MHS; Alonzo Pearson to William Becknell, August 8, 1829, ibid.; William Becknell to John S. Sappington, December 24, 1830, ibid.; *Mary Ann Mills Parsons v. Eliza Sappington*, Circuit Court Cases, 1841, Saline County [Missouri], box 3, folder 155, MSA (first, second, and fourth quotes); Erasmus D. Sappington to Meredith M. Marmaduke, June 18, 1830, Sappington Family Papers, box 2, MHS (third quote); *Journal of the House of Representatives of Missouri*, Sixth Gen. Ass., First Sess., 74, 82,

While the business opportunity in the family mercantile presented by the abrupt abdications of the eldest Sappington son-in-law might have offered an inducement for the merchant Jackson to marry one Sappington daughter, the rapid expansion of the pill business afforded him more than enough reason to try to remain in the family. By 1833, licorice-tasting "Sappington's Anti Fever & Ague Pills" had proven wildly successful throughout central Missouri—route salesman William J. Eddins wrote from Howard County that he "could sell any quantity"—and were included in the regular stock of many pharmacists and merchants, including Jackson, who knew the potential sales value of the pills. Jacob H. Headons, a merchant in Howard County, wrote to Sappington that "I have taken Dr Sappingtons Medicine myself, and that my family has had need for it, and used it, in six or seven cases, in all of which cares sd Medicine promptly proved efficacious in every care equal to, & in some far surpassing the directions." Headons recommended the pills to merchants as far away as Springfield, Missouri, on the Ozark plateau, and he related that he had "heard much said about it, & I have seen no person, who has made any expressment, of sd Medicine, who does not speak of it in the highest possible terms. There has been a large supply of it left at my office, in Springfield, Green Cty, for sale, it sold out in a short time, & there is pressing demands for a fresh supply of the same article, both there, & at many other places of deposit to my cirtain knowledge. it is cirtainly the best remedy for fevers, that I have ever seen or heard of." With such strong endorsements, and financial success in central Missouri, Sappington had become convinced that he should begin national marketing of his product, and began preparations for the venture as early as 1833, just as Jackson married a second of his daughters.[30]

95–96, 118, SHSM, hereafter cited as *Missouri House Journal; Journal of the Senate of Missouri*, Sixth Gen. Ass., First Sess., 101, 132–33, 164–65, 203, SHSM, hereafter cited as *Missouri Senate Journal*. Parsons fled to the Indian Territory before his scheduled trial, seeking refuge with the Cherokees on the Arkansas River. The close vote on annulment in the senate arose in part from some of its members' position that because Pearson had never divorced his first wife, the marriage to Eliza was never actualized and thus could not be annulled, but in additional part from the correct perception that Dr. Sappington, rather than Eliza, sought the annulment. See Lavinia Marmaduke to William B. Sappington, January 8, 1831, and Edward Bates to M. M. Marmaduke, January 4, 1831, Sappington Family Papers, box 2, MHS; William Becknell to Dr. John Sappington, December 24, 1830, John S. Sappington Papers, Mss. 1027, box 1, folder 18, SHSM.

30. William Eddins to John Sappington, July 19, 1837, John S. Sappington Papers, Mss. 1027, box 2, folder 26, SHSM; Affidavit of Jacob H. Headons, Howard County, Missouri, September 24, 1835, John S. Sappington Papers, Mss. 1027, box 1, folder 22, SHSM; Morrow, "Dr. John Sappington," 49–50. Eddins later married one of Alonzo and Eliza Pearson's daughters, Elizabeth, later Jackson's step-daughter, thus becoming Sappington's grandson-in-law.

In November 1835, Sappington created Sappington and Sons, in partnership with his sons, Erasmus and William, and his four sons-in-law, Jackson, Marmaduke, Layton S. Eddins, a Fayette businessman and farmer, and William Price, a physician. Sappington especially wanted Jackson's financial expertise in the company's operations; he would act as comptroller and chief financial officer, as well as being a district supervisor, requiring him to travel. Sappington began ordering hundreds of pounds of quinine from Philadelphia and New York and targeted those regions where the dreaded disease was most endemic, establishing distribution sites and hiring agents in target regions that centered in and around river valleys, traditional epicenters of malaria. One district, or route, would encompass the Ohio River Valley, including Kentucky, Illinois, and Indiana; a second would embrace the Lower Mississippi Valley, including Tennessee, Arkansas, Mississippi, and Louisiana; a third would take in the White and Arkansas River Valleys in southern Missouri and northern Arkansas; a fourth would offer pills in the Red River Valley in Texas; and a fifth would center upon the southern states of Alabama, Georgia, and South Carolina. Not surprisingly, given the title of the company or his dedication to family, Sappington employed his sons, sons-in-law, and even nephews in the business, generally as agents for distribution and collection in the southern states as well as for traveling purchasers to the eastern cities. The company quickly grew profitable; by 1837, gross receipts from the Lower Mississippi Valley alone totaled sixty thousand dollars, meaning sales of some forty thousand boxes of pills.[31]

Jackson probably anticipated the company's success when marrying Louisa. Someone so ambitious and calculating, and with intimate family connections and being a merchant who had sold the product himself, would have known well of the potential success of this company and could not have been unaware of Sappington's plans, however preliminary, to expand his business nationally. One of Jackson's correspondents certainly reminded him of the great fortune his seat at the bountiful family table offered, advising him to be "particularly gratified to have had all along the custom of the extensive connexions of Dr. Sappington's family who are amongst the oldest and most esteemed . . . not only in Missouri but in all the world." Jackson wasted no time parlaying this family connection into a business venture; by 1836 he had entered into a company with Marmaduke, based in Arrow Rock,

31. Burks, "Thunder on the Right," 64, 56–57, 62–66; Receipt from Cooper and Shroyer for M. M. Marmaduke [signed by C. F. Jackson], February 24, 1837, Sappington Family Papers, box 2, MHS; Morrow, "Dr. John Sappington," 50–52, 51n25; Burks, "Missouri Medicine Man," 100, 103–5; Riley, "John Sappington," 129–31. Merchants sold Sappington's pills on consignment for between 10 and 33 percent commission. Each boxed vial contained twenty-four pills.

that distributed pills to the Lower Mississippi Valley. Whether a marriage of ambition or of love, Jackson, with the horse sense of a native Kentuckian, grabbed tightly to the reins of the Sappington family thoroughbred.[32]

As Jackson positioned himself to become more and more involved in the Sappington pill business, initially as a traveling agent to St. Louis and beyond, which increasingly called him away from the store for long periods of time, he distanced himself from his mercantile operations. He had begun to withdraw from such businesses as early as 1833, when his partnership ended with Caleb Jones, who moved across the river to Boonville after selling his portion of the Arrow Rock store to Samuel B. Miller. Jackson signed a four-year contract with Miller, calling the firm Jackson and Miller. In a financial sense, Jackson probably did not need a partner at this point in his professional life; he could have employed a capable clerk to conduct business at the store while he traveled to the East for goods, as had his original employers, Hickman and Lamme. Having a partner unsaddled Jackson from the burdens of store management and offered the capacity for Miller to use company expenditures as business opportunities arose in his absence, something a mere clerk could not handle. To this end, each man invested three thousand dollars, with Miller agreeing to pay Jackson five hundred dollars a year if the former did not participate actively in the store's operation. Jackson was largely the company buyer, and often combined travel for both his and the Sappington businesses, purchasing from mercantile houses in Philadelphia for his own store while buying chemicals for the Sappington pill company.[33]

Jackson did not intend to fetter himself with the mercantile business for much longer. In 1836 he terminated his partnership with Moss Prewitt in New Franklin, selling the store for a substantial profit. In the spring of 1837, two years into a renewed four-year contract, Jackson and Miller sold their business to two aspiring merchants, W. A. Barnes and Jesse McMahan. While Miller continued in the mercantile business with other partners, Jackson had loftier visions and left the trade of merchant permanently. With established

32. E. M. Ryland and Company to C. F. Jackson, February 13, 1856, Sappington Family Papers, Accounts, box 8, MHS (quote); William B. Sappington to Jackson and Marmaduke, October 29, 1836, ibid., box 2, MHS.

33. Note of Deposit, October 12, 1835, John S. Sappington Papers, Mss. 1027, box 1, folder 22, SHSM; John Sappington Ledger, ibid., box 5, vol. 5, 41, SHSM; West, "Earlier Political Career of Jackson," 4–5; Burks, "Thunder on the Right," 75; Contract between Samuel Miller and C. F. Jackson, September 22, 1831, John S. Sappington Papers, Mss. 1027, box 1, folder 19, SHSM; Atherton, *Frontier Merchant in Mid-America*, 121; Receipt, Samuel Miller to C. F. Jackson, undated, ibid., box 1, folder 5, SHSM; Expense Book, 1836–1852, ibid., box 5, folder 3, SHSM; Notes of Exchange, Jackson and Miller to Samuel Hildeburn, Everly and Rees, Robert Toland, and Joshua C. Olmer and Co., March 3–11, 1836, ibid., box 1, folder 23, SHSM; *History of Saline County*, 403.

business and social connections, and with the Sappington name now firmly etched on his Boon's Lick pedigree, the once-merchant set fair for a new career that boded both far more lucrative and risky than his erstwhile bailiwick. Jackson entered the rough-and-tumble world of Missouri politics.[34]

34. *History of Saline County,* 403; Contract between Samuel Miller and C. F. Jackson, September 22, 1831 [appended September 22, 1835] and Deed, Samuel Miller to C. F. Jackson, October 18, 1837, John S. Sappington Papers, Mss. 1027, box 1, folder 19, SHSM; Atherton, *Frontier Merchant in Mid-America,* 121; Bill, Jesse McMahan to C. F. Jackson, June 1–December 28, 1857, John S. Sappington Papers, Mss. 1027, box 1, folder 24, SHSM. Soon after Jackson's withdrawal from their trading company, Samuel Miller formed a partnership called Lewis and Miller. By 1850, he had a modest position in government as the Saline County tax collector. See Receipt, Samuel Miller to C. F. Jackson, February 19, 1850, John S. Sappington Papers, Mss. 1027, box 3, folder 58, SHSM.

4

THE POLITICS OF PLENTY

MEN ARE CONSERVATIVES when they are least vigorous, or when they are most luxurious. They are conservatives after dinner.

RALPH WALDO EMERSON, "NEW ENGLAND REFORMERS"

By the mid-1830s, the Sappingtons were known throughout the Boon's Lick as strong Benton men. Eschewing political labels, Missourians affiliated most strongly with their leaders and thus factions, rather than formal parties, held sway in the state well into the 1830s. In the case of the Sappington men, they aligned strongly and quite naturally with their family friend, Thomas Hart Benton, one of the state's original U.S. senators and a pillar of the West. In 1824, though Benton had actively supported Kentuckian Henry Clay for the presidency until the race narrowed to one between Andrew Jackson and John Quincy Adams, Benton cast his lot with the westerner, Jackson, who lost the election after the celebrated "corrupt bargain." The move propelled Benton into the forefront of political popularity in Missouri, whose populace showed then for Jackson and even more strongly during the next two elections, which Old Hickory won easily. Andrew Jackson was, as Missourians saw him, the heir to the Jefferson throne. By the early 1830s, virtually the entire state political corps professed its claim to being "Jacksonian," though in reality a wide chasm existed within the leadership over the degree to which many adhered to Jacksonian principles and philosophy. By the 1830s, Benton's senatorial seat was nearly unassailable and his position as Jackson's stentorian spokesman thrust him into the position as the people's champion. His strong Democratic stands against a protective tariff, a national bank, a national system of internal improvements, and the elitist electoral college placed Benton firmly in the Jackson camp, though his popular image as a defender of the people belied his place at the center of the elite circle of the Boon's Lick gentry. Benton often celebrated victories with the Sappingtons at parties that lasted for days, and he stayed regularly at the fine home of Meredith M. Marmaduke, located a mile south of Pilot Hickory farm.[1]

1. McCandless, *History of Missouri*, 68–77; Shalhope, *Sterling Price*, 18–21; West, "Earlier Political Career of Jackson," 11; Richard P. McCormick, *The Second American Party System: Party Formation in the Jacksonian Era*, 304–25; Burks, "Thunder on the Right," 54*n76*.

Incumbent upon Claib Jackson as a Sappington clansman was his unqualified support of Benton as his political standard bearer. In this factional affiliation—one he accepted willingly—Jackson deviated sharply from the political alignments of most Boon's Lick merchants, who overwhelmingly favored Henry Clay's "American System" of national banking, internal improvements, and a high tariff, all planks in a commercial-based platform that was decidedly not Jacksonian in theory. By 1840, three-fourths or more of western merchants supported these policies to some degree, creating in Missouri a conservative "Opposition" faction of the Jacksonian juggernaut that would, in 1840, break away to form the state's Whig party. Claib Jackson saw astutely that despite his merchant status, his social connections with the Bentonite Sappingtons—and the widespread appeal of the traditional Jacksonian label among the farmers of the Boon's Lick, well more than 70 percent of whom Andrew Jackson had carried in 1828—would serve him far more facilely as an aperture into politics than any pro-business Opposition stance, no matter his commercial importance to the community. He took hold of the Benton oar and rowed with all his might, a decision that soon resulted in his receiving appointment as the first postmaster in Arrow Rock, a political appointment afforded by his Sappington-Benton patronage, with an annual salary of fifty dollars. At the time of the consolidation of Missouri's Democratic party in 1835, in which the Boon's Lick leaders played a dominant role, Jackson was an avowed Democrat. Though he would soon find himself in contradiction to planks of the party platform, Jackson the opportunist had cast his lot with the party of the Democracy.[2]

And, in 1836, again with the support of the Sappingtons and others in Saline, Jackson cast his hat into the Boon's Lick political ring as well. In the same year that Old Hickory bowed out of politics with an entire generation's political legacy established and a successor picked, Claib Jackson sought entrance into the realm of men of influence by announcing his candidacy as a Democrat for the Missouri House of Representatives for his county. He canvassed Saline through the spring and summer of 1836, asserting his standing among his peers as a merchant, postmaster, upstanding citizen and family man (his wife, Louisa, had recently given birth to two sons, William Sappington and John Breathitt), and loyal Jacksonian. Locals did not offer the inexperienced candidate much chance against local judge Elbert Hayes; one of the Sappington company's agents, Benjamin Brown, wrote to the Doctor from Arkansas to "tell Mr Jackson I would like to hare from the

2. Atherton, *Frontier Merchant in Mid-America*, 32–36; *History of Saline County*, 403–4; Shalhope, *Sterling Price*, 18; John Volmer Mering, *The Whig Party in Missouri*, 28–40; McCandless, *History of Missouri*, 90.

election in Saline[.] I do not believe in dreams myself though I dreamed Hays beet him six votes which I should be sorry to hare." Brown's dream was both prophetic and wrong; after a hard-fought campaign, the upstart Jackson actually won the election by those very six votes, the sole conservative Jacksonian to win election over Opposition opponents. The Sappingtons' influence was evident in his victory; Jackson had carried the Arrow Rock district—the home district of the Sappington clan—forty-seven votes to one. When the Ninth General Assembly convened on November 21, 1836, Claiborne Jackson answered proudly when the speaker called his name at morning roll. At that moment, at the age of thirty, he entered into a world in which the ancient rites of deference and privilege—of power—were cloaked in the egalitarian garb of the common man.[3]

While central Missourians' heritage might have been Jeffersonian and their politics Jacksonian in nature, their state legislature in 1836 was clearly Madisonian in fact. All claimed themselves to be Jacksonians, yet factions of Old Hickory's legion did battle daily in the raucous statehouse, and the alignments clearly reflected the state's—and the nation's—social and economic maturation as a whole. The 1832 debate over nullification (which, in South Carolina, might have commenced "the evolution from nationalism to sectionalism," as one historian has claimed) evoked a significantly different response in distant Missouri. There, the debate opened a breach among the state's Jacksonians not so much over the issue of state or national sovereignty or broad or loose construction theories of government, but rather in the extent to which the federal government should either intrude upon or enhance the economic practices of the western states and localities under its aegis. Of course, all of these issues conjoined in the impassioned rhetoric and political positioning of Missouri's leadership within a complex and capricious tangle of political alignments that derived more from its participants' posturing for personal aggrandizement than any deeply held ideological stance or commitment to the public good. As Claib Jackson found upon his arrival in Jefferson City, the state's assembly was already a house divided over how best to capitalize on mass democratic politics.[4]

3. *History of Saline County,* 403–4; Shalhope, *Sterling Price,* 22–23; Ellsberry, ed., *Cemetery Records of Saline County,* vol. 2, 36; Benjamin Brown to John S. Sappington, August 9, 1836, Sappington Family Papers, box 2, MHS; Burks, "Thunder on the Right," 97–99; John Sappington to Jeremiah Wilson, October 10, 1836, Sappington Family Papers, box 2, MHS.
4. William W. Freehling, *Prelude to Civil War: The Nullification Controversy in South Carolina, 1816–1836,* 134 (quote); McCandless, *History of Missouri,* 92–97; Mark W. Summers, *The Plundering Generation: Corruption and the Crisis of the Union, 1849–1861,* 16–36.

In 1836, all of Missouri's politicos yet considered themselves Jacksonian Democrats, though they debated endlessly the permutations of their self-styled label. "Whiggish" Jacksonians increasingly supported Henry Clay's "American system," a neo-Federalist plan to promote national growth and development by means of a protective tariff, centralized banking, and federally sponsored internal improvements to foster and promote American manufacturing. For Missourians, the system offered expansion of the domestic market for western raw materials, while facilitating the transportation of those materials to the industries of the East as well as returning manufactured goods from the East to the West. Conservative western Jacksonians such as Thomas Hart Benton found themselves perched on the horns of a dilemma; in theory, none could oppose the clear advocacy of western growth and the potential prosperity of the region through the increased availability of markets, whether domestic or foreign. Instead, Missourians divided over the states' rights theory of excessive exercise of the national government's authority made famous during the nullification controversy, as well as the potential for an unequal distribution of benefits that the American system would offer, both sectional and intrasectional. After 1832, Benton, who as a St. Louis editor once advocated a national system of internal improvements, and other state politicians adopted a selective adherence to democratic principles that derived largely from local and personal interests. The result was fractious. Benton and his supporters decried economic nationalists as "false Democrats," yet supported the National Road and improvements to the nation's internal river system. Claib Jackson and other representatives from the Boon's Lick soon fashioned a unique democratic political stamp.[5]

Not only had the state's leadership divided markedly over the extent to which they adhered to Jacksonian ideals, but the General Assembly also already reflected the dichotomy between the urban, industrial locus of St. Louis and the rural, agrarian countryside. In arguing for the efficacy of national republican politics in *The Federalist,* No. 10, James Madison might well have anticipated states such as Missouri, in which one faction dominated its political landscape. And during the 1830s and 1840s, such was indeed the case. The country Jacksonians of the Boon's Lick enjoyed a political oligarchy that dominated both party and state politics, enough for all of Missouri's representatives sent to Congress between 1830 and 1842 (elected, without districts, by state voters at large) to have come from those central river counties. These new gentry railed against the "business Democrats" of St. Louis as the elitist, anti-democratic Opposition and portrayed themselves as the phalanx of Jefferson and his heir, Andrew Jackson, in their championing of the democratic rights of the plain folk. More curious and yet true to its

5. McCandless, *History of Missouri,* 92–95.

Jeffersonian roots and Jacksonian platform, this hegemony was built upon a conservative and decidedly undemocratic social ideology.[6]

The Boon's Lick gentry's adherence to the Democratic party—and concomitant opposition to the "false Democrats" of whiggish dissent—forced upon them a decided paradox of conviction. Clay's American system appealed especially to men of wealth who benefited from economic exchange—merchants, bankers, factory owners, small-town entrepreneurs, commercial planters in the South, and farmers in the West who supported its implications for bank credit and internal improvements. Theoretically, Whig doxology offered perfect symmetry with the circumstance of the Boon's Lick leadership. Moreover, their home, the populous central river counties, carried significant political weight—and wealth—in Missouri. This was no region of poor, unpropertied men; the Boon's Lick was settled early on by men of property, whether large landholders or yeomen with moderate holdings, and with decided commercial interests. Profit through access to broad national and world markets actuated them in their daily lives and framed their political sensibilities. Ostensibly, the Boon's Lickers should have embraced the Whig opposition emerging within the Democracy's ranks. Most did not. The Boon's Lick conservatives convinced themselves and their western constituents that despite their relative wealth and power, they supported the Democratic party for reasons far more compelling than personal gain through business. The new gentry's rejection of whiggish principles, despite their obvious attraction to those of a commercial mind, and their attendant support for the Democracy proved largely a product of their and their constituents' self-assumed identity as frontier westerners.

Westerners found comfort in two aspects of the Jeffersonian tradition espoused in traditional Democratic party platitudes. The tenets of personal liberty, local rule, freedom from special privilege, and "least government" advocacy combined into a holy scripture, a western Talmud. The whiggish proposition of an active and even interventionist government in the promotion of economic development, thus a positive portrayal of government, cut across the grain of western mentality, which regarded an invasive governmental presence at best with suspicion and at worst with outright hostility. While these westerners could and did look in part to government as protectors of their commercial interests, they simultaneously drew firm boundaries to its intrusions, whether real or imagined. Moreover, the Democrats' allure to the mass of voters in the region owed nearly as much to party rhetoric that above all else it stood for the individual rights of common folk over special interests

6. Edmund S. Morgan, *Inventing the People: The Rise of Popular Sovereignty in England and America*, 267–70; Shalhope, *Sterling Price*, 19–21; West, "Earlier Political Career of Jackson," 10–11.

and any governmental support of privileged aristocrats. The Boon's Lick gentry, who stood apart from their constituents in their wealth and standing, both capitalized on and minimized this potentially damaging stigma with their steadfast support of Jacksonian principles, portraying industrial and business interests both in urban St. Louis and the capitalistic East as tyrannical threats to democratic principles. In offering their vision of a good national society by focusing upon the limited role of government in westerners' lives, the Boon's Lick gentry defined their concept of democracy selectively, offering their support to the Democratic precepts while maintaining their own privileged place at the head of their own society. In this, they maintained an ideological tie with the southern conservatives who railed against the radical democracy and egalitarianism attendant with the market revolution, both of which they now linked with the industrial North.[7]

The message played well with the mass of Boon's Lick residents who, too, defined democracy according to the exigencies of their individual lives in the Far West. Ironically, these rugged individualists' inherent concept of democracy proved as undemocratic as their leaders'. Collectively, the Boon's Lickers' independent nature allowed them little truck for those of simple means who might have looked to government for any leveling of the social order. The Boon's Lick political climate reflected its populace's commitment to a democracy of opportunity, but only insofar as they remained devoted to the principle of free access to the *means* of advancement, rather than to the actual achievement of it. On the frontier, where existed an egalitarianism of sorts, however imagined (in that at least theoretically all white settlers faced the same hardships of survival), the popular notion held that those who did not succeed in their quest for standing had no one to blame but themselves. In reality, of course, not all were equal, and no democracy existed in truth, and especially not after more than two decades of settlement in the Boon's Lick. Yet the illusion of accomplishment, of mastery, quite apart from any achievement of actual success, fostered the construction of their notions of independence as the freedoms available in the West, especially from governmental interference, afforded. This western philosophy was thus a peculiar hybrid, at once individualistic, democratic, and egalitarian while innately traditional, hierarchical, and conservative.[8]

Yet, ironically, the Boon's Lick gentry's opportunistic support for their region's democratic promise was firmly rooted in continued governmental

7. Lee Benson, *The Concept of Jacksonian Democracy: New York as a Test Case*, 86.

8. Turner, "Significance of the Frontier in American History," 215–27; Genovese, *The Southern Tradition*, 14–15, 22–23; Alexander Saxton, *The Rise and Fall of the White Republic: Class Politics and Mass Culture in Nineteenth Century America*, 131–36; Daniel Walker Howe, *The Political Culture of the American Whigs*, 32–42. Oakes, *Slavery and Freedom*, 64–68, 71–75.

support for frontier slaveholding. As these residents saw it, slavery was perfectly consistent with, even essential to, frontier development. Slave labor in this rural setting offered a distinct advantage to those who sought to tame the wilderness for economic benefit. And while not all possessed slaves, the prevailing theory held that with diligence, thrift, and sagacity any could obtain them if they wished. And once they obtained slaves, the individual had initiated progress, both for himself and for his society, as much as any northern free-labor ideologue claimed the same for their organic philosophy of labor and societal ascendance. The democracy thus envisioned by these westerners in effect justified inequality. While rural Democratic party leaders might have espoused anti-wealth, anti-privilege principles in their rhetoric, the Boon's Lick Democrats were actually conservative in their worldview and their leaders in reality were unprogressive and undemocratic in their various political positions. In supporting the Democratic party, the Boon's Lick gentry had their cake, and banqueted well—though, for appearances' sake, not too sumptuously—upon it.[9]

Nowhere was this paradox more apparent than in Claib Jackson's first term in the Missouri legislature. Despite his background as a merchant, which might have caused him to adopt whiggish principles, his votes and the bills he introduced reflected a consistent support for the conservative leadership of the Boon's Lick, men who had gained control of the 1835 Democratic nominating convention and to whom Jackson owed his legislative seat. Foremost among these leaders were Jackson's father- and brother-in-law, Dr. John Sappington and Meredith M. Marmaduke, as well as judges Thomas Reynolds and Owen Rawlins, editor of the *Boon's Lick Democrat* and later state supreme court justice William B. Napton, merchant Joshua W. Redman, and physicians John J. Lowry, George Penn (once a partner in a practice with Sappington), and Chauncey R. Scott. All hailed from either Howard or Saline County, were Benton stalwarts—none was a planter—and their collective influence in the Missouri Democratic party grew so pronounced that they were known widely and simply as the "Clique." Rawlins and Scott gained election to the state senate, while Redman served in the house alongside Jackson's brothers, Thomas and Wade, both sent from Howard County. In the ambitious Jackson, the Clique had chosen an able understudy, and immediately he assumed and consistently upheld the group's conservative posture in his legislative efforts. By the end of his first session, his peers would regard him as one of the three or four most indefatigable champions of conservative politics in the house.[10]

9. Horsman, *Race and Manifest Destiny*, 1–6, 83–97; John Mack Faragher, *Sugar Creek: Life on the Illinois Frontier*, 53–60; Foner, *Free Soil, Free Labor, Free Men*, 11–39.
10. *History of Howard and Chariton Counties*, 181, 252, 353, 1209; Shalhope, *Sterling Price*, 18–19; West, "Earlier Political Career of Jackson," 22; John S. Sappington

Ensconced within the Clique's protective fold, Jackson found himself at home in this congress of men. Most members of the house were aggressive, roughhewn, and overwhelmingly young—a reflection of Missouri society as a whole. At thirty, Jackson was one of the elder statesmen. He thrived in the backroom style of governance so characteristic of frontier America, learning quickly that the real masters of the art of politics painted their best canvases outside the galleries in which they would hang, in barrooms, hotel suites, and private rooms. Jefferson City proved no exception, though its small size and dearth of public houses forced some adaptations. Rows of long tables filled the spartan Assembly room at the new statehouse, around which many cabals gathered and held court, often at the extremities of the room so as to strategize or isolate and influence voting holdouts, and liquor was as prevalent in the crowded scene as tobacco stains on the plank flooring. One observer likened the boisterous assemblage to a "grog shop," and the demeanor and speechifying of its members little more accomplished than that of schoolboys. In this environment, Jackson's background as merchant politician served him well and he quickly exerted a strong voice and presence in the state assembly. Yet Jackson never rose to eloquence; one observer recalled that he was "a politician of moderate abilities and only tolerable courage, but of great partisan activity. . . . He essayed to be an orator, had much reputation as such, but his speeches developed little depth of thought or anything beyond the customary phrases which were the stock in trade of all the orators of his class." If anything, his limited abilities suited him perfectly to the pedestrian climate of a state legislature.[11]

From his first legislative project, Jackson learned that the true business of government was not so much leadership as the acquisition, conservation, and disbursement of public capital. He served on the noncontroversial House Education Committee, which drafted the basic act for the state's common school fund, appropriating to the public schools Missouri's share of surplus Federal Treasury revenues distributed among the states as well as investing the windfall in endeavors that would guarantee its consistent growth and long-term availability. He stood firmly in the small minority—outvoted as much as 56–6—who opposed the call for public improvements, especially railroads, put out by the St. Louis "business Democrats." While his stance might have been consistent with the Jacksonian platform, his motives also included his background as a merchant in Missouri river towns in the interior

---

to Charles M. Cravens, March 7, 1838, John S. Sappington Papers, Mss. 1027, box 2, folder 28, SHSM; Morrow, "Dr. John Sappington," 46; John Sappington to Jeremiah Wilson, July 23, 1836, Sappington Family Papers, box 1, MHS.

11. Shalhope, *Sterling Price*, 24 (first quote); McElroy, *Struggle for Missouri*, 20 (second quote).

of the state, which stood to lose much of their business—and which at the moment enjoyed a distinct advantage over most of Missouri's rural populace as a result of the river artery—once the railroads snaked into their region. He probably gained some satisfaction in that while the legislature chartered eighteen private railroads in Missouri, the companies received no state appropriations or public support. Yet Jackson's conservatism revealed itself most clearly during Missouri's legislative debate over the National Bank.[12]

When Claib Jackson took his seat in the Ninth General Assembly, he was thrust into the midst of a controversy that had gone on unresolved for four years and that not only would become the overriding issue of the current session but also would frame the state's political divisions as a whole. Gubernatorial candidate Lilburn Boggs—a staunch Jacksonian who would win the governorship in the fall 1836 election—put the issue perhaps as succinctly as anyone when he proclaimed during the campaign that "Missouri is the only state without a bank, so we are at the mercy of the money of other states. We get all the evils of a state bank and none of the benefits." Andrew Jackson's famed "war" on the National Bank placed millions of dollars of federal deposits in the hands of numerous state banks—"Pets"—whose directors used the windfall to fund speculative ventures, including loaning to yet other banks who then issued currency based upon these loans. Moreover, his veto of the rechartering of the Bank of the United States, with a branch in St. Louis, to take effect in 1836 threatened Missouri, particularly during the present business boom that would precede the Panic of 1837. With a destabilized money supply resulting from the myriad issuances of private banks, and with neither state bank nor national bank to regulate it, devaluation was rampant.[13]

Under these conditions, most Democrats of necessity might have joined with the St. Louis faction in support of the establishment of a state bank that could offer a stable yet flexible money supply, claiming "soft" principles consistent with the party's concern for the broadened mass of voters who undoubtedly suffered from the devaluation of currency. Instead, conservative Boon's Lick "Hards" held firm to a hard money policy, with a restricted paper money supply. Jackson, echoing Benton in his firm opposition to all banks, whether state or national, went so far as to claim in a campaign speech that

> [I]t is a popular delusion to suppose that an increase of currency adds to the wealth of a country and makes real money plenty. No Bank of any kind can

12. *Missouri House Journal,* Ninth Gen. Ass., 1836–1837, 45, 260–61, 447; *Laws of the State of Missouri, 1836–1837,* 137, 226–85; West, "Earlier Political Career of Jackson," 12–14; Burks, "Thunder on the Right," 111; McCandless, *History of Missouri,* 95–96.
13. Shalhope, *Sterling Price,* 23–26 (quote, p. 23); Glyndon G. VanDeusen, *The Jacksonian Era: 1828–1848,* 80–90; McCandless, *History of Missouri,* 101.

increase the capital of a country. All that Banks can do is to collect money from one class of people and even it to another. Every dollar of wealth added to a country is produced by *labor*, and Banks do not labor. They do not create, wheat, hemp, cotton, tobacco or rice,—neither do they grow hogs, sheep, cattle, mules or horses,—nor do they open mines, erect furnaces, build houses or work shops, or even make a coat or pair of shoes.

In his public opposition to the state bank, the former moneylender supported the conclusions of an 1821 Howard County assemblage who, skeptical after several disastrous earlier attempts, decried banks in general as little more than breeding ground for vice, "only lead[ing] to the support of a host of bank officers, speculators and swindlers at the expense of the honest and industrious part of society."[14]

Privately, however, Claib Jackson softened his stance on the National Bank considerably. While he agreed that the president should not renew the bank's charter, he conceded that the Jackson administration's policy of fostering state banks might well prove more harmful than any abuse that the bank might commit. Opposed to the National Bank in principle, Jackson believed that the state bank issue, which he predicted the Ninth General Assembly would face in its upcoming session, was a far greater evil because of the lack of restraints available to Missouri. Yet Jackson placed political allegiance well above any private stance he held about the National Bank. His deepest fear was that the Softs would use the banking issue to realign the Democracy, threatening the Clique's dominance and thus his patronage within the party. He reserved his greatest animus for the whiggish St. Louis faction of the party of Old Hickory.[15]

When the house voted on the bill entitled "An Act to Charter the State Bank of Missouri" in late January 1837, Jackson's thoroughly conservative posture became even more apparent. The bill's final version included an amendment that Jackson framed prohibiting bank officers from issuing currency at a higher rate of interest than the legal one under penalty of removal from office. In final discussion before the vote, he argued successfully for the prohibition of denominations below ten dollars, convinced that small denominations banished hard currency from circulation, were easily counterfeited, and thus forced the mass of residents to account for their losses. Though he failed to get the limit set at thirty dollars, Jackson was adamant

14. John Ray Cable, *The Bank of the State of Missouri*, 56; West, "Earlier Political Career of Jackson," 14–18, 23; Perry G. McCandless, "The Rise of Thomas Hart Benton in Missouri Politics," 16–29; Burks, "Thunder on the Right," 90; "Points to be considered in discussing Banking, Commerce, trade & money" [in Jackson's handwriting], undated, John S. Sappington Papers, Mss. 1027, box 1, folder 5, SHSM (first quote); *Missouri Intelligencer*, May 21, 1821 (second quote).

15. Burks, "Thunder on the Right," 91.

enough in his distrust of the bank to support making the stockholders responsible individually for any debt the bank might incur. The final bill was not sufficiently restrictive for Jackson's taste, and though the house passed the bill by a vote of 46–5, his vote was firmly in the dissenting minority. Despite his opposition to the bill's final form, Jackson had influenced its tenor profoundly. The state bank that the legislature established was a decidedly conservative institution; the governor and the General Assembly ultimately controlled the bank's general policies through the powers of electing bank officers and conducting investigations. More important for the Hards, the bank could not suspend specie payments without nullifying its charter. In the following years, with the onset and deepening of the Panic of 1837, in part a result of the proliferation of state banks, Jackson likely received some grim satisfaction from his unyielding stance on chartering the Bank of Missouri.[16]

Interestingly, the bank issue influenced Jackson more than he ever affected it. When the legislature voted to charter the bank, it created branch banks in a select number of cities and towns throughout the state. One of these branches would do business in Fayette, and the Clique made sure to allow it special latitude and power; the St. Louis bank was required to set aside one-tenth of all capital stock received for the Fayette bank and had no power to withdraw these funds. Because the Fayette officers had access to the St. Louis books, the positions became politically charged; the Clique would guarantee that Hards must govern the Fayette bank. When the legislature appointed a member of the Clique, John J. Lowry, as the branch's first president, he and the newly named board of directors—including Jackson's brother, Wade—maneuvered to name the Clique's protégé, Claib Jackson, as the bank's first cashier. The moved forced upon Jackson a dilemma. If he accepted, the appointment would not allow him time enough to act as state representative and would force him to leave Saline and thus negate his seat from that county. Recognizing the great financial opportunity, Jackson resigned his seat at the adjournment of the General Assembly in February 1837, packed his young family and their belongings, and returned across the river to Howard County, this time to Fayette. In September, with money borrowed from Dr. Sappington, he bought a modest lot and built a home in which they took up residence as Jackson began work at the bank. In supreme irony, the prophet, all but cast from the temple, was now a moneychanger.[17]

16. West, "Earlier Political Career of Jackson," 14–19, 23–24; Shalhope, *Sterling Price*, 23–25.

17. West, "Earlier Political Career of Jackson," 14–19; *History of Howard and Chariton Counties*, 181; Burks, "Thunder on the Right," 106–7, 113; Indenture between William R. B. and Tallitha Cotton and C. F. Jackson, September 15, 1837, John S. Sappington Papers, Mss. 1027, box 2, folder 38, SHSM; Division of Property of Dr.

Jackson's hiatus from representative politics would last five years, during which time he set to work building a solid financial and social base in Howard County in anticipation of a later return to the political arena. His base salary as cashier of two thousand dollars annually, later reduced to a still-handsome fourteen hundred dollars per annum, offered stability and material comfort attendant to his stature as a state and community sachem. Jackson augmented his comfortable position with a wide array of remunerative ventures, all of which combined to set him apart from the mass of Boon's Lickers. Jackson became a partner with Arrow Rock resident O. B. Pearson in a trading company that sold provisions—largely flour and meat—as well as horses, mules, and cattle to residents of Natchez, Mississippi, on the burgeoning southwest cotton frontier. The market for mules in the region only grew in strength, especially after the widespread adoption of mule- or horse-drawn or powered implements—plows, sweeps, harrows, and gins—to assist in cotton production during the 1830s and 1840s. Pearson carried the largest burden of the business while Jackson took a less active role, but the senior partner committed the lion's share of the company's operating capital.[18]

Moreover, released from his business investments, Jackson entered heavily into land speculation, the principal form of investment among nineteenth-century Americans. Far from being anathema to democratic principles, as many frontier residents considered nonresident speculation, locals such as Jackson acquired, held, and sold land parcels with Jacksonian aplomb. Many sold the land to buyers on credit, allowing cash-strapped settlers the opportunity to pay for their land with profits from its future harvest. As early as 1829, Jackson had engaged in speculation, starting small with two town lots on H Street in New Franklin, assessed at just twenty dollars each. Once in the Sappington fold, his speculative activities enlarged decidedly in scale. By the late 1830s, with the financial backing of his father-in-law, Jackson speculated in large tracts of land in his new home county, but especially outside it. In partnership with brother-in-law George P. Bass (a Tennessean who had married Jackson's younger sister, Susan), Jackson operated a land company in both Fayette and Arrow Rock, and bought land specifically for sale as well as acting as agent for many other prospective buyers. Moreover, Jackson both assisted and engaged the Sappington family in acquiring land in Missouri's Osage country, an area in the west-central part of the state that had recently opened to settlement. The elder Sappington's meticulous

---

John S. Sappington, December 30, 1843, Sappington Family Papers, Mss. 2889, folder 11, SHSM.

18. Contract between C. F. Jackson and O. B. Pearson, January 10, 1839, Sappington Family Papers, box 3, MHS; Moore, *Cotton Kingdom in the Old Southwest*, 37–72; Hurt, *Agriculture and Slavery in Little Dixie*, 147–50.

financial records indicate that Jackson borrowed money regularly from his benefactor, more than two thousand dollars in 1837 and a thousand or more on other occasions, far surpassing that borrowed by the other sons-in-law, and used the money to speculate in land in Howard and Saline Counties, as well as to acquire with his brothers-in-law more than thirty-five hundred acres of public land along the Osage River.[19]

Many of these individual speculative transactions appear to have been remarkably lucrative and formed a considerable income during the troublesome years of the early 1840s. Jackson held a number of houses and town lots in Arrow Rock, and purchased additional acreage next to town that he carved up into town lots, selling them for many times not only their purchase price but also their proportionate value of the original acreage. In May 1835, Jackson and his wife purchased twelve acres adjoining the town of Arrow Rock for two hundred dollars; less than three years later Jackson sold the same tracts for more than six times the original purchase price. By 1842, Jackson estimated that the public lands purchased for $1.50 per acre in 1839 had appreciated to as much as $8 an acre; by the late 1850s, he had sold all but 280 of his thousand-acre share of the Osage land. Jackson traveled to his Osage lands regularly and often for several weeks at a time, keeping close tabs on the condition of things in order to protect their investment, especially during the 1841 debate on the location of the county seat at Osceola. "I own a good deal of land in that County," Jackson wrote to newly seated Governor Thomas Reynolds, "and like most of us, feel some interest in the settlement of this question." From his position in the legislature, Jackson supported the improvement of the region's river system, including those to the south like the White River that ran into the wide and navigable Arkansas, an ambitious plan to bring commerce to the Osage country and thus increase the value of his investments there even further. In all, the deeds and tax records recorded in Howard, Saline, and St. Clair Counties reveal that Jackson purchased or sold more than thirty individual

19. Robert Swierenga, *Pioneers and Profits: Land Speculation on the Iowa Frontier,* 210–27; C. F. Jackson to M. M. Marmaduke, October 18, 25, 1837, John Sappington Family Papers, box 2, MHS; J. Locke Hardeman to M. M. Marmaduke, March 27, 1839, ibid., box 3, MHS; E. D. Sappington to M. M. Marmaduke, January 25, 1841, ibid., box 3, MHS; Howard County [Missouri] Tax Lists, vol. 2 (1829–1841), microfilm reel S244, MSA; Seventh U. S. Census, 1850, Population Schedule, Howard County [Missouri], NA; "Sketch of the Life of Dr. John Gano Bryan, 1788–1860," Mss. 2919, SHSM; Division of Property of Dr. John S. Sappington, December 30, 1843, John Sappington Family Papers, Mss. 2889, folder 11, SHSM; List of Notes, undated, John S. Sappington Papers, Mss. 1027, box 1, folder 9, SHSM; C. F. Jackson's Osage Lands unsold [St. Clair County, Missouri], undated, ibid., box 1, folder 1, SHSM; Legal Memorandum, 1839, John S. Sappington Papers, Mss. 1027, SHSM, quoted in Burks, "Thunder on the Right," 132–33.

pieces of property in those counties between 1829 and 1860—the bulk of which he acquired after 1835—totaling 1,281 acres.[20]

In keeping with his newfound stature in Howard County, Jackson acquired a home that reflected his place in society. In February 1841, he paid thirty-five hundred dollars for sixty acres of cleared land on an eminence lying two miles north of Fayette along the Glasgow Road. Using a dogtrot log cabin located on the grounds as the foundation, Jackson began construction of a two-story, federal-style frame home reminiscent of those found widely in Kentucky. With classic symmetry, its front facade boasted eight twelve-pane windows with full shutters—considerably more genteel than the homes of the neighboring farmers—as well as central doorways emerging from both floors, with handsome paned glass transoms and sidelights. A second-floor, railed deck supported by square wooden columns, external brick chimneys at each end of the house, and heavy panel doors completed the stately exterior. The home's four rooms, located on either side of wide entrance halls on both floors, were spacious and boasted deep fireplaces, walnut plank floors and wall panels, and locally carved walnut fireplace surrounds, mantels, and door frames, the latter more than six feet high to accommodate the home's tall owner. The stairway's gracefully turned newels, carved risers, and serpentine railing supported by simple, squared balusters lent the interior of the house an air of elegance without pretension. The cabin stood in the rear of the dwelling and served as a cookhouse for several years until Jackson used the structure as the foundation for a two-story rear addition to the home, complete with piazza and external stairwell, converting the home into what was commonly called an "L" house. Though impressive, Jackson's home—completed in 1847 and in which he and his family would live in various stages of completion for nearly fifteen years—stood a far cry from the elegant

20. O. B. Pearson to Abiel Leonard, May 16, 1847, Abiel Leonard Papers, Mss. 1013, box 9, folder 231, SHSM; Deed, Burton and Nancy Lawless to Claiborne F. Jackson, May 12, 1835, ibid., box 1, folder 22, SHSM; Deeds Records, Saline County [Missouri], vol. A, 254; vol. G, 284, 286, 571; vol. N, 271; vol. O, 296, microfilm reel C6227; vol. R, 3; vol. S, 395, 425, 580, 581; microfilm reel C6233; vol. T, 484, microfilm reel C6234; vol. U, 139, microfilm reel C6234; vol. W, 583, microfilm reel C6235; vol. X, 493, microfilm reel C6236, all MSA; Deed Records, Howard County [Missouri], book 1, 446, microfilm reel C2795; book 2, 438, 443, 445, 455, microfilm reel C2795; vol. L, 516, microfilm reel C2786; vol. O, 114, microfilm reel C2787; vol. P, 318, microfilm reel C2787; vol. T, 158, 161, 162, 458, microfilm reel C2790; vol. W, 164, 384, 385, microfilm reel C2792; vol. X, 101, 293, microfilm reel C2792, MSA; C. F. Jackson's Osage Lands unsold [St. Clair County, Missouri], John S. Sappington Papers, Mss. 1027, box 1, folder 1, SHSM; C. F. Jackson to Thomas Reynolds, May 25, 1841, Thomas Reynolds Papers, MHS (quote); J. H. Haden to M. M. Marmaduke, February 29, 1848, Sappington Family Papers, box 5, MHS. The talented young artist George Caleb Bingham purchased one of Jackson's Arrow Rock town lots. The one-story brick house that Bingham had built on the lot still stands, a tourist attraction of modern Arrow Rock's historic district.

splendor of Oakwood, the brick home of Abiel Leonard, which looked down regally upon Fayette from a ridge just east of town.[21]

Much of the land that Jackson acquired in Howard—unlike those properties in Saline and St. Clair Counties, which were largely speculative—adjoined his homestead, suggesting that Jackson sought more than mere profit in his land dealings in his home county. Jackson bought more than 450 acres of land in the vicinity of his home, most of the tracts contiguous. He sold almost none of it, a virtual inversion of his dealings in Saline County. What property he did buy for speculation in Howard tended to be city lots and houses in Fayette. Jackson appears to have been plagued by dual demons: an ambition to move beyond the world of his father, combined with nostalgia for the life in which he had been reared. His brothers' successes likely exacerbated this need to live the life of a country gentleman, albeit through urban sustenance, whether by salary or land sales. By 1841, Jackson's older brothers Thomas and Wade (the latter a local judge as well as a farmer) held 320 and 560 acres of land, respectively, in Moniteau Township, in the easternmost portion of Howard County, while William farmed 214 acres in Chariton Township, near Glasgow in the western part of the county. In that year, Claib, too, held 219 acres of Howard County land, a third of what he would own there eventually. Yet distinct from his brothers, by 1840 only he would claim to the census taker that his primary bailiwick was not agricultural.[22]

The house and land allowed Jackson to pursue another passion—horse breeding and racing, an endeavor for profit as much as for sport. As a Kentuckian, Jackson equated horseflesh with gentility, and as early as 1836 he was involved with his brother Thomas in breeding and selling horses, one to his father-in-law for a hundred dollars, bringing studs from as far away as New York. In 1840, Jackson entered into a partnership with two other men to breed racing horses. Advertising in the *Boon's Lick Democrat,* "the firm of Jackson, Cooper & Kinkle announce[d] that the well known *Duke Sumner* is now standing at stud." The firm charged as much as thirty-five dollars for the service, a hefty price for farmers in the West. A circular horse track

21. Indenture between Joel H. and Isabella Green and C. F. Jackson, February 10, 1841, John S. Sappington Papers, Mss. 1027, box 2, folder 38, SHSM; Howard County [Missouri] Tax Lists, vol. 2 (1829–1841), microfilm reel S244, MSA; Federal Writers' Project, *Missouri,* 351; West, "Earlier Political Career of Jackson," 6. My thanks to Mr. Denny Davis of Fayette, Missouri, for opening the Jackson home to me and for sharing his wealth of knowledge of Fayette, the Boon's Lick, and early American architecture.

22. Howard County [Missouri] Tax Lists, vol. 2 (1829–1841), microfilm reel S244, MSA; Deed Records, Howard County [Missouri], vol. T, 161, microfilm reel C2790; vol. W, 164, microfilm reel C2792, MSA; Broadsides-Horses, "Splendid—By Duroc.," April 21, 1836, MHS; Sixth and Seventh U.S. Censuses, 1840 and 1850, Population Schedule, Howard County [Missouri], NA; Seventh U.S. Census, 1850, Agriculture Schedule, Howard County [Missouri], NA.

graced the rear of Jackson's estate, on which he trained his thoroughbreds for competition and which reputedly can be seen from the air yet today. He regularly attended horse races, and presumably wagered on his and others' steeds and jockeys. In 1837, he tried to entice his brother-in-law Meredith M. Marmaduke to join him in Fayette for a day or more of racing: "Can't you come over and spend the coming week with us?—we shall have some good running I think, and no doubt a large concourse of people." Though not a farmer by trade, Jackson sought the life and stature of a country gentleman.[23]

By 1840, Jackson included slave ownership in the measure of his standing, both in the Howard County community and his own families by blood and by marriage. The Jackson brothers each possessed slave labor commensurate with the farms they ran and their stature in the family. The fifteen slaves who accompanied Mary Jackson from the family farm in Kentucky to Missouri at her husband's death in 1833 augmented the holdings of the sons. In 1830, Wade owned fourteen slaves, all but three of whom were males between the ages of ten and fifty-four; most of them probably were field hands who worked on the three Jackson farms. William owned two slaves (one male child and one female) while Thomas and Claib held none. By 1840, the Jackson brothers held forty-seven slaves collectively, including Claib, who held ten. A member of two prominent slaveholding families, Claib Jackson measured his success perforce by his ability to acquire and provide for chattel slave property. Despite owning more than two hundred acres of land, however, only two of Claib's bondmen were of working age. The rest—with the exception of two adult women, possibly spouses of the men—were children, and probably a gift of the elder Sappington's to the Jacksons for his daughter's comfort, a gesture he offered occasionally to each of his daughters as well as to his grandchildren. Because Jackson's farm was not a working one, he had little need for mature field laborers and hired such men when needed—by contrast, nine of Thomas's thirteen slaves, five of Wade's eighteen, and six of Dr. Sappington's fifteen bondpeople in 1840 were working-age males— and the ages and genders of his slaves reflect his use of his bondpeople to offer luxury as house servants and drivers, rather than to provide profitable agricultural labor as field hands. As cashier of the Fayette bank, former county representative, and the son-in-law of the esteemed Dr. John Sappington, Claib Jackson held slaves primarily for status. Slave ownership completed the

---

23. Handbill, "PUBLIC NOTICE," March 4, 1840, John S. Sappington Papers, SHSM, quoted in Burks, "Thunder on the Right," 133; Broadsides-Horses, "Splendid,— By Duroc.," April 21, 1836, MHS; E. D. and W. B. Sappington's Expense Book, 1836– 1852, October 1, 1839, p. 25, John S. Sappington Papers, Mss. 1027, box 5, folder 3, SHSM; West, "Earlier Political Career of Jackson," 8; Grissom, "Personal Recollections of Jackson," 505; C. F. Jackson to M. M. Marmaduke, September 22, 1837, Sappington Family Papers, box 2, MHS (quote).

illusion of gentility that Howard Countians—whether farmers, lawyers, or businessmen—wished to convey of their society, and of themselves.[24]

By the late 1830s, Jackson had carved a significant place in the Boon's Lick's societal hierarchy. He owed a large portion of that niche to his connections with the Sappington family, whether economically, socially, or politically. The exigency that Jackson attached to his place in the Sappington clan revealed itself nowhere more clearly than in 1838, when he suffered another family tragedy. In early May, Jackson's second wife, Louisa, age twenty-three, gave birth to a third son, whom the couple named Andrew. Within days, on May 9, 1838, the mother had died in a runaway accident, followed a month later—even more tragically—by the infant son. In an instant, the couple's two young children became motherless and Jackson was a widower for a second time. Whatever grief Jackson might have felt upon the premature death of yet another young wife was clearly and decidedly of secondary importance to his continuance in the Sappington fold, even more than at the death of his first wife. Jackson was acutely aware that at age thirty-two, as a former representative who harbored political ambitions still, this particular point in his life was pivotal yet precarious in terms of his ultimate ascendance. His stature in the region, as well as a youthful, if balding, appearance, as indicated by an extant painting done of him at this time, offered him entrance to the home and courting parlor of virtually any of the Boon's Lick gentry with a marriageable daughter. Yet just six months after Louisa's death, on November 27, 1838, Methodist minister William B. West married Jackson for a third time to a Sappington daughter at the family's home in Saline County. This time, his bride was Eliza Pearson, the eldest daughter whom the bigamist Alonzo Pearson had wronged so publicly.[25]

Jackson's latest marriage might well have been as much one of convenience for the Sappingtons as one of position for Jackson. Family tradition holds that on her deathbed Louisa had asked Eliza to care for her children if she were to die; the faithful Eliza kept her promise and the bond brought Jackson and his third wife together out of twin tragedies. The story presents problems. Just one month younger than Jackson and no beauty, as had been

24. Sixth U.S. Census, 1840, Population Schedule, Howard and Saline Counties [Missouri], NA; Receipt, Messrs. Hooks and Co. to B. H. Rives, October 20, 1836, Abiel Leonard Papers, Mss. 1013, Business Documents, 1835–1841, folder April–December 1836, SHSM; Deed Gift, March 7, 1844, John S. Sappington Papers, Mss. 1027, box 2, folder 45, SHSM; Division of Property of Dr. John S. Sappington, December 30, 1843, John Sappington Family Papers, Mss. 2889, folder 11, SHSM.

25. Jerena East Giffin, *First Ladies of Missouri: Their Homes and Their Families,* 78–79; Burks, "Thunder on the Right," 134; Marriage License of C. F. Jackson and Eliza W. Pearson, dated November 27, 1838, recorded February 11, 1839, Saline County [Missouri] Marriages, vol. A (1835–1851), microfilm reel C6266, MSA; Ellsberry, ed., *Cemetery Records of Saline County,* vol. 2, 36.

one or both of her dead sisters, Eliza brought five children to the marriage: daughters Sarah Jane, Lavinia, and Elizabeth, and sons John and Erasmus. Their ages ranged from John's seventeen to Elizabeth's eight, while Jackson's two sons by Louisa were yet under the age of four. The surviving records of Jackson's demeanor toward those children suggest that the Sappington patriarch might have played a strong hand in arranging the marriage. Fearful of his eldest daughter remaining unmarried the rest of her life as a result of a rogue's indiscretion, Sappington may well have presented his son-in-law a carrot and stick proposition, well aware of Jackson's ambitious nature and his own salience in the achievement of those aspirations. Missouri tradition (which one contemporary claims was a "standing joke told at [Jackson's] expense") suggests at least Sappington's recognition of the expedient marriage; when Jackson approached the doctor about marrying Eliza, or so the story goes, Sappington responded caustically, "You can take her, but don't come back after the old woman." Whether apocryphal or not, the ring of complicity in the tale is unmistakable; its public reification only punctuates the point.[26]

Whatever the arrangement or offer, Jackson never adopted the Pearson children, nor did he assume from Sappington their financial support, which the doctor had provided from the day he banished their father from the family and from the Boon's Lick. On regular occasion, and for the duration of the marriage, Jackson submitted to the Sappington patriarch expenses he incurred for the children's maintenance, whether educational or otherwise. Sappington kept a separate fund specifically devoted to his grandchildren's upkeep, which he drew from the Arkansas branch of the pill business as well as the southern proceeds from the sale of his book, *The Theory and Treatment of Fevers,* published in 1844. Erasmus attended private school in Arrow Rock, Lavinia and Sarah Jane attended the Fayette Female Academy, John attended an academy in the river town of Madison, Indiana, preparatory to studying medicine, and Elizabeth, a seamstress in Fayette, charged cloth at a local mercantile, all of which bills ended up with the Sappingtons, either directly or through Jackson for reimbursement. Whether arranged or not, the agreement was not public knowledge, and perhaps was kept even from Eliza. As a result, to the residents of Howard and Saline Counties, Jackson's marriage to the long-suffering woman looked especially gallant and was thus politically important, counteracting the whispers that his three marriages

---

26. Burks, "Thunder on the Right," 134–35; Park and Morrow, *Women of the Mansion,* 124–25; John F. Darby, *Personal Recollections of Many Prominent People Whom I Have Known, and of Events—Especially of Those Relating to the History of St. Louis—During the First Half of the Present Century,* 465 (first quote); Giffin, *First Ladies of Missouri,* 78–79 (second quote).

to Sappington daughters were blatantly opportunistic. As important, the marriage entrenched him permanently in the Sappington clan.[27]

Jackson would need—and he did tap—the largesse that his family connection offered. The onset of a financial panic in 1837 brought huge occupational and political problems to the cashier of the Fayette bank. Jackson was horrified when the exchange banks of the East, followed by smaller banks throughout the country, began suspending specie payments in order to save themselves from failure. Despite heavy penalties that the charter threatened for such suspensions, both branches of the state bank—including the one at Fayette—quit paying specie during the dark winter months of 1837 and well into 1838. As late as August of the latter year, the St. Louis bank forced Jackson to take forty-nine thousand dollars' worth of Illinois Bank notes due the Fayette bank instead of the specie the directors had promised him. Specie payments resumed nearly immediately afterward in Missouri—the first state in the nation to do so—and the state bank offered specie through the remaining depression years. Benton's steadfast insistence on hard-money policies earned both the enmity of many cash-starved Missourians as well as the nicknames "Old Bullion" and "Gibraltar of the West," the defender of the Jeffersonian order. Benton's fiscal conservatism and considerable influence in Missouri (along with the bullion coming into the state from the Santa Fe trade) allowed its politicos to hold fast to hard-money policies, opposing any relief measures. Jackson faced the real problem of holding unstable and devaluated currency from other state banks, while facing angry patrons who could not redeem the currency for hard cash at the bank after the board of the state bank voted in November 1839 not to accept paper issued by

27. Ellsberry, ed., *Cemetery Records of Saline County,* vol. 2, 36; Park and Morrow, *Women of the Mansion,* 125–30; Deed of Sarah Jane Baskett et al., to William S. Jackson, undated, John S. Sappington Papers, Mss. 1027, box 1, folder 4, SHSM; Boyers, Blythe and Trigg to John S. Sappington, undated [1835], ibid., box 1, folder 22, SHSM; Account of Elizabeth Pearson with C. Billingsley and Brothers, August 24, 1844, ibid., box 2, folder 46, SHSM; Bill, John D. Perry and Co., to E. Pierson [*sic*], August 12, 1844, Charged to acct of S J Billingsley, January 1, 1845, ibid., box 2, folder 46, SHSM; Bill from Darius Reed to William Sappington for Erasmus Pearson's school tuition during fall and winter term, 1844, March 8, 1845, ibid., box 2, folder 47, SHSM; John S. Pearson to William B. Sappington, May 20, 1845, ibid., box 2, folder 48, SHSM; Mortgage, James Ward to John S. Sappington for negro girl Maria, January 7, 1846, ibid., box 2, folder 50, SHSM; E. D. and W. B. Sappington's Expense Book, 1836–1852, ibid., box 5, folder 3, SHSM; Receipt, H. Boon, Trustee of the Fayette Academy, to John S. Sappington, for Tuition fees for Miss Pearson's at the Second Session, October 31, 1836, ibid., box 4, folder 94, SHSM; Receipt, C. F. Jackson for Jno. Sappington and Sons, October 1, 1844, ibid., box 4, folder 95, SHSM; Morrow. "Dr. John Sappington," 55–56. Ellsberry incorrectly cites Eliza's birth date as March 4, 1806, which was actually Jackson's birth date. According to the inscription on Jackson's and her tombstone in the Sappington Family Cemetery, Eliza was born on April 4, 1806.

any other bank. As late as 1842, John Sappington—his interstate business keenly affected by discounted currency—had eight hundred dollars' worth of devalued paper currency on hand, while neighbors held even more, which "constitute[d] probably seven-eighths of our present circulation and if it does not come up again it will produce a durned sight harder times than it has heretofore."[28]

While Missouri's brave stand gained national attention and even prestige, the deepening crisis only widened the state's emergent political chasm. The onset of the banking crisis and its economic corollaries created disaffection among the voters of the state for the traditional Democratic party leaders and toward hard-money policy. Led by St. Louis Softs who were antagonistic to both the hard-money policies and political domination of the river county representatives, whiggish leaders and editors began tarring the "Central Clique," as they termed the Howard Democrats, with their own brush, portraying them as anti-democratic, anachronistic monopolists whose unresponsive and even obstructionist leadership had exacerbated the economic crisis. By 1840, the political controversy boded poorly for the Democratic party in the upcoming election, and candidates of the upstart Whig party—organized from the growing ranks of opposition Democrats—challenged incumbents at all levels.

In reality, Missouri's Whigs proved anything but a stark contrast to the state's Democrats in most ways, especially when compared with those in the Boon's Lick. Neither aristocrats nor dirt farmers, the party represented a middle class of sorts in its conservative devotion to commerce and industry and in its leaders' high level of education. Consequently, the party drew special strength from the river counties, and thus merchants and professionals figured prominently in the Whig ranks and leadership, but not so much as to ostracize the party from the independent farmers of the region, for they were numerous in the party as they were in the Democratic party. Whig leaders represented a wide spectrum of wealth and standing in the populace at large, also similar to the Democrats, though the concentration of merchants in the state's Whig leadership gave them something of a financial edge, distinguishable only at the middle ranks. Yet the Missouri Whigs did differ from the Democrats in one important way: their perception among the population at large was one of snobbishness and aristocracy, largely born of the educational gap, the lack of strong proslavery and anti-Mason planks

28. Nagel, *Missouri,* 112–13 (first and second quotes); West, "Earlier Political Career of Jackson," 25–29; Statement of William C. Boon, *Missouri House Journal,* 12th General Assembly, 1842–43, 751–52; John Smith to M. M. Marmaduke, January 10, 1840, Sappington Family Papers, box 3, MHS; William Bradford to W. B. Sappington, March 1, 1842, John S. Sappington Papers, Mss. 1027, box 2, folder 38, SHSM (third quote).

in the party's platform, and the fact that its leaders emerged largely from an urban and town-dwelling corpus. Many associated the Whigs with St. Louis, a damning charge to the common man in Missouri's interior.[29]

To overcome this formidable obstacle, the Missouri Whigs proved that they had learned their Democratic political lessons well, especially in the Boon's Lick. They augmented their political challenge by adopting the symbolism and strategies of their former party, "out-Jacksoning the Jacksonians" with barbecues, torchlight parades, songs, and cartoons, complete with a war hero for a presidential candidate of invented "hard cider and log cabin" origins. Claib Jackson lamented that "you Cannot go into one single house in this County without finding it litterally [*sic*] crammed with 'Stockholders,' 'Old Soldiers,' 'Log Cabin Hero's' and all such papers." By all appearances, the Missouri Whigs were poised to inhabit what was once the ancestral house of Jefferson.[30]

They did not. The 1840 election indeed witnessed a Whig ascendance into state governments throughout the country, as well as in Congress, and Whig candidates took the presidency from the firm hands of the Jacksonians. Yet in Missouri, the results were decidedly more mixed, especially in the Boon's Lick, where the two parties were so much alike. The governorship and lieutenant-governorship remained in the hands of Boon's Lick Democrats, with Thomas Reynolds of Howard County and Jackson's brother-in-law Meredith M. Marmaduke of Saline County taking November oaths of office as the state's highest officers. At the local level, however, the Boon's Lick bore the effects of the Whig juggernaut. The years of economic distress and seemingly endless daily deprivations suffered by central Missourians had taken their toll on the Boon's Lick's voters. Democratic charges of Whig "federalism," once a damning charge in republican America, could not stem the tide. Stuffy or not, Whig candidates swept into office throughout the region, carrying Cooper, Saline, Lafayette, and Audrain Counties, as well as numerous other counties throughout Missouri. Receiving the "miserable news" in the week after the election, Jackson "heard of nothing but defeat after defeat from all quarters. . . . we are gone hook and line, so far at least, as the Legislature is concerned." Fissures now rived the once-granite pediment of the Boon's Lick Democracy.[31]

29. McCandless, *History of Missouri*, 125–26; Mering, *Whig Party in Missouri*, 2–28.

30. St. Louis *Daily Missouri Republican*, April 21, 1841 (first quote); Shalhope, *Sterling Price*, 30–35; West, "Earlier Political Career of Jackson," 30–31; VanDeusen, *The Jacksonian Era*, 143–44 (second quote), 145–48; Daniel Ward Howe, *The Political Culture of the American Whigs*, 51–58; C. F. Jackson to M. M. Marmaduke, August 7, 1840, Sappington Family Papers, box 3, MHS (third quote).

31. McCandless, *History of Missouri*, 124–26; C. F. Jackson to M. M. Marmaduke, August 7, 1840, Sappington Family Papers, box 3, MHS (quotes).

In the spring of 1840, after three years as cashier of the Fayette bank, weathering the storms that increasingly more of the public believed had been brought about by inflexible Jacksonian banking policies, Claib Jackson feared that a widespread Whig victory in the autumn elections would jeopardize his position at the bank. He had good reason to fear such a turnover; the Whigs had taken particular aim at the state's banking officers in their criticisms of Democratic leadership. In an effort to forestall deep Whig inroads into the Missouri political landscape and to secure a remunerative position in the event of losing his cashiership after a political turnover, Jackson saw a need to reenter politics even more quickly than he might once have envisioned. In the spring of 1840, he declared his candidacy for the state house in Howard County. Jackson might have gained some small satisfaction from the fact that, unlike most of the Boon's Lick, Howard County would stand by the Democratic party, but he was bitterly disappointed that he finished third in the caucus election for candidates. The August elections only confirmed the Whig victory in the region, jeopardizing his own place at the bank. Writing disdainfully but with resolve to Marmaduke, Jackson claimed that "the whigs here, are exulting at a great rate. I understand they have already selected my successor. Be it so; I am ready and willing to leave the Bank, and go to work with my friends throughout the Country to regain the loss already sustained."[32]

The means by which Jackson intended to regain losses sustained and by which he would oppose Whig leaders in the Boon's Lick became evident soon after his unsuccessful candidacy for the state legislature. The result was nearly deadly. On August 26, 1840, just three weeks after the election, an article appeared in the *Boon's Lick Democrat,* a Fayette party organ, that had been published originally in the *Ozark Standard,* a Polk County newspaper, claiming that Whig organizers had printed and distributed false ballots to unsuspecting Democratic voters in several counties in the southwestern portion of the state. The ballots, colored to match the Democratic ballots printed by that party's organizers in those counties and labeled "Union Democratic Ticket," correctly bore the names of John C. Edwards and John Miller, Democratic candidates for Congress, and Meredith Miles Marmaduke, Democratic candidate for lieutenant-governor on the party ticket. Yet the ballots also bore the name of the Whig candidate for governor, John B. Clark of Fayette, nestled amid the other names. The perpetrators designed the ruse to fool Democratic voters who, thinking they were casting straight party ballots, used them to vote unwittingly for Clark. The *Democrat* exposed

32. C. F. Jackson to M. M. Marmaduke, August 7, 1840, Sappington Family Papers, box 3, MHS (quote); Shalhope, *Sterling Price,* 33; West, "Earlier Political Career of Jackson," 31–35.

the charges of fraud to Howard Countians, but did not implicate Clark in the scheme.[33]

Two weeks later, on September 7, a letter to the editor appeared in the Fayette paper signed "Anti-Fraud," which claimed to have intercepted a letter written in July at the height of the campaign from Clark to James H. Birch, a chameleonlike, perpetual candidate from Clinton County who ran in the recent election for Congress as a Jacksonian, though without the Democratic party's support. Avowing that his "object [was] to lay before the 'public eye' the names of the federal leaders who plotted this foul conspiracy, and put under way this unholy and damnable attempt to swindle the unsuspecting portion of the democratic party out of their dearest rights," "Anti-Fraud" charged that Clark, a native Kentuckian, Indian war veteran, and Fayette lawyer who was now a Howard County circuit court judge and major general of the Missouri militia, had committed fraud and provided "the whole letter, . . . *verbatim et literatim*, . . . word for word, comma for comma, i for i and dot for dot, and *rascal* with a K." To leave no doubt as to Clark's complicity in the scheme, "Anti-Fraud" italicized the sentence that most incriminated the respected judge in which he asked Birch *"would it not be well to have two sets of tickets printed one with my name and the balance Democratic and forward them to those counties with directions how to use them."*[34]

The author's inelegant pseudonym offered only the thinnest of veils to the residents of Howard County; to the target of the author's invective, his cover was completely transparent. Pressuring the editor of the *Democrat*, J. T. Quesenberry, into divulging the author's identity, Clark had his suspicions confirmed: "Anti-Fraud" was indeed Claiborne F. Jackson. A Clique member, Owen Rawlins, claimed to have found the letter in a set of borrowed saddlebags he had used in the recent election (Clark charged that Rawlins stole the letter from Clark's hatband as it sat on the podium while he delivered a speech), and upon his return to Fayette showed it to Jackson at his office at the bank. Jackson, smarting from his own recent defeat and eager for revenge, sent it to the editor of the *Democrat*. Enraged, Clark initiated a correspondence with Jackson, delivered by seconds, over the course of a week in which the former sought redress for the "derogation of my personal honor." The principals each recognized the ominous content of these overly polite missives; they were in actuality preliminary challenges in the macabre and very public ritual of dueling. While characterized as a cultural phe-

---

33. *Jefferson Inquirer*, September 24, 1840. During the mid–nineteenth century, political parties, rather than state government, customarily printed the ballots used in elections. Without regulation, fraud was not uncommon.

34. Ibid.; McCandless, *History of Missouri*, 99–100; *History of Howard and Chariton Counties*, 252–53.

nomenon exclusive to the antebellum South, the *code duello* in fact assumed a much wider field in America prior to the 1830s. New Yorkers—foremost among them being Alexander Hamilton and Aaron Burr—assumed the field of honor similar to Georgians, if not as often, to settle deeply held personal grievances; only in the final antebellum decade was the practice exclusive to the southernmost states of the American cultural landscape. The mixed culture of the West preserved the grisly ritual, particularly in Missouri where Kentuckians and Virginians conjured cavalier notions of chivalry. The ritual, largely practiced by young professional men rather than established planter parvenus, was not exclusive to rural areas; as many as eight individual duels occurred in St. Louis even before statehood, and many more afterwards, resulting in numerous deaths, one by the hand of a young Thomas Hart Benton. Many took place on Mississippi River islands straddling the borders of Illinois and Missouri; frequent duels caused St. Louisans to refer to one near the city as "Bloody Island."[35]

As newspapers capitalized on the fraud and locals gossiped publicly about it, the formalities accelerated both quickly and dangerously. Clark believed that Jackson had sullied his integrity, even his manhood, and because he had gained no satisfaction from Jackson, who steadfastly refused to recant his statement, arguing that his intent was only "to expose the political fraud which, I consider, had been put under way to deceive the Democratic party, and in that matter my views remain wholly unchanged," the general demanded from the banker "a personal interview." Clark's meaning was clear; he had challenged Jackson to "mortal conflict." As Clark was a devout Methodist, whose church held out firm doctrinal strictures against dueling (including expulsion), his challenge offers at how deeply wronged Clark believed himself. The following day, September 15, after conferring with Dr. Chauncey Scott and perhaps other members of the Clique, Jackson sent his card with the terms. He would meet Clark at six o'clock on the following morning, the sixteenth, at any place Clark selected "within one mile of the town of Fayette, . . . the parties to be armed with rifles, with calibers to carry balls weighing not less than fifty-six to the pound. The distance to be seventy yards." No one but seconds and surgeons would be admitted to the "field of

35. Owen Rawlins to James M. Birch, September 16, 1840, in *History of Howard and Chariton Counties*, 316; John B. Clark to C. F. Jackson, September 11, 1840, in ibid., 316 (quote); *Jefferson Inquirer*, September 24, 1840; *Boon's Lick Times*, September 26, 1840; Bertram Wyatt-Brown, *Southern Honor: Ethics and Behavior in the Old South*, 350–61; Edward L. Ayers, *Vengeance and Justice: Crime and Punishment in the 19th-Century American South*, 15–17; William Nisbet Chambers, "Pistols and Politics: Incidents in the Career of Thomas Hart Benton, 1816–1818," 5–17; Elbert B. Smith, *Magnificent Missourian: The Life of Thomas Hart Benton*, 58–65; Foley, *History of Missouri*, 204; Foley, *Genesis of Missouri*, 186.

honor." These were no gentlemen's terms, no mere affair of honor; Jackson's was an end game. Rifles of that caliber were precise at that distance and any wounds to the torso, where the combatants would aim, would kill instantly or maim, likely resulting in a lingering, agonizing death. These two soldiers had experience with such weapons, and Jackson was known in Fayette as a crack shot, making unlikely an error in at least his aim. Someone would be killed or grievously injured in this fight, and locals were betting that it would be Clark.[36]

Yet Jackson's alarming response may have been a well-calculated bluff. By Missouri law, dueling was forbidden within the state's borders, subject to six months' imprisonment and a five-hundred-dollar fine for either dueling or for posting a challenge. Jackson knew the penalty as well as Clark's second, Judge Abiel Leonard, when he demanded that the "interview" take place within a mile of Fayette, and likely calculated that Clark would decline for that reason. As hoped, Leonard as second responded immediately to the challenge by objecting to the site of the proposed meeting, stating that "so far as the knowledge of the practice of this state in matters of this kind extends, . . . such a meeting would subject both principal and friends to penalties and inconveniences" and requested a change of venue. When Chauncey Scott refused Leonard's request, Clark issued a public card, "pronounc[ing] Claiborne F. Jackson a cold-blooded slanderer, a reclaimless scoundrel and a blustering coward," and vowing to prove it in a public forum. Jackson responded by submitting to the *Democrat* not only the entire series of correspondences but also a statement that branded Clark a cowardly "*dastard* who feels that his indiscretion has brought him into a position in which his *heart* will not sustain him." Newspapers throughout the state carried the correspondence in its entirety, and the *Boon's Lick Times* declared that "the *noise* sounds as little like 'Bloody Island' . . . as a disgraceful house yard fight." Privately, the incident had damaged Clark's reputation far more than Jackson's, and for much longer: one politico wrote to Marmaduke from St. Louis soon afterward that "the affair of Mr Jackson and Genl. Clark has resulted in favor of the former and much to the disparagement of the latter,"

---

36. *Boon's Lick Times,* September 26, 1840; C. F. Jackson to John B. Clark, September 11, 1840, in *History of Howard and Chariton Counties,* 317–18 (first quote); John B. Clark to C. F. Jackson, September 14, 1840, in ibid., 318 (second quote); *Jefferson Inquirer,* September 24, 1840 (third and fifth quotes); C[hauncey]. R. Scott to A[biel]. Leonard, September 15, 1840, in *History of Howard and Chariton Counties,* 318 (fourth quote). Five of the original copies of the correspondences surrounding the duel—John B. Clark to C. F. Jackson, September 14, 1840, Jackson to Clark, September 14, 1840, C. R. Scott to Abiel Leonard, September 15, 1840, Leonard to Scott, September 15, 1840, and Scott to Leonard, September 15, 1840, are in Abiel Leonard Papers, Mss. 1013, Box 7, folder 148, SHSM.

while as late as 1852, the editor of the *Glasgow Times* offered a sarcastic reminder to his Boon's Lick readership and to Clark, then a candidate for Congress, to "Remember that affair of honor, which covered you all over with glory, and which has no parallel in the record of chivalry, save the great Wingleberry duel immortalized by the pen of Dickens." With the exception of a final, plaintive note by Clark explaining away his letter in question, the entire episode passed without further incident, and though neither man had lost blood, Clark clearly had lost face. One impression came even clearer; Claib Jackson was not a man with whom to be trifled, and he was fully willing to put personal safety at stake for public appearances and reputation, whether for himself or for his party.[37]

Jackson's attack on Clark probably stemmed from personal, as much as party, frustrations. Though the Democrats were able to elect their slate of candidates over the strong opposition of the St. Louis Whigs, the victory came at a cost to the Central Clique. The Softs' relentless attacks upon the group as self-serving padrones of state political offices—and especially their focused portrayal of the state's rigid monetary policies as a product of poor leadership—had exposed the Democracy's soft underbelly. When the combined assembly convened in December 1840 to elect officers for the state bank and its branches, a full slate of Whig candidates opposed those named by the Boon's Lick Clique at every position. Moreover, a house investigation of the state bank for violating the hard-money policies of its charter and the bitter attacks by the Soft directors of the St. Louis branch against the Hards of the Fayette branch further threatened the Clique's credibility. Having escaped with a narrow statewide victory in this election—despite the losses in the Boon's Lick—but recognizing that the banking issue made the party vulnerable to a widespread defeat in two years if the depression continued, the Clique offered a sacrificial lamb: Jackson. They withdrew the candidacy of the incumbent directors of the Fayette branch of the state bank in favor of other, less Hard and thus less controversial Democrats: representative Sterling Price of Chariton (who had just led the Chariton militia against the Mormons) and William C. Boon of Howard. Claib Jackson had learned a painful reality of mass politics. The party beast's insatiable hunger for victory outstripped the appetite of any one member, no matter how seemingly important.[38]

37. The entire series of correspondence is published in the *Jefferson Inquirer,* September 24, 1840 (first and second quotes); *Boon's Lick Times,* September 26, 1840 (third quote); George Penn to M. M. Marmaduke, October 4, 1840, Sappington Family Papers, box 3, MHS (fourth quote); *Glasgow Weekly Times,* August 12, 1852 (fifth quote).

38. *Missouri House Journal,* Eleventh Gen. Ass., First Sess., 52, 113–39, 172–73, 337–38, 386–87, 468–501, SHSM; West, "Earlier Political Career of Jackson," 30–35; Shalhope, *Sterling Price,* 27–29, 33; Notarized protestation of refusal of note redemption, October 21, 1844, John S. Sappington Papers, Mss. 1027, box 2, folder 47, SHSM;

Though it might have forced upon him an indefinite officeholding hiatus, the Democrats cast neither Jackson nor Lowry aside completely. The election of 1840 bloodied the party, but the Clique remained strong and took the lead in preparing new strategies for the political wars ahead. In an effort to forestall any further Whig inroads, the Democrats called a young men's convention to meet in Jefferson City in October. Foremost in the minds of the delegates was the need for a thorough organization of the party to present a united front in the upcoming elections (both the state, in August, and the national, in November) and to mend the party schism, though at the point of a sword. Armed with political capital from the recent election, the Clique sought to entrench its hegemony within the state Democratic party while drawing a blueprint for party dominance within the state. When Thomas Harvey of Saline, a Clique confederate, introduced a series of resolutions providing for more party organization, the proposals included one that called for the creation of a state central committee that would orchestrate the plan's implementation at the county and township levels. Not only were the nine men to be from Howard County, but they had full power to fill any vacancies that might occur in the committee, thus creating a perpetual Boon's Lick or even Howard County oligarchy. The proposal passed easily, and the convention named John J. Lowry as the central committee's first chairman. Claib Jackson became one of the committee's nine charter members. While not holding office himself, Jackson had a powerful influence on those who did. Party members regularly frequented his Fayette home and office on party matters, and Jackson took the lead in nominating and securing petitions in support of Democratic candidates for various offices and appointments.[39]

Out of a job, Jackson fell back upon his place in the Sappington family and business. For income, he became a traveling supervisor, salesman, and banker, coordinating the pill company's operations in Arkansas, Louisiana, and Texas in the distribution and sales of both pills and books. The responsibility required him to be away from his family for long stretches of time, an imposition not lost on family members who commented on the suffering

---

Howard County Circuit Court Proceedings, May 19, 1842, House Impeachment—Judge John D. Leland, Capitol Fire Documents, 1806–1957, microfilm reel CFD-118, folder 10737: Twelfth General Assembly (1842–1843), MSA.

39. *Jefferson Inquirer,* October 15, 1840; Shalhope, *Sterling Price,* 30–31; William E. Parrish, *David Rice Atchison of Missouri—Border Politician,* 32; McCandless, *History of Missouri,* 122–23, 124; L. J. Eddins to M. M. Marmaduke, November 21, 1840, C. F. Jackson to M. M. Marmaduke, December 20, 1840, both in Sappington Family Papers, box 3, MHS; C. F. Jackson to Thomas Reynolds, January 6, 1841, and C. F. Jackson, L. S. Eddins, John J. Lowry, et al., to His Excellency, Thomas Reynolds, Governor of the State of Missouri, January 1, 1841, and John W. Price to Thomas Reynolds, April 11, 1843, all in Record Group 3: Governors' Papers—Thomas Reynolds Papers, Correspondence, box 2, folders 57–58, MSA.

his family endured during his long absences as he frequented St. Louis, Little Rock, Alexandria, and New Orleans on regular occasion. Because of his banking background, Jackson carried an even heavier burden; the Sappingtons charged him with finding solid investments to exchange for the unstable paper currency taken in by the company in the region. The lingering depression and banking problems plagued the Sappington company; one merchant in Vicksburg, Mississippi, wrote that "Alabama money is the almost entire circulating medium and it is 20 per cent below par now. [T]hey tell me Dr Sappington may go to hell if he will not take such money as other people do. [T]hey say that they will law him as long as there is a pea in the dish if he does not take the Alabama money and then not pay him." Jackson now confronted the grim reality of devalued currency from the perspective of both a businessman and a banker. In January 1842, he wrote soberly to the Sappingtons from Little Rock that "I am here at the very worst and most unfortunate time that has been for the last twelve months. Had I been here one month sooner, I could have saved the Company at least $3000 more than I shall now be able to make out of the wreck." He railed against the depression, and especially the Soft currency policy, which only confirmed his Hard financial philosophies: "Damn the money & the country. Such a set of damn scoundrels & rogues never before went unhung. Heaven only Knows the manner in which the people of this state have been swindaled [*sic*], and the poor devils take it as kindly as though it were the best of treatment." He predicted a revolution that would "raze their banking houses flat to the ground," only heightening his confirmation of conservative principles, fiscal and otherwise.[40]

Personal influences made this arrangement temporary for Jackson. Working within the Sappington business might have been financially rewarding—even sustaining—for Jackson, but it was not personally gratifying. He seriously considered moving to St. Clair County to find challenges in his life, to farm and rejuvenate his mercantile trade and perhaps to escape the irrepressible ennui of his present. Moreover, the tragedies of the past decade had conspired to rob him of his youth. The oppression of spirit occasioned by the deaths of two spouses, a convenient, if not arranged, third marriage within the Sappington family, and the added responsibilities he shouldered

40. L. W. Parsons to O. B. Pearson, May 29, 1843 (first quote), and C. F. Jackson to John Sappington and Sons, January 24, 1842 (second, third, and fourth quotes), both in Sappington Family Papers, box 3, MHS; C. F. Jackson to M. M. Marmaduke, January 4, 1842, ibid., box 3, MHS; William Price to M. M. Marmaduke, March 18, 1844, ibid., box 4, MHS; James H. Saunders to C. F. Jackson, April 2, 1841, John S. Sappington Papers, Mss. 1027, box 2, folder 37, SHSM; William Bradford to W. B. Sappington, March 1, 1842 [two letters], ibid., box 2, folder 38, SHSM; William Price to John S. Sappington, March 3, 1844, ibid., box 2, folder 45, SHSM.

for five children who were not his and four who were (Eliza had in the past two years borne him a son, Claib, Jr., and a daughter, Louisa), along with a position within a family business that he did not control and that took him often and far away from home, all conjoined to spark a hunger that neither financial reward, family patriarchy, nor even a cloaked position of importance in the Democratic hierarchy could satisfy. This vacuum of personal insecurity only expanded as he neared middle life and, at thirty-six, confronted the timeless paradox of men his age: neither the body he once had nor the life he had once conceived and had struggled a lifetime to build was one he now controlled. He remained clean-shaven despite the Victorian trend toward full beards, and began wearing a toupee to cover the balding crown of his head while keeping his own hair long, flowing over his neck and onto his shoulders. Moreover, this epiphany moved him to seek again the realm of public men, that complex combination of competition and camaraderie known as politics. Whether to prove a manhood he secretly questioned, or to recapture the days and haps of a lost youth, or to resurrect the exhilarating and rootless spirit of adventure that had actuated his and his ancestors' moves to the frontier, Jackson ran again for office in 1842.[41]

Jackson entered his campaign for the General Assembly under inauspicious circumstances. The Democrats had managed to maintain a single majority in the Eleventh General Assembly; at the state nominating convention held in June in Jefferson City, the Boon's Lick Hards—who had produced all of Missouri's congressmen during the past decade—had not been able to secure even the nomination of one candidate for Congress. Claib Jackson had been one of those disappointed aspirants, and his inability to secure a nomination revealed a deep division among the once-solid Boon's Lick Democrats. More ominous, in that same month Congress had ordered that all states divide themselves into electoral districts equal to the states' representational apportionment, effectively eliminating county-based, at-large elections (a general ticket had allowed voters to vote for as many candidates as the state had seats, without regard for geographic balance) and thus reducing the clout of the populous Boon's Lick and especially Howard and Saline. The Clique's

---

41. E. D. Sappington to M. M. Marmaduke, January 25, 1841, Lavinia Marmaduke to M. M. Marmaduke, November 25, 1841, and T. P. Bell to M. M. Marmaduke, August 28, 1841, all in Sappington Family Papers, box 3, MHS; Seventh U.S. Census, 1850, Population Schedule, Howard County, Missouri, NA; Grissom, "Personal Recollections," 506. Grissom relates an incident from the late 1850s, when Jackson "was state bank commissioner, and was in St. Louis in connection with his official business. While he was driving a buggy one day along Third street near Vine, he was run into by a dray, which upset his vehicle and threw him out. His wig fell off, and even his personal friend did not at first recognize him in his bald, shining head. He was greatly exasperated by the accident and vented his wrath at the drayman who, he thought, was responsible for it."

steadfast opposition to the redistricting bill—seeing rightly that its passage would end their virtual monopoly on Missouri's congressional seats—quickly brought charges of undemocratic nepotism, further weakening the party's position in the upcoming election. The Clique's future hold on Missouri politics seemed tenuous, and its members realized that only through active local electioneering could they "revive their importance and influence."[42]

Securing even a party nomination was a difficult task, and after a late entrance into the field and some inventive maneuvering of the Clique, Jackson received it by an abrupt caucus on the lawn of the Fayette courthouse. The lone conservative in the field, he campaigned against a number of opponents in Howard who had aligned in varying degrees with the Softs. Jackson stood true to his 1840 promise to Meredith M. Marmaduke, offering traditional Boon's Lick Democratic principles in his speeches in firm opposition to the Whigs. He strongly opposed both soft-money policy and congressional redistricting, which he decried as unconstitutional. The great risk paid off; in a close election for three seats in the state legislature, Jackson finished second to Dr. Chauncey R. Scott, once his second in the near duel with John Clark and now a Clique defector who drew heavily from local Whigs in the absence of a candidate of their own. The *Boon's Lick Times* claimed that a combination of "three elections and by bringing out a ticket headed by their surest shot and strongest man [Jackson] and using every possible effort they succeeded in electing one Clique man." Jackson's election to the legislature caused Governor Thomas Reynolds, a resident of Howard County, to write elatedly to his lieutenant-governor, Marmaduke, that he was "much gratified at the result of your [Howard County's] election, but not half so much so as when I found out that Jackson had beaten the disaffected of his own party and the combined power of Whiggery."[43]

Claiborne Jackson's second entrance into the Missouri legislature would serve as a springboard to prominence not just in the state, but soon the nation. His election was as much symbolic as it was personal, the first of several such victories in his political life. Armed with political capital accumulated over years of local political leadership, as well as a resolve for conservative principles steeled by economic hardship in the state, if not in his

42. *Boon's Lick Times,* November 2, 1844, July 2–August 6, 1842, August 13, 1842 (quote); West, "Earlier Political Career of Jackson," 35–42; Burks, "Thunder on the Right," 142–50; McCandless, *History of Missouri,* 230–31.

43. Secretary of State Election Returns, August 6, 1842, Capitol Fire Documents, 1806–1957, microfilm reel CFD-183, folder 16236, MSA; *Boon's Lick Times,* October 8, 1842, August 13, 1842 (first quote); *Jefferson Inquirer,* June 9, July 7, 1842; *Columbia Patriot,* June 17, 1842; Burks, "Thunder on the Right," 142–50; West, "Earlier Political Career of Jackson," 35–42; Thomas Reynolds to M. M. Marmaduke, August 22, 1842, Sappington Family Papers, box 3, MHS (second quote).

own life, and personal conflicts over fiscal policy, Jackson would soon play a leading role in propelling Missouri into the great sectional debate already sweeping the nation. In Claib Jackson, Missourians would find a lens through which to interpret national events that had seemed far away both physically and ideologically as late as the 1830s, yet which by the 1840s were literally on their doorstep. As the nation marched toward them, Missourians would find reason to fear the issues and events into which they felt increasingly dragged. Yet Claib Jackson's conservatism would represent to Missourians more than simply a comforting sentinel of an increasingly anachronistic order. His voice would soon offer a clarion by which these once-westerners would begin to reimagine both their world and themselves.

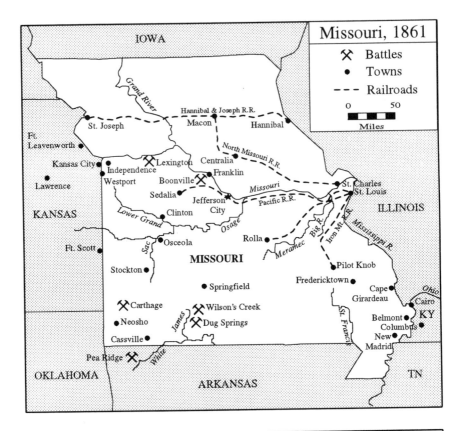

Missouri, 1861

⚔ Battles
● Towns
- - - Railroads

0   50
Miles

IOWA

Grand River

Hannibal & Joseph R.R.
Macon   Hannibal
St. Joseph

Ft.
Leavenworth

North Missouri R.R.

Kansas City   Lexington   Centralia
Independence   Boonville   Franklin
Westport   Missouri
Lawrence   St. Charles
                    Sedalia   St. Louis
                              Jefferson Pacific R.R.
KANSAS   Lower Grand   Clinton   City   ILLINOIS

                              Osage

Ft. Scott   Osceola   Rolla
              Sac   Meramec   Big R.   Iron Mt. R.R.   Mississippi R.

              MISSOURI   Pilot Knob

Stockton   Fredericktown
                                                                        Cape   Ohio
              Springfield   Girardeau   Cairo

        Carthage   Wilson's Creek   Belmont   KY
                                                                              Columbus
    Neosho   Dug Springs   New
                James   Madrid
Cassville
                                                St. Francis

Pea Ridge   White

OKLAHOMA   TN
              ARKANSAS

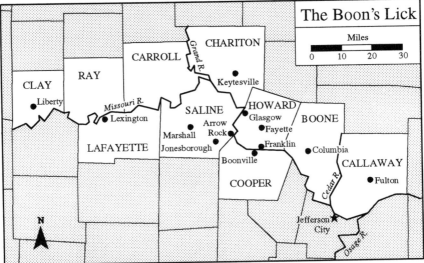

The Boon's Lick

Miles
0   10   20   30

CHARITON

CARROLL   Grand R.

CLAY   RAY   Keytesville

Liberty   Missouri R.   SALINE   HOWARD   BOONE
              Lexington   Glasgow
                              Arrow   Fayette
                    Marshall Rock
LAFAYETTE   Jonesborough   Franklin   Columbia
                              Boonville
                                          CALLAWAY
                        COOPER   Cedar R.   Fulton

N
                                    Jefferson
                                    City   Osage R.

Claiborne Fox Jackson, ca. 1850. Drawing, artist unknown.
Courtesy State Historical Society of Missouri, Columbia.

Dr. John Sappington, ca. 1840. The wealthy Boon's Lick physician and entrepreneur patented quinine-based medicine for treatment of malaria. Jackson married three of his daughters. Courtesy State Historical Society of Missouri, Columbia.

Mrs. Eliza W. Jackson, ca. 1860. Jackson's third wife, and eldest daughter of Dr. John Sappington. Courtesy State Historical Society of Missouri, Columbia.

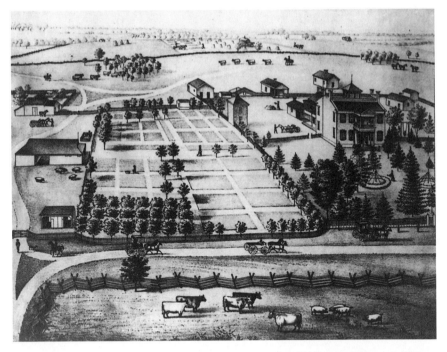

Prairie Park, estate of William B. Sappington, west of Arrow Rock, Missouri. The family's demonstrable wealth caused an ambitious Jackson to seek and retain entry into the Sappington clan. Courtesy State Historical Society of Missouri, Columbia.

Fayette, Missouri, city square, looking east, ca. 1860. The town served as Jackson's home from 1837 to 1853, and was the base of the state's Central Clique. Partially visible at the extreme right is Oakwood, Abiel Leonard's stately home. Courtesy State Historical Society of Missouri, Columbia.

Jackson's home, northwest of Fayette. It was constructed in stages around an existing log cabin and completed in 1847. The home still stands on State Highway 5. Courtesy State Historical Society of Missouri, Columbia.

Missouri Statehouse, Jefferson City, ca. 1853. Begun in 1837, it witnessed nearly the entirety of Jackson's political career, serving as the state capitol until destroyed by fire in 1911. Courtesy State Historical Society of Missouri, Columbia.

Thomas Hart Benton, Missouri's original senator, ca. 1856. Jackson was instrumental in ending his thirty-year tenure in 1851. Oil painting by F. T. L. Boyle. Missouri Historical Society, St. Louis. Courtesy State Historical Society of Missouri, Columbia.

William B. Napton. Jackson's political mentor and Saline County neighbor, he was the author of the Jackson-Napton resolutions, used to end Benton's Senate career. Courtesy State Historical Society of Missouri, Columbia.

CROSSROADS

[WITH] ONLY A loose, and often ephemeral attachment to places and institutions, many Americans felt a compelling need to articulate their loyalties, to prove their faith, and to demonstrate their allegiance to certain ideals and institutions. By so doing they acquired a sense of self-identity and personal direction in an otherwise rootless and shifting environment.

DAVID BRION DAVIS, "SOME THEMES OF COUNTER-SUBVERSION:
AN ANALYSIS OF ANTI-MASONIC, ANTI-CATHOLIC, AND
ANTI-MORMON LITERATURE"

For residents of the Boon's Lick such as Claib Jackson, St. Louis had always been a foreign city. Viewed alternately with inspired awe and intense hatred, either reaction stemmed entirely from their oppressive fear of the city's uniqueness. St. Louis had been the first city of the great West, established before the Revolution and already home to more than a thousand souls—nearly a quarter of them slaves—in the midst of a vast frontier when the piedmont yeomanry began their ineffable march to Missouri's interior after the turn of the nineteenth century. French customs and Spanish rule left lasting marks on this once Creole capital; its narrow streets, steep-roofed cottages, and especially the odious Catholic presence suggested to American Protestants far-too-visible images of a chained European past and present. The bricked city boasted people of wealth, sophistication, and genteel urban tastes with names such as Laclède, Chouteau, Gratiot, and Labbadie, and its reputation as a center of opulent urbanity continued after the influx of Anglo-Americans began with the acquisition of the Louisiana Territory. Long into the ensuing century, sons and daughters of Virginia, Tennessee, and especially Kentucky's finest city-dwelling families—primarily from Louisville, Lexington, Richmond, and Nashville and educated in the East, in Europe, Canada, or at Transylvania—struck out for St. Louis to practice law or business and to intermarry with partners bearing the elite family names of their respective homes, such as Breckinridge, Blair, Benton, Preston, Gratz, and Crittenden. As country folks like Claib Jackson passed inevitably through the gateway city on their way to the Boon's Lick, they could not help but be either impressed or repulsed, or both.[1]

1. Nagel, *Missouri*, 76–77; Charles N. Glaab and A. Theodore Brown, *A History of Urban America*, 29–30; Richard C. Wade, *The Urban Frontier: Pioneer Life in Early*

The passage of two score years only created a St. Louis ever more distinct from the Missouri hinterlands. Within two decades of statehood, two Missouris existed, each reflecting the character of the respective fecund rivers that animated them. One was located along the wide Mississippi, mother of rivers and artery to civilization, while the other straddled the wild Missouri, a secondary vessel and the avenue to the frontier. St. Louis was the crown jewel of the Mississippi, while much of the rest of the state was identified with the Missouri. The Boon's Lick struggled to belong completely to neither. The commercial colossus that was St. Louis drew from both Missouris, and both rivers were its lifeline. Lying astride the Mississippi and just below the great river's confluence with the Missouri, one observer noted that the city "occupies as it were the central point, from which the great natural highways of the Union diverge in different directions. . . . The Missouri connects it with the Rocky Mountains, the Ohio with the Alleghenies, the Upper Mississippi with the Great Lakes, the lower with the ocean." Indeed, the city owed its very life to trade, and its ideal location at the mouth of the nation's great internal river hydra had always allowed it to feed well. The arrival of the country's first great revolutionary mode of transportation, the steamboat, commenced an engorgement. In 1832, 532 steamboats docked at St. Louis wharves; by 1845 that number had reached two thousand, and by the 1850s St. Louis received annually more than three thousand steamboats carrying 1.5 million tons of freight. So recognizably important was the vehicle to the city's life that the city council, in its first official act, designated that the centerpiece of the city seal "shall be a steamboat carrying the United States flag." Scottish observer Alexander Mackay marveled at the incessant "bustle, enterprise, and activity" in the city he proclaimed "the great internal entrepôt of the country." One resident, Henry Marie Brackenridge, declared St. Louis "the Memphis of the American Nile."[2]

By 1840, St. Louis appeared to most Missourians to be more a product of the East than it ever had been a city of the West. Its leaders—most notably five-term mayor William Carr Lane, a Pennsylvanian—consciously solicited and then adopted patterns for municipal organization and laws already established in the eastern cities or New Orleans. Railroads only cemented the bond. Beginning in the 1830s, St. Louisans pushed the indifferent state legislature to charter railroads to link the state with the city, anticipating the

---

Pittsburgh, Cincinnati, Lexington, Louisville, and St. Louis, 2–7; Foley, *Genesis of Missouri,* 35–36, 84–85, 185–86.

2. Glaab and Brown, *History of Urban America,* 74 (first and fourth quotes), 85 (third quote); Selwyn K. Troen and Glen E. Holt, eds., *St. Louis,* 49 (second quote); Wade, *Urban Frontier,* 191; Nagel, *Missouri,* 64; McCandless, *History of Missouri,* 137; *Missouri Gazette,* March 21, 1811, quoted in Wade, *Urban Frontier,* 64 (fifth quote).

boom as neighboring middle western states contracted their own prolonged railroad fever in order to link themselves—and ultimately St. Louis—to the burgeoning industrial centers of the East. This obtrusive fact was decidedly not lost on the Boon's Lickers whose trade loyalties lay down the muddy yet natural rivers to Memphis and New Orleans, not along artificial iron rails to the sooty cold of Philadelphia and New York. Boon's Lick residents had watched bemused as neighboring Illinois nearly bankrupted itself courting the canal and railroad companies, then with horror as St. Louis representatives urged the state to do likewise, with the city as the hub, clearly intent upon wresting complete dominance of the state's trade. By the early 1850s rural Missourians feared the usurpation of the once-democratic hegemony of the rivers in favor of the exclusionary tyranny of the iron horse. The fact that these railroads connected St. Louis with the corrupted world of the East only confirmed their distrust of the city that lay on the fringe of what most considered as the traditional Missouri, whether social, political, or economic. Yet with Whig support both in St. Louis and the interior, between 1836 and 1837 the state chartered eighteen railroad companies, though rural Democratic influence in the legislature succeeded in stymieing any funding of those companies until the 1850s.[3]

As unsettling to rural Missourians was St. Louis's industrial growth. As late as 1815, St. Louis owed its commercial importance largely to trade activity rather than manufacturing, its largest industry connected to the fur trade. In 1829, one New England observer "estimate[d] the commerce and trade of St. Louis, at this time, at ten millions of dollars annually. It cannot be less, I think, and may be more, much more." This slow growth of industry accelerated during the 1840s and 1850s. Led by flour and mill processing, sugar refining, and meat packing (and followed by such collateral industries as brewing, distilling, brick and iron manufacturing, cordwaining, and stove making), the city boasted manufactured products valued at $27 million by 1860, ranking seventh among American cities, while being sixth nationally in the number of manufacturing firms. By 1854, *De Bow's Review* proclaimed boldly that "St. Louis is destined to become commercially more than Venice ever *was*—and in manufactures what *Lowell is!*"[4]

---

3. McCandless, *History of Missouri*, 34; Wade, *Urban Frontier*, 316, 277–79; David Thelen, *Paths of Resistance: Tradition and Dignity in Industrializing Missouri*, 12–13; Nagel, *Missouri*, 66–67.

4. Caleb Atwater, *The Writings of Caleb Atwater*, 213; Wade, *Urban Frontier*, 202; James Neal Primm, *Lion of the Valley: St. Louis, Missouri*, 201–10; Jeffrey S. Adler, *Yankee Merchants and the Making of the Urban West: The Rise and Fall of Antebellum St. Louis*, 89–90; *De Bow's Review* 17 (1854): 397 (third quote). Despite its industrial growth in the antebellum years, St. Louis's manufacturing sector remained comparatively underdeveloped.

Rural Missourians considered such economic changes in St. Louis of secondary importance to the alarming sea of humanity that the city attracted after 1840. For these Jeffersonian legatees, St. Louis's mushrooming population was the most visible specter of evil. The city represented a blot on the agrarian landscape they envisioned for their western utopia, the serpent materialized in the Missouri Eden. The city had always been the largest in the region, never remotely unseated as Missouri's metropolis despite the optimistic predictions of Franklin's founders. Yet the city had achieved only a fraction of its eventual growth prior to the century's fifth and sixth decades. In 1820, St. Louis had boasted just more than 10,000 inhabitants; by 1830 the town had 14,125 people, and a decade later its population had grown to just 16,500. Yet between 1841 and 1850, the city's population exploded; by 1842, it approached 30,000 (double that of a decade before) and by 1850, 77,860 people crowded into the river city that over the same period had expanded from less than a square mile to nearly five. By 1860, St. Louis would boast some 160,000 residents, nearly ten times that of just twenty years earlier and representing more than 13 percent of the state's population as a whole.[5]

Rural Missourians' perception of St. Louis as an increasingly alien city drew into sharp focus with the arrival of thousands of immigrants during the 1830s. The earliest and most pronounced of these new arrivals came from the German principalities, spurred by the writings of Gottfried Duden, a Malthusian lawyer and promoter who lived in Missouri from 1824 to 1827 and portrayed the state as "a second *Vaterland*" and the Missouri and Mississippi Valleys as a Rhineland in the West. His "Report," published in 1829, served as an instruction manual for emigration and soon initiated a prolonged exodus of Germans, both from eastern cities and from their native homes, disappointed with the failure of the liberal revolutionary movements of 1832 and 1833. St. Louis served as a staging place for many groups of educated "Latin farmers" who ultimately settled on the hills and bluffs of the interior river valleys west of the city, founding towns such as Hermann, Rhineland, Wittenberg, Dutzow, and Westphalia, as well as becoming the permanent home for many more skilled and semi-skilled urban tradesmen who opened breweries, tanneries, shops, and markets in the southern and western parts of St. Louis. One visitor marveled later at the "whole sections of the city where the Teuton predominates." By 1850, one in three residents of St. Louis was of German origin—as compared with just 7.2 percent of

---

5. Fourth, Fifth, Sixth, Seventh, and Eighth U.S. Censuses, 1820–1860, Population Schedules, St. Louis County, Missouri, NA; William E. Parrish, *Frank Blair: Lincoln's Conservative*, 11; Burks, "Thunder on the Right," 150; Primm, *Lion of the Valley*, 147–49.

the state population as a whole outside St. Louis—and their numbers would double to more than fifty thousand during the ensuing decade.[6]

Though numerically the largest, Germans were not the only immigrant group to diversify even further the historically cosmopolitan river city. During the 1840s, in the years after the infamous potato blight and resulting famine, Irish people flocked to St. Louis, concentrating in two sections northwest of the business district in communities soon called Vinegar Hill and Kerry Patch. Less affluent, educated, or skilled than the Germans, Irish immigrants had little capital with which to buy land and thus leave the city or to start businesses after they had stayed. Consequently, the Irish hired out as day laborers, the most menial of occupations, and as railroad laborers and dock workers, routinely receiving meager wages for their efforts. Their communities were as exclusive as were those of the Germans, their benevolent organizations, Hibernian societies, and other such communal associations safeguarded cultural sodality as much as they promoted societal progress. More ominous to Anglo-Americans in Missouri than these "secret societies," particularly to those in the countryside, was the rock-ribbed adherence of the descendants of Erin to the Catholic Church, which these rural Protestants regarded with outright hostility. The French and Spanish legacy of Catholicism in St. Louis offered the new Irish communicants a certain degree of clemency within the city limits (prompting one observer to remark that its "people generally are much more tolerant [of Catholicism] . . . than they are in England"), but outside the metropolis this newest influx of Catholics only deepened long-standing rural and decidedly Protestant mistrust. By 1850, the more than ten thousand Irish-born residents would represent a full 13 percent of the city's population; a decade later, Irish immigrants would constitute nearly 16 percent of the city's whole. Altogether, more than half of St. Louis's population was foreign-born—as compared with just 8.3 percent in the Boon's Lick in 1850—more than 80 percent of the immigrants being either German or Irish. By a twist of fate, these two cultures soon dominated the city that the French had established, the Spanish had nurtured, and the Americans had purchased.[7]

6. McCandless, *History of Missouri*, 35, 38–41; Gottfried Duden, *Report of a Journey to the Western States of North America, and a Residence of Several Years on the Missouri (during the years 1824, '25, '26, and 1827), dealing with the Question of Emigration and Excess Population*, in Troen and Holt, eds., *St. Louis*, 66–68 (first and second quotes); Nagel, *Missouri*, 95–99; King, "The Great South," 264 (third quote).

7. Ray Allen Billington, *The Protestant Crusade*, 322–44; John Chester Greville, *Transatlantic Sketches in the West Indies, South America, Canada and the United States*, 243–44, 245 (quote); Troen and Holt, eds., *St. Louis*, 74; McCandless, *History of Missouri*, 40–41; J. D. B. DeBow, ed., *The Seventh Census of the United States: 1850*, 663.

Political changes forced by St. Louis's spectacular sprawl only widened Missouri's long-standing urban-rural dichotomy. St. Louis's traditional image as a city—never a mere village—in the wilderness, established in the French and Spanish colonial era, had become iridescent for generations of rural residents who by the 1820s instinctively separated it from the Missouri whole. The state's government, as with its politics, evolved along the Jeffersonian model so as to keep its size small and its focus as local as possible. With numerous counties created and represented, government would thus remain—at least theoretically—responsive to local interests, needs, and networks and, as important, the preponderance of its power would remain in the hands of the rural majority and outside of St. Louis. As early as 1820, the editor of the *Missouri Gazette* put the matter bluntly: "It has been said that St. Louis is obnoxious to our legislature—that its growth and influence . . . are looked on with a jealous eye, and its pretensions ought to be discouraged." Yet already by 1824, all of Missouri's representatives in Washington—two senators and one representative—as well as the state's governor hailed from St. Louis. The serpent appeared coiled around the Garden's residents.[8]

The advent of mass, democratic elections prompted urban leaders to seek remedy for the disproportionately low representation afforded the growing and prosperous city in the state legislature. They met continuous and steadfast opposition from country interests protective of the traditional order and their dominance of the political realm. The story was in no way Missouri's own; similar scenarios played out in nearly all states born of rural circumstance and which now confronted a voracious and threatening urban presence. The specter of St. Louis lay at the center of the congressional redistricting storm during 1840 and 1841. The city's solidly Whig allegiance provided only a backdrop for the power politics that had enveloped the legislature; its booming population offered the interior representatives their greatest challenge. As the state's population grew and spread, rural leaders in the General Assembly used their clout to increase the number of counties from sixty to seventy-seven, but managed to stymie any proportionate growth of the total number of representatives, allowing only two new seats. Consequently, the house grew only from ninety-eight seats to one hundred, the constitutional limit, and because the state constitution guaranteed each county at least one representative, the larger counties—especially St. Louis but also Howard—actually lost seats and votes in the house at the expense of the newer counties. Furious St. Louisans would decry the "unholy shackles that prevent the City of St. Louis from developing in accordance with divine and natural law," but

8. Bernard Bailyn, *The Origins of American Politics,* 101–5; Thelen, *Paths of Resistance,* 21–22; *Missouri Gazette,* December 6, 1820; Wade, *Urban Frontier,* 337; McCandless, *History of Missouri,* 71–72.

they would not "strike the fetters" imposed by the rural populace's hereditary distrust until 1876 when the new state constitution granted the city home rule, offering it virtual political independence from not only the county but also the state.[9]

The unnatural colossus that blighted rural Missourians' idyll offered in reality a convenient symbol. The scorn heaped upon the city arose from a fear far more complex and yet less understood than that born of any simple rural-urban dichotomy. Urbanization, industrialization, immigration, innovation, transportation, commercialization, and cosmopolitanization—all recognizable facets of the St. Louis experience during the Jacksonian period—were merely substrata of the process of modernization, a sweeping transformation of American life that these Missourians in part publicly rejected, privately embraced, and on the whole proved unable to avoid. While at once they celebrated the steamboat's mastery of the rivers that had defined Missouri heretofore and now connected its rural people more completely with an outside world, they as easily condemned the railroads, seemingly for the same reason. This caprice was attributable neither to mere protection of "Nature's legacy"—the steamboat augmenting that which was unalloyed and the railroad introducing that which was not—nor any overweening custodianship of public appropriations characteristic of Jeffersonians/Jacksonians. Rather, this bucolic dualism stemmed largely from these westerners' perceptions of the worlds to which they were, or feared they would be, linked. That St. Louis would benefit most from the introduction of the railroad by serving as the state's hub only punctuated the rural Missourians' eschewal of the new technology, for the eastern, modernized world with which the iron horse would connect Missouri already counted St. Louis as one of its principal cities.[10]

THE CONFLICT OVER the railroad was the opening salvo in what would ultimately prove to be nearly a century-long struggle between Missouri and the coming of the new industrial and social order. Yet this was no struggle between premodern and modern forces, between feudalism and capitalism; these were neither precapitalist peasants nor mean subsistence farmers. Boon's Lickers actively sought and achieved material acquisitiveness as they embraced free-market commercialization. Yet their participation in the market revolution was limited, grounded—at least as far as they were concerned—in western concepts of individualism. These rural residents occupied a middling station in the painful transition within American capitalist

9. McCandless, *History of Missouri,* 230–31; Office of the Mayor, *A Plea to the Constitutional Convention of Missouri for Enlargement of Boundaries of the City of St. Louis,* 5 (quotes); Nagel, *Missouri,* 77–80.

10. Richard D. Brown, *Modernization: The Transformation of American Life,* 3–22; Nagel, *Missouri,* 49 (quote), 50–52, 63–71.

development, a place described by one historian as a "dynamic and modern social formation tied to the world market but not fully of it." With a staple crop economy on which they relied but were not dependent, a labor system that would at once permit independence and encourage commerce, and an inclusive legal and governmental nexus that offered access to property of many kinds and protected it against external threats, the "hybrid" economy and society of the Boon's Lick had evolved into the living embodiment of the West in that above all else, freedom of choice in capital and societal advancement prevailed. As yeomen in central Missouri believed, being neither purely industrial nor even agrarian offered the purest form of liberty, boundless like the West itself.[11]

As with their capitalistic proclivities, the Boon's Lick society knew limits. Rural Missourians could and did accept the commercial largesse of modernization only so long as it augmented, rather than challenged, the traditional order they had established and cultivated. In their concept of a western Eden, generations of rural Missourians such as those in the Boon's Lick had conceived an image of "a birthright reclaimed," as one historian has described this vision of freedom in which traditional agrarian values reigned. The very nature of the inhabitants' flight into the region and away from an increasingly impersonal market society demanded such. Built upon the bedrock of such institutions as family, neighbors, and church—traditional patterns of community—these Missourians' social order, created out of a yearning for normalcy in their new environment, bore the mark of what had become a schizophrenic conception of individual liberty. Obligation, born of these unsure residents' construct of localism—rooted in the past—curbed rural Missourians' ambitions—centered in the future—and thus ineluctably tempered the West's promise of freedom. Consistent with this conservative vision, the inhabitants' economic pursuits operated in harmony with both the natural and social landscapes, a moral economy of sorts in which "traditional rights and customs . . . were supported by the wider consensus of the community." Part fantasy, part fact, the rights and customs of residents of middle Missouri owed their life at once to the capitalistic visions of their migration and the embedded concepts of deference and place that themselves marked boundaries. Within this realm, residents rewarded familiarity with peace while countering unfamiliarity with contempt and even violence.[12]

11. Kulikoff, *Agrarian Origins of American Capitalism*, 24–27 (quotes).

12. Hofstadter, "The Pseudo-Conservative Revolt," and Seymour Martin Lipset, "The Sources of the 'Radical Right,'" both in Bell, ed., *Radical Right*, 82–91, 336–40; Michael Cassity, *Defending a Way of Life: An American Community in the Nineteenth Century*, 6 (quote), 10–11; Thelen, *Paths of Resistance*, 274; Anthony P. Cohen, *The Symbolic Construction of Community*, 11–15; E. P. Thompson, "The Moral Economy of the English Crowd in the Eighteenth Century," 78–79 (quote); James C. Scott, *The*

The social ritual of tobacco production and the collective identity derived from its cultivation nested with the Boon's Lick residents' innately conservative conception of community, one that stressed personal networks and close if not intimate economic relations. Social hierarchy, established by years of residence, local leadership, and consistent excellence of leaf production (which in itself became a self-fulfilling prophecy in that name recognition as much as tobacco quality garnered the highest prices at auction) tempered the inevitable distraction of competition associated with commercialization. Tobacco was thus more than a mere commodity; it was a "social good," as one theorist has described salable products that hold deep cultural meaning far beyond their economic status as a commodity. Social goods satisfy human needs and desires far beyond the material, and as such have a socially determined value and meaningfulness. Being social, such goods become defensible not solely from their economic value, but from their cultural imprint, or as one theorist has concluded, from their "wider [meaning historical, collective, and shared] process of conception and naming."[13]

More even than their capacity for generating profit, tobacco's broad leaves thus offered a shared sign of community health, and its production was a symbol of membership. Even the terms with which planters John and Henry Bingham described the leaf's reception in foreign markets—"esteemed" and "admired"—suggests the value of the crop far above that of livestock or grain. Just as planters grew and honed long thumbnails as badges of acceptance as much as implements of tobacco production, tobacco offered a source of identity and harmony that buttressed the societal status quo and resisted the power of the market economy to detract from it. Similar to one scholar's depiction of cattle among the African Nuers, tobacco was the Boon's Lickers' "social idiom." Thus the Planters' Hotels in the salient tobacco markets of Weston and St. Louis pandered to local consciousness rather than working any emulative conjuring of a yet undefined and distant plantation culture.[14]

Moral Economy of the Peasant, passim; John Scott Strickland, "Traditional Culture and Moral Economy: Social and Economic Change in the South Carolina Low Country, 1865–1910," 145; John Walton, *Western Times and Water Wars: State, Culture, and Rebellion in California,* 193–97; T. Clay Arnold, "Rethinking Moral Economy and Political Science," 4–8. The story of rural Missouri's resistance to the imposition of the industrial order throughout the nineteenth century is well told by the combination of Cassity and Thelen's books.

13. Breen, *Tobacco Culture,* 47–58; Geertz, "Thick Description: Toward an Interpretive Theory of Culture," 3–30; Mary Douglas and Baron Isherwood, *The World of Goods,* 56–62; Michael Walzer, *Spheres of Justice: A Defense of Pluralism and Equality,* 6–7 (second quote), 8–10. My thanks to Professor Clay Arnold for introducing me to the concept of social goods, and for sharing with me his argument for pairing the concepts of social goods and moral economy.

14. Hurt, *Agriculture and Slavery in Little Dixie,* 81 (first and second quotes); E. E. Evans-Pritchard, *The Nuer: The Political Institutions of a Nilotic People,* 17–19 (third

Judging by Missouri's tobacco production, the state's residents regarded the crop as an especially important social idiom during the 1840s, one that indeed defied the economic conditions of the final antebellum decades. In 1839, tobacco planters in Missouri marketed just more than nine million pounds of the leaf, sixth most in the country but behind North Carolina by nearly half. A decade later, despite a steep and prolonged downturn of tobacco prices that caused declines in all of the other major producing states save Kentucky, Missouri had nearly doubled its output to more than seventeen million pounds and leapfrogged Carolina to become the nation's fifth-largest producer of tobacco. Yet with the inception of the 1840s came a deep trough of tobacco fortunes that lasted a full decade, in which New Orleans tobacco prices plunged to less than five cents a pound and remained mired there for more than five years. In fact, during two-thirds of the first twenty-seven years of Missouri's statehood, New Orleans tobacco brought less than five cents per pound, and Missourians could expect at best four cents for their best-quality leaf. The 1850s saw a stirring of prices that for the better part of the decade held above eight cents per pound, climbing as high as 14.6 cents in 1857, only to suffer yet another sharp downturn. Yet Missourians again seemed less tied to this upswing of prices; between 1849 and 1859, all of the other tobacco-producing states but Maryland doubled or tripled their output as planters took advantage of the abnormally high prices. Missourians witnessed a more moderate gain of 47 percent, the lowest by far of any tobacco-growing state; the Boon's Lick's output increased by less than 8 percent, from 5.1 million pounds in 1850 to 5.5 million pounds in 1860—half of that in Howard County alone. As a social good, tobacco and its fortunes in Missouri drew strength from symbolic, cultural factors often distinct from economic realities.[15]

Tobacco alone did not create or sustain any such social idiom for the people of the Boon's Lick. Just as these capitalistic rural people could not stand apart from the market revolution and participated in it to the extent that their local conditions would tolerate, their social goods did not exist in isolation from one another. Rather, such goods were nested, intertwined into a complex tangle of values and processes that concerted into its people's collective identity. Because such social goods are shared and mutual rather than convergent, even the valuation rituals attendant with their status as commodities—tools, implements, work rhythms, modes and venues of exchange (tobacco auctions were social events far beyond mere

---

quote, p. 19; Meredith Ramsay, *Community, Culture, and Economic Development: The Social Roots of Local Action*, 9.
    15. Gray, *History of Agriculture in the Southern United States*, vol. 2, 759, 765, 1038; Hurt, *Agriculture and Slavery in Little Dixie*, 80, 99.

business transactions), and forms of labor associated with production—become satellites of local culture and identity whose social value equals or even exceeds the monetary value of the social good they support. As central Missourians clustered the concepts they associated with tobacco production, another, more essential social good soon emerged and by the 1840s dictated their perceptions of their world, their lives, and themselves even more profoundly than ever had tobacco. That social good was slavery.

By the late 1840s, slavery had become a load-bearing joist of the Boon's Lick's societal edifice. The Jacksonian-era liberal doxology had only further entrenched these westerners' hereditary commitment to individual freedoms, which in turn gave license to the proliferation of slave ownership in the region. At precisely the same time that Missouri confronted the disruptive changes wrought by modernization, slavery became more firmly entrenched in the Boon's Lick than ever in its past. While in 1840 nearly 16,300 slaves labored in the central river counties, a decade later the region boasted 27,408 bondpeople—an increase of more than two-thirds—and by 1860, its 36,787 slaves represented a growth rate of more than 55 percent in two decades. This increase fueled the remarkable expansion of the slave population in Missouri, which itself grew by 97 percent during the final two antebellum decades. Ironically, slavery's expansion in Missouri ran counter to the trend of slave populations in the other border slave states—Kentucky, Virginia, Maryland, and Delaware—which grew moderately or actually decreased during those same years. Rather, with one signature exception, Missouri's and the Boon's Lick's explosion of slave numbers from 1840 to 1860 approximated and even exceeded that experienced in the Lower South states, where the population of slaves increased by more than 90 percent.[16]

Economics alone cannot explain the phenomenal expansion of slavery in Missouri's river counties during the period any more than for tobacco production. If anything, slavery's fortunes there proved inversely proportional to that of tobacco and unlike that of cotton in the Deep South states. While the 1840s were marked by great fluctuations of cotton prices—ranging from the crop's all-time lows of 4.9 and 4.7 cents per pound in 1842 and 1844, respectively, to a decade high of 12.2 cents per pound in the fall of 1849—the 1850s proved flush times for cotton planters. Sparked by the late-decade surge, demand for cotton—and subsequently the supply of it—reached an all-time high in 1860, nearly tripling over the previous two decades. The decade of the 1850s not only witnessed sustained price increases—cotton doubled in price in that decade alone and nearly every year was one of above-normal profits, often wildly so—but also the cotton boom encouraged an

16. Ira Berlin, *Slaves without Masters: The Free Negro in the Antebellum South*, 396–403.

accelerated and widespread settlement of the southwestern frontier, which by 1860 dominated the nation's cotton production and per capita slave owner-ship. Missouri's tobacco production witnessed no such sustained boom and appeared especially susceptible to national economic downturns. Between 1820 and 1860, with the exception of just three sharp and brief spikes (in 1837, 1850, and 1854, lasting two, one, and three years respectively and followed each time by precipitous drops), tobacco prices at New Orleans auction houses fetched consistently between four and eight cents per pound; Missouri planters routinely received no more than three cents—and as low as a penny and a half—even during the periods of high prices, prompting charges of price-fixing by local commission merchants. Increased produc-tion from western tobacco fields, heavy European duties, and recurring and protracted worldwide depressions contributed to an uneven, often lackluster tobacco market, hardly as encouraging to any potential owners of slaves in the Boon's Lick's tobacco culture as to those in Mississippi's and Louisiana's burgeoning cotton kingdoms.[17]

Yet slave numbers grew in the Boon's Lick and in broad sections of Missouri, seemingly apart from staple crop realities. Missouri's agriculture indeed expanded; by the 1850s Missourians demonstrated a hunger for cleared land that far exceeded that in any of the southwestern cotton states. During the final antebellum decade, Missouri farmers more than doubled the state's total cultivated acreage by bringing 3.3 million new acres under cultivation, a full 60 percent more than its nearest rival, Alabama, nearly double that of Mississippi, and well more than double that of Louisiana. Yet in their number and size, Missouri's farms more closely resembled those of the Northwest (now extended into the new states of Wisconsin and neighboring Iowa) than those in the Southwest. By 1860, its 64,216 individual farms (fourth highest in the slave states) boasted an average of just more than 97 cleared acres each (fifth lowest of those states), dwarfed by Louisiana's 156 cleared acres per plantation, smaller than in space-starved Maryland, and virtually equal to those in elfin Delaware.[18]

17. Robert W. Fogel, *Without Consent or Contract: The Rise and Fall of American Slavery,* 63–64, 69–70, 95–98; Gray, *History of Agriculture in the Southern United States,* vol. 2, 697, 765–69, 1027, 1037–38; Hurt, *Agriculture and Slavery in Little Dixie,* 91–93, 98. Tobacco inspectors estimated that negligence on the part of the planters, especially in packing, cost them 15 to 20 percent of the crop's value. Hurt estimates that planters routinely reduced their incomes by two dollars per hogshead, in addition to freight costs and commissions.

18. Joseph C. G. Kennedy, *Agriculture of the United States in 1860; Compiled from the Original Returns of the Eighth Census,* 88–95; Gray, *History of Agriculture in the Southern United States,* vol. 2, 708–9, 730, 751, 776; Hurt, *Agriculture and Slavery in Little Dixie,* 101, 110. Cultivated acreage increases in other southwestern cotton states, in millions of acres, were: Alabama, 2.03; Tennessee, 1.72; Mississippi, 1.71; Arkansas, 1.15; and Louisiana, 1.14.

More telling, Missouri's farmers devoted only a small portion of their newly cleared land to the production of any staple crops. The combined yields of all the staple crops planted in Missouri—tobacco, hemp, cotton, rice, and sugarcane—account at best for 125,000 acres, or just 1.9 percent of the state's 6.25 million cultivated acres. Even the 46.6 percent increase of acreage devoted to tobacco production from 1849 to 1859—from 17,114 to 25,086 acres—did not alter the minuscule percentage of Missouri's soil used for the cultivation of tobacco or any other staple crop. Of the slave states, only Maryland and Delaware devoted less acreage to staple crops than Missouri. By contrast, the southwestern states of Alabama, Mississippi, Texas, and neighboring Arkansas each devoted between 16 and 24 percent of its cultivated land to staple crops, while Louisiana put only slightly less than half of its 2.7 million acres of improved land into staple crop production, a whopping proportion that more than doubled that of any of the plantation states, eastern or western. By the 1850s, Missouri might have been a slaveholding western state, but its agricultural landscape—and thus labor needs—were decidedly unlike those of the states of the Southwest, whether Old or New.[19]

As a social good, slavery in Missourians' perception transcended any economic necessity. As a democratic institution, slavery conjoined rather than stratified the populace at large. No distinct rural-urban dichotomy with regard to slavery's spread followed the emergence of St. Louis, though the city did not share in the antebellum growth of slavery in Missouri. In 1830, slaves made up nearly one-fifth of the city's population, and as late as 1850, 2,656 slaves continued to labor for urban masters, only slightly less than two decades earlier. Only in 1860, after the massive influx of immigrants to St. Louis bloated the city's unskilled labor market as well as its overall population (now 160,773 strong), did the number of St. Louis's slaves fall precipitously. Its 1,572 slaves constituted just 1 percent of the city's overall population, numerically and proportionately the smallest of

19. Kennedy, *Agriculture of the United States in 1860*, 88–95, 207; Gray, *History of Agriculture in the Southern United States*, vol. 2, 708–9, 730, 751, 776; Hurt, *Agriculture and Slavery in Little Dixie*, 101, 110. I obtained my figures for acreage devoted to staple crops by dividing the total state output by the average yield per acre of the particular crop, assuming the lowest possible yield so as to figure the highest possible acreage. For example, in 1859 Missourians produced a total of 19,267 tons of hemp, with the average yield per acre being seven hundred pounds, hence a total of 55,049 acres. The actual total staple crop acreage in Missouri was 121,800, which I rounded up to 125,000 to account for any smaller yields per acre, the margin of error being 2.7 percent. Applying the same formula, the percentage of improved acres devoted to staple crops in the other slave states, in descending order, are: Louisiana, 49.5 percent; Mississippi, 23.8 percent; Arkansas, 19.1 percent; Texas, 16.9 percent; Alabama, 16.0 percent; Florida, 11.8 percent; Georgia, 11.1 percent; South Carolina, 10.2 percent; Tennessee, 5.1 percent; North Carolina, 3.0 percent; Kentucky, 2.9 percent; Virginia, 2.0 percent; Missouri, 1.9 percent; Maryland, 1.3 percent; and Delaware, 0.01 percent.

any major slave-state city.[20] Outside St. Louis, the political structure of the state reflected no broad elision with regard to slaveholding. If anything, political office in Missouri—the litmus of societal ordering—proved distinct from other slaveholding states in that regard, and nearly at all levels of government. At the county level, by 1850 nonslaveholding landowners dominated those lesser offices held traditionally by the lower gentry. In Pettis County prior to 1850, while nearly two-thirds of county court judges and sheriffs were slave owners, two of every three of the county's election judges were nonslaveholders. Nearly six in ten of Missouri's justices of the peace owned no bondpeople—as compared with but one-fourth in mother Kentucky—despite the fact that 80 percent were propertied farmers; Claib Jackson's brother, Wade, a justice in Howard County's Moniteau Township and the owner of nineteen slaves, was a decided exception. More surprising, no slaveholding elite emerged to dominate Missouri's legislature. Despite the state's increase in slave population, in 1850 Missouri's legislature again ran counter to all those in the slave states in that nonslaveholders held a majority of seats—just less than two-thirds—a stark contrast to Alabama and Mississippi, where three-fourths of the legislature owned slaves. In Missouri, slaveholding did not so much reflect the hegemony of any master class as it represented, as one historian has written of the Boon's Lick, "an equilibrium between the gentry and the people."[21]

Slavery's status as a social good in central Missouri was not a completely unconscious construct of community. For many residents, the institution symbolized democratic ascendance and offered both a vehicle for and a yardstick of material progress. For those who either engaged in the practice or sought to, slavery's expansion served as an expression of membership in the community as a whole, for the commonality of purpose, and provided an "ambit of comparison" for social identification. Even more than tobacco production, ownership of slaves offered a sign of inclusion in the culture their forebears had built and that they continued to perfect. Its proliferation beyond mere economic need affirmed the principle of free choice inherent in the western experience. Yet just as they employed slavery as a measure

20. Wade, *Slavery in the Cities,* 325–27.

21. D. Alan Williams, "The Small Farmer in Eighteenth-Century Virginia Politics," 98–99; Kulikoff, *Tobacco and Slaves,* 280–95; Fifth, Seventh, and Eighth U.S. Censuses, 1830, 1850–1860, Slave Schedules, Howard County [Missouri], NA, and St. Louis [Missouri], cited in Richard C. Wade, *Slavery in the Cities: The South, 1820–1860,* 327; Cassity, *Defending a Way of Life,* 24–25 (quote); Ralph A. Wooster, *People in Power: Courthouse and Statehouse in the Lower South, 1850–1860,* 54–55, 125, 143; Ralph A. Wooster, *Politicians, Planters and Plain Folk: Courthouse and Statehouse in the Upper South, 1850–1860,* 63, 114–17, 168; Robert M. Ireland, *The County Courts in Antebellum Kentucky,* 13; Oakes, *Ruling Race,* 144.

of sameness, so too did mid-Missourians erect slavery as a cultural boundary. Slavery as symbol masked the existence of diversity within Missouri's society, a sentient component of its people's deflection of the changes that modernization had imposed. However far a culture or community internalizes its icons, extrinsic threats to the occupancy of its social space propel those symbols to the forefront of its people's consciousness. Indeed, the Japanese citizenry evoked just such a social metaphor, in this case short-grain rice, a sacred symbol of purity and ancestry, during the late 1980s when the government considered importing cheaper and more plentiful—yet foreign—California rice (ironically, sown from stocks original to Japan). Though most of its residents have adopted other western foods and customs, a wide raft of Japanese people protested so vigorously and widely that such importations of "impure" rice posed a threat to social identity and autonomy that their government scrapped the plan. As one anthropologist has written, "if outsiders trespass in that [social] space, then its occupants' own sense of self is felt to be debased and defaced. This sense . . . depicted as under threat, . . . is a ready means of mobilizing collectivity." Rice both defined and confined the collective self, but only completely once a threat to that self had presented itself.[22]

A century and a half prior to the Japanese example, Missourians, too, conjured a full image of community only after an external threat had manifested itself toward one of its social constructs, in this case their supreme social good—slavery. Missourians, perhaps more than any other American people, denounced the discordant cant of abolitionism. As early as 1835, the president of the newly established Marion College near Palmyra lost his position and was run from the state for speaking out against slavery. The nation's first abolitionist martyr, the Reverend Elijah P. Lovejoy, proprietor of the *St. Louis Observer,* first suffered the lash of righteous Missourians in May 1836 after daring to criticize the mob lynching—in this case a burning—of a mulatto sailor accused of murder. Not only did the judge uphold the vigilantism on the grounds that Lovejoy's inflammatory, abolitionist editorials had provoked temporary insanity, but also the mob soon dumped Lovejoy's press in the Mississippi and threatened his and his family's lives, hastening their removal across the river to Alton, Illinois. Missouri's legislature responded to the incident by passing in February 1837, without one dissenting vote in the house, a stringent law prohibiting abolitionist activism under penalty of life imprisonment. Lovejoy's torment only continued in Alton, resulting in three more destroyed presses—one he was defending before being shot to death

22. Theodore Schwartz, "Cultural Totemism: Ethnic Identity, Primitive and Modern," 108 (first quote); Cohen, *Symbolic Construction of Community,* 70–75, 108, 109 (second quote); Emiko Ohnuki-Tierney, *Rice as Self,* 95–111.

in the fall by a mob led by current and former Missourians. While New Englanders memorialized Lovejoy in sermons and speeches (John Quincy Adams proclaimed the murder "a shock as of an earthquake throughout this continent") and both Wendell Phillips and John Brown dedicated their lives to the destruction of slavery in Lovejoy's honor, Missourians celebrated the event as democratic justice. Passions had in no way cooled by 1841 when, in his inaugural address, newly elected Governor Thomas Reynolds— a resident of Howard County—thundered against the abolitionists' "head long fury . . . [to] trample upon the rights of the slaveholding states and expose us to all the horrors of a servile war," declaring that Missourians would be "wanting in self-respect . . . were we to suffer the least interference with this delicate question, from any quarter."[23]

As a result, Missourians' intolerance of abolitionists and the infernal doctrines in their midst had deep root. In reality, Missouri's crusade against antislavery derived from factors far more complex than any perceived internal threat to the peculiar institution. The state itself was the first born amid the gathering national storm over the institution of slavery. Its statehood petition opened a gaping wound in the national psyche and the resulting controversy forced Missourians to exist perpetually under a sword of Damocles with regard to slavery. As the northernmost and westernmost slave state (at least until the admission of Texas in 1845), for nearly two full decades Missouri drew unobstructed the nation's eye as its people gazed westward in contemplation of their own destiny. When Missourians celebrated the transition from the Jeffersonian to the Jacksonian era as a triumph of egalitarian assumptions, they did so in part as a vindication of the deeply recollected pain suffered during their own natal struggle.[24]

The controversy surrounding Missouri's entrance to the Union did not deliver a precise volley into the state's proslavery ranks so much as it signaled the completion of sectional alignment in the original seaboard states along slavery lines. Between 1790 and 1820, the middle western states—Kentucky, Tennessee, Ohio, Indiana, and Illinois—each engaged in local debates over slavery whenever Congress wrangled over constitutional issues. The additions of the southwestern states of Alabama and Mississippi honed an edge to "the Missouri question" in their support of western rights to property, but did not in themselves create a slave state phalanx. People in the slaveholding

---

23. McCandless, *History of Missouri*, 61–63; Nagel, *Missouri*, 93; Louis Filler, *The Crusade against Slavery, 1830–1860*, 78–79, 80–81 (first quote, p. 81); Merton L. Dillon, *The Abolitionists: The Growth of a Dissenting Minority*, 93–98; Benjamin Merkel, "Abolition Aspects of Missouri's Antislavery Controversy 1819–1865," 240, 242–46. Reynolds's speech is quoted in *Missouri House Journal*, 11th General Assembly, 1st Sess., 1841, 30 (second and third quotes).

24. William W. Freehling, *The Road to Disunion: Secessionists at Bay*, 144–61.

states had not yet become an alert sectional minority, they were not yet southerners in a politically conscious sense. Only the shock to the systems of these Christian sons and daughters of the Revolution delivered by the abolitionists' moral attacks completed their complex process of identification. For Missourians, however, the abolitionist assault was more an unpleasantry for which they, even more than residents of the other western states and certainly more than South Carolinians, were not unprepared. Their response to New Yorkers such as James Tallmadge, who sought to block slavery's extension into Missouri during the debate over statehood, was well schooled and personal, not the distant indignation of a courtly cotton planter. While sensitive to attacks on slavery, Missourians would not be moved by them, for they had already developed an identity—however imperfect—not just as westerners, but as far westerners, and in 1835 they were far from being ready for a dramatic reappraisal of themselves along one or more sectional lines onto which they did not perfectly fit. In two decades, that reluctance would subside, but not yet.[25]

Missourians' virtually immediate and wholly violent response to abolitionism did not stem from any southern exposure. Rather, their clarion was a growing fear of the too-rapidly advancing nation, and of the changes being wrought in the Middle West—a region of which they were yet a part. As late as 1835, an Illinoisan could write to his Missouri acquaintance that "it is a fact that people in upper Missouri Live too far out of the world." By the 1840s, to many rural Missourians' great discomfort, that world had grown much smaller, and their social good now caused these residents to believe themselves ever more vulnerable to the outside world's approaching tempests. For Missouri was a slaveholding island in a democratic sea of free labor, the most exposed of the slave hinterlands. The state jutted into the New Northwest so completely that more than eight-tenths of its land space lay north of the Ohio River's mouth, shielded from the slave states in 200 of its 320-odd longitudinal miles by the free state of Illinois, a fact not lost on Congress when it demarcated the southern, not the northern, boundary of Missouri as the Far West's Mason-Dixon line. Consequently, Missouri was the only slave state to have a free-labor neighbor to the east, and it had an uninhabited frontier to the west.[26]

Perhaps more important, with the entrance of Arkansas and Iowa in 1836 and 1846, respectively, Missouri faced the anomaly of being the only state in the Union bordering both a free state and a slave state with no natural boundary—such as a river—between either of them, rendering the line all

25. Tise, *Proslavery*, 55–57.
26. James Gilbert to M. M. Marmaduke, October 18, 1835, Sappington Family Papers, box 2, MHS (quote).

the more artificial, even preternatural, in its people's eyes. That all but one of Missouri's largest slaveholding counties lay north of St. Louis in 1850—a decade later, all of them were north of the city—only made more glaring the state's seeming geographic incongruity with regard to slavery. The nation's westward march had forced Missouri onto a now uncomfortable middle ground, and as the New West grew nearly to surround them, assuming the sectional aspects of the nation's economy as well as its people, Missourians found themselves living firmly astride a fault line.[27]

The geographic discomfiture that Missourians found themselves in could have arisen only with the accompaniment of a changing demographic, and thus ideological, landscape of the West from which Missourians once drew comfort. Though their neighboring westerners had embraced the institution of slavery, whether practiced or not, as part of a middle heritage, by the 1840s a decided alteration had occurred that rendered the peculiar institution unacceptable to large segments of the population of the Old Northwest. While the first migrants who had populated the southern portions of the states above the Ohio had accepted slavery as part of the natural order, a second stream of immigration from New York and the New England states into the northern parts of those states had changed the complexion of their people and the tenor of their politics. By 1848, so many of these Yankees had settled in northern and central Illinois that the state replaced the provision in its original 1818 constitution that prescribed the county as the state's sole local administrative agency in order to accommodate the Puritan governmental archetype, the township. One Indianan summed up the new dialecticism of the Old Northwest when he stated that in his state, "we have various phases of public opinion; the enterprising Yankee of Northern Indiana, despises the sluggish and inaminate [*sic*] North Carolinian, Virginian, and Kentuckian in the southern part of the State." Indeed, as the northern residents of the Old Northwest increasingly became enamored of the free labor ideology, transforming themselves at once into antislavery and anti–free black advocates in the pursuit of a homeland where "all men are created equal—except niggers," their prejudices moved them increasingly to see the entire West as a place where the dream of a white man's country—meaning free of both free blacks and slaves—could be realized. Democracy, the western catholicon, revealed deep fissures.[28]

Missourians recognized implicitly that democracy was a two-edged sword

27. Hurt, *Agriculture and Slavery in Little Dixie*, 220; Freehling, *Road to Disunion*, 538.

28. Howard, *Illinois*, 255–56, 260; J. Herman Schauinger, ed., "The Letters of Godlove S. Orth: Hoosier Whig," 367 (first quote); Eugene H. Berwanger, *The Frontier against Slavery: Western Anti-Negro Prejudice and the Slavery Extension Controversy*, 47 (second quote) and passim.

and ultimately could hurt as much as it could help slavery's existence in the decentralized West. As free-labor ideologues in the Old Northwest began condemning the slaveholders' democratic vision, glorifying the progressivism of northern labor with the inherently anti-wealth slogan "free soil, free speech, free labor, free men" and decrying the existence of slavery in Missouri and other portions of the free West, Missourians bristled at the clearly sharp divergence of democratic notions in their once-pastoral region. While the Jacksonian creed had held that democracy entitled all laborers to social advancement regardless of avenue, free-labor adherents now evinced a pronounced intolerance of any such progress when achieved through the use of slave labor. Employing pejorative terms such as "Mulatto Democracy" and "black democracy," these New Northwestern critics pointed out the intrinsic incompatibility of slave labor with a truly modern society, characterizing slave society as stagnant, degraded, reactionary, and inefficient while positing free-labor society as dignified, industrious, egalitarian, and above all else, progressive. They tarred Missourians with the same brush they used to condemn the Missouri Compromise, once "canonized in the hearts of the American people," for allowing slavery to cross the Mississippi, invoking the same utopian principles that the state's Jacksonians had once used in celebration of the creation of their West.[29]

The cognizance of these antagonistic visions for the present and future of the West moved Missourians to action. The free West that they had claimed for liberty and for themselves was being threatened by outsiders once distant and now in their midst, interlopers in Eden. Sterling Price, soon to be governor, likened these antislavery invaders to the Germans in St. Louis; they were "exceptions to the law abiding and dutiful citizens, and doubtless to their phrenzied [*sic*] zeal, may be justly attributed the presumptuous liberties which even *Foreigners* themselves, felt sometimes disposed to take." Price's language—and his allusion—were carefully chosen. Though distinct, Missouri was no island, for the antislavery transformation of the upper middle western states was under way as well in much of the state, and outside of St. Louis. During the 1850s, the number of Missouri residents from the northeastern states increased by more than 200 percent, and when coupled with the German immigration and the influx of Mormons to the state, those immigrants born in non-slave states outnumbered those from states where slavery was sustained. By 1860, Missouri's 160,541 foreign-born residents (a subpopulation that had increased by nearly 110 percent over the past decade) doubled those in the nearest slave state rival, Louisiana, and dwarfed those 3,298 foreigners in North Carolina. When coupled with

29. Foner, *Free Soil, Free Labor, Free Men,* 18–23 (first quote), 40–72, 89, 92–94, 95 (fourth quote); Berwanger, *Frontier against Slavery,* 131 (second and third quotes).

the 155,540 northern-born Missourians in that year, nearly three of ten in the state hailed from places the self-styled native Missourians increasingly considered not only alien, but hostile.[30]

Such immigration triggered alarm in part because the patterns of settlement and spatial arrangements that the invaders brought to Missouri proved distinct from those of the state's early years and wholly unlike those of the other slave states. In 1860, for census enumeration, Missouri organized itself into a full 728 towns, cities, townships, and districts, a figure seven times that of its nearest competitor, Virginia, and which constituted 62 percent of the slave states' total and represented more than one and one-half times that of all those other states combined. The small-town nature of Missouri far more closely reflected that of Illinois and Indiana—which in 1860 boasted 934 and 1,017 towns and cities, respectively—than Kentucky or Georgia (with 63 and 36, respectively), much less for Tennessee, South Carolina, and Alabama, with either 16 or 15 each. This community construction was more than clerical. While not all Missourians ascribed to these various districts actually lived within the physical boundaries of these towns, they still affiliated with the towns nearest their farms; those such as the Sappingtons and Marmadukes were clearly country-dwellers, but considered themselves residents of the Arrow Rock township, just as Claib Jackson lived a full two miles from Fayette yet considered himself a resident of that town. Consequently, nearly 90 percent of Missouri's entire population affiliated themselves with these small towns and cities, as compared with just a third of both Maryland's and Louisiana's populations and in stark contrast with the 3 percent of Mississippians and Arkansans who dwelled in such towns. Missourians' sense of self included the capacity for self-delusion. Just as they trumpeted the rugged individualism of their region and their lives, they had organized themselves around the model of those they now began to resist.[31]

Thus the changes wrought in the region as a whole were not merely external, they were also from within. William B. Napton, a rural Missourian who proved a keen observer of his state's town-country dichotomy, noted that "the little towns and villages scattered throughout the country opposed to the mass of the country people—it is here the little politicians and would-be great men of the day congregate, here the newspapers are taken and read, party schemes are hatched and all the tactics of party warfare put into complete operation." Coupling the changing community landscape with

30. Sterling Price to Josiah Foster et al., November 22, 1853, in *Jefferson Inquirer,* December 3, 1853 (quote); Steven C. Rowan and James Neal Primm, eds., *Germans for a Free Missouri: Translations from the St. Louis Radical Press, 1857–1862,* passim; Nagel, *Missouri,* 100; Kennedy, *Population of the United States in 1860,* 301; DeBow, ed., *Seventh Census of the United States: 1850,* 663.

31. Kennedy, *Population of the United States in 1860,* 288–98.

the antislavery Germans' and Yankees' advocacy of a "free Missouri," many Missourians perceived a massive threat to their way of life. Napton was clearly alarmed at the geographic inroads that antislavery had made into Missouri: "[T]hat little band of Yankee abolitionists & German radicals have gotten possession of St. Louis & have made the place as thoroughly hostile to slavery as Chicago. From St. Louis the idea has crept up & down the rivers—has found location in the river towns—& gradually & slowly pervaded to a slight extent into the country."[32]

Rather than focus upon the towns that were so much a part of their lives, however, rural Missourians began their onslaught against these internal menaces not by seeking out those who were avowedly antislavery, but by waging war upon those completely peripheral to the issues at stake: the state's Mormons. As early as the winter of 1830–1831, a small group of Saints had settled in Jackson County, on the western edge of the Boon's Lick, but their unconventional religious beliefs, theocratic rule, and church-funded acquisition of land did not provoke any notable response for more than two years. And while their northern heritage and ambiguous views on slavery heightened the perception of these newcomers as foreign, they did not generate any immediate antipathy among the Boon's Lickers. Rather, the "gathering" of the Saints, who numbered ultimately as many as ten thousand, and their potential economic and political dominance of the region aroused the passions of the natives. One "gentile" Missourian declared, "if we do not make them [leave the state] now . . . they will be so strong in a few years that they will rule the country as they please." Democracy that threatened to consume both itself and its architects moved Missourians to action.[33]

In the summer of 1833, after the Mormon newspaper *Evening and Morning Star* published what locals interpreted as an intention to lead an uprising of Indians to eliminate the non-Mormon population and an encouragement for free black emigration, Jackson Countians began assaulting their three thousand Mormon neighbors, forcing their withdrawal to the new and sparsely populated counties in the northwestern portion of the state. In August 1838, when local Saints engaged in an election-day fracas in Daviess County to protest their being barred from the polls, the new climate of fear propelled central and western Missourians into a renewal of extralegal violence against their Mormon neighbors. When the beleaguered Saints lashed out against vigilante "house-burnings, field-wastings, insults, whippings, [and] murders," they triggered an unprecedented response from

32. Napton Diary, folder 1, p. 46, MHS (first quote); Rowan and Primm, eds., *Germans for a Free Missouri* (first quote); William B. Napton to C. F. Jackson, October 3, 1857, Miscellaneous Manuscripts, Mss. 1879, SHSM (second quote).

33. Stephen C. LeSueur, *The 1838 Mormon War in Missouri*, 2–3, 245–55 (quotes) and passim.

the state governor, Lilburn Boggs, who rashly ordered out the state militia to attack the Mormons, who "must be exterminated or driven from the state if necessary for the public peace." Ironically, only the militia commanders' refusal to comply fully with Boggs's "exterminating order" (they believed that such actions would "disgrace the State . . . by acting the part of a mob") prevented genocide. The militia did, however, force the surrender of the belligerent Saints, then coerced them to sign away their land and drove them east to Illinois, a fitting end for those who attempted to bring change to the Old West.[34]

Thus, when abolitionist voices began attacking slavery as a national evil, referring to the slave states as "ONE GREAT SODOM," they struck a raw nerve among Missourians who might have understood such condemnations but were anything but desensitized to them and who by now silently feared as much as they publicly heralded the ascension of democratic principles. The democratic promise of the West now revealed itself to Missourians to be as threatening as it was comforting. The concept of individual freedom they had come to associate instinctively with their region—and of which slavery was an essential part—they now found themselves forced to defend. The sense of self they once derived from their unfettered liberties in the West now became a point of vulnerability, the patrimony that Missourians traditionally assumed now hung in balance not from anything they had done, but from that which they concluded had been done to them. These Missourians had not changed, or so they believed; rather, the latecomers in the northern portion of their region were now using the Missourians' social good, slavery, as a shibboleth in their attempt to re-create the social landscape of the entire Far West—a region that these intruders had not created so much as inherited from its first pioneers. The real creators would now exert with increasing vigilance their proprietary right. Democracy—indeed, the West— had reached a crossroads.[35]

In his efforts to legitimize the culture he believed he understood amid the expansion of a nation he did not, Claiborne Fox Jackson would offer a light to Missourians who too approached the West's Scylla. Yet in resisting the agencies that threatened to founder the Missouri he once knew, Jackson actually swept his state toward the Charybdis its people struggled in vain to avoid.

34. Ibid., 6–7 and passim; Parrish, *David Rice Atchison*, 17–28; McCandless, *History of Missouri*, 105–11; Shalhope, *Sterling Price*, 26–28; *Document in relation to the disturbance with the Mormons*, 48–49 (first quote), 50–63, 75–77; John P. Greene, *Facts Relative to the Expulsion of the Mormons or Latter Day Saints, from the State of Missouri, under the "Exterminating Order*," i (second quote), iv–v (third quote).

35. Berwanger, *Frontier against Slavery*, 131; Cohen, *Symbolic Construction of Community*, 109; Walton, *Western Times and Water Wars*, 333–35.

THE WIRE-PULLER

I LIKE [JACKSON] yet personally—But he is politically everlastingly making bargains.
BENJAMIN F. MASSEY TO JOHN F. SNYDER, SEPTEMBER 6, 1859

For two years, Claib Jackson had been honing his axe, preparing for his reentry into Missouri's political forest. Embarrassed by his sudden fall from grace as director of the Fayette Bank in 1840, he was not so much licking his wounds as readying himself for an inevitable return to public life. The landscape looked inviting. With fellow Boon's Lickers in office—Thomas Reynolds now governor, brother-in-law Meredith M. Marmaduke the lieutenant governor, John C. Edwards and John Miller in Congress, Owen Rawlins and Dr. William Penn in the state senate, and Sterling Price and Wade Jackson, Claib's brother, in the Missouri house—the "Democracy of Boons Lick" still maintained a formidable presence in state politics. Yet for five years, and especially for the last two, Jackson had been an outsider. His place on the state's Democratic central committee had provided a partial return to the fold and thus some comfort, but mere stewardship was not enough to satiate his driving ambition. His election to the house in the fall of 1842—complete with three dollars per diem and twelve cents per mile for traveling the 130-mile round trip between Fayette and Jefferson City—now offered him more than mere restoration. Jackson sought vindication, not only for his own actions as bank director but also for his party's actions in response to the Panic of 1837, especially after the Whigs' bitter denunciations had allowed the rival party to make inroads into Missouri politics and ousted Jackson from his position at the bank. Most important, he sought redemption from the obviously divergent course that outsiders, whether Whigs, liberal Democrats, Germans, Irish, Mormons, Yankees, abolitionists, or St. Louisans, were causing his state to take. The path they pursued differed greatly from what the state's founders—of which Jackson considered himself one—had intended for not only Missouri but also the entire West.[1]

1. Shalhope, *Sterling Price*, 31–33; Thomas Reynolds to Meredith M. Marmaduke, April 12, 1841, Sappington Family Papers, box 3, MHS (quote); House Accounts: J, Capitol Fire Documents, 1806–1957, microfilm reel CFD-115, folder 10440: Twelfth General Assembly (1842–1843), MSA; C. F. Jackson to John Sappington, August 13, 1842, private collection, cited in Burks, "Thunder on the Right," 151*n28,* and 153–54.

When Claib Jackson entered the Twelfth General Assembly in late November 1842, he did so as a Benton stalwart. He had in part built his reputation upon the broad shoulders of "Old Bullion," the nickname that the senator had received for his obdurate support of hard-money policies. In August 1842, as the election drew near, Benton campaigned for the "Fayette junto," as one St. Louis newspaper labeled the Clique and its candidates, reminding listeners in Jefferson City of his place as paladin of conservatism during his crusade against the National Bank. "I began the war against this Bank," Benton trumpeted, "almost *'solitary and alone'* . . . and have lived to see the institution in dust and infamy." Jackson's resolute advocacy of "hard" policy established during his previous term in the house and as Fayette Bank cashier, only reaffirmed during his recent campaign, had crystallized his conservative agenda on behalf of those who had reelected him to the state legislature as a Benton disciple. He set upon Jefferson City with an avowed purpose now incumbent upon him, and the members of the house itself—with a Democratic majority and Hard plurality, despite the Soft/Whig successes of the past few years—appear to have recognized the depth of Jackson's resolve as well as his organizational ability. After the delegation selected fellow Boon's Licker Sterling Price as house speaker, held over from the previous session, the Clique maneuvered the Hards into voting in caucus for Jackson as majority floor leader and parliamentarian, an important position that had practical political implications. Nearly overnight, the outsider had moved nearly as far within the legislative machinery as possible.[2]

While the charismatic Price served as figurehead, Jackson as floor leader was the faction's tactician, setting the agenda for the Hards during the session. Armed with Benton's political capital and a mandate from the Hard majority, Jackson drew down on those Softs and Whigs (more the former than the latter, especially now that the entire St. Louis delegation were "soft" Democrats) who had embarrassed him by unceremoniously removing him from the Fayette Bank. Still smarting, he wasted no energy obscuring either his targets or his motives. Indeed, he had no need to do so, for the issues that he confronted upon his return to the house offered him ample opportunity to wage a personal war with his enemies with impunity, carried out in the name of both the party and the public trust. The debate over state banking and currency reform that he had entered into in his first brief legislative tenure had not been resolved—if anything, it had only grown more divisive during the five-year-long chill of hard times that had peaked in 1842. Jackson now

2. William Nisbet Chambers, *Old Bullion Benton: Senator from the New West*, 202, 261 (quote); Shalhope, *Sterling Price*, 37–40; Burks, "Thunder on the Right," 153–54; *Boon's Lick Times*, September 7, 1842.

hunted the proverbial two birds, relishing the chance to finish that which he once started as well as to defeat those whom he now despised.[3]

By the outset of the session, Jackson had already conceived a two-pronged plan of attack. As expected, he would first turn his attention to the issues of banking and currency, culling support for Hard candidates for the directorships of both the Fayette and St. Louis Banks and pushing currency legislation that would drive all extraneous paper money out of Missouri. Jackson then would take aim on redistricting, intent upon rescinding the law that had complicated the hegemony of the "Fayette junto" as well as his own recent election to the house. By targeting the directorship and policies of the state banks, Jackson underscored what he and other Hards considered the most fruitful approach to resolving the state's most vexing political issue, namely the currency issue (more directly, Jackson sought to correct in his opinion its most glaring error). Yet the resolution of the issue revealed the depth and breadth of the chasm that now marred the state's once-consonant Democratic political and ideological vista. With Jackson at the helm, the Hards' struggle for mastery over the Soft/Whig coalition would dominate the ensuing session of the legislature.[4]

In keeping with his plan of attack, Jackson fired his first salvo at the St. Louis Bank, under Soft control. Jackson's cannon was neither loose nor errant; prior to the session, Governor Reynolds had appointed a special commission to investigate the bank's decision to accept depreciated currency in violation of state law. Moreover, because state law prescribed that the next house election of bank officers would occur on December 5, Jackson etched the date in his mind as he planned Hard strategy with Clique confederates. With impeccably calculated timing, just three days before the scheduled election, Jackson introduced into the house a bill that aimed to discredit the leadership of the bank (especially one its directors, Ferdinand Kennett, currently a Soft candidate for bank president) as well as to curtail its power and autonomy within the state's banking system. Jackson sought to capitalize on the controversy by exposing the loose business practices of the bank, thus swinging public opinion toward Hard policy as well as shoring up the candidacy of Clique member Dr. George Penn for bank president. Jackson's resolutions called for a detailed report from the bank's cashier regarding the acceptance of Illinois currency, including the amount taken in, the losses suffered as a result of the paper's depreciation, the amount due to state depositors and not paid as a result of the depreciation, and the business

3. Shalhope, *Sterling Price*, 39; McCandless, *History of Missouri*, 229.
4. Chambers, *Old Bullion Benton*, 260 (quote); C. F. Jackson to W. B. Sappington, November 23, 1842, cited in Burks, "Thunder on the Right," 154–55.

agreements between the St. Louis Bank and the Bank of Illinois that might have influenced the directors' decision to accept the currency.[5]

Jackson's gambit forced the Softs to scramble for a response. Shadrach Penn, a Louisville, Kentucky, editor (who had recently relocated to St. Louis after purchasing the *St. Louis Argus,* now renamed the *Missouri Reporter* and the state's most prominent Soft organ), quickly initiated a vitriolic smear campaign against the Hards' bank war, targeting Benton and the group he now referred to as the "Central Clique" as purveyors of anachronistic economic policies and Jackson as their principal antagonist in the state itself. Penn's charges of "Centralism"—his code word for the Clique's dominance of state politics—soon echoed in other newspapers throughout the state, emplacing both terms in the public lexicon and focusing attention on Jackson, the architect of the currency bill, as "being chained to Colonel Benton's car and subject to his direction." Nearly half of the state's Democratic papers soon opposed Jackson's bill, as well as its author, especially in the areas outlying the Boon's Lick. The bitter attacks on Jackson prompted the Democratic editors in the region to come to his defense, claiming the Fayettan to be one "of our friends in the Center," and decrying his having "been bitterly assailed for his course in the election of a president of the bank." No longer a freshman legislator, Jackson had stepped from the shadows and quickly found the light white-hot.[6]

As the Soft press identified and vilified Jackson, house Softs quickly parried his thrust at the bank director. Objecting strenuously not only to the prospect of a Hard but also of a Boon's Licker as leader of the St. Louis Bank, Thomas B. Hudson, a prominent St. Louis Soft and able foe, countered Jackson's undisguised effort to manipulate the upcoming election by amending the scope of the bank resolutions to include the Fayette branch. Moreover, Hudson maneuvered the Softs into a steadfast refusal to caucus with the Hards in order to align party support for a candidate for the upcoming elections, wary of the Clique's prowess in such a venue. Hudson preferred the open floor for Kennett's candidacy, where he could bring to bear Whig votes. On the day of the election, after a last-minute resolution orchestrated by Jackson failed to postpone the vote until after the house had received the report of the bank's cashier, the Hards recognized the strength of their

---

5. *Missouri House Journal,* Twelfth Gen. Ass., 1842–1843, 88–89; Shalhope, *Sterling Price,* 38–39; Burks, "Thunder on the Right," 154–57.

6. Chambers, *Old Bullion Benton,* 260–61; *Missouri Reporter,* November 1, 1842; *Columbia* [Missouri] *Patriot,* June 17, 1842 (first quote); *Jefferson Inquirer,* February 16, 1843 (second, third, fourth, and fifth quotes); Shalhope, *Sterling Price,* 35–37, 41; Burks, "Thunder on the Right," 168–70. Also opposing Jackson's bill were the *St. Louis Argus,* the *Ozark Eagle,* the *Liberty Banner,* the *Grand River Chronicle,* and the *Missouri Register,* among others.

opposition and that Penn's candidacy would fail. As a way of saving face for the Clique and for Penn, the Hards threw their support at the last minute to Robert Campbell of St. Louis, who lost to Kennett 91–38. Though the Hards had lost their first battle under Jackson's leadership, the Soft/Whig victory was not complete; the Hards maintained complete control of the Fayette Bank, including the reelection of Clique member John J. Lowry as president and the election of Wade Jackson, Claib's brother, as one of its directors.[7]

Jackson recognized that the implications of the defeat he and the Hards had suffered in the bank election could potentially cast a wide net. Though the investigation of the St. Louis Bank might yet offer some leverage in the fight for the party direction, Jackson no longer believed that avenue of approach to be fruitful. Less than a week after the election, he offered to withdraw his resolutions against the bank management. The new president refused, insisting that "the hand be played out." He and the Softs now counterattacked, initiating a series of mirror resolutions that challenged the Fayette Bank's management, effectively tarring its directors with the same brush that Jackson had wielded so heavy-handedly just days before. Implicating Lowry and Jackson directly, the resolutions called for disclosure of paper currency that the Fayette Bank accepted and loaned, and then questioned expenditures for construction of the bank building and even impugned the work ethic of its directors, charging that Jackson while cashier had on occasion closed the bank for business to attend horse races. Infuriated, Jackson pressed on with his original resolutions, and subsequent investigations revealed what he had charged all along: from 1838 to 1842 the St. Louis Bank had sustained losses of more than sixty-one thousand dollars, far exceeding those of the Fayette Bank, while the latter had actually returned anywhere from a 6 to a 12 percent profit. Though no evidence came to light that proved any malfeasance, the figures alone more than implicated the previous St. Louis administrators for poor management. Thus Claib Jackson's rendition of the "bank war"—as well as his own tenure as Fayette cashier—had received full vindication.[8]

Yet the banking report left the majority floor leader anything but appeased. His bank war strategy had two fronts, and he had not yet ordered his troops to join battle on the second. After a brief Christmas respite, in February 1843 Jackson introduced a bill in the house that he had personally driven

7. *Missouri House Journal,* Twelfth Gen. Ass., 1842–1843, 92–94, 100–102, 111–16, 125–28; *Boon's Lick Times,* December 17, 1842; *Jefferson Inquirer,* December 29, 1842; Burks, "Thunder on the Right," 157–59; Shalhope, *Sterling Price,* 38–39; McCandless, *History of Missouri,* 229.

8. *Missouri House Journal,* Twelfth Gen. Ass., First Sess., 1842–1843, 114, 750–52; *Boon's Lick Times,* December 17, 1842 (quote); Burks, "Thunder on the Right," 159–61; West, "Earlier Political Career of Jackson," 47–49.

through the Select Committee on Currency and Banking. The bill cobbled together four separate bills that various legislators had introduced during previous sessions and that were aimed collectively at currency reform. Jackson's "Currency Bill" combined and adjusted the previous bills into an acceptable compromise package that, above all else, severely regulated the circulation of paper currency. Jackson's bill rendered illegal the passage or acceptance of such currency less than ten dollars by any public or private corporation, moneylender, or exchange broker. Moreover, Jackson's bill declared that these bodies should not circulate any suspended or non-specie-paying bank notes, nor should any corporation exercise any banking function (such as issuing or discounting notes and receiving deposits in paper), reserving that right exclusively for the Bank of Missouri. As a significant revision of the previous bills, Jackson's currency bill refrained from making it unlawful for individual citizens to circulate such currency, consistent with the Democratic platform that the last five fractious years had nearly obscured. Instead, the bill assessed heavy penalties—from $250 to $1,000—on those corporate bodies and individuals who might profit from the exchange of currency, "shinplaster" or otherwise.[9]

Following so closely on the heels of the battle over the bank, Jackson's bill proved immediately controversial. Softs immediately labeled it the bill of "Pains and Penalties," and took aim at the restrictive nature of the legislation, decrying the unavoidably deleterious effects that such drastic measures would have on businesses—and thus individuals—in the state. Yet Jackson the Democrat had crafted his bill skillfully, targeting those bodies outside the party's political umbra and thus least defensible. The debate on the bill raged in the house for more than a month as the majority leader maneuvered the Democrats adroitly (with consistent Clique backing) against stiff and repeated challenges, this time more from Whigs than from Softs, who could not so easily ignore the implications of their defection from such a clear party-line bill. To shore up party adherence, Jackson applied to "Old Bullion," who mentioned publicly his support for "a most excellent bill." The efforts paid off handsomely; the house approved the bill 53–40, and the senate in turn passed it on the first ballot without a recorded vote. Jackson had won his first complete victory as floor leader; moreover, his legislative peers had passed into law the first bill he had sponsored.[10]

---

9. *Missouri House Journal*, 11th General Assembly, First Sess., 1840–1841, 400–438; *Missouri House Journal*, Twelfth Gen. Ass., First Sess., 1842–1843, 134–43; *Missouri Register*, April 9, 1844; Burks, "Thunder on the Right," 161–65; West, "Earlier Political Career of Jackson," 49–52; *Jefferson Inquirer*, February 9, 1843; C. F. Jackson to Thomas Reynolds, March 12, 1843, Thomas Reynolds Papers, MHS (quote).

10. McCandless, *History of Missouri*, 229 (first quote); *Missouri House Journal*, Twelfth Gen. Ass., First Sess., 1842–1843, 437, 469–71, 530–33; *Missouri Senate Journal*, 12th

Jackson's currency victory had gained far more for his own prestige and for his party than any election of bank officers or fiscal investigations had ever stood to achieve. He not only had demonstrated the ability to initiate and complete a piece of legislation, thus earning him the reputation of a finisher, but also had succeeded as party chieftain in aligning the polarized Democratic factions enough to face down opposition to a controversial bill. By severing the Gordian knot, Jackson had established himself as a leader in more than name, no mere parliamentarian but a skilled orator with an indefatigable public presence. In this, Jackson proved an effective complement to House Speaker Sterling Price, who lacked oratorical skills but whose acumen in backroom politics brought those recalcitrant legislators into line that Jackson was unable to manage on the floor. Yet unlike the charismatic Price, Jackson's confrontational style and doctrinaire conservatism made him a lightning rod for criticism if not outright enmity and entrenched factional divisions both in the party and in the house as a whole. The pressure he exerted in pursuit of currency and banking reforms and the polarization that resulted only foreshadowed his relentless drive for further conservative reform as well as the deepening political divisions that would cloud Missouri's horizon for decades to come.[11]

Jackson used his currency triumph as a signal to renew another old fight, this one against redistricting. The coming storm was no surprise; he had sounded his call in December 1842, claiming that his Boon's Lick constituents had elected him specifically to oppose congressional redistricting, which would rob the region of its political dominance. The reapportionment issue proved divisive largely because of the growth of Missouri's population, especially in St. Louis. The state's constitution limited the number of house seats to one hundred, with at least one representative from each of the state's counties. When the General Assembly increased the number of counties to seventy-seven in 1841 (and then again to ninety-six in 1845, largely by adding counties in the northwestern portion of the state), keeping intact the provision for at least one representative from each county without increasing the number of seats overall, the rural counties maintained the preponderance of power while the more populous counties such as St. Louis screamed for reapportionment.[12]

General Assembly, First Sess., 1842–1843, 414; *Boon's Lick Times,* December 30, 1843 (second quote); Burks, "Thunder on the Right," 161–66; West, "Earlier Political Career of Jackson," 49–54.

11. Shalhope, *Sterling Price,* 39.

12. William E. Parrish, Charles T. Jones, and Lawrence O. Christensen, *Missouri: The Heart of the Nation,* 98–99; *Boon's Lick Times,* December 10, 1842; Bradford, "Missouri Constitutional Controversy of 1845," 35–37; *Missouri House Journal,* Twelfth Gen. Ass., First Sess., 1842–1843, 334.

Throughout the winter Jackson consistently coordinated delaying tactics against bills proffered on behalf of redistricting. In a dramatic move, on January 24, 1843, Jackson and fifteen other Hard Democrats—the core of the Boon's Lick conservatives—absented themselves on the day scheduled for a vote for the enabling act for a constitutional convention, which would conjoin with the redistricting issue to rob Howard and the Boon's Lick of representatives and thus political power. Jackson's dubious act of protest— he knew he would lose—as well as his fight were blatantly partisan. The traditional alignments of power no longer reflected the reality of who these Missourians now were, whether in their residence or their heritage. Jackson was well aware of his state's population shift, and his fear of Missouri's changing character moved him both to an unmasked protestation against a new constitution (he publicly tied his opposition to banking reform, arguing weakly that a new constitution would allow the Softs to replace the banking restrictions recently emplaced) and then to a vigorous opposition to the popular issue of redistricting rather than witness the certain loss of his home region's political and social hegemony. While the state might have changed, the issue—and Jackson's motivations—had not; as redistricting's inevitability had grown more pronounced, its opponents had only become more obvious, and more desperate.[13]

Though marshaling virtually the same supporters as he had for his fight for currency reform, Jackson employed a somewhat different strategy against redistricting. Instead of initiating a bill to overturn current legislation, the Hards used their influence to oppose a senate bill introduced into the house on February 22, 1843. The bill created five congressional districts (equal to its allotted seats) spread uniformly throughout the state, and appeared popular enough for the *Boon's Lick Times* to report that a majority of as many as twelve to fifteen house members were in favor of it at the beginning of the session. The current at-large system, whereby all voters statewide cast ballots for each congressional seat—thus allowing the Clique to dominate such elections because of its ability to control nominations—was in jeopardy. Jackson, with plenty of warning with which to fashion his plan of attack, attached to the bill an amendment in the form of a rider that would call for the election of congressmen by general ticket, rather than by district, thus effectively establishing districts but not implementing them for voting purposes. The editor of the *Times* held that Jackson used "every known device of persuasion, and apparently some that are known only to him" to effect a 58–30 passage of the bill with the rider attached. The effort managed to achieve what Jackson had intended; the senate promptly rejected the rider, and when the reamended bill returned to the house floor, House

---

13. Burks, "Thunder on the Right," 171–73; *Missouri Register,* October 17, 1843.

Speaker Price ruled it out of order on the grounds that the body had already considered a bill with the same provisions and could not consider the measure again during this session. Jackson's delay tactics had worked to postpone any implementation of congressional districts at least until the fall. The general ticket system would remain for the 1844 election.[14]

As the first session of the 1843 legislature adjourned in March, Claib Jackson returned home to Fayette a party magnate. His leadership of the house majority had been effective, and his place on the party's central committee brought office-seekers from all levels to his home all through the summer in hopes of patronage appointments. Even Sterling Price, who contemplated leaving the house for a more lucrative position as land commissioner, traveled from nearby Keytesville to Fayette, seeking Jackson's largesse from the party's patronage pool. When Jackson " 'rule[d] him off the track' at least for that berth" by reminding him that such a position required a working knowledge of surveying, Price suggested an appointment as tobacco inspector and superintendent of tobacco warehouse construction or "something out of the general distribution of favors." Jackson then asked jokingly whether he would be satisfied "even . . . if it should be a pair of old breeches. He [Price] replied that he would be thankful for the smallest favors." Despite the obvious levity that underscored the scene, the roles clearly revealed that Jackson's presence in the party infrastructure was even more apparent than Price's. Jackson was now the lion of the Clique, and both he and it were very much alive and well in Missouri politics. Smugly, he wrote from Fayette during the recess to Governor Reynolds: "Mr. [Shadrach] Penn may cry 'central clique' as much as he pleases, it will not avail him—the people are not fools."[15]

As Jackson exulted at home during the recess, reacquainting himself with his family, preparing for the Democratic state convention, and riding over his Osage lands, another political observer in the state wrote a telling letter to Lieutenant Governor Marmaduke. "All the noise about currency bills, conventions & District systems," he claimed, "can not direct any ones mind from the real object in view [—] the defeat of Benton—Mask their batteries how they will, he is their mark & every body knows it." The writer was neither a political insider nor was he prescient; he reacted primarily to the relentless and public war that the Softs had waged against "Old Bullion" for the better part of a decade. Anyone who had followed the recent legislative

14. *Missouri Register,* December 10, 1842 (quote); Burks, "Thunder on the Right," 166–68; West, "Earlier Political Career of Jackson," 54–55; C. F. Jackson to Thomas Reynolds, March 12, 1843, Thomas Reynolds Papers, MHS; *Missouri House Journal,* Twelfth Gen. Ass., First Sess., 1842–1843, 391–92, 509–10; Shalhope, *Sterling Price,* 40–41; McCandless, *History of Missouri,* 230–31.

15. C. F. Jackson to Thomas Reynolds, March 12, 1843, Thomas Reynolds Papers, MHS (quotes).

debates in the newspapers could easily have surmised the Softs' collective intent to rid the Democratic party of "an arrogant and arbitrary dictator." What the correspondent probably did not envision was the storm that would soon rage within the ranks of the Hards, and even within the Benton phalanx itself. And what the writer could never have envisioned was that the leader to emerge in the chaos of this revolution would be Claiborne F. Jackson.[16]

Indeed, Benton's stranglehold on the political life of Missouri was both intransitive and complete. In 1842, he had personally approved 90 percent of the federal appointees in the state, a power that might not have proven so controversial had Benton not come to expect it. To many, Benton appeared to believe his own legend, and his speeches in the state sounded egocentric, if not self-idolatrous. A. B. Chambers, editor of the St. Louis *Missouri Republican,* a Whig organ, condemned Benton's published statement on behalf of currency reform as "a specimen of bombast and egotism which could hardly be excelled . . . the pronouns *I* and *me* are the most conspicuous words in the letter, and it is evident the writer thinks himself the Hercules of the day." Yet Benton had irritated more than just Whigs and Softs; he rarely consulted the party heads in the state in decisions he made and stances he took, evoking cries of "private judgment" on many fronts. Benton employed the party machinery to maintain his seat in the Senate yet rarely greased its cogs, a sin no longer venial for many Benton stalwarts once they became increasingly vulnerable during the depression that lingered well into the 1840s. Many Hards found themselves impaled on the horns of a dilemma; they owed their political fortunes to their posturing as Bentonites, yet found that their master's position on currency jeopardized those very seats. Shadrach Penn warned Benton that "the silence and wire pulling of your office-hunting followers prove that they are alive to the dangers with which they have been surrounded to the sufficiency and indiscretions of their chief." As his legions bared their political throats—and often found them slit—during the currency battles in the name of their leader, many found themselves less likely than they once had been to prostrate themselves before the Benton throne.[17]

With Benton up for reelection in the next assembly, Jackson spent the summer of 1843 campaigning for the party's monarch, who had returned to Missouri to prepare for the contest. Both Benton and Jackson made great exertions in Howard County, meeting largely in informal caucuses with local party lieutenants and fighting the "dictator" charge against Benton. The time he spent in the Boon's Lick—away from his family in St. Louis—

16. Anonymous, to M. M. Marmaduke, undated [1844], Sappington Family Papers, box 4, MHS (first quote); *Missouri Reporter,* November 1, 1842 (second quote).

17. Burks, "Thunder on the Right," 153, 178–81; *Daily Missouri Republican,* November 1, 1842, quoted in Shalhope, *Sterling Price,* 37 (first quote); Chambers, *Old Bullion Benton,* 260 (second quote); *Missouri Register,* December 19, 1843 (third quote).

and public statements he made characterizing Shadrach Penn as being no longer of the party made it clear to the Softs that Benton intended to secure his traditional power base with "the malign influence of the Central Clique" at the exclusion—even the expense—of themselves and St. Louis. Benton's view of the party obviously did not include them, opening him to even more vehement criticism and complete withdrawal of Soft support. Indeed, the party leader openly thanked Governor Reynolds and the General Assembly for their efforts on behalf of his hobby horse—currency reform— and especially "to Messrs. Jackson and Howard . . . my thanks are particularly due for their respective bills and meritorious exertions on this subject."[18]

Indeed, Jackson did more for Benton than simply marshal votes for currency reform. He openly supported Benton, organizing a public fête in Fayette in Benton's honor for the fall of 1843. More publicly, Jackson toed the Jacksonian Democratic mark by writing a series of resolutions adopted at a Howard County meeting in October 1843, and published throughout the Boon's Lick. In the strongly worded resolutions, Jackson declared Howard Countians opposed to a National Bank and supportive of Benton and of the Democratic party convention's choice for president—whoever it might be, though Jackson motioned that the meeting endorse New Yorker Martin Van Buren, Benton's candidate —in the upcoming national election. At the state level, the resolutions expressed the "fullest confidence" in Governor Reynolds and, to deflect charges of "Centralism," claimed to support a state convention as "the fairest means of choosing state candidates." Holding out Missouri—"governed by the Democrats"—as a model for other states, Jackson boasted of the success of the Hards' fiscal policies and his currency bill, claiming that "no heavy debt hangs upon our necks like an incubus; no combination of overgrown mushroom shinplaster manufacturers stalk abroad in the land . . . [and] no monuments of decaying railroads and half-finished canals meet the eye of the stranger who comes to mark the folly." And saving his strongest rhetoric for "the infamous falsehoods of Shadrick Penn . . . [and] the fiendish attacks of certain other presses professing to be Democratic," Jackson claimed that the Softs had "forfeited the confidence of the Democratic party . . . by exciting the border counties against the center, by the libelous assertion of a central Clique dictating to the state, . . . [and] by attacking the best friends of Benton and evidently acting with his enemies while pretending to be for him."[19]

18. Chambers, *Old Bullion Benton,* 269 (first quote), 260–68 (second quote, p. 268); Burks, "Thunder on the Right," 185; *Missouri Register,* November 14, 1843, quoted in West, "Earlier Political Career of Jackson," 69 (third quote).

19. *History of Howard and Chariton Counties,* 183; *Boon's Lick Times,* December 14, 1843; *Boonville Register,* October 17, 1843, quoted in West, "Earlier Political Career of Jackson," 70–72 (quotes); McLaughlin, *Lewis Cass,* 215–19. The Democratic convention,

Apart from his role as Benton's Peter, Jackson fought on Old Bullion's behalf out of more than simple party or individual loyalty. Clearly, he was angling for higher office; Jackson desired a congressional seat. All five of the state's congressmen were pro-Benton, and despite the Softs' attacks on Benton's "dictating," no one could realistically foresee any deviation from that pattern in the near future, explaining Jackson's steadfast support for Benton despite his eroding support within the Democratic rank and file. Moreover, Benton's wavering stance on districting and the constitutional convention forced Jackson to deny publicly that he opposed either reform, compromising his positions on both in the name of the Benton faction. Maintaining both his fidelity and his probity proved burdensome to Jackson, as many others of Benton's once-loyal legions had discovered. Jackson would soon grow weary of his unrewarded efforts.[20]

Jackson's first break with Benton in effect began precisely as he took the greatest pains to pledge his allegiance to him. In early October 1843, Senator Lewis Linn died unexpectedly at his home at Ste. Genevieve, leaving vacant the seat that many coveted. Governor Reynolds held the power of appointing a replacement, and Jackson believed that his close acquaintance with the governor (and having his brother-in-law and business partner as lieutenant governor), as well as his yeoman service for Benton and the Clique and strong showing as party floor leader in the recent legislative session, combined to make him a leading contender for the position. Within days, at his behest, supporters of Jackson joined the throngs who wrote to Reynolds lobbying for their respective candidates: "I must say to you though some objections may be made," wrote James D. Bouloin of Fayette, "I cannot come to any other conclusion than to beleave [sic] that our unflinching Democrat friend Mr C. F. Jackson would give your constituents, as general satisfaction [as] any other Gentleman in this State." Similarly, Thomas L. Belt wrote that "[Jackson] is a man in the bloom of political life, has shared largely in the odium which the mongrel politicians of the day have *attempted* to attach to your name, and who would be vigilant of the interests of his constituents on the new theatre on which he might be called to act." Unknown to Jackson, Marmaduke, too, wrote to the governor, endorsing former governor John C. Miller for the vacant seat. Anticipating a tremendous backlash if he had named one of the Clique as senator, much less an ardent Bentonite, Reynolds waited less than a fortnight to name Linn's replacement: David Rice Atchison, a

held in Baltimore on May 27, 1844, would nominate James K. Polk of Tennessee as its presidential candidate. The Missouri delegation was the only one from the slave states to cast its ballots for Van Buren.

20. Chambers, *Old Bullion Benton,* 266 (quote); *Boon's Lick Times,* December 30, 1843, February 10, 23, March 30, 1844; West, "Earlier Political Career of Jackson," 73–74.

circuit judge from Platte County, the first senator from the western portion of the state, who had in no way lobbied for the position and who at thirty-six was the youngest senator from the state. Though the decision shocked many in the party, Benton wrote to Reynolds within days of the appointment that "I for one am much pleased with it," though privately he had endorsed Miller—not Jackson—as well. Claib Jackson had learned again the hardest lesson of political life, that conscience—and in this case family—has little to do with politics.[21]

Jackson's disappointment grew more bitter in the spring of 1844, when he set about campaigning for his party's nomination for Congress in preparation for the April state Democratic convention. He traveled extensively, stump speaking throughout his legislative district, whose very existence he opposed, if now privately. Publicly, he began to distance himself from Benton, however slightly, on the issue of districting and the constitutional convention. At least three prominent papers—the *Boon's Lick Democrat,* the *Jefferson Inquirer,* and Benton's *St. Louis Missourian* (in part as a payoff for Benton's refusal to support Jackson's candidacy for Linn's vacant Senate seat) backed him for representative. Yet his boycott of the constitutional convention vote now haunted him; so pronounced were the criticisms that Jackson authorized the *Missourian* to deny that he had opposed the call for such a convention during the last legislative session. When the state Democratic convention met in Jefferson City, the error of Jackson's ways became apparent in the tense, divisive atmosphere. Despite a clear and militant Hard majority who made devotion to Benton their test oath (and who refused to seat Soft delegations), the debate over districting and a constitutional convention influenced the balloting. On the third day, Jackson saw his candidacy swallowed up by the Hards' commitment to statewide factional unity at the expense of the Boon's Lick Democracy. In the nomination contest for his second district, Jackson finished a distant second, accepting the nomination as an elector for the second district. Only then did he learn that Benton had endorsed another candidate.[22]

21. James D. Bouloin to Thomas Reynolds, October 11, 1843, Thomas L. Belt to Reynolds, October 13, 1843, and M. M. Marmaduke to Reynolds, October 16, 1843, all in Thomas Reynolds Letters, Mss. 1737, SHSM (see also Thomas Reynolds Papers, Record Group 3: Governors' Papers—Correspondence, box 2, folder 58, MSA); Parrish, *David Rice Atchison,* 34–37; Chambers, *Old Bullion Benton,* 269–70.

22. West, "Earlier Political Career of Jackson," 74–76; *Boon's Lick Times,* February 10, 2, 23, March 30, April 13, 1844; *Missouri Register,* April 9, 16, 1844; Shalhope, *Sterling Price,* 41–43; Burks, "Thunder on the Right," 190–94; *Missouri Statesman,* April 12, 1844. D. C. M. Parsons received seventy-two ballots to Jackson's thirty-three. Benton reportedly endorsed John Jameson. In 1845, the General Assembly passed legislation establishing congressional districts and aligned its voting procedures with congressional directives. In 1849 it approved a provision for reapportionment so that the principle of

If Claib Jackson's thwarted ambition convinced him that he had been betrayed by Benton, if the experience of the past six months had opened an irreparable breach between the disciple and his prophet, and if the wounded pride of Jackson drove him to oppose Benton hitherto at every opportunity, no record exists. At least one biographer has concluded that "Jackson held Benton entirely responsible for his failure to secure Congressional nomination, . . . [and] for the vast abuse that had been heaped upon him during the years 1843–1844." Another historian posits that at this point Jackson assumed the leadership of an insurgency against Benton that would span the course of seven years. Neither interpretation has offered evidence, whether direct or indirect, to substantiate the charge. On the contrary, much evidence points to a much later severance between the two. While Jackson's disappointment is unquestionable, and his subsequent actions during the summer leave no doubt that the Fayettan would soon break—if he had not already done so—with his former mentor, any past indiscretions that Benton might have made were likely mere prologue to the vortex that he set into motion less than a month following the Democratic state convention, and in which Jackson would leap to the center.[23]

The issue was Texas. On April 22, 1844, President John Tyler, a states' rights Whig, signed a treaty written by Secretary of State John C. Calhoun annexing Texas immediately from Mexico. As the bill went before the Senate, cotton state ideologues (including Calhoun) enmeshed it in the politically charged issues of slavery's expansion into the Southwest and constitutional protections of the peculiar institution. As extremists cried "Texas or Disunion," Tyler and Calhoun pressed senators to support the bill. Missourians roundly supported annexation and assumed Benton would as well. "We are all Annexation men, & Polk & Dallas men!" wrote Clique member John J. Lowry from the Fayette Bank, "Col. Benton is a Texas man too, & one of the best friends Texas has got. . . . & no man can, in truth say to the contrary!" However, Benton refused to be caught up in the clearly sectional overtones of the debate; five days after Tyler presented the treaty to the

county representation was maintained, but allowed additional seats for populous counties through a ratio system with no restriction on the total delegation. See Parrish, Jones, and Christensen, *Missouri,* 100.

23. Burks, "Thunder on the Right," 194–95 (quote), 196; Charles H. McClure, *Opposition in Missouri to Thomas Hart Benton,* 56–70 and passim. Both authors have put great emphasis on the impact that Thomas Reynolds's suicide made on Jackson. On February 9, 1844, Reynolds shot himself in the governor's mansion, leaving a note saying that "the slanders and abuse of my enemies [had] rendered my life a burden to me." While Jackson addressed a Howard County memorial for Reynolds later that month, no other record indicates that the death set Jackson on an anti-Benton crusade. See *Jefferson Inquirer,* February 15, 1844; *Boon's Lick Times,* February 17, 1844; Parrish, Jones, and Christensen, *Missouri,* 99.

Senate, Benton denounced annexation, claiming that such an act without the Mexican government's recognition of an independent Texas was tantamount to an act of war—an unnecessary and unjustified war. By mid-May, Benton had offered an unexpected and, in most Missourians' minds, blasphemous addendum to his reasoning: during a Senate chamber harangue that lasted nearly three days, Benton thundered against the political maneuvering of the president "to explode the Texas bomb" just prior to the Democratic national convention. Then Benton made what would prove a fatal declaration: the slaveholder bellowed—not completely accurately—that "I will not engage in schemes for [slavery's] *extension* into regions where it was never known . . . where a slave's face was never seen."[24]

Missouri exploded upon learning of Benton's speech. Many could accept that Benton opposed the annexation short of war, accepting his claim that the United States could acquire Texas by legal and even honorable means. That the Senate soundly rejected Tyler's treaty (and the fact that seven Democrats other than Benton voted against it, though David Rice Atchison was not one of them) offered evidence to Missourians that Benton was not merely acting the rogue. Yet however much Old Bullion argued that his position on slavery had not changed—that the institution was an affliction that posed the greatest threat to the Union and that the slave states alone must in time resolve the institution's future without its injection into national politics, and that his loyalties were still with the yeomanry and he wanted continued Texas emigration to equalize the disproportionate power of its small planter class prior to statehood—Missourians were in no mood for rationalizations on his part. For many, Benton had committed a mortal sin, not so much for his apparent abolitionist stance (though the opposition press vilified him with the epithet, Missourians had known Benton too long to believe such rubbish) as for questioning the right of slavery's extension into the West. These westerners, long since having fused the concepts of slavery and westernness, now reacted in defense of their region and its future, of which Texas was part. The *Missouri Register* captured the essence of this pervasive feeling, warning Missourians that Benton "must not be permitted to stand

24. Chambers, *Old Bullion Benton,* 273–75 (first quote, p. 273), 276 (third and fifth quotes); Resolutions of the General Assembly of the State of Missouri on the annexation of Texas to the United States, Capitol Fire Documents, 1806–1957, microfilm reel CFD-121, folder 11065: Thirteenth Gen. Ass. (1844–1845), House Resolutions (1844–1845), MSA; J. J. Lowry to M. M. Marmaduke, June 12, 1844, Sappington Family Papers, box 4, MHS (second quote); William M. Meigs, *The Life of Thomas Hart Benton,* 346–47 (fourth quote), 348; McCandless, *History of Missouri,* 233; Burks, "Thunder on the Right," 181–82, 196–97. Secretary of State Calhoun's response to the British foreign minister, Lord Aberdeen, that expressed his government's general desire for slavery's extinction, argued that slavery and its protection by the federal government was a core issue in the Texas issue. The letter found its way into the public press.

in the way of the onward and upward march of our country to those high and holy destinies to which God and nature seem to have designed . . . [and] thus sacrifice the highest hopes and the dearest interests of his native land."[25]

With his house seat up for election in the fall, Claib Jackson moved to capitalize on what clearly was no mere peccadillo on Benton's part. Indeed, annexation immediately submerged any former litmus that might distinguish candidates—particularly their allegiance to Benton. In addresses given in May, prior to Benton's Texas speeches (widely published in national newspapers), as part of his campaign for elector in his district, in towns such as Bloomington, Paris, and Huntsville, as well as Fayette, Jackson pledged loyalty to Benton, echoing the conclusion of a recent Howard County meeting, but with reservation.[26] Once Jackson had received nomination for one of three seats in the house at another county meeting on June 1, the day after the national Democratic convention nominated James K. Polk, an ardent expansionist, rather than Martin Van Buren, whom the Soft press had tied Jackson to earlier, he began to criticize Benton's stand on Texas without excoriating the senator himself. At a "Texas Meeting" in Fayette that he called two weeks later, Jackson disputed Benton's history of Texas that had argued that Mexico still claimed Texas, and called unequivocally for immediate annexation. Even this language was too strong for the Clique; John J. Lowry wrote to Marmaduke, imploring him to convince Jackson—whom Lowry considered excessively ambitious—not "to drag Col. Benton unnecessarily into the Canvass—Benton is for Texas but he wants business done properly! Let us not give the Whigs the advantage of us, . . . our friends may be imprudent, by unnecessarily drawing Col. Benton into this Texas question & thereby injure him."[27]

Though the relationship was strained, clearly Jackson had not yet broken—at least publicly—with his prophet. After Benton's speech in Fayette, Jackson had risen first from his seat to lead the ringing applause. When the Whig press began reporting that Jackson had pledged not to vote for Benton (state legislatures, not the public at large, elected U.S. senators) if returned to the legislature, he issued a statement through the *Boon's Lick Democrat* to the

25. Smith, *Magnificent Missourian*, 188–89, 200 (quote); Parrish, *David Rice Atchison*, 45; Chambers, *Old Bullion Benton*, 273–74.

26. *Missouri Statesman*, May 3, 1844; *Boon's Lick Times*, June 22, 1844. At this meeting, Thomas Jackson, Claib's brother, offered an amendment that the meeting condition its support for Benton upon his remaining loyal to the party in all matters. Though rejected, Jackson's suggestion would ultimately frame the notable 1849 Jackson-Napton Resolutions, named for Claiborne Jackson, who introduced them to the Missouri legislature.

27. J. J. Lowry to M. M. Marmaduke, June 12 (quote), June 29, August 10, 1844, all in Sappington Family Papers, box 4, MHS; West, "Earlier Political Career of Jackson," 81–83, 86–90.

contrary, though this was tempered by an editorial supporting Jackson's call for immediate annexation. Moreover, at a July 17 meeting at the courthouse in Boonville, at which Benton was not only present but also the keynote speaker—the meeting was publicized widely as a showdown between Jackson and Benton—the Fayettan followed Benton's three-hour speech with a brief rejoinder in which he pledged himself strongly to the senator, despite Old Bullion's stand on Texas, but impressed upon Benton the need to vote as the state legislature instructed him on the matter. Many perceived Benton to have assented to such obeisance. Resolutions that the Boonville assemblage adopted (drawn by a committee that Jackson chaired), approving the Baltimore platform and calling for immediate annexation, confirmed such notions for many.[28]

Jackson's strong stand on the Texas issue—and his firm yet politic resolve in opposition to Benton's—paid greater dividends than merely securing his reelection to the Missouri house (though by the narrowest of margins; Jackson was the only Democrat elected from Howard County and received less votes than either of the Whig candidates elected). The political capital he had accrued positioned Jackson for the speakership, now vacant with Sterling Price's election to Congress. Some anticipated Jackson's ascendance as a natural, given his strong floor leadership during the previous session; others charged fancifully that the position "will buy him [Jackson] off from contending against Colonel Benton for the senatorship." Ironically, the annexation controversy had rendered Jackson, if temporarily, a compromise candidate: his disingenuous posturing in favor of congressional districting and a constitutional convention played well with the Whig opposition, and his firm stand for immediate annexation and apparent reining in of Benton solidified him with the Democrats, whether Hard or Soft.[29]

When the session convened in late November, and with little Democratic opposition, Jackson received election as speaker. His clear posturing for Benton in obtaining the position was not lost on the legislative correspondent for the *Missouri Republican*. "C. F. Jackson is to be elected speaker," spat the disgusted writer. "All applicants for office were required to pledge to support Colonel Benton. . . . Jackson, whose reported split with Benton on the Texas question has been so rife, goes the whole figure." The reporter knew of what he spoke. Upon assuming the gavel as speaker, Jackson offered a brief acceptance in which he graciously thanked the assembly while expressing with

28. *Boon's Lick Times,* June 8, 22, 1844; *Jefferson Inquirer,* August 1, 1844; Shalhope, *Sterling Price,* 43–44; *Boonville Observer,* July 24, 1844.

29. Secretary of State Election Returns, 1844, Capitol Fire Documents, 1806–1957, microfilm reel CFD-183, folder 16244, MSA; *Missouri Republican,* November 22, 1844 (quote); West, "Earlier Political Career of Jackson," 89–97; Burks, "Thunder on the Right," 207–13.

"regret that I am not able to bring with me more of experience and more of ability." Then—as he had promised more than once—Jackson promptly cast his vote among seventy-four who elected Benton once again to the U.S. Senate, despite a number of papers reporting regularly that the new speaker "intend[ed] throwing Colonel Benton out of the Democratic ship."[30]

Moreover, in his first act as speaker, Jackson did not marshal forces to coerce Benton into adhering to Missouri's support for immediate annexation of Texas. When the house debated a bill that introduced a strongly worded, immediatist series of resolutions on the issue (a debate in which Jackson participated but did not vote), their final form refrained from demanding that Benton vote for immediate annexation. Jackson went so far as to advocate a draft that omitted the word "immediate" from the original resolutions. Questioned about his taciturnity on an issue upon which he had campaigned stridently for an entire summer, Jackson responded dubiously—and weakly— that he personally favored immediacy, but that the majority of Missouri voters opposed it. The opposition press ridiculed his newfound willingness to compromise; the Democratic press did likewise for his inconsistency. One reporter observing the debate in the statehouse noted the irony of Jackson's changing stance on Texas, remarking that "the Speaker . . . was not as powerful or eloquent as I expected him to be. He charged however that the Whigs, were ever changing their name. . . . [yet] admitted that heretofore he had been in favor of 'immediate' annexation, and that he was yet, but that he was now also willing to compromise on the subject; and therefore he was now in favor of annexation 'at the earliest practicable period'. . . . 'Immediate' you know, means *now,* but *'the earliest practicable period'* means nothing."[31]

Most likely, the Clique convinced Jackson that presenting such a unified front at this point would be far more important to the Boon's Lick Democrats than would pinning Benton into a corner; one member, John J. Lowry, warned that "this nation ought not to be too hasty, but do its business correctly & our friends not break our prominent men down, which might do an irreparable injury to the good old Cause. I am fearful that some of our friends may be imprudent, by unnecessarily drawing Col. Benton into

30. 13th General Assembly (1844–1845): Senate Messages, Capitol Fire Documents, 1806–1957, microfilm reel CFD-129, folder 11715, MSA; *Missouri Republican,* November 22, 1844 (first quote); West, "Earlier Political Career of Jackson," 89–97; *Missouri Democrat,* November 30, 1846 (second quote); *Boon's Lick Times,* October 19, 1844 (third quote). Despite widespread criticism, only after winning reelection to the house did Jackson resign as elector from the Second District, the two positions clearly being a conflict of interest. See *Jefferson Inquirer,* September 19, 1844.

31. *Missouri House Journal,* 13th General Assembly, 1844–1845, 121–22; *Boon's Lick Times,* November 23, December 28, 1844; Burks, "Thunder on the Right," 212–14; West, "Earlier Political Career of Jackson," 97–99; *Missouri Statesman,* January 3, 1845 (quote).

this Texas question & thereby injure him. . . . On the defeat of Benton, the Democracy, not only in Missouri, but in the U. States receives paralytic stroke." If Jackson contemplated any mutiny, the loyal lieutenant offered no indication to either his captain or crew that he would be throwing the breadfruit overboard. Such fidelity, however feigned, would soon reach its end.[32]

32. Burks, "Thunder on the Right," 212–14; West, "Earlier Political Career of Jackson," 97–99; J. J. Lowry to M. M. Marmaduke, June 12, August 10, 1844, Sappington Family Papers, box 4, MHS (quote).

"LET LOOSE THE DOGS OF WAR"

BENTON FORCED HIS enemies to conspire to kill him that they might live.

JAMES H. BIRCH

Late on the sultry spring afternoon of June 8, 1845, Andrew Jackson drew his last spasmed breath as he lay propped on pillows in his massive four-poster bed on the first floor of the Hermitage. Beyond the extinction of physical life, the death of the great chieftain offered no grand symbolism of the passing of an era. If anything, Jackson had given life to a two-party system that was only now beginning to walk. Yet his own passing did offer a metaphor of sorts. Only days before, he had dictated one of the last letters of his life to William B. Lewis, a close acquaintance, which Lewis would hand-deliver to Thomas Hart Benton. "The Colonel," the Old Hickory whispered, "is not only an able and distinguished statesman, but a warm and sincere patriot, and his country is under great obligation to him." While the dying statesman's note more reflects a personal recognition of the Missourian's lifelong devotion to the party he had organized as well as to himself, the coincidence of the message offered a grim irony, one which Old Hickory might well have perceived: as Jackson's life ended his era did not, yet while Benton lived on his epoch in Missouri politics was fast closing.[1]

Despite his combative life, Andrew Jackson had passed on during a lull between two storms. As the seemingly endless economic depression at last loosed its iron grip, the nation witnessed the inauguration of Democrat James K. Polk, an ardent expansionist, as the nation's eleventh president. Polk's acceptance of his predecessor's push for immediate annexation of Texas caused Benton to stir from his recumbence, but only enough to voice disapproval of a measure he had only recently damned. Temporarily at least, the Texas drama submerged under a nearly clinical series of negotiations for the acquisition of Oregon. The battle cry "Fifty-four Forty or Fight" rang hollow without sectional overtones. The outbreak of the war with Mexico, whether induced or not, and the overwhelming congressional and popular support for it (especially among westerners) all but subsumed any controversy

1. Chambers, *Old Bullion Benton,* 293; Marquis James, *Andrew Jackson: Portrait of a President,* 500; John Spencer Bassett, ed., *Correspondence of Andrew Jackson,* vol. 6, 414–15n2.

that had once raged about Texas, the furor over Benton becoming lost in the swirl.[2]

In Missouri, too, an eddy emerged in the oft-raging political current. A constitutional convention met in the fall of 1845 (with Claib Jackson not only a member, but vice president, despite his original opposition to the convention, ostensibly for reasons of expense) to address its inadequacies, among them apportionment. The competing interests present at the convention proved a self-fulfilling prophesy; the mixed bag the gathering produced died with a whimper as the diverse populace of the state rejected the ineffectual document. Not wishing implementation of reapportionment at the expense of his Clique anchor, Jackson refused to campaign for the constitution and was anything but disappointed at its defeat in referendum. Subsequent debates in the General Assembly on judicial reform, monetary policies and the state bank (Jackson's hobby horses), internal improvements, land distribution, and state-supported education evoked less the normal, fiery divisiveness of previous sessions than a comfortably routine partisanship.[3]

As Missouri sat becalmed during the war years, Claib Jackson's personal fortunes witnessed great stirring, as well as great change. As the financial misery attendant with the Panic of 1837 at last eased—later than in other states, ironically, as a result of Jackson's hard-money crusade—Jackson began turning his home place into a working farm. With more than four hundred acres of contiguous land along the Glasgow Road, as well as another two hundred Howard County acres lying nearby, during the mid-1840s Jackson began raising sizable numbers of livestock: cattle, horses, sheep, and swine. He also bought a number of mules and oxen with which to cultivate cover crops such as hay and flax and large amounts of food crops such as wheat, corn, and oats, the former to feed his livestock and the latter for profit. By 1850, Jackson owned a thousand dollars' worth of implements, more than double that of any of his brothers or Sappington in-laws. His farm also produced for its owner's family's consumption, including Irish and sweet potatoes, peas, beans, and orchard fruits. Jackson slaughtered much of his beef, turned the milk from his dairy cattle into butter—six hundred pounds' worth annually by 1850—and sold his raw wool and flax fiber and seed in the neighboring markets. By that year, the value of his homemade manufactures doubled that of any of his brothers or in-laws. Moreover, Jackson cultivated

---

2. Chambers, *Old Bullion Benton*, 288–94.

3. Parrish, Jones, and Christensen, *Missouri*, 100; Secretary of State Election Returns, 1845, Capitol Fire Documents, 1806–1957, microfilm reel CFD-183, folder 16269, MSA; West, "Earlier Political Career of Jackson," 100–126; Burks, "Thunder on the Right," 236–51; McCandless, *History of Missouri*, 238–41. The voters of Missouri rejected the new state constitution by referendum in August of 1846.

at least ten acres of dew-rotted hemp that yielded him three tons of the fibrous crop by 1850, exclusively for sale to the consignment merchants in the river towns of Glasgow and New Franklin. By the middle of the decade, Jackson estimated his combined income from both the farm and the pill business to be more than seventeen thousand dollars annually.[4]

None of this expansion would have been possible had Jackson not increased his slaveholdings significantly, both in number and in composition. While just a few years earlier Jackson's bondpeople had been largely house servants, by the late 1840s his chattel property began to resemble more those of a working plantation than a gentleman's farm. In 1850, Jackson owned nineteen slaves, five of whom were males between the ages of sixteen and fifty; only four of his slave women were of this prime working age. Local newspapers noted Jackson as frequenting auctions, bidding for both land and slave property at this time, as well as buying slave men from local residents. Jackson bought male slaves from Dr. Sappington on occasion, and as the doctor neared the end of his life he granted young female house slaves to his daughter and her children for their use, freeing up funds for Jackson to purchase even more male field hands. By the mid-1840s Jackson appears to have largely ceased hiring male slaves, as he had done frequently during the previous decade, relying more on his own servants and borrowing those of his brothers. By 1860, Jackson's chattel holdings would have tripled.[5]

The expansion of Jackson's farm from a largely self-sufficient operation to a full-fledged commercial plantation derived some impetus from his own family evolution. Jackson's two sons by his second wife, Louisa, and five stepchildren from his third wife, Eliza, created immediate responsibilities at the time he and his third wife were married in 1838. Moreover, Jackson and Eliza soon began their own family, and between 1839 and 1844 the clan welcomed three more young Jacksons to the fold: Claib, Jr., Louisa Jane, and Ann Eliza. Because the Pearson stepchildren were older at the time of Jackson's marriage to their mother, they soon left the house. The eldest son,

4. Seventh U.S. Census, 1850, Howard County [Missouri], Agricultural Schedule, NA; Burks, "Thunder on the Right," 253.

5. *Glasgow Weekly Times,* December 9, 1852; Bill of Slave for Slave Cyrus, May 8, 1855, John S. Sappington Papers, Mss. 1027, box 3, folder 63, SHSM; Estate of Jos[eph] Sears, undated, ibid., box 1, folder 2, SHSM; Bill of Sale for Slave Aaron, April 30, 1846, ibid., box 2, folder 50, SHSM; Settlement and division of Slaves made between Jesse M. Baskett and Claiborne F. Jackson, January 1, 1853, ibid., box 3, folder 61, SHSM; Bill of Sale for Slave George, November 20, 1854, ibid., box 3, folder 63, SHSM; Mortgage and Endorsement for Slave Maria, January 7, 1846, ibid., box 2, folder 50, SHSM; Receipt, Messrs. Hooks and Co. to B. H. Rives [*sic*] for Servant Man Lun, October 20, 1836, Abiel Leonard Papers, Mss. 1013, Business Documents, 1835–1841, folder April–December 1836, SHSM; Seventh and Eighth U.S. Censuses, 1850 and 1860, Slave Schedule, Howard County [Missouri], NA.

John, attended medical school in the East, then returned to Arkansas and set up practice, while Erasmus, a Presbyterian minister, lived in the town of Louisiana, Missouri, in Pike County on the upper Mississippi. Sarah Jane married a local farmer, Virginia-born Jesse M. Baskett, and they moved to the river town of Hannibal in Marion County. Elizabeth, a Fayette seamstress, married William J. Eddins, also a native Virginian and Howard County farmer whose brother, Layton S. Eddins, had married Eliza's younger sister, Susan, and was a partner in the Sappington Pill business. In 1841 Lavinia married Dr. Charles M. Bradford, a New Yorker who, like Dr. Sappington, was a Penn-educated physician and had moved to Arrow Rock in 1839, setting up his practice the following year. Bradford assisted the doctor with the perfection of his quinine formula before marrying Lavinia and accepting partnership in the Sappington company. Jackson appears to have had only a distant role in his stepchildren's courtship rituals; the stepfather the Pearson children with comfortable respect called "Pa" was so often away, either on business or for political matters, that Jackson witnessed few of their rites of passage into adulthood, including courtship, leaving a self-professed "lonesome" Eliza to write long letters to Jackson and other family members describing her impressions of her daughters' suitors, explaining decisions, and occasionally asking advice. Clearly, the long Sappington shadow had stretched into the career and marital choices of the Pearson children more than did that of one of the state's most visible—and powerful—public servants.[6]

That a gladiator such as Claib Jackson should offer little more than am-bivalence in his stepchildren's first life choices was no coincidence. Jackson's life was one of complete calculation, a quest for dominance over others, whether political or personal. In all things, Jackson exerted control or fought

6. Sarah Jane Baskett to William B. Sappington, March 3, 1852, William B. Sappington Papers, Mss. 1421, folder 1, SHSM; Deed Gift of Sarah Jane Baskett et al. to William S. Jackson, undated, John S. Sappington Papers, Mss. 1027, box 1, folder 4, SHSM; Luda [Louisa] J. Lamb to Eliza W. Jackson, July 29, 1860, ibid., box 3, folder 71, SHSM; E. D. Pearson to W. B. Sappington, January 10, 1872, ibid., box 3, folder 79, SHSM; E. D. Pearson to Eliza W. Jackson, August 9, 1860, ibid., box 3, folder 71, SHSM (first quote); Eliza W. Jackson to W. B. Sappington, January 13, 1845, ibid., box 2, folder 47, SHSM (second quote); Family tree of John Sappington and Jane Breathitt Sappington. ibid., box 1, folder 1, SHSM; Burks, "Missouri Medicine Man," 50*n*4; Seventh, Eighth, and Ninth U.S. Censuses, 1850–1870, Population Schedule, Howard, Marion, and Pike Counties [Missouri], NA; Obituary of Mary Ellen [Cossitt] Pearson, undated clipping [1851], Sappington Miscellany, Mss. 1036, folder 4, SHSM; Last Will and Testament of Claiborne Fox Jackson, December 6, 1862, Will Book B, Saline County [Missouri], 138–40, microfilm reel C11591, MSA; National Society of the Colonial Dames in the State of Missouri Papers, 1968–1974, Mss. 3584, folder 1, SHSM; C. M. Bradford to Lavinia M. Pearson, August 21, 28, October 2, 15, 1841, Saline County Papers, MHS; Eliza W. Jackson to C. F. Jackson, December 30, 1859, John S. Sappington Papers, Mss. 1027, box 3, folder 69, SHSM.

relentlessly to get it, even over the management and career decisions of his blood children, as family letters indicate. In stark contrast, Jackson's indifference to the Pearson children's raising offers one of several clear signals of a breach between the Sappington nobility and its once head courtier. By the late 1840s, having gained aperture into what now appeared a boundless professional ascent, Jackson might well have resented the limitations, even subordination, endured within the Sappington patriarchy. Having achieved success among men, Jackson had reached the point in mature life when he felt strong enough to stride alone, scorning that and those who reminded him of fragile, youthful steps. Yet being part of the Sappington retinue offered Jackson the daily recognition that he was neither king nor even heir to that or any throne. Though Jackson was speaker of the house, and though he might have been married to the eldest Sappington daughter (for that matter, three daughters), whether for convenience or for love, Miles Marmaduke's election as lieutenant governor, then elevation to governor upon Thomas Reynolds's suicide, served as grim reminder that Jackson had not attained a position of such prominence, whether in the state or even in the family. Marmaduke's refusal to support Jackson for the vacant U.S. Senate seat in 1843 only worsened the strained family situation. Jackson's relationship with his erstwhile partner eroded first; his once-cordial personal letters enjoining Marmaduke, "Can't you come over and spend the coming week [in Fayette] with us?" ceased quickly, and their land partnership dissolved systematically within a few years. Indeed, in 1848, when Jackson and Marmaduke competed for their party's gubernatorial nomination, Layton Eddins would write to Marmaduke that "Mr. Jackson and his friends are dead against you," while Clique member George Penn would claim that "Jackson is . . . more in the way of your Success than any one else."[7]

While jealousy played a hand in Jackson's breach with Marmaduke, greed too contributed to the concomitant deterioration of Jackson's relationship with the Sappington patriarch. Jackson had grown wealthy on the family pill business, but only with considerable effort on his part. Jackson's districts of

7. McCandless, *History of Missouri*, 236; W[illia]m S. Jackson to C. F. Jackson, September 13, 1857, Sappington Family Papers, box 6, MHS; W[illiam] S. Jackson to C. F. Jackson, May 17, 1860, John S. Sappington Papers, Mss. 1027, box 3, folder 71, SHSM; C. M. Bradford to C. F. Jackson, January 1, 1860, ibid., box 3, folder 70, SHSM; Eliza W. Jackson to C. F. Jackson, December 30, 1859, ibid., box 3, folder 69, SHSM; C. F. Jackson to M. M. Marmaduke, October 18, September 22, 1837, Sappington Family Papers, box 2, MHS (first quote); C. F. Jackson to M. M. Marmaduke, March 16, 1845, ibid., box 4, MHS; Deed for Osage Lands, April 10, 1857, John S. Sappington Papers, Mss. 1027, box 3, folder 67, SHSM; Deeds Records, Saline County [Missouri], vol. S, 365, microfilm reel C6233, MSA; L. S. Eddins to M. M. Marmaduke, May 28, 1848, Sappington Family Papers, box 5, MHS (second quote); George Penn to Marmaduke, June 2, 1848, ibid., box 5, MHS (third quote).

the company included the Arkansas and Louisiana regions, lands that boasted some spectacularly rich planters but far more impoverished plain folk. In its excessive stratification, the area contained the most fragile economy in the entire nation. Jackson had struggled mightily to collect from the poverty-stricken masses in his district during the depression years, and now witnessed his brothers-in-law, including Marmaduke, who controlled the company's choicer regions, earning larger profits for the company with less effort than him and reaping greater financial benefit. Moreover, Jackson had borrowed liberally from the Sappington coffers. The doctor kept meticulous records of this, as well as of the amounts he contributed to the Pearson children's upkeep, requiring Jackson to pay back every cent with interest. Feeling his various contributions to the company unappreciated, Jackson confronted the ineffable realization that the chickens had indeed come home to roost: his Faustian pact had actually made him an outsider, rather than an insider—as he had grown accustomed in the political arena—within the Sappington fold.[8]

Frustrated, Jackson vented his anger at the elder Sappington. Just after Christmas 1843, ironically just months after Jackson's betrayal by Marmaduke, Dr. Sappington determined to make a division of his business and property among his living kin. Writing to his stepson-in-law Charles M. Bradford (who stood to gain from the Sappington division in that the doctor would be dividing the company into seven parts, one of which Bradford would head for the benefit of the Pearson children for whom Jackson had provided no financial support), Jackson "Express[ed] the disinclination . . . for reasons best known to myself . . . toward having anything whatever to do in the settlement and division of property which Dr. Sappington has just been making." Yet he agreed to "come over and assist in the valuation of the negroes . . . sooner than be considered obstinate or perverse in the matter." Jackson then made clear that his disaffection stemmed from the clear favoritism employed in the method by which the Sappington resources had been "parcelled out and then divided by 'lot.'" "I see no possible room for reflections," Jackson wrote angrily, "I am glad the settlement is made. I think it ought to have taken place long since. How it has been made, of course, I know nothing. *But be it what it may,* I say a-men." Jackson would indeed accept his slice of the rich Sappington pie—the Illinois and

---

8. List of Debts to John Sappington, undated, John S. Sappington Papers, Mss. 1027, box 1, folder 4, SHSM; List of Notes held by John Sappington, undated, ibid., box 1, folder 9, SHSM; Division of Negroes, undated [1844], ibid., box 3, folder 62, SHSM; Account Statement due J. E. Walsh, Denis, and Cockran, St. Louis [note on back written by C. F. Jackson], December 13, 1845, ibid., box 3, folder 65, SHSM; Settlement Agreement, September 2, 1848, ibid., box 4, folder 95, SHSM; Separation of Estate of John S. Sappington, December 30, 1843, John Sappington Family Papers, Mss. 2889, folder 11, SHSM.

Kentucky districts, far less lucrative than others in the plantation states, even the Arkansas and Louisiana districts, which Sappington willfully bestowed on the Pearson children—but rationalized that his refusal to genuflect for such largesse signaled a mastery over both the family and his own former dependence upon it. More realistically, the hollow act of defiance merely punctuated Jackson's cognizance of his supplication—one that despite any such gesture would stretch over nearly a quarter century.[9]

Interlaced with the developing personal chasms within the Sappington family was Jackson's driving political ambition, which helped to create these years of meteors in all aspects of his life. While maintaining his seat in the state legislature from 1842 to 1852 (three consecutive terms in the house and one in the senate), Jackson ran regularly for higher political office during the late 1840s and 1850s: state senator, U.S. representative, governor, as well as posturing unsuccessfully for appointment as U.S. senator when Atchison's and Benton's respective seats came open in 1848 and 1850. One correspondent of Marmaduke's related in 1847 that "I see both Hughes & King are attending all the Meetings in the Platte Country and Jackson told me since I saw you that he intended to stir about. Too much modesty won[']t win in this Country." Far from being modest, Jackson's incessant pursuit of office soon prompted some of the state's newspapers to anoint him with the sarcastic sobriquet, "the Eternal Claib," while others—simply yet knowingly—called him "the Fox." The *Jefferson Inquirer* published a scathing history of "Fox" Jackson's political steeplechase between 1844 and 1849, claiming his "having more impudence than intellect—more zeal than patriotism, and more selfish aspirations than merit, he has constantly thrust himself forward as the exponent of party doctrines . . . [yet] has been on both sides of every important political question since he entered upon public life."[10]

Missouri politicos—even members of the Clique—recognized and now disapproved of Jackson's ceaseless quest for higher office. While these consummate wire-pullers once had welcomed the young votary and encouraged his political aspirations, some now saw his behavior as destructive, not only

9. Division of Negroes, undated [1844], ibid., box 3, folder 62, SHSM; Account Statement due J. E. Walsh, Denis, and Cockran, St. Louis [note on back written by C. F. Jackson], December 13, 1845, ibid., box 3, folder 65, SHSM.

10. West, "Earlier Political Career of Jackson," 130–39; William Shields to M. M. Marmaduke, October 11, 1847, Sappington Family Papers, box 4, MHS (first quote); Shields to Marmaduke, November 8, 1847, ibid., box 4, MHS; *Missouri Statesman*, May 14, 21, 1852 (second quote), June 22, 1849; *Jefferson Inquirer*, July 14, 1849 (third and fourth quotes); Grissom, "Personal Recollections," 506; *Missouri Democrat*, May 18, 1846; Parrish, *David Rice Atchison*, 70–72, and *Frank Blair*, 35; Chambers, *Old Bullion Benton*, 287, 368–73. Daniel Grissom claims that William Switzler, editor of the Columbia *Missouri Statesman*, first labeled Jackson "the Fox."

to himself but also to the Democratic party. John J. Lowry wrote from the Fayette Bank that "Jackson has been nominated by the Glasgow convention, a candidate to represent Howard & Chariton in the state Senate. I did not think that he ought to have run, I think that he will injure himself, by his unbounded ambition. His friends thought the state Senate, a stepping stone to the U. States Senate, but my opinion was, that he would be equally prominent on his farm at home, & probably more so!" Similarly, Benjamin F. Massey of Joplin cautioned that "there was a time when I thought more of Jackson both personally and politically than I did of any man in the state. And I like him yet personally—But he is politically everlastingly making bargains."[11]

Myopic, if not quite blind, ambition soon embroiled Jackson in the greatest controversy of his life, one that would accelerate the process by which Missourians forever changed their conceptions of their country, their region, and themselves. Hungry for power, Jackson—now unmoored from the Sappington pier—sought avenues for advancement with little regard for the once-comforting aegis of the Boon's Lick Democracy. Yet he was stymied at every turn, passed over repeatedly for nominations and appointments, even accused by the *Jefferson Inquirer* of being a wire-pulling "trickster" for his bald intrigues in pursuit of Atchison's Senate seat. Thomas Gray reported almost gleefully to Marmaduke from a party caucus in January 1848 that "we succeeded in puting [*sic*] once more the faction down and instructed our delegates both to the State and District Convention to Vote for Marmaduke & Rawlin[s]. . . . Jackson was present, and His Name was not even mentioned." Desperate at the thought that his quick success at the state level might now have blocked any further ascent, Jackson needed to establish a reputation not as merely a small-town or even county street brawler, but as a skilled pugilist capable of national competition. He might well have recognized that his efforts to enter Missouri's upper political presbytery would require a magnum opus, one that would propel him from the vestibule to the altar. No mere blood-letting would do; Jackson needed a sacrifice. Yet this was no Herod ordering up the head of John the Baptist, the powerful bringing low the commoner; rather, Jackson the attendant sharpened his knife for Missouri's high priest, Thomas Hart Benton.[12]

---

11. J. J. Lowry to M. M. Marmaduke, March 20, 1847, Sappington Family Papers, box 4, MHS; Lowry to Marmaduke, June 29, 1848, ibid., box 5, MHS (first quote); B. F. Massey to John F. Snyder, September 6, 1859, John F. Snyder Collection, box 1, MHS (second quote).

12. *Jefferson Inquirer,* July 14, 1849 (first quote); Thomas Gray to M. M. Marmaduke, January 9, 1848, Sappington Family Papers, box 5, MHS (second quote); George Penn to Marmaduke, January 11, 1848, ibid., box 5, MHS; J. H. Haden to Marmaduke, February 29, 1848, ibid., box 5, MHS.

In reality, Jackson did not so much choose the role of king killer as Benton anointed himself a target of the Missouri Democratic party. Old Bullion raised the ire of the state's party membership by being, in one historian's words, "increasingly negligent as a politician, seldom mending fences back home, and regarding his seat more or less as personal property." Jackson's earlier affray with Benton indeed served as prelude to a renewed attack, yet he was but one of a multitude of those who had waged such assaults on Benton. Indeed, Francis Preston Blair, Sr., influential editor of the *Globe* and father of two of Missouri's prominent young politicos (each a Benton legal protégé), wrote to then-president Martin Van Buren, likening Benton's stature among the state's politicians to "a great Bear surrounded by a yelping pack of whelps. He slaps one down on this side—another on that," wrote the elder Blair, "and grips a third with his teeth, then tosses him with his snout." The colorful description aptly depicted the Missourians as harrying, but not felling, the mighty Benton. Indeed, Benton had grown accustomed, to the point of hubris, to such attacks, recounting to Montgomery Blair a remark he recalled made by a friend to one of the conspirators upon learning of a movement "to overthrow me near twenty years ago." "Billy Kinney told [the assailant]," Benton boasted, "that he had seen many persons attack Benton & he had seen them all fall dead at his feet. That was his fate. We will see what will be the fate of the present assailants. I say assailants for I mean to make them throw off the disguise of plotters & come openly to the work."[13]

Though Benton appeared reined somewhat after his Texas annexation stance had met with such strong response among his Missouri constituents in 1844, Old Bullion quickly demonstrated that the maverick could not long be ridden. In 1846, though he had been an ardent supporter of the West and of national expansion throughout his career—earning him the sobriquet "Gibraltar of the West"—Benton had advocated a settlement of the Oregon controversy that accepted the forty-ninth parallel as the permanent boundary between British Canada and the Oregon Territory. In April of that year, in two addresses before the Senate chambers, he strongly condemned those "Fifty-four forty men"—including fellow Missouri Senator David Rice Atchison, who became a leader of the "ultras" in the Senate—who advocated that parallel. Recounting the history of the joint occupation of the region in order to deny all American claims to the entire territory, Benton privately advised President Polk to accept the compromise boundary. He ultimately voted in favor of advising the president to accept the forty-ninth parallel, then again for the official treaty that incorporated the measure (which the Senate

13. Smith, *Magnificent Missourian*, 252 (first quote); Schlesinger, *Age of Jackson*, 473 (second quotes); Nagel, *Missouri*, 114; Montgomery Blair to M. M. Marmaduke, February 22, 1849, Sappington Family Papers, box 5, MHS (third quote); Burks, "Thunder on the Right," 258–59.

ratified 41–14) and which Polk ultimately signed. The majority of Missouri's Democratic newspapers favored Atchison's—and decried Benton's—stance on Oregon, and county meetings called throughout the state loudly echoed the criticisms, none of which prevented Benton from boasting his having saved the nation from inviting "the calamities of a war upon mistakes and blunders."[14]

While Benton's contrary Oregon position piqued the anger of Missouri's Democrats, his stance on the war with Mexico—and especially the conflict's ultimate resolution—inflamed their passions. Upon first word of the hostilities between Mexicans and U.S. troops at the Rio Grande, Benton—chairman of the Senate Military Affairs committee—steadfastly opposed this war as inconsistent "with the honour of the country." He insisted that American troops were on Mexican—not Texas—soil when attacked, even in private meetings with the president and key cabinet members. Missourians disagreed, and loudly; a Howard County Democratic meeting—for which Jackson served on the resolutions committee—passed unanimously a series of resolutions affirming "That the present war was commenced by Mexico in support of pretensions unwarranted by reason or justice; [and] that it is the duty of our government to prosecute it vigorously to a successful termination, . . . and that we condemn those, who would oppose the action of the government in the efficient and energetic prosecution of the war." Once Congress had voted overwhelmingly to wage war, however, Benton quickly began to support its prosecution, consistent with his position as chair of the Senate Military Affairs committee and encouraged by the success of his son-in-law, John C. Frémont, in the "Bear Flag Revolution" in California. None of his actions or stances was clear to Missourians, for Old Bullion stayed away from the state during it all, ignoring its people's mandates and allowing newspaper editors and a growing phalanx of political opponents to make their own war upon Benton as the country fought with Mexico. Old Bullion's return to Missouri in 1847, to heap praise upon the returning Missouri volunteers at a St. Louis celebration, rang hollow to many listeners.[15]

The Mexican War thrust Benton anew into the center of the Missouri political storm. Benton had ample warning of this tempest's approach, enough to avoid its clearly marked path or even any potentially powerful ground

14. Nagel, *Missouri,* 117 (first quote); Parrish, *David Rice Atchison,* 59–63; Meigs, *Life of Thomas Hart Benton,* 301–17 (second quote, p. 301); McCandless, *History of Missouri,* 238–39; Shalhope, *Sterling Price,* 52; Smith, *Magnificent Missourian,* 212 (third quote).

15. Smith, *Magnificent Missourian,* 210–11 (first quote), 212–15; *Missouri Democrat,* April 18, 1847 (second quote); Meigs, *Life of Thomas Hart Benton,* 358–61; Parrish, *David Rice Atchison,* 70–71; Chambers, *Old Bullion Benton,* 305–11; Robert W. Johannsen, ed., *To the Halls of the Montezumas: The Mexican War in the American Imagination,* 141.

strike. Yet Benton strode directly into the spate, defiant or perhaps reckless, believing himself impervious to the charged elements after nearly three decades in the Senate. In early 1847, as Congress debated the contentious Wilmot Proviso, which called for the prohibition of slavery in any territories gained from Mexico as a result of the war, a jittery Missouri General Assembly sent a clear message to Benton of its stance on the issue by passing a resolution instructing the state's senators to hold unerringly to the terms of the Missouri Compromise. While Benton had voted consistently against the Proviso to that point, he resented the public leashing, and especially that his junior colleague, David Rice Atchison, should have presented it as such in front of the full Senate. Owing his career to the compromise, the Gibraltar of the West needed no instructions on that score; rather, the legislature's resolution chafed Benton in that it assumed that the 36°30' parallel—the boundary between free and slave in the former Louisiana Territory with the decided exception of Missouri—now would extend to the soon-to-be acquired far western territories. Benton would have none of this fiction; his anger only heightened when, four days after Missouri legislators issued their instructions, John C. Calhoun presented to the Senate a series of resolutions that challenged the constitutionality of the Missouri Compromise, calling for the right of persons to carry slave property to all territories without restriction. To settle the issue and old scores, Benton returned for the first time in several years to Missouri.[16]

In May 1847, Benton gave public addresses in St. Louis and in the statehouse at Jefferson City, all of which centered on his steadfast opposition to Calhoun's "fire brand resolutions." Confident of his support in the river city, Benton also believed that in the Boon's Lick he was speaking among friends, especially after a Howard County Democratic meeting—chaired by Wade M. Jackson—during the previous winter had nominated him as the party's candidate for president in the upcoming election, and asked his permission "in presenting your name to the nation." In his gracious refusal, Benton claimed that, owing to "the glaring fact that, in above fifty years existence of this federal government, the democracy of the north had given but one President to the Union," he believed that the current climate demanded that "the course of things would have to be changed, otherwise there would be an end of the democratic party." Echoing such sentiments in his public speeches, Benton took up the "new slavery question," drawing down on Calhoun by decrying the "propagandism [that] is now the doctrine of the political sect which assumes to be the standard bearer of all the slave holding states and to plant slavery, by law, in all the Territories of the United

16. McCandless, *History of Missouri*, 243–44; Schlesinger, *Age of Jackson*, 450–57; Parrish, *David Rice Atchison*, 65–67.

States . . . becomes the design and the attempt!" "Heretofore," Benton reminded the audiences, "we the slave holding states, have stood together upon two points—Defence and Compromise—the defence of property and institutions and the compromise of the laws and of the constitution; and on these two points . . . both political parties, have been able to stand with us." The fate of the Union, Old Bullion thundered, now was at stake, as Calhoun and the other fire-eaters schemed to make "the sole principle of slavery propagandism" the new litmus for presidential aspirants, threatening the entire political party structure and jeopardizing the "harmony and stability of our federal Union." This "subversion of the Union," Old Bullion warned, was "one on which no northern man can stand."[17]

By drawing the sectional lines of this debate into Missouri, Benton left listeners—already confused over his anomalous stances on Texas and the Mexican War, themselves obscured by his years of absence—bewildered about not only his position on the future of the West but also as to his own sectional identity. Rather than condemn Benton's latest obfuscation, the state's Democratic editors, unable to decipher Old Bullion's intent, virtually ignored the issue, leaving a deafening silence hanging over Missouri's political landscape for the entire summer and fall of 1847. Charles M. Bradford wrote disquietingly from Arrow Rock that "things are at best mostly dandily *mixed* even here," even among the once solidly pro-Benton Sappingtons. Indeed, Bradford related that a frustrated Dr. Sappington suggested that "an invitation be given to Benton & [Jackson] to address the citizens of this county on some day soon that the object be stated in the letter of invitation—he said if Benton refuses then he may be dam'd." As winter set in, Claib Jackson moved to the center of the din. At a December meeting in Howard County, John J. Lowry (still a Benton stalwart) called for a resolution supporting Benton for his leadership of the war effort and for a special military commission that would make him supreme commander of the war in Mexico. Jackson, along with D. R. Scott and others, immediately objected, claiming that they were dismayed with Benton's stance on slavery in the territories. After a lengthy and heated debate, the assembly voted down the resolution. One editor recognized this clear "repudiation" of Benton as a signal that Old Bullion's grip on the Boon's Lick—indeed Missouri—was "on the wane and that the ice is now being broken against him." More directly, the action turned even more of the once-solid Fayette Clique—

17. Thomas Hart Benton to Wade M. Jackson, May 7, 1847, printed in *Missouri Democrat,* May 24, 1847 (first, third, fourth, sixth through ninth, eleventh quotes); Jackson to Benton, January 13, 1847, in ibid. (second quote); Chambers, *Old Bullion Benton,* 316–17, 318 (fifth and tenth quotes); *Jefferson Inquirer,* May 29, 1847; McCandless, *History of Missouri,* 244–45; Shalhope, *Sterling Price,* 78–80.

including John J. Lowry, who had earlier that year supported Jackson for Benton's vacant seat if he had been appointed commander-in-chief of the forces in Mexico—against Jackson as a viable party candidate.[18]

Jackson's failed gubernatorial and senatorial bids in 1848 propelled him into an all-out conflict with Old Bullion. During the winter of 1847, as the war neared a close, Jackson had begun pressing hard for his party's nomination. The newspaper editors gossiped freely, claiming that Jackson was cutting deals with local party leaders with abandon—including rival editors who might agree to remain silent during the campaign—promising appointments to them if he were to be elected. Indeed, Schuyler County Democrats instructed their delegates to vote at the spring nominating convention for Jackson, "the sterling democrat, . . . second to no man in his advocacy of the Hard money doctrine, and the champion of equal rights to all, . . . who with zeal and ability has stood foremost in fighting the battles of democracy in this State." Yet in his stirring about, courting the state's Democratic leaders, Jackson learned how pervasive was his reputation as being anti-Benton, now the factional litmus that had replaced the Hard-Soft schism that had once prevailed over Missouri politics. He traveled to St. Louis a few days prior to the nominating convention, as George Penn related, "with the view of disabusing the public mind upon this subject. . . . The numbers here in his support is much smaller than I had anticipated . . . now since the proceedings of the Howard meeting, voting a resolution down complimentary to Benton, Jackson has not gotten the proper hold and [that] may put him down." Penn was correct in his assessment of Jackson's bid for governor; after twenty ballots, he lost the nomination to Austin A. King, a Soft from western Missouri—who ultimately carried the election—and, adding insult to injury, the convention adopted a set of resolutions strongly supporting Benton. The anchor once securely cast in the General Assembly now appeared to chain Jackson agonizingly to port.[19]

That Benton stayed away from Missouri during one of its—and the nation's—most politically charged summers only eroded further his already precarious support in the state. The presidential election proved anything but a banal affair between two lackluster candidates; the entrance of a

18. Smith, *Magnificent Missourian*, 217–18; C. M. Bradford to C. F. Jackson, June 2, 1847, Sappington Family Papers, box 4, MHS (first quote); *Boon's Lick Times,* December 11, 1847, cited in Shalhope, *Sterling Price*, 80 (second and third quotes); J. J. Lowry to M. M. Marmaduke, March 20 (fourth quote), December 25, 1847, Sappington Family Papers, box 4, MHS.

19. *Missouri Democrat,* January 12, 19 (first quote), 1848; Shalhope, *Sterling Price*, 80–81; McCandless, *History of Missouri*, 245; Parrish, *Frank Blair*, 35; George Penn to M. M. Marmaduke, January 11, 1848, Sappington Family Papers, box 5, MHS (quote); West, "Earlier Political Career of Jackson," 141–42.

third party—the Free-Soilers, made up of seceded antislavery "Barnburner" Democrats, Liberty party abolitionists, and disgruntled Whigs, among others of the same stripe, and its candidate, former president Martin Van Buren, pitched Missouri into its newest slavery-induced fever. As Van Buren's old friend and confidant, Benton remained silent as to his choice of candidates, prompting the Missouri press and politicians to whip-saw the state's electorate over Old Bullion's affinities. The *Missouri Republican* declared that Benton would bolt the Democrats to support Van Buren while the *Saint Louis Daily Union,* with Samuel Treat, a member of the Democratic National Committee, as editor, declared consistently that Benton would remain loyal to the party and support its candidate, Lewis Cass. Moreover, Frank Blair only fueled the controversy over Benton's possible party defection. Blair, who had chaired the resolution committee at the state Democratic nominating convention, gave speeches in New York and St. Louis claiming Benton's support of Van Buren as well as orchestrating the publication of a new St. Louis newspaper, *Barnburner,* a pro–Van Buren, free-soil campaign organ, with endorsements and editorials from his father and brother, both party magnates. When in September Benton finally announced himself for Cass and the Democratic party, the gesture proved too late for the comfort of most of Missouri's Democrats, especially after he had, as late as August, supported a House bill that established a territorial government for Oregon which prohibited slavery. Old Bullion's clear flirtation with the Free-Soilers—who lost badly in Missouri—goaded the state's alarmed proslavery adherents to action. Missouri politico James H. Birch wrote, tellingly, "Benton forced his enemies to conspire to kill him that they might live."[20]

One of those who now leaped to Benton's throat was Claib Jackson. Jackson waged his assault both overtly and covertly, drawing popular attention to Benton's affiliation with the free-soil cause while working backroom politics to galvanize the Democratic opposition—the most direct threat to Benton's seat. Stumping the western and southwestern counties in support of Atchison's reelection to the U.S. Senate, Cass's candidacy for president, as well as for his own candidacy for the state senate (which he would soon receive, his only successful popular election to a position other than in the house prior to 1860), Jackson denounced the secessionist Barnburners as traitors to the Democratic party. At a party caucus in Jefferson City in late December, Jackson began stealth approaches on Benton. Sol J. Lowe, a pro-Benton representative to that caucus, related that "the Atchison men (almost

20. Parrish, *Frank Blair,* 35–39, and *David Rice Atchison,* 70–72; Shalhope, *Sterling Price,* 80–82; St. Louis *Daily Missouri Republican,* June 5, 6, 1848; *Saint Louis Daily Union,* June 30, 1848; McCandless, *History of Missouri,* 245–47; Meigs, *Life of Thomas Hart Benton,* 408 (quote).

without exception) pursued a course which might in its consequences to him have been disastrous but for the coolness & perfect temper of those who had no very great *feeling* in the matter. . . . [James M.] Hughes & Jackson came to my room the other night & after feeling round me (Knowing my political sympathies) boldly broached the matter [of breaking with Benton]—I hesitated & charged them in a jovial way of being influenced more by revengeful than party or political motives—they hesitated, not to acknowledge it."[21]

Within two weeks of the new year, Jackson launched a more direct assault on Benton, one that eclipsed even his 1844 reconnaissance-in-force following Old Bullion's initial response to Texas annexation. On January 15, 1849, upon taking his new seat in the Missouri Senate after the Christmas holiday recess (he managed to win election from Howard County in the fall 1848 election), Jackson introduced a set of resolutions designed to put on record the state's unadulterated future stance on the issue of slavery in the territories, and thus to curb Benton's incongruent free-soil proclivity as Missouri's senior senator. More directly, the resolutions sought to force Benton to noose his own elusive neck by means of imposing upon him instructions which its authors knew the senator could not at this point follow. The "Jackson Resolutions," the name immediately attached to the four submissions, might forever carry his name, but they were decidedly not of the new state senator's device; rather, William B. Napton, a staunch proslavery Democrat who had been educated at Princeton and the University of Virginia, practiced law in Fayette (where he briefly edited the *Boon's Lick Democrat*), and who had served as the state's attorney general and for the past decade as a justice of the Missouri Supreme Court, had written them. Shortly after the session had convened, Jackson and two other anti-Benton Democrats had met in Napton's office in the Capitol and after a lengthy discussion hatched the plan to force Benton's hand. Moreover, the effort was hardly secret; as early as November 1848, the *Missouri Republican* announced that "an effort will be made at the coming session of the legislature to instruct Col. Benton out of his seat in the Senate." Moreover, Napton had shown the resolutions to Sterling Price (an act that Price later would have to explain away to Benton), among others, prior to Jackson's introduction of them to the legislature.[22]

21. Parrish, *David Rice Atchison*, 38, 70–71, 136, 153; West, "Earlier Political Career of Jackson," 151–52; *Missouri Statesman*, September 1, 22, 1848; Shalhope, *Sterling Price,* 80–81; Sol J. Lowe to M. M. Marmaduke, December 31, 1848, Sappington Family Papers, box 5, MHS (quote). Hughes was a representative from Liberty, Clay County.

22. Secretary of State Election Returns, 1848, Capitol Fire Documents, 1806–1957, microfilm reel CFD-184, folders 16304–5, MSA; Napton Diary, box 3, folder 10, pp. 934, 986, 992–94, 998–99, MHS; Hugh P. Williamson, "William B. Napton: Man of Two Worlds," 208–11; *Reports of Cases Argued and Determined in the Supreme Court of the State of Missouri*, i–iv; McCandless, *History of Missouri*, 247–48; Parrish, *David*

The Jackson-Napton Resolutions declared boldly and unequivocally that Congress had no right to legislate against slavery in the territories, thus securing Missouri to consistent opposition to free-soilism and abolitionism and those who supported either position. Additionally, the resolutions upheld the position of popular sovereignty in the territories themselves, claiming it to harmonize and even equalize the union of states, whether future or present—a veiled condemnation of northern antislavery politics. The third resolution unmasked the sectional culprits, "regard[ing] the conduct of the northern states on the subject of slavery as releasing the slave holding state from all further adherence" to the Missouri Compromise, but "for the sake of harmony, and for the preservation of our Federal Union," Missourians would sanction the application of the compromise's principles to the recent territorial acquisitions (namely that those unorganized territories below the 36°30' parallel should be reserved for the introduction of slaves without congressional interference) "if by such concessions future aggressions upon the legal rights of the states may be arrested and the spirit of anti-slavery fanaticism be extinguished." The resolutions then drew two lines in the sand, one by claiming that if Congress were to pass any act contrary to them, "Missouri will be found in hearty co-operation with the slave-holding states," and the other—as expected and positioned strategically last, for impact— by instructing "our Senators in Congress . . . to act in conformity to the foregoing resolutions." With little debate, both the senate and the house quickly passed the resolutions with large majorities; by March, Governor King had signed them as well. Missouri, reminding the nation of its natal pain, claimed its birthright.[23]

Upon learning of the Jackson-Napton resolutions, Benton declared them the "offspring of the Calhoun address" and thus "fundamentally wrong," and refused outright to comply with them. He had already refused to attend the caucus of slave state senators and congressmen—among them John C. Calhoun and David Rice Atchison, newly reelected to the Senate—and had rejected the resultant set of resolutions known as the "Southern Address," issued days after the introduction of the Jackson-Napton resolutions. Similar in both wording and substance to those resolutions, the Southern Address

Rice Atchison, 86–87; *Missouri Republican,* November 7, 1848, quoted in Parrish, *Frank Blair,* 39 (quote), 40–42; West, "Earlier Political Career of Jackson," 162–63; Edward Bates Diary, 1848–1852, Edward Bates Papers, box 8, October 25, 1849 entry, MHS; Shalhope, *Sterling Price,* 82–83; *Jefferson Inquirer,* September 7, 1849, June 4, 1853.

23. Napton Diary, box 3, folder 10, 993–94, MHS (quotes); McCandless, *History of Missouri,* 247–48; Parrish, *David Rice Atchison,* 86–87; *Laws of the State of Missouri,* Fifteenth Gen. Ass., 1848–1849, 667; *Missouri Senate Journal,* Fifteenth Gen. Ass., First Sess., 1848–1849, 175; *Missouri House Journal,* Fifteenth Gen. Ass., First Sess., 1848–1849, 461.

bore the signatures of only 48 of the 121 senators and representatives from the slaveholding states in Congress; Atchison was the only supporter from Missouri's seven-man delegation. Though Benton considered the Southern Address treasonous, the sixty-seven-year-old senator saved his unalloyed wrath for the impudent Jackson-Napton resolutions and its chief architect, Jackson. Through his supporters in Missouri, Benton learned that dissension indeed existed within—and thus without—the statehouse regarding the Jackson-Napton resolutions; one representative lamented on the day of the resolutions' introduction that the affair was "one of the most arbitrary acts of one man['s] dictation for selfish purposes that it may ever my lot to witness. . . . Rumor on what foundation I know not has assigned as a reason for Jackson's course . . . [to have] a great party made to subserve the private ambition of a few men, at the expense of a partial sacrifice of the principles of that party, and a probable disruption of the element here composing it. . . . [T]he Democratic party of the State may ere long have to fight the battle of 1844 over again." Benton indeed intended to fight, but not within customary channels. Refusing to resign despite his avowal not to abide by the Jackson-Napton instructions, Benton—the great bear—took his case directly to the electorate.[24]

Returning to Missouri in May, Benton embarked upon the most strenuous speaking tour of his three-decade-long career in the Senate. From St. Louis, he issued a lengthy and blunt letter to "The People of Missouri" that denounced the Jackson-Napton resolutions. Then, on May 26, in the house chambers in Jefferson City, Benton bitterly denounced John C. Calhoun as the "prime mover and head contriver" of the position of the southern "nullifiers," or "ultras," bent on "the subversion of the Union." Twenty-one of the twenty-three newspaper columns required to print Benton's diatribe centered upon Calhoun, whom he accused of orchestrating a conspiracy against him. Answering a half-decade of criticism and perhaps carried away by the force of his passionate rhetoric, Benton declared unmistakably his final position on slavery, whether in the West or elsewhere. Though a slaveholder himself (a circumstance for which he all but apologized, portraying himself as benevolent victim), he thundered now that "if there was no slavery in Missouri today, I should oppose its coming in; if there was none in the United States, I should oppose its coming into the United States; as there is none in New Mexico or California, I am against sending it to those territories." Benton reserved his most savage invective for Calhoun's confederates in

24. *Missouri Statesman*, June 8, 1849 (first and second quotes); Parrish, *David Rice Atchison*, 87–88, and *Frank Blair*, 40–42; McCandless, *History of Missouri*, 248–49; Sol J. Lowe to M. M. Marmaduke, January 15, 1849, Sappington Family Papers, box 5, MHS (third quote); William E. Smith, *The Francis Preston Blair Family in Politics*, vol. 1, 252–53.

Missouri, on whom he now declared war. "Now I have them," he screamed, "and between them and me, henceforth and forever, *a high wall and a deep ditch!* and no communication, no compromise, no caucus with them."[25]

Benton's fury at the Missouri Calhoun element may have been both provoked and measured. The Blairs had related to Old Bullion that Jackson's newfound spleen stemmed from a secret deal with Atchison that if Jackson would support him for reelection to the Senate (the state's newspapers had made it clear that as late as the last day of September 1848, Jackson had stumped for Atchison's seat, rather than for his reelection), Atchison would throw in for Jackson when Benton's seat came open. The logic of the scheme far outweighed the evidence. Regardless, Frank Blair wrote under a pseudonym that "The Wolf Is on His Walk Again," echoing the plot in the *Missouri Republican.* The following June, another of Benton's friends, Whig state senator James S. Rollins, communicated to Old Bullion Jackson's complicity in another, more inventive plot against him, claiming that the Fayettan was using his position on the Senate Education Committee to target pro-Benton leaders of the state university at Columbia:

> There is a small clique in this State (*more* than a *baker's dozen*) who I think have very much mistaken the public sentiment on the subject of Slavery—the Wilmot or *Calhoun* proviso &c; acting with you politically but *long* secretly and violently opposed to you, they have siezed [*sic*] upon the subject, and they present time for your overthrow. . . . You are not the only person who has been marked as a victim to be sacrificed, on account of your "freesoil" sentiments. The elegant gentleman and erudite scholar Mr. Lathrop, who presides over the University is to be driven from the State, on account of his supposed coincidence of feeling and views with you, on this subject. The same clique, who got up Jacksons resolutions, carried thro' the Legislature a law, changing the . . . government of the college—locating the board of curators, in the affluent circuits, under the pretext of giving to it more the character of a state Institution, but really with a view of thrusting aside the old board, and placing in power, men whose opinions and actions could be controlled by Jackson & Co and thus, to displace the President.[26]

Enraged, Benton now devoted six months to the state—in many of its residents' opinion, he had all but neglected it for more than a decade—to

25. Parrish, *David Rice Atchison,* 87–88, and *Frank Blair,* 40–42; *Jefferson Inquirer,* May 19 (first quote), May 26, 1849 (second through sixth quotes); Chambers, *Old Bullion Benton,* 247–49; Shalhope, *Sterling Price,* 84–85.

26. Chambers, *Old Bullion Benton,* 342; Meigs, *Life of Thomas Hart Benton,* 411; Montgomery Blair to M. M. Marmaduke, February 22, 1849, Sappington Family Papers, box 5, MHS; Burks, "Thunder on the Right," 282–83; *Missouri Republican,* January 3, 13, February 1, 1849; *Glasgow Times,* January 4, 1849; Parrish, *David Rice Atchison,* 87–88, and *Frank Blair,* 40–41, 42 (first quote); James S. Rollins to T. H. Benton, June 6, 1849, James S. Rollins Papers, Mss. 1026, folder 15, microfilm reel 2, SHSM (second quote). John Hiram Lathrop was the first president of the University of Missouri.

punishing these conspiratorial whelps as he "let loose the dogs of war," as one newspaper described Old Bullion's political style. He now attempted to move Missouri toward his vision of the West, all the while securing his position in the Senate. Benton now accepted all invitations to speak, especially in the Boon's Lick, traditional center of his support, now the epicenter of the revolution against him. At Boonville, New Franklin, Lexington, Columbia, Glasgow, Platte City, Liberty, and Fayette, Benton found the dusty roads choked with wagons as throngs of farmers crowded into the courthouses, churches, and town squares to attend his well-publicized speeches. Fighting for his political life, Benton employed all his prodigious oratorical acumen honed during thirty years of senatorial battles, as well as the personal courage with which to wage those battles in the face of a multitude of enemies. The Blairs feared daily that he would be assassinated.[27]

Benton's once-solid Central Clique now cleaved in their allegiances to Old Bullion. The volatile party stalwart John J. Lowry (who as recently as February wrote to Montgomery Blair that he supported Benton and "forswears Jackson. . . . He is too ambitious altogether") communicated to Marmaduke in late May that while he still could not support Jackson (he was "not a man after my own heart!") he now considered Benton "a Wilmot provisoist. . . . [who] abandons the south & the West! I mourn over him as one of the Democracy's champions, & a great mind in perfect error. Well, with heart felt emotions, I now leave him! I am for my country, for the South & the West, & the North, the whole union, but can never agree that the South & West shall be shorn & deprived of their constitutional rights! No never." George Penn, on the other hand, "had at all times every desire to sustain Col. Benton . . . for the valuable services that he can still tender of which the party in Missouri as well as the nation may & likely will greatly need." Capitalizing on this chasm, Benton took personal aim at Napton, Atchison, and especially Jackson at every turn, hoping to discredit them in Old Bullion's commanding presence. At one speech, seeing his principal antagonists in the audience, Benton pointed them out for scorn, crying, "And here are Claib Jackson [and the others, naming them] as demure as three prostitutes at a christening." At Lexington, Benton brought roars of laughter when he claimed the lineage of the Jackson-Napton resolutions: "CALHOUN, *the father;* NAPTON, *the Granny;* CLAIB JACKSON, the nurse, and clout washer." At New Franklin, after a two-hour harangue, when Jackson (who was in attendance) approached the podium unannounced to respond, "Col. Benton took his hat and marched off without deigning to cast a look even of scorn upon the pigmy defender of the disunion resolutions—

27. *Boon's Lick Times,* July 30, December 17, 1842 (quote), September 30, 1848; Parrish, *Frank Blair,* 40–42.

so called by Col. Benton." A large portion of the crowd left with him, leaving Jackson, as one observer related, with "the clique only for listeners."[28]

Despite Benton's entertaining, even awing, of many of those in his rapt audiences throughout the Boon's Lick, many more listeners were far from satisfied with what they heard from their elder statesman under the fiery summer sun. A violent newspaper war preceded the senator at virtually every stop: "OBEY OR RESIGN" blared the *St. Louis Union*. Atchison himself fueled "the fire in the rear," in his published words "making open war upon [Benton]" by stumping the region in opposition to the senior senator's appeal, often preceding, sometimes shadowing Old Bullion's appearances. Locals distributed and posted handbills to influence the listeners, while Democratic meetings (many organized by Jackson and his supporters) prepared the audiences with condemnations of Benton (such as those offered by Jackson at a Fayette meeting) as "a full brother of Van Buren, Wade, Giddings, Chas. Adams, and the whole brood of Abolitionists of the North," passing resolutions supporting the Jackson-Napton resolutions and Atchison's reading of them in the Senate. Benton often found hostile audiences, who jeered and cat-called his comments; at Fayette, where Benton spoke uninvited, "pistols and Bowie-knives were largely in demand," and Benton received threats that he would be tarred and feathered and if he did not answer questions he would have to walk over dead bodies in order to leave the Central College chapel. After speaking in Platte City—Atchison's home—the editor of the *Argus* printed that Benton had cried "*GOD DAMN* Platte City,—*GOD DAMN* it, I wouldn't make another speech there to save it from the fate of Sodom and Gomorrah." The opposition to Benton was as resolute as Old Bullion was determined; one writer declared, "I am against Benton and the 'Wilmot proviso[.]' I am against Benton, and in favor of the right of instruction. I am against Benton and the whole troop of northern fanitics [*sic*], and abolitionists his new allies. I believe in the principals set forth in the 'Jac[k]son' resolutions, and hold if they even were wrong yet Benton is bound to obey them. Benton is certainly down in Missouri as Van Buren, and can never rise again, and all prominent men who sustain him in his apostasy will immolate themselves forever."[29]

28. Shalhope, *Sterling Price*, 86–87; Montgomery Blair to M. M. Marmaduke, February 22, 1849, Sappington Family Papers, box 5, MHS (first quote); J. J. Lowry to M. M. Marmaduke, May 13, 1849, ibid., box 5, MHS (second quote); George Penn to M. M. Marmaduke, July 25, 1849, ibid., box 5, MHS (third quote); Meigs, *Life of Thomas Hart Benton*, 456 (fourth quote); *Glasgow Times*, July 26, 1849 (fifth quote); Smith, *Magnificent Missourian*, 250–51, 252 (sixth quote); *Missouri Statesman*, June 22, 1849 (seventh quote).

29. *St. Louis Union*, July 23, 1849 (first quote); *Missouri Statesman*, March 23, 1849 (second quote), June 8, 1849 (third quote), September 7, 1849 (fourth quote);

Jackson also stumped for the resolutions he publicly declared to have written, and for it took the beating of his political life. He faced venomous criticisms from all sides, within and without the Clique, both for leading the attack on Benton and for the introduction of the resolutions to which he lay claim. Publishing an appeal of his own, he defended the resolutions as consistent with his beliefs as well as for the wishes of the people of Missouri and vowed that if the voters should support Benton's stance on "Wilmot, Van Buren, and the Free Soil party, I shall resign my seat in the Senate." His impassioned stance failed to impress many of the local newspaper editors; the *Jefferson Inquirer* decried him as "the great Missouri nullifier . . . [whose] ridiculous ignorance and political depravity, has secured for him no small share of notoriety. . . . They [the voters] have often repudiated him—they do it now, and will ever continue." Columbia's *Missouri Statesman* ridiculed Jackson's subaltern effort against Benton at Fayette, its correspondent claiming to have "heard before now of the Weasel and of the Lion; of pitching straws against the wind; of firing pop-guns at the rock of Gibraltar; of the mole-hill and of the mountain, and I saw all of these comparisons illustrated in the speeches of Benton and of Jackson." A number of regional papers hounded Jackson about claiming authorship of "these traitorous resolutions," deriding him and his credibility for claiming to be "the begetter of the bastard which [Napton] fathered" and at least one renamed them, more accurately, the "Napton-Calhoun Resolutions."[30]

More ominous, a number of editors saw Jackson's once-bright political future now dim. One argued that "if some of the would-be leaders of the Democratic party (Jackson, Wells, and Company) survive the shock of Col. Benton's appeal, we think they could easily recover from Cholera itself," while another claimed to have "told him long ago that he was getting his head in a hornet's nest and now he will soon see the result." One was clear, if poetic, on Jackson's inevitable fate: "Poor Jackson. I fear he has embarked 'upon a sea of troubles,' and that the tide of his political fortune is beginning to ebb." Between July and mid-October, the *Jefferson Inquirer* reported that at least fifteen Missouri counties had gone on record as being against the Jackson-Napton resolutions, and at least six newspapers that had pledged support to Jackson in the fight against Benton came out for Old Bullion as he took his tour to the southwestern and southeastern portions of the state. One editor who followed Benton's campaign estimated that he delivered

Burks, "Thunder on the Right," 289–91; Chambers, *Old Bullion Benton,* 346–47; Smith, *Magnificent Missourian,* 252–53 (fifth quote, p. 252); Parrish, *David Rice Atchison,* 90–91; Lisbon Applegate to M. M. Marmaduke, June 18, 1849, Sappington Family Papers, box 5, MHS (sixth quote).

30. *Jefferson Inquirer,* July 14, 1849 (first quote), June 4, 1853 (third, fourth, and fifth quotes), August 11, 18, 1849; *Missouri Statesman,* September 7, 1849 (second quote).

three hundred speeches in just five months. True to his word, he refused to compromise with his Missouri antagonists; when learning of a proposed peace meeting with the opposition, Benton declared that he "would sooner sit in council with the six thousand dead who died of cholera in St. Louis, than go into convention with such a gang of scamps."[31]

Allegiance or opposition to Benton now defined the camps within Missouri's Democratic legion. The summer of 1849, in one contemporary's recollection, "was characterized by a bitterness of invective and popular excitement without parallel in the history of Missouri," making unavoidable the maelstrom that was the 1850 elections. Benton's apparent defection to the free-soil cause had done damage enough to his support in the state, but his savage attacks on Jackson and Calhoun, too, had taken a toll. Several of the leading newspapers of the state, including the *Jefferson City Metropolitan*, speculated that "Colonel Benton has lost his reason and is now the prey to his wicked and ungovernable passions. . . . [H]e is every day losing the respect and confidence of his friends, he seems determined on self-ruin." Benton did not return to Missouri during the election year, trusting to the long oar he had pulled the previous summer. Similarly, Jackson's conspicuous leadership of the anti-Benton forces and unwillingness to disavow any complicity in a plot to rob Benton of his seat doomed any chance he might have had for election to the Senate should Old Bullion not prevail.[32]

The bitter prelude to the late summer contest had served the Whigs well, and as the summer of 1850 wore on, most perceived that they, not the Democrats, held Benton's fate. Hopelessly fractured over Old Bullion and the Jackson-Napton instructions, the Democrats were unable to unite on any issue, much less Benton's seat. In the August congressional elections, the Whigs captured three of five districts; in the elections to the legislature, the party of Clay elected sixty-four members, as compared to fifty-five pro-Benton and thirty-seven anti-Benton Democrats; in the state senate, thirteen Benton Democrats, twelve Whigs, and eight anti-Benton Democrats (including Jackson) prepared to do battle. Benton was confident that the results of the election would work to his favor. Hungry for their first Senate seat, the Whigs began bargaining with the anti-Bentonites in the General Assembly, so much so that one correspondent intimated that they intended "to hand the Whig party body and soul to the Nullifiers." Jackson's "corrupt bargain"

---

31. *Missouri Statesman*, May 18, 1849 (first quote), June 8, 1849 (third quote); *Daily Missouri Republican*, May 10, 1849 (second quote); Burks, "Thunder on the Right," 291–92; *Jefferson Inquirer*, April 6, 1850 (fourth quote). The nation's cities, including St. Louis, experienced a cholera outbreak in 1849, thus the cluster of references to the deadly disease.

32. Meigs, *Life of Thomas Hart Benton*, 411–12 (first quote); *Jefferson City Metropolitan*, October 30, 1849 (second quote); Burks, "Thunder on the Right," 305; Shalhope, *Sterling Price*, 94–97; Parrish, *David Rice Atchison*, 91–93, 110–14.

with Atchison for Benton's seat appeared unfounded; his name did not enter into the debate for nominees when balloting began in joint session. After forty ballots, Henry S. Geyer, a proslavery Whig (until recently a Democrat) from St. Louis emerged the winner, but only after a last-minute bargain that allowed the anti-Benton Democrats all positions elected by the assembly. The longest consecutive reign of any U.S. senator was over; the sacrificers had knifed Missouri's Caesar.[33]

Missouri's Brutus, too, was soon buried. Many blamed Jackson for the split in the Democratic party that resulted in the Whig victory. Moreover, within days of Benton's defeat a vindictive Jackson introduced separate motions to censure the former senator for his "treason" to the Democratic party and to remove Benton's painting from the wall of the senate chamber in Jefferson City, turning many more against him. Jackson found the backlash against him stronger than during his campaign against Benton, compounded by the realization that for many, Benton had become alternately a martyr to the Democratic cause or a victim to Jackson's chicanery. Outside Fayette, Jackson witnessed his support eroding in the Boon's Lick, even among those in Howard and Chariton Counties who had sent him so recently to the state senate. In late 1851, rumors surfaced that Jackson had purchased a farm near Hannibal in Marion County (where two of his stepchildren lived) and that he intended to leave the Boon's Lick, prompting the *Missouri Statesman* to note coldly that "the Hannibal *Courier* congratulates the people of that part of the State upon the Major's removal among them. There are those who will just as heartily congratulate the people of this part of the State upon the Major's removal from them. Politically, the Major is an awful sinner."[34]

Knowing he could not win, Jackson chose not to run for his senate seat when it came open in 1852 and instead focused on a return to the house. By the narrowest of margins he won the election (as well as being chosen as one of eight of his district's electors for the fall's presidential election) largely with the vote of the rabid proslavery element in unrepentant Howard County. Upon assuming his seat in the winter of 1853, Jackson found his resolutions assailed, led by the newly elected representative from St. Louis, Frank Blair, who sought to repeal the Jackson-Napton abominations in part to avenge Benton's defeat. Jackson himself was anything but exempt from the attacks; he was in fact as much the target as were the resolutions. Blair attacked the resolutions not along the issue of slavery, but because they represented

33. Chambers, *Old Bullion Benton*, 374–77; Burks, "Thunder on the Right," 307–12; Shalhope, *Sterling Price*, 92–93; Parrish, *David Rice Atchison*, 112–13; McCandless, *History of Missouri*, 251–53; McClure, *Opposition in Missouri to Thomas Hart Benton*, 211–16.

34. *Democrat Banner*, January 13, 1851, cited in Burks, "Thunder on the Right," 315, 316; *Missouri Statesman*, January 17, December 19, 1851 (quote).

a plot by "demagogues who compose the bulk of the Anti-Benton party [and who] have repudiated the principles and sentiments of Jefferson and the other patriarchs of the Democratic party." The *Jefferson Inquirer* used stronger words:

> On one side is presented the cause of the people; on the other, that of a few dishonest politicians; the question to be decided is, whether the State shall continue longer officially committed to the false and odious doctrine of nullification, nay, whether the Jackson resolutions shall remain, not only as the solemn legislative declaration of a falsehood, but as the unimpeached and unimpeachable evidence of a criminal conspiracy to destroy a faithful public servant, in which the Legislature itself was fraudulently made the instrument to accomplish the purpose, and thus perpetuate a disgrace to which every honest citizen of Missouri is wrongfully made a party.

The counterattack forced Jackson, on his heels, to define and defend their—his—doctrines as consistent with those of other slaveholding states who together faced the national ramifications of the westward march. After weeks of debate, the Whigs and "Anties" in the legislature came together to table the debate for fear of rending themselves yet again. The Jackson-Napton resolutions stood, but on unsteady legs.[35]

By summer, Jackson was a candidate for Congress. He faced Whig James J. Lindley in the Third District, occupying eighteen counties in northern Missouri. Campaigning in July, Jackson defended his record and his resolutions before mixed crowds, attempting to downplay his role in the division of the Democrats and even his stand against Benton. A rumor that he had traveled to Washington to assist Atchison with patronage in Missouri brought renewed charges of wire-pulling. The Benton press excoriated him; the *Jefferson Inquirer* wrote that "If the spirit of the Sage of the Hermitage, did not rebuke a true democrat for voting for Jackson, a wounded conscience would. . . . Let such men be laid aside, and soon peace and quiet will be found in the ranks of the democracy:—Support such tricksters, and we may ever expect to see bickering and strife throughout the whole State." In August, Jackson was defeated in a district that many charged was configured to secure his success, and largely by anti-Benton Democrats voting against him. Even in Scotland County, the strongest anti-Benton Democratic county in the state, Jackson lost by more than two hundred votes. The *Paris Mercury* gloated over the defeat: "What an awful sight must have been for Jackson, to see his own party marching up by platoons and casting their votes for

---

35. Secretary of State Election Returns, 1852, Capitol Fire Documents, 1806–1957, microfilm reel CFD-185, folders 16333–43, 16346, MSA; *Jefferson Inquirer,* February 12, 1853 (first quote), February 19, 1853 (second quote), March 12, 1853; *Glasgow Weekly Times,* February 17, 24, 1853, April 7, 1853; *Missouri Statesman,* March 11, 24, 1853; Parrish, *Frank Blair,* 50–53.

Lindley. . . . Jackson completely vanquished on the stump—routed 'horse, foot and dragoons,' in a district which the year before had given 1800 democratic majority—and that, too, by a young man who had never before engaged in a political contest, was almost entirely unknown in many of the counties of the district! Is there another *such* a defeat or *such* a triumph on record?" Ironically, in the same election, residents of Missouri's First District elected Thomas Hart Benton overwhelmingly to Congress as their representative, his first popular election in more than three decades. Ambition's debt had been well paid.[36]

36. *Jefferson Inquirer,* July 1, 9 (first quote), 16, 23, 1853; *Glasgow Weekly Times,* March 24, April 7, August 11, 22, September 1 (second quote), 15, 1853; *Missouri Statesman,* July 22, 1853; Parrish, *Frank Blair,* 52.

THE CRIME AGAINST MISSOURI

ONE OFTEN FINDS in . . . communities [in transition] the prospect of change being regarded ominously, as if change inevitably means loss. A frequent and glib description of what is feared may be lost is "way of life"; part of what is meant is sense of self.

ANTHONY H. COHEN, *THE SYMBOLIC CONSTRUCTION OF COMMUNITY*

Missouri's nearly decade-long political nightmare accomplished more than a simple pogrom of the state's leading factional antagonists. As witnessed by the bitter struggle for Benton's U.S. Senate seat, this was no mere contest between legislative rivals or even cabals for an election-year plum; the depth of the animosities alone offers such. Rather, this was by 1850 a jihad, a holy war for the state's—for the West's—soul. That Missouri's most visible (and most perpetual) office-seeker toppled the state's original senator from his proprietary throne was in fact incidental to the truest nature of the conflict, one refined or even altered by the very tumult that surrounded the coup. Slavery, once conquest right, then social good, and now political shibboleth in Missouri, defined its residents no longer as part of the western landscape they had created, but instead as resisters against an invasion that was defiling their once-pristine home.

The language of power employed during Benton's long torment points clearly toward a transition of mind in Missouri with regard to the place of slavery in the state and the region. Old Bullion's damning sin had been neither his wayward party demeanor nor his imperious nature (earning him the derisive nickname "the great I AM"); each of these infelicities had been in place well prior to his precipitous fall from grace. His immolation resulted from his apparent outright embrace of the free-soil doctrine that in itself signaled a sea change in his philosophy of the West. Benton considered his stance consistent; he had long championed the right of individuals, of common men, consistent with his devotion to Jacksonian principles. Yet while this conviction had once found an audience with western farmers who formed the core of the party's membership, by 1850 the mass electorate in the maturing northern cities—workingmen, artisans, and shopkeepers— had eclipsed them within the Democratic party ranks and now steered the machine. Ironically, the maelstrom of popular politics also drove the people's party sharply away from individual liberty and toward majoritarianism, a fact certainly not lost on Benton's nemesis, John C. Calhoun. In the West, one of the transition's first targets was slavery; one of its first victims was Old Bullion, who bet his stake on the future of the nation according to the new eastern model and lost much of it in his by now bellicose Missouri.[1]

Indeed, Missouri's newly risen star—David Rice Atchison—ascended to his place by adopting Calhoun's rhetoric, if not his world. An able confederate of Calhoun who assisted in the drafting of the Southern Address and then proved the lone Missourian to sign it, Atchison actively championed it in his home state. To his own Platte Countians, he avowed that he "expect[ed] always to be found acting with the southern men in the Senate chamber and out of it, in defence of the rights of the southern States." Moreover, Atchison publicly supported Missouri's Jackson-Napton resolutions, the General Assembly's refraction of the Calhoun address, claiming that "as a Senator from Missouri and as a citizen of a Slave State, it is my duty to resist every attempt to change her institutions, and every assault upon her rights."[2]

However fiery his words, Atchison was no planter, not in Missouri's reckoning, much less that of the plantation states. He was not even a farmer, but a bachelor lawyer and circuit court judge prior to attaining the Senate. Atchison, son of a small slaveholding Bluegrass yeoman, had removed from Kentucky not to Missouri's Boon's Lick, the state's slaveholding heart, but to far western Clay and Platte Counties, vestibules to the slaveholding river counties that by 1850 boasted regionally as many as 50,000 of the state's 103,671 chattels, worth an estimated twenty-five million dollars. Atchison quickly became seignior of the region's common whites and, if judged by his words—and ultimately his deeds—in defense of slavery in the West, he proved indistinguishable from the fire-eaters of South Carolina and Mississippi. Yet one incontrovertible fact set him decidedly apart from those rabid cotton state defenders of the peculiar institution: Atchison owned at most one bondman.[3]

---

1. *Missouri Statesman,* May 18, 1849 (quote); Schlesinger, *Age of Jackson,* 401–8, 413–21.

2. *Liberty Tribune,* June 29, 1849, quoted in Parrish, *David Rice Atchison,* 79–80 (quote).

3. Nagel, *Missouri,* 126; Parrish, *David Rice Atchison,* 1–5; Trexler, *Slavery in Missouri,* 43–44; Sixth U.S. Census, 1840, Population Schedule, Clay County, Missouri, NA; Seventh U.S. Census, 1850, Population and Slave Schedules, Platte County, Missouri, NA; Eighth U.S. Census, 1860, Population and Slave Schedules, Clinton County, Missouri, NA. William Freehling offers a description of Atchison's F Street "mess," or the Washington boardinghouse that he shared with three fellow senators from slaveholding states, Virginians William O. Goode and James M. Mason and South Carolinian Andrew P. Butler, that includes three black domestic servants. No record indicates that any of these slaves belonged to Atchison. Indirect evidence suggests that at this time he might have had a personal servant named George. By August 1865, Atchison clearly had slaves in his

Atchison was anything but alone as a non-slave-owning Missourian. Missouri's year of meteors—1850—coincided with a precipitous proportional downturn in the state's slaveholdings; in that year, slaves represented 12.8 percent of its total population, down from more than 15 percent a decade before. By 1860, after the waves of immigrants had poured into the state, Missouri slaves accounted for just 9.6 percent of its residents, the smallest of the slave states save Delaware. More to the point, in that year slave-owning families represented just 18.4 percent of the state's total, lowest of any of the slave states save Delaware and a far cry from South Carolina, where more than half of all free white families owned bondpeople. By 1860, Missouri's twenty-four-thousand-odd slaveholders would constitute just 2.3 percent of its total free population; they and their families represented just 12.5 percent of Missouri's white families.[4]

Clearly, Atchison's peculiar crusade for the peculiar institution was no mere charade designed to win political support among slaveholders or anyone else—his ultimate relinquishment of his Senate seat over the issue settled that question. That Missouri's most ardent defender of slaveholding was himself not the master of slaves offers a revealing insight into the complex evolution that the issue of slavery had undergone in the minds of Missourians, slave-holding and not. The dualistic nature of slavery in the state only complicated the issue further. Rather than signaling any death knell in the state, raw slave numbers in Missouri actually increased during the same period, and they did so far more dramatically than their proportion within the state's overall population declined. Between 1830 and 1850, Missouri's slave population more than tripled to 87,422; by 1860, that number had increased by another third to 114,931, an all-time high. More than 35,000 of these labored in the central river counties. Inflated prices of slaves offered no indication that chattel bondage was waning in Missouri. Prime field hands fetched routinely as much as fifteen hundred dollars in Howard County, while annual prices for hired laborers caused one resident of Prairieville to write to Claib Jackson late in the decade that "every thing is rising in value—especially negro property—

---

possession; indeed, a letter written from Grayson County, Texas, to his brother in Clay County, Missouri, states that "I have all the rest of the Negroes on my hands and know not what to do with them." The letter does not state whether he owned these slaves. If he did, Atchison likely acquired them after retiring from the Senate in 1855 to a 250-acre farm in Platte County. Possibly he had taken his brother's slaves to the relative safety of northern Texas while his brother remained in war-torn Missouri. See Freehling, *Road to Disunion*, 550; A[ndrew] P. Butler to Atchison, March 5, 1856, David Rice Atchison Papers, Mss. 71, folder 6, SHSM; D. R. Atchison to William Atchison, August 12, 1865, ibid., folder 6, SHSM, quoted in Parrish, *David Rice Atchison*, 220–21 (quote), and 115.

4. Gray, *History of Agriculture in the Southern United States*, vol. 1, 482; McCandless, *History of Missouri*, 35–36, 59–60; Hurt, *Agriculture and Slavery in Little Dixie*, 219–23; Nagel, *Missouri*, 128.

hirelings went at most exorbitant prices on New Year's day—men generally at about $230 for the year. . . . Slave labor has never been any thing like so high." In the last antebellum decade, slavery was thriving.[5]

Given the proliferation of slavery in Missouri, the storm clouds that gathered with the coming of abolitionism became a tempest during the debate over Texas, Mexico, free soil, and Benton. With roots sunk firmly into a bedrock of individual and democratic rights, these westerners found it easy to construct an active response to the threat posed to their social good by the antislavery host. Armed with the battle cry of liberty, they waged war first against William Lloyd Garrison's undemocratic minions, then against any of their own who turned against the cause. In this new sectional realm, Missourians targeted those they knew best, their free-state antagonists—now including Benton, who advocated a northern president— who sought to subvert democratic ascendance in the West. "It was the fixed design of the Free States," Atchison howled, "not only to prevent the Slave States from any further participation in the Territories of the United States, but by a series of measures to reduce the latter to a state of *helpless inferiority,* and to subject them and their institutions to the mercy of Abolitionism. And that Missouri would be the first victim sacrificed upon the altar of this infernal spirit." Echoing this sentiment, justice William B. Napton wrote in 1850 that "the persistence of the North is regarded as a proof of her fixed and settled purpose, not only to prevent the increase of slave territory but gradually to undermine and ultimately to destroy the institution itself. This will be resisted as an unconstitutional interference with our domestic concerns." Recognizing slavery's power in Missouri's consciousness, artist George Caleb Bingham remarked astutely in 1854 that "the slavery agitation is too convenient an instrument in the hands of demagogues to be dispensed with."[6]

As abolitionists within and without attacked Missouri's social good, its democratic right, an alarmed populace quickly parroted proslavery arguments articulated by Calhoun and other positive good apologists. Napton was one of the state's most ardent polemicists; the justice accused free-soilers of duplicity as well as hypocrisy "in trying to shut up slavery within the old states and exclude it from the new territories, which shows clearly their motives to be not of a philanthropic character—but merely based upon a thirst for political power. . . . If slavery is an evil . . . it is most manifest that

5. Gray, *History of Agriculture in the Southern United States,* vol. 2, 650–56; Hurt, *Agriculture and Slavery in Little Dixie,* 222–23; Trexler, *Slavery in Missouri,* 37–43; McCandless, *History of Missouri,* 35–36, 57; P. Carr to C. F. Jackson, January 15, 1859, John S. Sappington Papers, Mss. 1027, box 3, folder 95, SHSM (quote).

6. Parrish, *David Rice Atchison,* 73 (first quote); Napton Diary, folder 1, pp. 50–51, MHS (second quote); McCandless, *History of Missouri,* 270 (third quote).

emigration to new territories will ameliorate the condition of the slave as well as his master. Our own experience here in Missouri establishes this, not as a conjecture, plausible and reasonable, but as a fact every day under observation. If these Freesoilers then are all governed by love for the negro race, they would advocate the extension and diffusion of slavery—rather than its being shut up in narrow limits." A rock-ribbed agrarian utopian, Napton promoted the classical republican image of superior slave-based societies, including Missouri, arguing that

> whatever may be thought or said of the evils of slavery, and no people are more fully apprised of or regret them more than the intelligent slaveholders themselves, it is certain that the institution has the effect of ridding society of a great many evils which infest countries where free labor alone is found and tolerated. . . . Hence a certain degree of dependence and loftiness of sentiment pervades even the poorer and humbler classes of citizens, which among the idle and higher classes, is united with intelligence, taste, and refinement. . . . We are clear of these evils here . . . . To slavery we owe this distinction.[7]

While Napton's rhetoric on slavery and social progress might have invoked the language of Deep South apologists, Missourians yet clearly considered the South a distinct place of which Missouri was not a part. While their culture might have derived largely from a slaveholding heritage sectionalized now to the extent that in common parlance their institution was "peculiar," Missourians still considered themselves and their state part of the West, or now—in the sectional era—more specifically the Middle West, "the heart of the American continent." Boone County proslavery politico James S. Rollins cautioned his son, a cadet at West Point, to "say to the Northern and Southern cadets—that you belong to *neither section*—that you are a true son of the great West." In their language, Missourians—even those in the Boon's Lick—regarded the South and certainly the North as distinct, even foreign regions from their own. One proposal submitted to the state house as an alternative to the Jackson-Napton Resolutions claimed that Missouri, "being one of the most north western Slave States . . . occupies a central portion in this grand valley of the Mississippi [whose] geographical position in this Union presents a unit in interest, whether considered commercially, socially or politically—such a unity of interest can never be permanently severed." B. Gratz Brown, a newly elected state representative, saw Missouri as "a central state, at present the advanced leader of the Western states." Even

---

7. Napton Diary, folder 1, p. 77, (first quote), folder 2, pp. 100–101 (second quote), MHS; Tise, *Proslavery*, 349–60; William S. Jenkins, *Pro-Slavery Thought in the Old South*, 65–81. For a fuller discussion of the classical republican theories of slavery, see Clyde N. Wilson, *Carolina Cavalier: The Life and Mind of James Johnston Pettigrew*, and Shalhope, *John Taylor of Caroline*.

Atchison, responding to arguments linking Missouri with the South, quickly reminded a middle western colleague in the Senate who had differentiated his region from those that practiced slavery that Missouri was indeed "one of the northwestern States, although it is generally, from its institutions, classed as one of the southwestern States." True to its western identity and to its pledge to "take a just and conservative position . . . and arrest the fire brands hurled by the violent and fanatical portion of the North and the South," Missouri sent no representatives to a "Southern convention" held at Nashville in 1850, though the topic of debate concerned the maintenance of slavery. Clearly, Benton's damning sin may well have been his seeming conjoining of Missouri with the North rather than with the West.[8]

As the national debate over slavery drew the new West into its scope in the wake of the war with Mexico, Missourians saw the debate over their own statehood rekindled and thrust into the national forum. The very boundary that was their southern border—the 36°30' parallel—became alternately the seed of harmony and discord between slavery's restrictionists and extensionists. As Congress debated afar the future of the vast territories taken from Mexico and as the nation's politicians contorted over it in the subsequent electioneering mayhem, the sacred parallel became a regular topic as a practical compromise line upon which to organize the entire region. Just as the debate laid the state's name yet again on the lips of the nation's leaders, so did it isolate Missouri even further as potentially the only slave state situated above the parallel. The Compromise of 1850 essentially sidestepped the issue by avoiding the Louisiana Purchase entirely, allowing all the remaining portion of the Mexican cession save California to organize on the murky principle of popular sovereignty. Missouri was thus segregated even further, the only state allowed to have slavery in a northwestern region which, by permanent decree, forbade the institution. More confusing, Missouri was now situated alongside the remaining northern expanse of the Louisiana Territory, whose future was barred from slaveholding by the very act that had breathed life into Missouri. As Missourians did all in their power to maintain their allegiance to the democratic Middle West, the nation's newest paroxysm over slavery forced them glaringly into the role of outsiders.[9]

Yet Missourians refrained from adopting the language of power emanating with increasing volume from the cotton states. Cries of disunion and

8. *Missouri Statesman,* March 9, 1849 (first and fifth quotes); James S. Rollins to My Dear Son, November 14, 1858, James S. Rollins Papers, Mss. 1026, box 2, folder 55, SHSM (second quote); *Appendix to the Congressional Globe,* 33d Cong., 1st sess., 301 (third quote); Norma L. Peterson, *Freedom and Franchise: The Political Career of B. Gratz Brown,* 74 (fourth quote); Thelma Jennings, *The Nashville Convention: Southern Movement for Unity, 1848–1851,* 187–211; Parrish, *David Rice Atchison,* 101.

9. Morrison, *Slavery and the American West,* 62–63.

secession, grown louder during the territorial debate, met with stony silence in Missouri. Claib Jackson was forced to fend off widespread attacks as a "nullifier"—a once-democratic hallmark now linked to the Calhoun camp and thus condemned as being disunionist—a charge that he was unable to shake, costing him his seat in the Missouri Senate as well as his candidacy for the U.S. House. More important, in their defense of slavery, Missourians embraced a strangely selective stance on federal power within the Republic, one that accepted Congress's authority to legislate on slavery while accommodating the states' rights to protect its residents' property, so long as neither interfere with individual liberties. "I take the ground, that neither Congress, nor even the state in convention have anything to do with slave property," wrote John J. Lowry from Fayette,

> any more than any other species of property. . . . I assume that there is no such thing as *absolute state sovereignty,* because, even in a state convention, such convention can only make fundamental regulations, which rules are guides for subsequent Legislatures whereby to shape their state laws—Congress then has no powers delegated whereby that body can give any preference over any species of property, or prevent the individuals removing to any part of the U. States, & carrying with them their property. . . . I am satisfied with the "Missouri compromise," or any other compromise, if the people acquiesce in them, & they will sement [*sic*] the Union of these states. . . . This is high ground, . . . but it is the only tenable ground, which I can discover in accordance with the true rights of property.[10]

Indeed, Missourians remained vigilant against those, proslavery and not, who manipulated the already blurred lines surrounding the debate over slavery's extension into the West to their own advantage. The editor of the *Glasgow Weekly Times* cautioned readers that "whilst we are as decidedly and as unalterably opposed to Abolitionism, 'Freesoilism' and all sorts of slavery agitations as any *live* man on the face of the earth, we, nevertheless, regret to hear the charge of Abolitionism and Freesoilism applied indiscriminately to all men who do not feel disposed to threaten 'blood and thunder' against every man hailing from a free State, and especially against those who, whilst they believe that Congress has the constitutional power to legislate upon the subject of slavery in the Territories, are yet decidedly opposed to its exercise." Indeed, in 1853, Claib Jackson found himself forced to explain his understanding of the term "free-soiler" on the floor of the state senate, after having used the charge ubiquitously against political opponents. Jackson quickly equivocated, claiming that "he did not consider a man who believed Congress had the power to exclude slavery from the Territories of the United

10. *Missouri Statesman,* May 14, 1852 (first quote); J. J. Lowry to M. M. Marmaduke, September 8, 1848, Sappington Family Papers, box 5, MHS (remaining quotes).

States a free soiler; but those who advocated the *exercise of the power,* were free soilers."[11]

Seeking a middle ground in the growing struggle, Missourians remained steadfastly loyal to the Union while supporting the democratic process as the foundation of liberty. In 1855, Boon's Lickers called for a Union state convention for the purpose of "averting the calamities which a separation of the States would bring upon us"; a year before, residents of Weston called a "Law and Order" meeting and declared unwavering fidelity to the government, taking as their motto "The Union first, Union second, and Union forever." Yet because of the past decade's debates, the politicized issue of slavery—once Missouri's social good—had become for its residents democracy's litmus. The ground upon which slavery and liberty had coexisted peacefully was becoming increasingly slippery.[12]

In an attempt to keep their footing as slaveholders and Unionists, Missourians sought to convince the nation's sections that a fourth section of the country existed, apart from the North, South, and West, one that ameliorated the antagonistic influences in their daily lives and which, if recognized, could do so with the country as a whole. The middle, or border, states formed a natural alignment, whether of culture, heritage, climate, or geography. More important, all were slaveholding states, but of conviction rather than of economy. As Henry S. Geyer noted before the U.S. Senate, "south of 36°30' is the cotton region, where slave labor may be profitably employed, . . . There, soil & climate settle the question; . . . but in the latitude above that and below 41° is the debatable ground. That is the latitude of the middle states—Virginia, Maryland, and Kentucky. The emigration from these States is small. . . . The inducements [to import or own slaves] in point of soil are only those portions which will produce hemp and tobacco." Able to separate themselves from the sectional debate over slavery, the middle border states, "the heart of the American continent, containing at this time nearly one half of the population of the U.S. should, and must, at no distant day, exercise a potent influence in giving tone, character and direction to our national legislation." The concept of a middle confederacy of sorts as healer of the ailing nation appealed to many Missourians who felt caught in the increasingly vituperative sectional climate. More important, the concept vindicated their place as virtuous slaveholders within the Republic.[13]

Yet as the nation cleaved over the issue of chattel slavery, Missourians

---

11. *Glasgow Weekly Times,* March 29, 1855 (first quote), February 19, 1853 (second quote); *Missouri Statesman,* June 15, 1855, quoted in Hurt, *Agriculture and Slavery in Little Dixie,* 283.

12. Shoemaker, "Missouri's Proslavery Fight for Kansas," 232.

13. *Appendix to the Congressional Globe,* 34th Cong., 1st sess., 465 (first quote); *Missouri Statesman,* March 9, 1849 (second quote).

heard well in the northern condemnations of slavery the heavy tolls of an accepted superiority—both moral and economic—of a free society over a slave society. Though in the sectional arena the abolitionists directed these jeremiads largely at southerners, Missourians found themselves squarely in two lines of fire, one the abolitionists'—aimed at slaveholders—and another the free-soilers'—directed at slaveholding westerners. Abolitionists such as William Lloyd Garrison condemned slaveholders indiscriminately as "murderers of fathers, and murderers of liberty, and traffickers of human flesh, and blasphemers against the Almighty," vowing Old Testament retribution and trumpeting that "the motto enscribed on the banner of Freedom should be NO UNION WITH SLAVEHOLDERS," a slogan that soon pealed from the mouths of radical northern politicians in the halls of Congress. Free-labor and free-soil advocates in Washington condemned southern slave society as socially stagnant, without incentive and degrading to laborers, and touted the West as holding the future greatness of America—a vista achieved only by the prohibition of slavery from the region. One of the Old West, Ohioan Salmon P. Chase, held that a free West, removed of slavery, would offer "freedom not serfdom; freeholds not tenancies; democracy not despotism; education not ignorance . . . progress, not stagnation or retrogression." To Missourians, Frank Blair proclaimed boldly that "the wealth and the political power of the country will in a little time reside at its Geographical centre," adding almost wistfully that once crossing the river into Illinois, one could not view "the splendid farms of Sangamon and Morgan, without permitting an envious sigh to escape him at the evident superiority of free labor."[14]

More offensive, the northern assault on slavery and the restrictionist effort intrinsically relegated southern slaveholders to the status of inferiors, whether moral or numerical. Indeed, Atchison became John C. Calhoun's southern rights standard-bearer not from any long-standing belief in his or Missourians' general southern heritage, but because of the specter of a northern majoritarianism. His dead captain's "Disquisition on Government" put the matter in language unmistakable to these beleaguered westerners: far from simply calling for any general restriction of governmental power in order to preserve individual freedoms, Calhoun argued that too much liberty in the hands of those unfit to exercise it was democracy's curse. Those so unfit, in the sectional era, were northerners, especially those now influencing the national government as they sought to "monopolize" the territories. "To extend the powers of government, so as to contract the sphere assigned to liberty," wrote

---

14. Smith, *Blair Family in Politics,* vol. 1, 203 (first quote); James Brewer Stewart, *Holy Warriors: The Abolitionists and American Slavery,* 112 (second quote); Foner, *Free Soil, Free Labor, Free Men,* 56 (third quote), 55 (fourth quote), 63 (fifth quote), and 46–72 passim.

the South Carolinian, "would have the same effect, by disabling individuals in their efforts to better their condition." The triumph of democracy had, in effect, empowered an unequal yet majority people, extending them the right—the power—by virtue of the mass franchise to claim the nation's future. By advocating a series of governments to assure the sovereignty of the nation's various "communities," Calhoun's proto-Marxian logic and imagery were clear to Missourians such as Atchison. "Some communities," Calhoun argued, "require a far greater amount of power than others to protect them against anarchy and external dangers; . . . such as exposed and unprotected frontiers, surrounded by powerful and hostile neighbors." Those dangers now poised on two of Missouri's community borders—and by virtue of the Missouri Compromise, their third, western border, once populated—would inevitably doom Missouri as a slaveholding peninsula in an angry sea of free soil.[15]

The charge of inferiority combined with the attempt to limit slavery's extension caused Missourians to see the northern antislavery element as a tyrannical majority intent upon oppressing an enlightened minority. In attempting to limit the South's ability to carry their property wherever they chose, the North was clearly limiting their constitutional freedoms. Denying slaveholders their constitutional right to property, to freedom, was in effect the denial of equality, yet another proof that Free-Soilers, not slaveholders, intended to destroy democracy in the nation. The defense of slavery gave way to one more germane for westerners: that of the defense of white minority rights within the Republic, a concept that both Atchison and Geyer grasped firmly. In the debate over the organization of Nebraska, Atchison vowed to "oppose the organization or the settlement of that Territory unless my constituents and the constituents of the whole South, of the slave States of the Union, could go into it upon the same footing, with equal rights and equal privileges, carrying that species of property with them as other people of this Union. . . . I will vote for a bill that leaves the slaveholder and non-slaveholder upon terms of equality." Atchison had learned his mentor's lessons well; Geyer argued similarly. "The antagonism and hostility between the States and the people, engendered by the agitation of the slavery question," he charged, "is aggravated by hostile legislation and the struggle for political power by a sectional party warring upon the institutions of one half the States of the Union."[16]

---

15. Richard Hofstadter, *The American Political Tradition and the Men Who Made It,* 68–92 (first quote on 86); Crallé, ed., *Works of John C. Calhoun,* vol. 1, 52–59 (remaining quotes). Calhoun's antimajoritarian polemicism prompted Hofstadter to offer his now-famous analogy of the proslavery Calhoun as "Marx of the master class."

16. Foner, *Free Soil, Free Labor, Free Men,* 89–94; Morrison, *Slavery and the American West,* 59–62; William J. Cooper, Jr., *Liberty and Slavery: Southern Politics to 1860,* 257–

Indeed, the defense of individual rights soon drew Missourians into a general acceptance of the concept of southern rights, with slavery at the notion's core. " 'Southern rights,' as they are termed," scoffed one Boon's Lick editor who saw clearly the separative implications of the term, implicitly involved defiance against majoritarian authority. More ominously, its sympathetic and widespread use in country parlance suggested a retreat from the middle western identity that had so shaped its past and a move toward a distinctive identity based upon separation—party and otherwise—and all over slavery. In the heat of the sectional debate, that identity clearly found sympathy in the plight of the beleaguered South, prompting one western Missouri newspaper to adopt as its moniker, the *Southern Advocate*. Alarmed, the aforementioned Democratic editor saw need to remind Boon's Lick readers who claimed such southern affiliation out of their politics that

> Many conscientious men both Whigs and Democrats doubted the policy of repealing the Missouri Compromise; but our idea is that all those of every party who *acquiesce* in that *repeal,* and who are opposed to *interfering* with the question any longer, are *good friends* to Southern rights; yea, as good friends as any others; for *therein* consists the *test* of loyalty to the South. Southern people can make nothing by casting off such men; but, on the contrary, have all to lose. As for ourselves, we think the repeal of the Compromise was *right,* in itself, and that so the good sense of the whole country will consider it when reason shall have resumed its throne.[17]

Yet Missourians found solace in the victimization imagery embedded in the concept of southern rights. Already condemned by abolitionists as moral degenerates, Missourians conjured from the moral chords the not-too-distant memory of Missouri's natal struggle—a memory of northern contempt and diminution that inflamed its residents' passions yet again. Clearly, as Henry S. Geyer dutifully reminded his Senate colleagues, "there were some in western Missouri who remembered how little their rights were respected by the North in the memorable struggle of 1820." Indeed, Geyer appears to have been one of those with long memory; he went on to condemn the "barbarian wall erected by this government, arresting the progress of settlement and civilization westward." Napton echoed these sentiments, claiming that "the injustice of the old Missouri Compromise is manifest from its very terms. It recognizes the great principle of popular sovereignty south of the line of 36°30'—but north of that line establishes a guardianship over the people and imposes an absolute restriction. It is as much adverse

---

58; *Congressional Globe,* 32d Cong., 2d sess., 1111–12 (first quote); *Missouri Republican,* September 16, 1853, quoted in Parrish, *David Rice Atchison,* 126 (second quote); *Appendix to the Congressional Globe,* 34th Cong., 1st sess., 464 (third quote).

17. LeSueur, *Mormon War in Missouri,* 57–58; *Glasgow Weekly Times,* March 29, 1855 (quote).

to the spirit of our Constitution as the famous Wilmot Proviso." David Rice Atchison was more direct and, as ever, more colorful. Debating the Nebraska bill in 1854, Atchison claimed a "higher principle" contained in the bill, and vowed that "although there might be not only one, but one thousand obnoxious principles contained in it, I would vote for it, because it blots out that infamous—yes, sir, I think it is a proper term to be used—that infamous restriction passed by the Congress of 1820, commonly called the Missouri 'compromise.' "[18]

The concert of exclusion—anathema to egalitarianism—intoned by the North against the South quickly conjured among Missourians images of their ancestors waging their own revolutionary struggle against a tyrannical majority. Indeed, Napton defended "the great principle of popular sovereignty, for which our ancestors in the revolution fought." Yet this new struggle did not signal a new revolution, at least not in terms of any revolt against the federal government. Rather, democratic Missourians must act as sentinels against antislavery zealots bent upon the Union's destruction. "Certainly it is not the part of a good patriot to do anything, or say anything," Napton cautioned, "by which the tendency to disunion may be hastened—and it is well enough to hold up *in terrorem* all the evils which fertile imagination may conceive, as to the necessary results of such an occurrence." John J. Lowry's condemnations of Benton echoed the same themes: "Col. Benton is the *Disunionist* then, & not the Legislature of Mo. & Mr. Calhoun! . . . He will divide the Democracy of this Union & be the cause of a *Disolution* [*sic*] of the confederated states! No patriotism, no philanthropy, in brief a Calagula [*sic*] in North America in 1849. . . . I am for my country, for the Union & for the constitutional rights of the whole of the people of the confederated states!"[19]

Yet as northerners united against slavery and the Slave Power by adhering to the free-soil movement, many Missourians heard much more than condemnations of the South; they heard themselves condemned first as slaveholders, then—by yet another sin, that of association—as southerners. When Frank Blair, an aggressive free-soil Democrat who would soon take up the Republican banner, received election to Congress from St. Louis in 1856, the *National Era* hailed the victory of this "man of the West, of the age" as a harbinger of regional, even national, politics, predicting confidently that the border would soon become an antislavery, thus Republican, bastion. "Our principles have become *aggressive*," trumpeted the paper's editor. "We

18. *Appendix to the Congressional Globe,* 34th Cong., 1st sess., 465 (first and second quotes); Napton Diary, folder 1, 78–79, MHS (third quote); *Appendix to the Congressional Globe,* 33d Cong., 1st sess., 1303 (fourth quote).

19. Napton Diary, folder 1, 78–79, MHS (first and second quotes); J. J. Lowry to M. M. Marmaduke, July 26, 1849, Sappington Family Papers, box 5, MHS (third quote).

no longer stand upon the defensive. We have crossed the line, and are upon slaveholding ground." The boast crossed a line indeed, smacking—at least to Missourians—of a taunt.[20]

More repugnant, in dishonoring southerners by proclaiming their institutions—and thus their society—as inferior and thus unworthy, northerners dishonored Missourians who shared the southerners' commitment to chattel slavery. Northerners and northwesterners, in lumping Missourians together with the South as a result of one lone, shared institution, ignored the "identity of interest, feeling and destiny" that Missourians hoped yet prevailed over the western states. Considering theirs the freest society in the world, both because of their western, rural residence and their pervasive egalitarianism and commitment to liberty, Missourians opposed the free-soil arguments as slanderous attacks by an undemocratic host upon a free and loyal people. Now, listening to the widespread attacks upon the South and upon them, many Missourians at last began—however cautiously—to consider their interests distinct from those of their once northwestern neighbors and consistent with those of the beleaguered, slaveholding South. Indeed, a sense of honor was at stake, as William B. Napton observed: "The South regards it as a point of honor not to submit and the North regards it as a point of honor to persist, so it is merely a point of honor upon which we split. This is however enough." Though Napton was a former editor, his choice of "we" was no mere editorial form; Missouri's southernization had begun.[21]

In direct response to the northern attacks against the South and slavery, Missourians—proslavery or even free-soil—adopted the mantra of southerners. Prior to the 1840s, little evidence exists of Missourians having applied the term to themselves, in large part because the nation itself had not yet sectionalized so as to create the region in a national consciousness. The term "southern," as Missourians employed it initially, was a metaphor for slaveholder, regardless of the individual's stance on slavery's extension. In 1844 Benton responded defiantly to his free-state antagonists by affirming that "I am Southern by birth; Southern in my affections, interest, and connections. . . . I am a slaveholder, and shall take the fate of other slaveholders in every aggression upon that species of property." Similarly, in 1853 Frank Blair, also a slaveholder, sought to temper the firestorm that would inevitably attend his effort to repeal the Jackson-Napton resolutions by proclaiming that "I am a southern man by birth, and identified with southern institutions by my interest and education."[22]

20. *National Era,* August 14, 1856 (first quote), May 14, 1857 (second quote), both in Foner, *Free Soil, Free Labor, Free Men,* 121.

21. Bertram Wyatt-Brown, *Yankee Saints and Southern Sinners,* 183–213; Napton Diary, folder 1, 50–51 (quote), 57, MHS.

22. Chambers, *Old Bullion Benton,* 276 (first quote); *Jefferson Inquirer,* February 12, 1853 (second quote).

By the time of the Texas debates, however, with the cant of abolitionism well amplified, Missourians took up the cognomen more widely but largely as a defense of the peculiar institution. More important, Missourians generally reserved its use for the company of those from the free states who had labeled them solely as a result of their slaveholding adherence, or to Free-Soilers in their midst. Just as Benton occasionally adhered to the badge of "southerner" in debates with antislavery politicians, Atchison did so defiantly in the presence of northern colleagues in general. Yet even Atchison saw limits to the term's usage; tellingly, he and others did not employ it in the company of other proslavery Missourians. To the Democrats of Livingston County he offered his take on the recent Compromise of 1850: "Although in my opinion the slave States did not get equal and exact justice, yet we escaped dishonor and degradation. Let us hold our northern brethren to a strict observance of all the terms of settlement; they must comply with their part of the bargain." To another group, he affirmed that "as a Senator from Missouri, and as a citizen of the Slave States, it is my duty to resist every attempt to change her institutions, and every assault upon her rights." Atchison's clearly selective use of language suggests that adherence to slavery did not yet warrant any exclusive southern identity, at least not to others of the same stripe. The employment of the terms "southern" or "southerner" by Missourians was reserved exclusively for the benefit of outsiders, those who now posed a threat to the institution.[23]

Though even the most ardent of Missouri's proslavery adherents refrained from using these terms with one another, the ligature between southern identity and the slaveholding imperative had become powerful. By the mid-1850s those who evinced anything short of wholesale support for the institution and its extension to the western territories were subject to bitter political attack. James J. Lindley, who had won the congressional seat sought by Claib Jackson in 1853, addressed the U.S. House in 1856, claiming that Missouri's proslavery Democrats "assume to have taken into special custody the slave interest of Missouri, and freely denounce as Republicans and Abolitionists men of southern education, slaveholders, and all others who do not conform to and maintain every arbitrary tenet which they set up; . . . I am charged by the orators & presses of the anti-Benton faction in Missouri as a Free-Soiler— I who have been raised and educated to believe in the propriety of southern institutions, and who have never uttered one word against slavery, either as it exists or in the abstract." Those born in nonslaveholding states proved especially vulnerable. Gratz Brown captured this distinction most completely

---

23. David Rice Atchison to W. Y. Slack, W[illia]m. Hudgins, & Others, November 19, 1850, in *Missouri Republican,* January 7, 1851, reprinted in *MHR* 31 (July 1937): 443–44 (first quote); Parrish, *David Rice Atchison,* 74 (second quote).

when responding to New York–born state senator Robert M. Stewart's attack on Benton as an abolitionist. Pointing out Stewart's northern birth, Brown—a Kentuckian—threw doubt on Stewart's proslavery stance based upon it. Unlike Stewart, Brown argued, "I am a Southern man, in feeling and in principle, . . . the place of my birth forbids the ridiculous nonsense of abolitionism!" Frank Blair noted that "the absconding abolitionists from the north, who, in my county at least, are the principle leaders of the Anti-Benton party, find it necessary to turn pro-slavery nullifiers to free themselves from the suspicion which attends their place of birth." Blair added smugly that "I can well afford to entertain the opinions of Washington and Jefferson, upon the subject of slavery, and to express them without incurring the suspicion of disloyalty to the institutions of the south."[24]

Blair was wrong about his own immunity from suspicion attendant with his place of birth—in his case, like Gratz Brown's, Kentucky. Perhaps more than those in any other state, many Missourians of the 1850s drew the sharpest distinctions between their neighbors based not upon sectional hailing, but by their adherence or opposition to slavery. Lying astride two now-contested borders, one north-south and the other east-west, these Missourians did not enjoy the luxury of granting exemptions to anyone, even those born in slaveholding states. Indeed, with grim irony William B. Napton took aim at those of Benton's and Blair's ilk while pointing out the imperfection of the new southern identity swirling about Missouri. "A man's opinions are not to be determined by the place of his birth," he observed:

> Because a man is born and raised in a slave state does not prevent him from being a free-soiler or an abolitionist. . . . Kentucky is a slave state, yet I will venture that one half of the Kentuckians who emigrate here are free-soilers—one fourth out-and-out abolitionists. They are not slave holders though born and raised in a slave state, and wherever they are they still entertain anti-slavery sentiments. . . . The political adjuncts of the northern free-soilers stay scattered here and there throughout the South and "born and raised" in slave states are the most dangerous of the whole tribe. Such declarations are therefore entitled to little or no importance, except that they should cause the men who make them to be closely watched.

Atchison concurred: "Put confidence in *no man* for any station of public trust," he cautioned a group of supporters, "who is not known to be true to the institutions of the State and the rights of our citizens."[25]

---

24. *Appendix to the Congressional Globe,* 34th Cong., 1st sess., 673 (first quote); Thomas L. Snead, *The Fight for Missouri from the Election of Lincoln to the Death of Lyon,* 13; *Jefferson Inquirer,* February 5, 1853, quoted in Peterson, *Freedom and Franchise,* 28–29 (second quote); *Jefferson Inquirer,* February 12, 1853 (third and fourth quotes).

25. Napton Diary, folder 1, pp. 92–93, MHS (first quote); David Rice Atchison to W. Y. Slack, W[illia]m. Hudgins, and Others, November 19, 1850, in *Missouri Republi-*

Against this backdrop, in 1854 Congress created the Kansas and Nebraska Territories. Had the bill to open the westernmost portion of the Louisiana Territory to settlement been offered a decade earlier, it likely would have met with little resistance in the frenzied atmosphere of expansion that then prevailed. But a lifetime had passed in the last decade, the result being that the Kansas-Nebraska Act—which effectively repealed the Missouri Compromise in that it allowed popular sovereignty into the region long assumed as being forever free from slavery—emerged from a congressional debate of a magnitude the nation had not before seen. More important, the act unleashed a sectional storm that would eclipse any controversy that surrounded its passage.

Debated for nearly a decade, the Kansas-Nebraska Act owed much of its final form to the vision of Illinois Senator Stephen A. Douglas. More concerned with the opening of the West to white settlement—at the expense of the Indians of the region—than with the slave question, Douglas nevertheless kept a hungry eye on the presidency in the coming years as he acted as chairman of the powerful Senate Committee on the Territories. When proposals for a transcontinental railroad to connect California with the rest of the nation peppered Congress, Douglas (who favored a northern route so as to benefit his home state as well as his own speculative holdings near Chicago) spied an opportunity to break the logjam over slavery's extension while bolstering his own prospects for the Democratic nomination in 1856. Yet the Missouri Compromise, held as sacred by much of the North and Northwest for more than three decades, proved the greatest political obstacle to any successful resolution. With the railroad debate having been spawned amid the fervor over slavery's extension, a group of southern Democrats (with Atchison at its helm) determined to force into line its party's northern Free-Soilers by refusing to vote for any bill organizing Nebraska without slavery. Douglas recognized that any solution would require either modification or outright repeal of the Missouri Compromise.[26]

Douglas's bill involved considerable political risk, but its crafting proved its author's mastery of the art of political reciprocity. Moreover, Douglas demonstrated a keen sense of the historically latitudinal pattern of westward migration already demonstrated in the nation's marchlands. As offered, the bill carved the once-expansive Nebraska Territory into two territories—Kansas and Nebraska—each of which would organize on the basis of popular

can, January 7, 1851, reprinted in *MHR* 31 (July 1937): 443–44 (second quote, italics mine).

26. David M. Potter, *The Impending Crisis, 1848–1861,* 146–58; Freehling, *Road to Disunion,* 546–49; Roy F. Nichols, "The Kansas-Nebraska Act: A Century of Historiography," 201–4; Foner, *Free Soil, Free Labor, Free Men,* 155–56.

sovereignty, consonant with the territories acquired from Mexico. Coincidentally, Kansas would approximate the latitudinal boundaries of Missouri (significantly, the latter overlapped the former's northern and southern borders, thus largely sealing its emigration), while Nebraska would occupy the rest of the area. This was hardly an even division of territory; Nebraska would retain a full four-fifths of its land space. Indeed, this partition was deliberate, for Douglas dangled only a small carrot before southerners while retaining the largest for future northern—and presumably free—habitation. Kansas, in the nation's center, could be a crossroads; its climate—particularly that in the eastern portion of the territory, closest to Missouri—was conducive to staple crops, namely tobacco. In all likelihood, however, neighboring Missourians—by design—would populate the territory. As Douglas conceived the proposal, all under the psalm of popular sovereignty, the possibility of losing one future state to slavery when cast alongside the probability of four free states was a small price to pay for national harmony and the preservation of the Union itself.

When Douglas forecast "a hell of a storm" to attend his bill, he spoke exclusively of the legislative fight. In that prediction he was accurate; northern legislators evenly divided over the bill while slave state congressmen and senators, long stymied in their quest for room, overwhelmingly supported it, and after months of tortured debate, the House narrowly approved the bill and President Franklin Pierce signed it into law in May 1854. What Douglas could not have foreseen was the bitter border war that would ensue in the Kansas Territory, revealing the fiction that was popular sovereignty. More important, by stating in the bill itself that "all questions pertaining to slavery in Territories, and in the new States to be formed therefrom, are to be left to the people residing therein," Douglas and Congress had—unwittingly, and with clinical prose—set into motion the transformation of American democracy. And at the center of this national crisis, for a second time in a generation, lay Missouri.[27]

Missourians saw in the opening of Kansas several opportunities for progress. By allowing popular sovereignty to dictate the settlement of territories, western agrarians (who would settle the region) would carry to the future their brand of democratic promise and thus triumph over a distant, urban, industrial, and thoroughly inferior East. One Missourian who settled in Kansas immediately after the territory's organization believed that because of proximity and through concerted action, westerners could stymie "the

---

27. Potter, *Impending Crisis*, 158–77 (first quote); William L. Barney, *The Road to Secession: A New Perspective on the Old South*, 6–17; Freehling, *Road to Disunion*, 552 (second quote); James A. Rawley, *Race and Politics: "Bleeding Kansas" and the Coming of the Civil War*, 70.

hosts of the Lazarroni from the Eastern States and Cities and paupers from Europe that will be thrown into this country, . . . a curse equalling, at least, in its pestiferous character, the plagues of Egypt, in being made the unwilling receptacle of the filth, scum and offscourings of the East and Europe." Moreover, the Kansas-Nebraska Act signified that though challenged, even blunted for a time, the practicability of democracy had reasserted itself and in its purest form, outside the invasive influence of government, whether national or state. "Let neither Congress, nor state conventions," exulted John J. Lowry, "enact any arbitrary laws to regulate property, then will our political institutions smoothly progress, & then will *soil & climate* point out where the slave-holders ought to locate." In Kansas, liberty appeared to triumph over influence.[28]

Beyond the abstractions over slavery and government, however, Missourians, perhaps more than any other residents of the Union, considered the debate over the Kansas Territory in a practical sense. While slave-state residents in the Deep South attached symbolic political importance to winning Kansas, the matter offered far more immediate implications to those closest to the storm's center. Indeed, beyond the southern arguments for the winning of Kansas being "a point of honor," a means of regaining parity in the Senate, or even a last, best hope for the spread of southern culture and institutions in an expanding nation that had routinely constricted the South, Missourians saw Kansas as a gift. Even the term commonly used by Missourians when debating Kansas—"the Goose question"—connoted the sense of largesse implicit in the Kansas issue, in this case a Christmas goose. By virtue of the natural progress of American westward expansion, Missourians claimed a "natural right' to expand into the territory immediately west of them. Just as Kentucky had been settled by Virginians, Tennessee had been settled by North Carolinians, and Iowa had been settled largely by Illinoisans, so Kansas would be settled by Missourians. William B. Napton noted in 1850, in the midst of the debate over the Mexican cession, that "the natural order of events" would have brought slaveholding southerners into those regions, but northern machinations had interrupted the process by claiming California.[29]

---

28. William Walker to David R. Atchison, July 6, 1854, David Rice Atchison Papers, Mss. 71, folder 4, SHSM (first quote); J. J. Lowry to M. M. Marmaduke, September 8, 1848, Sappington Family Papers, box 5, MHS (second quote); Bill Cecil-Fronsman, " 'Death to All Yankees and Traitors in Kansas': The *Squatter Sovereign* and the Defense of Slavery in Kansas," 25–27.

29. Don E. Fehrenbacher, "Kansas, Republicanism, and the Crisis of the Union," in *The South and the Sectional Crisis,* 53–56; William E. Gienapp, "The Crime against Sumner: The Caning of Charles Sumner and the Rise of the Republican Party," 238–45; Barney, *Road to Secession,* 6–17; Cooper, *Liberty and Slavery,* 260; William J. Cooper, Jr., *The South and the Politics of Slavery,* 351–56; Morrison, *Slavery and the American*

More pressing even than this was the notion that if Kansas should not become a slave state, Missouri would become the first such state bordering a free state to its west, effectively sealing slavery from further progress and changing the complexion of westward expansion, likely forever. Napton certainly recognized the implications of this point. "If we cannot carry slavery into Kansas," he reasoned, "it is quite obvious that we cannot succeed anywhere else. The result will be that no more slave states will be created. The majority of the North over the South will in a few years become overwhelming, in both houses of Congress. This majority can mould the Constitution to their own purposes. What will constitutional guarantees be worth under such circumstances?" This precedent held a weighty charge, one that led Missourians to conclude that Kansas, by mandate, was theirs to shape. Indeed, Atchison declared to a northerner who opposed slavery in Kansas "that I and my friends wish to make Kansas in all respects like Missouri. Our interests require it. Our peace through all time demands it, and we intend to leave nothing undone that will conduce to that end and can with honor be performed. . . . We have all to lose in the contest; you and your friends have nothing at stake."[30]

The nearly immediate mobilization of Emigrant Aid societies in New England threw Missourians into a frenzy, in part from the fear that the most dangerous of interlopers would soon entice their bondpeople to escape. Hundreds, even thousands, of these "Hessian band[s] of mercenaries" were to be "sent here as hired servants, to do the will of others," and were poised "to pol[l]ute our fair land, to dictate to us a government, to preach Abolitionism and dig underground Rail Roads," William Walker predicted. Indeed, even before Congress authorized settlement in Kansas, Claib Jackson wrote from his farm in Howard County to Atchison that "I say let the Indians have it [Nebraska] *forever*. They are better neighbors than the abolitionists, *by a damned sight*. If this is to become 'free-nigger' territory, Missouri must become so too, for we can hardly Keep our negroes here now." In turn, Atchison wrote Jefferson Davis later in 1854 that "the men who are hired by the Boston Abolitionists to settle and abolitionize Kansas will not hesitate, to steal our slaves," prompting him to counsel one group of prospective emigrants from western Missouri "to give a horse thief, robber, or homicide a fair trial, but to hang a negro thief or Abolitionist, without judge or jury."[31]

West, 165–67; Gunja SenGupta, *For God and Mammon: Evangelicals and Entrepreneurs, Masters and Slaves in Territorial Kansas, 1854–1860*, 118 (first quote); Napton Diary, folder 1, pp. 50–51, MHS (second quote).

30. Parrish, *David Rice Atchison*, 162 (first quote), 165 (third quote), 168; Napton Diary, folder 3, p. 208, MHS (second quote).

31. *Squatter Sovereign*, October 16 (first quote), March 6, 1855 (second quote); William Walker to David R. Atchison, July 6, 1854, David Rice Atchison Papers, Mss.

Slave stealing by abolitionist invaders was bad enough, but far more detestable to Missourians was the well-publicized method by which New Englanders organized their swarming. With a capitalization of five million dollars approved by the Massachusetts legislature, and plans for mills, a hotel, a newspaper, towns, and tens of thousands of subsidized settlers, the Emigrant Aid Societies intended nothing like squatter sovereignty. Rather, they appeared intent upon replicating the North rather than any Jeffersonian vision. Indeed, the rabidly proslavery *Squatter Sovereign,* a territorial newspaper founded by Missourian John H. Stringfellow in Atchison (named conspicuously for Missouri's proslavery champion, largely as a result of Stringfellow's urging) forecast Kansas's grim future if invading urban Yankees gained sway, creating "sores in the body politic . . . [with] great wealth gathering in the hands of the few, the toiling millions struggling for bread; the one class is corrupted by luxury, the other debased by destitution." These northern hirelings, dupes of eastern money, could never be free, independent men of the land and thus had no legitimate rights in the West.[32]

Most ominous to Missourians was the grim realization that their "vilest enemies" would use the democratic process to usurp popular sovereignty as the Missourians understood it. As one Missouri Kansan predicted, "the Abolitionists will compass sea and land[,] heaven & hell to prevent the establishment of slavery in this Territory." What Eli Thayer and Amos A. Lawrence intended, even orchestrated, was an invasion, one initiated not so much to populate the region as to subvert the system on which they pinned their futures, as well as the nation's. In effect, just as Missourians breathed a sigh of relief that the southern phalanx had at last dragooned Congress into making liberty and democracy once again consonant by virtue of the principle of popular sovereignty, New Englanders now threatened the vulnerable alloy. Indeed, the New Englanders sought to out-Jacksonian the Jacksonian heirs in Missouri, envisioning the same strategy employed by western slaveholders to master the frontier and its inhabitants—but carried out by other means. Industrial capitalism would now provide the edge over individualism; slavery would be its first casualty. To destroy slavery, not by competition but by the state-making process, free-labor northerners would use both popular sovereignty (the democratic tool Missourians believed would open the West to slavery) and state sovereignty (the slave states' Cerberus as a minority within the Republic) against those very slaveholders

71, folder 4, SHSM (third quote); C. F. Jackson to David R. Atchison, January 18, 1854, David Rice Atchison Papers, Mss. 71, folder 4, SHSM (fourth quote); Atchison to Jefferson Davis, September 24, 1854, Jefferson Davis Papers, Duke (fifth quote).

32. *Squatter Sovereign,* February 13, 1855 (quote); Shoemaker, "Missouri's Proslavery Fight for Kansas," 226–27.

who championed these doctrines' theoretical actuality as well as depended upon their political viability. Indeed, the democratic process now threatened to consume the West's heart—liberty.[33]

Cornered, unable now to oppose popular sovereignty or to trust the natural democratic order, Missourians lashed out with fury at the New England interlopers. "Kansas meetings" held throughout the state quickly led to the formation of "self-defensive societies" and later "blue lodges" and other secret societies that sought to prevent abolitionist emigrants from reaching Kansas. One historian has estimated that as many as ten thousand Missourians pledged allegiance to such organizations, a thousand alone in Platte County. William Walker wrote to David Rice Atchison from the settlement at Wyandotte, Kansas, just across the Missouri River from Westport, soliciting aid from the other slave states. "A heavenly time we will have of it if they gain the ascendency here!" Walker exclaimed. "I tremble when I contemplate the threatening prospect. Our Southern friends must be up and stirring. Virginia, Tennessee and Kentucky ought to send her hardy sons out to claim their rights and maintain them too. Missouri, as far as she can, is doing nobly for a new State."[34]

Walker's plea did not go unheeded; Missourians and other slave-state men formed emigrant aid societies of their own. At Atchison's urging, thousands of Missourians—including Claib Jackson—crossed the Kansas border to claim exemptions or to vote illegally in territorial elections. Newspapers sounded the call. "We are in favor of making Kansas a 'Slave State' if it should require half of the citizens of Missouri, musket in hand, to emigrate there," declared the *Liberty Democratic Platform*. The editor of Howard County's *Glasgow Weekly Times* reminded residents in the summer of 1854 that "if Missourians desire Kansas to be slave territory, they must do something more than hold public meeting, and pass high-sounding resolves; they must be on the move, and that speedily." As the territorial elections approached the following spring, he employed a more urgent tone:

> If we would protect our hearth-stones, and defend our most sacred principles, we must act promptly.—Let no one hug any longer the defensive hope of security, for there is none; already the torch of desolation has been lighted, and

33. Hurt, *Agriculture and Slavery in Little Dixie*, 281 (first quote); William Walker to David R. Atchison, July 6, 1854, David Rice Atchison Papers, Mss. 71, folder 4, SHSM (second quote); Cecil-Fronsman, " 'Death to All Yankees and Traitors in Kansas,' " 25.

34. William Walker to David R. Atchison, July 6, 1854, David Rice Atchison Papers, Mss. 71, folder 4, SHSM (first quote); Shoemaker, "Missouri's Proslavery Fight for Kansas," 230–33; Elmer LeRoy Craik, "Southern Interest in Territorial Kansas, 1854–1858," 376–95; James C. Malin, "The Proslavery Background of the Kansas Struggle," 285–305; SenGupta, *For God and Mammon*, 116–18; Hurt, *Agriculture and Slavery in Little Dixie*, 290.

is now in the hands of fanatics . . . [and] nothing but prompt and determined action on our part can avert a catastrophe. . . . It is highly essential to the slave interest in Missouri, that Kansas should be a slave State, but it will take slavery votes to make it so. . . . There is no time for delay—and those who do not expect to go there at present, if at all should assist those who intend, and want to go this spring, in getting off immediately.[35]

Once the voting fraud in Kansas became known, widespread condemnations issued from the northern states. Missourians did anything but disavow their activities; in fact, they defended them vigorously as a virtuous defense of liberty against the undemocratic New Englanders. One Linn County meeting claimed to "deeply regret the necessity for any action on our part against any considerable portion of the citizens of the United States; but such has been the course of the Abolitionists and Freesoilers, that duty to ourselves and families and a love for the Union of States require it of us, at the present time." A Boone County Democratic meeting justified the actions of the Missouri voters in Kansas, claiming they were merely "neutralizing said abolition efforts, and preventing the fraud attempted by the importation of hireling voters into that territory." Similarly, a Kansas meeting held in Fayette offered eighteen resolutions, the second of which "heartily approve[d] the action of our friends who met in Kansas, and defeated the machinations of the enemies of the Union and equal rights, the 'aid society' emissaries, thereby maintaining the principles of the constitution and the Kansas bill, by which that Territory is recognized as common property open to settlement by citizens of all the States."[36]

The Fayettans' statement offers a revealing insight into what had clearly become these Missourians' uniquely sectionalized construction of democracy. Though admitting that the territories, including Kansas, were open to the settlement of all, not all were indeed welcome. Only those who evinced a willingness for slavery to extend into the West would be allowed to settle in the region. This conception now transcended old sectional lines to embrace only those who understood the democratic process, unbastardized by the corruptive influences of industrialization. Only westerners and southerners, the agrarian backbone of the nation, would gain free access to the fruits of Kansas; slavery would be the litmus. "Companies coming from slave States," wrote John H. Stringfellow in the *Squatter Sovereign*, "will be heartily welcomed by our citizens, as well as those from free States who are all 'right on the goose'. . . . There will be many a good citizen settle among us

35. Shoemaker, "Missouri's Proslavery Fight for Kansas," 233–34 (first quote, p. 233); *Jefferson Inquirer,* July 21, 1860; *Glasgow Weekly Times,* June 14, 1855 (second quote), October 19, 1854 (third quote), March 15, 1855 (fourth quote).

36. *Glasgow Weekly Times,* June 28 (first quote), June 14, 1855 (second and third quotes).

from Illinois, Indian[a], and Ohio, whose notions of slavery are parallel with our own." Indeed, the *Squatter Sovereign* made great distinction between residents of and emigrants from free states based largely upon their views of cultural geography:

> There are two classes of people who come from the free States, the independent and the dependent. The first have some means and intelligence. They are observant and practical as well as theoretic [and would themselves become slaveholders] if they find the country better suited to slave labor. The other class are the subjects of the "emigration Aid Society," who come without means and with Utopian anticipations and are sadly disappointed and curse the men who sent them hither.[37]

To protect liberty, Missourians targeted New England abolitionists, debauchers of the democratic process, and not free-soil westerners, procreators of this greatest—and most vulnerable—of American systems. "We are not contending against the honest, but mistaken Free-Soiler, but with *the scum and filth of the Northern cities;* sent here as hired servants, to do the will of others; not to give their own free suffrage," wrote John H. Stringfellow in his *Squatter Sovereign.* "No one can fail to distinguish between an honest, bona fide emigration, prompted by choice or necessity, and an organized colonization with offensive purpose upon the institutions of the country proposed to be settled." Westerners, the virtuous majority, would save democracy from the hands of a conspiratorial, corrupted minority. Kansas offered their best hope.[38]

The bloodshed in Kansas brought ill repute to Missourians. Northerners expanded their condemnations of Missourians from that of slaveholding sinners to that of frontier savages, barbaric bullies, uneducated "pukes." The caning of Massachusetts Senator Charles Sumner in defense of free-state Kansas only confirmed the notions of most northerners that Missourians were indeed violent southerners; the event entwined in public perception the slaveholding perpetrators of the Kansas and Sumner crimes. Condemned as southerners, many Missourians during the Kansas conflict internalized the characterization in a fuller political sense. Those Missourians looked beyond New Englanders or northerners as the enemy of liberty and democracy in the West and toward the federal government. An angry group of more than two hundred slaveholders—including Atchison, Napton, Lowry, Sterling Price, and Claib Jackson—from twenty-six counties assembled in Lexington in July 1855 to condemn abolitionism, but in their language pledged themselves to

37. *Squatter Sovereign,* February 20 (first quote), May 29 (second quote); Cecil-Fronsman, " 'Death to All Yankees and Traitors in Kansas,' " 25–29.
38. *Squatter Sovereign,* March 6 (first quote), October 16, 1855 (second quote); Morrison, *Slavery in the American West,* 169–78.

a conflict that transcended the current one in Kansas. Calling slavery a "God-given . . . Natural right," James Shannon, president of the state university at Columbia, argued that neither individuals nor governments could interfere. "Let us hope for the best, and prepare for the worst;" Shannon implored the audience, "and then having done all that men can do to save the Union, if a dissolution is forced upon us by domestic traitors . . . then I, for one say . . . we will stand to our arms." Six years earlier, Claiborne Jackson had declared similarly. In defending his resolutions as not advocating disunion or any call to arms against the federal government, he added defiantly "but yet Congress might go so far, that he would resist to the death."[39]

As the struggle for Kansas revealed painfully to Missourians, the promise of democracy would not be realized in the West. Constant exertions, including armed forays into Kansas, continued interference with territorial elections, and recurrent violence in the hopes of intimidating abolitionist residents did not stem what became a flood tide of antislavery migration. This influx came not from New England, however, but from the western states, the same pragmatic people that Missourians had predicted would support slavery in Kansas. These Free-Staters, well outnumbering proslavery settlers in Kansas, waged their own war with the proslavery element in the territory, delegitimizing the legislature and ultimately forcing a congressional showdown when Kansas applied for statehood in 1857. By the time the territorial legislature proffered its ill-fated Lecompton Constitution to Congress for approval— with its infamous option to vote *"for* the Constitution with slavery, or *for* the Constitution without slavery"—even Missourians grudgingly conceded that the proslavery clauses in the document no longer reflected the constituency of Kansas and condemned the document as undemocratic. "All this is . . . the work of a few political demagogues," declared the *Jefferson Inquirer,* "who are seeking to bring about a dissolution of the Union, and are reckless of the means to which they resort to accomplish their purpose." For the sake

---

39. Michael Fellman, *Inside War: The Guerrilla Conflict in Missouri during the American Civil War,* 13 (first quote); Hurt, *Agriculture and Slavery in Little Dixie,* 283–86, 287–88 (second quote); *Glasgow Weekly Times,* July 26, 1855; *Liberty Weekly Tribune,* July 20, 27, 1855; Parrish, *David Rice Atchison,* 175–76; *Missouri Statesman,* June 8, 1849 (third quote). Preston S. Brooks, a congressman from South Carolina, attacked Senator Charles Sumner on the floor of the U.S. Senate, days after Sumner had delivered a two-day speech, "The Crime against Kansas," an excoriation of the government's Kansas policy as well as Senator Andrew Butler (Brooks's cousin) and his recent public apology for the violence in Kansas. The savage caning forced Sumner to absent himself for three and a half years from the Senate, while northerners galvanized against "Bully Brooks" and a perceived proslavery extremism. See Gienapp, "Crime against Sumner," 226–29, and Rawley, *Race and Politics,* 125–29.

of the Union, Missourians accepted—however bitterly—Kansas's destiny as a free state.[40]

More important, the events in Kansas pointed out clearly that a new alliance had emerged, one in which the northern and northwestern states had united in their conspiracy against slavery. No longer was the West a place of liberty; the democracy that had once buttressed Missourians' belief in western independence now threatened the institution that embodied those liberties, and not only in the territories but also in the existing states. In 1856, William Napton's forecast was as ominous as it was prescient: Missourians, he concluded, "look upon the establishment of a free state on their border, and *such* a free state as Kansas must be under present auspices, as equivalent to the destruction of slavery here and in this they do not err. It is therefore self preservation that forces them to resist the aggressions of the abolitionists upon Kansas. They have no alternative. Kansas and Missouri await the same fate. . . . [I]t will end in a civil war—first a border war, but soon a general state of hostility between the two sections of the Union, slaveholding and non-slaveholding."[41]

The democratic process had robbed Missouri of its own progeny. That same process now threatened Missouri. The end of the decade would demonstrate, as the editor of the *Jefferson Inquirer* avowed, that the border was indeed fertile ground for demagogues. Events had created a climate of fear and rage that left Missourians ripe for one who could rouse their choler, who could turn their resentment into action. Missouri now sought an avenging angel. Long stymied, Claiborne Fox Jackson saw his time as now come.

40. *Jefferson Inquirer,* December 5, 1857 (quotes).
41. Napton Diary, folder 2, p. 180, MHS.

Claiborne Fox Jackson, ca. 1861. Missouri's secessionist governor. Engraving from an oil painting that formerly hung in the Arrow Rock Tavern. Courtesy State Historical Society of Missouri, Columbia.

Thomas Caute Reynolds. An ardent disunionist and Jackson's lieutenant governor, he differed with Missouri's chief executive on strategy for the state's secession. Courtesy State Historical Society of Missouri, Columbia.

Sterling Price, ca. 1850. Former Missouri governor and moderate chairman of the state's 1861 secession convention, Price led the Missouri State Guard against federal forces before gaining a Confederate command. Daguerreotype by Thomas M. Easterly. Courtesy Missouri Historical Society, St. Louis. Easterly 179.

Nathaniel Lyon, ca. 1854. Commander of federal troops in Missouri in 1861, his military campaign from St. Louis to Jefferson City and beyond exiled Jackson and secessionist legislators. Carte de visite, Webster's Photo Gallery, Louisville, Ky. Courtesy Missouri Historical Society, St. Louis. Portraits L92.

Rioting in St. Louis streets following the Camp Jackson affair, 1861. Lyon's attack on the State Guard encampment provoked the Missouri state legislature to offer Jackson more military power. From *Harper's Weekly,* June 1, 1861. Courtesy Hargrett Rare Book and Manuscript Library, University of Georgia Libraries.

Pro-Union cartoon depicting Jackson and the battle at Boonville, June 1861. Courtesy Library of Congress.

Jackson addresses surrendered federal troops following the battle at Lexington, September 1861. From *Harper's Weekly*, October 19, 1861. Courtesy Hargrett Rare Book and Manuscript Library, University of Georgia Libraries.

Grave of Claiborne Fox Jackson and Eliza W. Jackson. Located in the Sappington Cemetery, west of Arrow Rock. Courtesy State Historical Society of Missouri, Columbia.

INTERMEZZO

LET THEM (the border States) stand as a wall of fire between the belligerent extremes, and with their strong arms and potential counsel keep them apart. Let them stand pledged, as they now are, to resist any attempt at coercion, plighting their faith, as we do not hesitate to plight the faith of Missouri, that if the impending war of the Northern States against the Southern shall, in defiance of our solemn protest and warning actually occur (which God in his mercy forefend!) we shall stand by Virginia and Kentucky and our Southern sisters—sharing their dangers, and abiding their fortunes and destiny—in driving back from their borders the hostile feet of Northern invaders. *Of* the South, we are *for* the South.

WILLIAM F. SWITZLER, *MISSOURI STATESMAN*, APRIL 15, 1861

Exiled now twice from political office, Claib Jackson could only watch as the momentous events unfolded in Kansas, unable to exert any appreciable impact. Jackson was indeed a pariah, blamed widely for the precipitous fall of Benton. Already in 1852, rumors abounded in the Boon's Lick that Jackson intended to leave Howard County, largely precipitated by his recent ignominious defeat for Congress. One rumor had him relocating to near the Mississippi river town of Hannibal in Marion County, while the *Glasgow Weekly Times* now reported that with his political career at an end, Jackson would leave for Texas. Many Missourians publicly vilified the former Democratic champion's attempts to justify his war on Benton:

> It is not unusual for sinners, when they find their days of existence drawing to a close, to endeavor to make out as favorable a case for themselves as possible; . . . they frequently manage to bamboozle themselves into the comfortable conviction that they have not been such desperate rascals after all. This, we think, is the case, to some extent with Maj. C. F. Jackson of Howard. Aware that his political life is rapidly hastening to a close, and apprehending that he has done little to excuse him from the wrath to come, he is trying to balance accounts with himself, in order that he may at least avoid the additional burthen of an uneasy conscience when he comes finally to repose in that "deep ditch" prepared for all such as have waged impious warfare against the Jupiter Tonans of Missouri.[1]

1. *Missouri Statesman*, December 19, 1851, January 30, 1852; *Glasgow Weekly Times*, October 28, September 16, 1852 (quote); McCandless, *History of Missouri*, 182.

Jackson did indeed leave Fayette, though not for any motive that the papers might have conceived. Whether Jackson contemplated a move from shame or from the pursuit of political fortunes seemingly lost proves no more than speculation, for his relocation derived from opportunism of a different type. In the fall of 1853, Dr. John Sappington, recognizing his approaching demise, divided up his ample property holdings among his heirs. Ever meticulous, on September 1 Sappington called upon Jackson, the former banker, to itemize all notes due his estate as well as the interest due on those notes; the ledger totaled $52,720, from which Sappington deducted a number of individual debts to various family members and those business debts to the pill company that would likely never be recouped. Those who assumed those debts would be able to draw equally from the remaining siblings for their repayment, if they proved unable to collect them. Sappington then inventoried and appraised all of his property—real, personal, and human, valued at more than sixty-seven thousand dollars, bringing the entire estate to well more than one hundred thousand dollars—so that by valuation he could ensure a fair distribution. Once the assessments were complete, Sappington told Jackson that he intended to divide the value of his property in its entirety into seven equal shares (his wife, Jane, having died the previous December, Sappington did not need to reserve any property for her lifetime) and allow the legatees to determine how their property should thus be divided. He also reserved much of his wealth until after his death; a full twenty thousand dollars he set aside for the establishment of a school fund to benefit the children of Saline County.[2]

Calling his family together at Pilot Hickory Farm, Sappington announced his complicated plan of divestiture. The clan negotiated the allotments by value and by category—real property, liquid and business assets, and chattel property. Sappington allowed for one notable exception to the plan; he

---

2. Description and particulars of the Sappington property settlement derive from the following sources: List of Notes Due John Sappington and Interest on same, September 1, 1853, John S. Sappington Papers, Mss. 1027, box 3, folder 61, SHSM; Allotment of lands [owned by John S. Sappington], undated [1853]; ibid., box 1, folder 3, SHSM; Division of Negroes and Notes, September 23, 1853, ibid., box 3, folder 62, SHSM; Settlement and division of Slaves made between Jesse M. Baskett and Claiborne F. Jackson, January 1, 1853, ibid., box 3, folder 61, SHSM; Claims in Notes, money and medicines [for] Children of Daughter Eliza Jackson, December 30, 1843, Sappington Family Papers, Mss. 2889, folder 11, SHSM; Will of John S. Sappington, October 24, 1853, in Burks, "Thunder on the Right," 479–80; Ellsberry, ed., *Cemetery Records of Saline County*, 34; Morrow, "Dr. John Sappington," 57–59; *Missouri Statesman*, October 14, 1853; *Glasgow Weekly Times*, October 20, 1853. The Sappington School Fund continued in trust well into the twentieth century, weathering legal challenges by descendants to secure those funds for themselves, and thus assisted thousands of Saline County students through outright grants.

dictated terms for one of the seven shares, that of the Pearson children whom Jackson did not support during his marriage to Eliza. Indeed, Sappington stipulated that the portion of the pill business allotted to these grandchildren should come in large part from Jackson's portion of the business. Though not yet dead, the elder Sappington sent a clear message to Jackson that he would not benefit from his marriage of convenience at his stepchildren's expense.

Sappington allowed his heirs to bargain for the lands and slaves among themselves, paying others by value for their choices out of their allotments. By general consensus, Sappington sold off a number of his twenty-five slaves rather than divide them by person; the sons, William and Erasmus, each had nearly as many as their father, while the sons-in-law owned between nineteen and twenty-seven each. Including the proceeds from the sales in the estate settlement, Sappington reserved some eleven slaves, largely women and children, specifically for the use of his Pearson grandchildren. Dr. Charles Bradford and his wife, Lavinia, who used their eight slaves largely as domestic servants, did not wish for more. Those legatees who wished to receive slaves settled with those who had received them after the assessment and before the remaining slaves were sold. Jackson quickly bargained with the others for those slaves he considered to be most useful to him, taking working-age males and selling women, children, and older males to those parties who wished for house servants, including his stepchildren. Indeed, by 1860, the configuration of Jackson's slaveholdings had changed dramatically; a full third of his bondpeople were males between the ages of thirteen and thirty-four.[3]

Jackson's reasons for this strategy quickly became evident; he intended to buy the home place from the other parties. Jackson chose the single most valuable piece of property that Sappington owned—the home place along with 820 acres, together worth $9,840, a decision that forced him to pay each of the other heirs more than sixteen hundred dollars for it. Eliza probably had some influence in this decision; whoever might acquire Pilot Hickory would assume care and upkeep for the family's patriarch until his death before acquiring clear title to the property. Because Eliza was the eldest daughter, such a responsibility easily devolved upon her and thus afforded Jackson some privilege in acquiring the home farm, though not without charge. Indeed, the elder Sappington would live on for a full three years until a

---

3. Seventh and Eighth U.S. Censuses, 1850 and 1860, Slave Schedule, Howard and Saline Counties [Missouri], NA; List of Slaves [with Ages and Birthdates] of John Sappington, undated [1853], John S. Sappington Papers, Mss. 1027, box 4, folder 94, SHSM; Bill of Sale, M. M. Proctor to C. F. Jackson for slave George, November 20, 1854, and Receipt from C. M. Bradford to C. F. Jackson for slave boy Isaac, January 9, 1855, both in ibid., box 3, folder 63, SHSM.

brain tumor took his life in the fall of 1856. Jackson, however, despite his wife's entreaties, did not take on Pilot Hickory Farm purely from any spousal benevolence. Acquisition of the Sappington estate signified the culmination of a life's ambition; Jackson—once prince, now mere viscount—occupied the king's palace. With clear intent, Jackson remade the Sappington seat in his own image; he renamed the former Pilot Hickory Farm as Fox Castle.[4]

Jackson did not intend to occupy this farm as mere ceremony. Whereas in Fayette he wrote political letters to the *Missouri Democrat* under the pseudonym "Farmer of Howard," in Saline he intended to take up the mantra of planter in a full antebellum sense. Out of politics and its employment, Jackson devoted his energies to making his farm a profitable agricultural venture. Numerous receipts indicate that he engaged immediately in large-scale hemp production—producing by 1860 more than ten tons of dew-rotted hemp—as well as selling wheat, oats, corn, wool, lard, bacon, and livestock, namely hogs and cattle. He contracted with various St. Louis commission merchants and Glasgow shippers to market his produce, and purchased hemp presses and seed, as well as "Kentucky Manufacture Jeans, Linseys, [and] Osnaburghs" to clothe his laborers. Fittingly, to complete his status as a full-time planter/farmer, Jackson joined the Central Missouri Agricultural Society and regularly attended the state agricultural fair not in legislative finery, but as "a plain, gentleman-farmer-looking man, wearing a dry and dusty wig, and a still dustier hat with a broken rim," as one observer recalled. The image of the common farmer was merely for display; Jackson sought wealth and found means of profit from his farm other than agriculture. A creek bed on his property revealed visible deposits of cannel coal, a hot-burning bituminous, and Jackson contracted with a St. Louis mining company to extract as much as ten thousand tons of coal per year, which would yield him seventy-five hundred dollars annually. In all, the assessed cash value of his farm was a princely twenty-one thousand dollars.[5]

4. Eliza Jackson to Dear Daughter [misidentified as Mrs. John Sappington to Mary Price], January 20, 1856, Sappington Family Papers, box 6, MHS; Eliza W. Jackson to C. F. Jackson, December 30, 1859, John S. Sappington Papers, Mss. 1027, box 3, folder 69, SHSM.

5. West, "Earlier Political Career of Jackson," 139; *Glasgow Weekly Times*, October 20, 1853; C. F. Jackson in Account with Huston and Thompson, April 29 to December 30, 1854, John S. Sappington Papers, Mss. 1027, box 3, folder 62, SHSM; Eighth U.S. Census, 1860, Agricultural Schedule, Saline County [Missouri], NA; J. and E. Walsh to C. F. Jackson, June 26 and August 23, 1855, both in ibid., box 3, folder 63, SHSM; Account of C. F. Jackson with William H. Wood and Co., 1856, ibid., box 3, folder 64, SHSM; E. M. Ryland and Co. to C. F. Jackson, February 13, 1856, ibid., box 3, folder 64, SHSM; Bill from C. L. Lewis to Col. C. F. Jackson, July–November 1857, ibid., box 3, folder 65, SHSM; Bill for Hemp Press from J. and E. Walsh to C. F. Jackson, February 14, 1857, ibid., box 3, folder 66, SHSM; Receipt for Sales of Hemp rec[eive]d for St[eamer]s

Jackson employed an increasingly large slave labor force on his farm. He appears to have been especially active during his hiatus from political office in obtaining as many slaves as he could manage and afford; by 1860 he owned forty-seven bondpeople, far more than any of his siblings or brothers-in-law. Indeed, during the decade he managed to increase his slaveholdings by thirty-one, or by more than 60 percent, a figure that put him in the upper echelon of slaveholders in the entire Boon's Lick and certainly in Saline County. This increase occurred in part by natural increase and in another part by the bondpeople he inherited from his father-in-law. Yet evidence indicates that Jackson scoured the neighborhood for surplus bondpeople to purchase, routinely attending estate sales and foreclosures in order to obtain slaves as cheaply as possible, as well as purchasing young male slaves from persons in the area. Moreover, he often hired out his slaves when work was slack, to the county for road work and to individuals in town and on neighboring farms, thus maximizing his investment in human labor. Indeed, by all indications Jackson's farm was thriving; by 1860, it boasted a slave quarter of eight cabins. He appeared to all who noticed to epitomize all he had once stood for as one of the state's most dogmatic proslavery politicians.[6]

Jackson employed his elder sons John (or "Breathitt") and William (or "Will"), who acted as managers in running his farm. With his youngest daughters, Louisa (or "Luda") and Ann Eliza, having been schooled (one in St. Louis, the other in Arrow Rock), married, and living in distant Hannibal and near Fayette, respectively, and with young Claib, Jr., still attending school at a private academy near Sedalia in Pettis County and thus having only a

---

Kate Howard and Carrier for acc[oun]t Mr. C. F. Jackson, March 4–10, 1858, ibid., box 3, folder 68, SHSM; Bill from D. W. Bell to C. F. Jackson, March 22, 1858, ibid., box 3, folder 68, SHSM; Logan D. Dameron to C. F. Jackson, October 29, 1859, ibid., box 3, folder 69, SHSM; Certificate of Membership in Central Agricultural Society, April 23, 1860, ibid., box 3, folder 71, SHSM; Grissom, "Personal Recollections," 506 (quote); Indenture between C. F. Jackson and J. R. Finlay and Co., May 4, 1859, ibid., box 3, folder 69, SHSM; C. F. Jackson Account Book, Bank of the State of Missouri, February 14, 1857 to February 14, 1860, ibid., box 5, vol. 10, SHSM; Account Receipt from Commission Merchant to C. F. Jackson, May 6, 1858, ibid., box 3, folder 68, SHSM.

6. Seventh and Eighth U.S. Censuses, 1850 and 1860, Slave Schedule, Howard and Saline Counties [Missouri], NA; Hurt, *Agriculture and Slavery in Little Dixie,* 217–24; *Glasgow Weekly Times,* December 9, 1852; Bill of Slave from John Miller to C. F. Jackson for slave Cyrus, May 8, 1855, ibid., box 3, folder 63, SHSM; Bill from C. L. Lewis to Col. C. F. Jackson, July–November 1857, John S. Sappington Papers, Mss. 1027, box 3, folder 65, SHSM; Account of Dr. William Price with C. F. Jackson for Slave Isaac, January 1, 1854, ibid., box 3, folder 66, SHSM; W. G. Cheeney to C. F. Jackson, September 24, 1857, ibid., box 3, folder 67, SHSM; Receipt from John S. Nowlin, Overseer, to Claibourn [*sic*] F. Jackson, November 17, 1855, to June 5, 1856, ibid., box 3, folder 64, SHSM; Sarah Jane Baskett to William B. Sappington, July 4, 1851, William B. Sappington Papers, Mss. 1421, folder 1, SHSM.

limited, seasonal interest in the farm operations, Jackson depended greatly upon his eldest boys and was not above disciplining them for dereliction of their responsibilities. On one occasion in 1854, Jackson sternly rebuked his son, Will, while away at school for *"rowdyism & licentiousness"* and frivolous spending habits (Jackson routinely sent them money) after receiving poor reports from his preceptors. He nonetheless reminded his son that he had "by no means lost my confidence in you, but on the contrary fully believe that in the end you will render a good account of yourself. I cannot—I *will not* dispair [*sic*]," he wrote, and signed the letter "Your affectionate father." His sons in turn appear to have respected their father's authority, admitting personal failures in the knowledge that they had his unqualified support. On one occasion his son Will admitted candidly to being "stunned and mortified, distressed and humiliated" at finding himself nearly nine hundred dollars in debt, admitting that "a good sum of this has been expended foolishly." Having learned the values of his banker father, he asked Jackson for a loan that he would repay in a timely fashion—with interest—and would forego the study of law during his indebtedness and would sell his horse and buggy to pay the first installment of the loan. "By this arrangement . . . made with that spirit of liberality & candor which has ever characterized the past actions of your life towards me . . . you will save my credit and my feelings, by affording me the means to pay my debts punctually, and giving me time to liquidate without Sacrifice. . . . I am now a sober and I think a prudent man." Whether Jackson agreed to the arrangement is unclear, yet clearly his demeanor toward his blood sons was altogether different from that evinced toward his stepchildren.[7]

---

7. Sarah Jane Baskett to William B. Sappington, March 3, 1852, William B. Sappington Papers, Mss. 1421, folder 1, SHSM; Eliza W. Jackson to C. F. Jackson, December 30, 1859, John S. Sappington Papers, Mss. 1027, box 3, folder 69, SHSM; William S. Jackson to C. F. Jackson, September 9, 1857, ibid., box 3, folder 67, SHSM; Receipt for children's tuition, Lucky and Pritchett to C. F. Jackson, June 23, 1853, box 3, folder 61, SHSM; Bill from G. B. Newton to C. F. Jackson, October 10, 1857, ibid., box 3, folder 67, SHSM; Bill from John T. Tracy to C. F. Jackson, September 23, 1858, ibid., box 3, folder 68, SHSM; Receipt for boardinghouse of Howard High School, January 11, 1859, and Bill from Spencer Smith to C. F. Jackson for Board and Tuition of daughter, February 23, 1859, both in ibid., box 3, folder 68, SHSM; C. M. Bradford to C. F. Jackson, January 1, 1860, ibid., box 3, folder 70, SHSM; C. F. Jackson Account Book, Bank of the State of Missouri, February 14, 1857 to February 14, 1860, ibid., box 5, vol. 10, SHSM; C. F. Jackson to John Brown, Esq., July 5, 1858, ibid., box 3, folder 68, SHSM; C. F. Jackson to My Dear Son, March 9, 1854, photostat in Burks, "Thunder on the Right," 473–74 (first and second quotes); W. S. Jackson to C. F. Jackson, May 17, 1860, ibid., box 3, folder 71, SHSM (third and fourth quotes). Louisa Jane, or "Luda," married Charles L. Lamb, a physician born in New York, and the two relocated to the river town of Hannibal; Ann Eliza married John A. Perkins, a Virginia-born schoolteacher, and lived in Saline County. William S. Jackson attended law school at the University of Virginia. See Eighth

Despite his settling into the routine of farming, Jackson could not remain divorced from the political milieu. As early as 1854, he subscribed to as many as nine different Missouri newspapers, from St. Louis to the Boon's Lick, in order to keep abreast of the Kansas controversy and other public matters. Moreover, in 1858 he and William B. Napton established the *Marshall Democrat* in Saline. Men of influence, both in Missouri and in Congress, sought his opinions and counsel; he worked locally in opposition to the abolitionists in Kansas, rekindling his earlier association with now-neighbor William B. Napton—a strong Ultra—who advised him routinely on the political and legal implications of the struggle. Napton became something of a mentor for Jackson, who quickly determined to return to politics. In the summer of 1855, Claib served as a delegate from Saline County to the state Slaveholders' Convention, held at Lexington, hoping it would signal his reemergence into the realm of public men. Later that fall he was an orator, along with congressman John S. Phelps, in Jefferson City as the General Assembly deliberated over candidates for the Senate seat vacated by David Rice Atchison as he waged war in Kansas. In reviving his political aspirations, Jackson nearly lost his life; invited to Jefferson City on November 1, 1855, for a celebration for the opening of the Pacific Railroad, he narrowly survived the state's worst train accident when in a heavy rainstorm the uncompleted bridge over the Gasconade River gave way under the weight of the locomotive and it along with fourteen cars plunged thirty feet down the embankment. As many as thirty-four people died, many of their bodies horribly mangled, while more than a hundred others were injured; luckily for Jackson, he received only "considerable bruising" according to the newspaper reports. Yet he could not parlay his harrowing ordeal into political success; in 1856, he unsuccessfully sought the replacement seat of congressman John C. Miller. Indeed, the *Jefferson Inquirer* ridiculed the Georgetown convention for nominating "a man who does not act openly and boldly, but slips into committee rooms and plots the overthrow of good men, in order to secure office for himself." Time had not yet rescued Jackson from public scorn.[8]

U.S. Census, 1860, Population Schedule, Marion and Saline Counties [Missouri], NA; *Missouri Statesman,* August 6, 1880.

8. Account of C. F. Jackson with L. J. Herron, January 1, 1855, John S. Sappington Papers, Mss. 1027, box 3, folder 62, SHSM; John S. Phelps to C. F. Jackson, January 18, 1856, ibid., box 3, folder 64, SHSM; Thomas G. Dyer, " 'A Most Unexampled Exhibition of Madness and Brutality': Judge Lynch in Saline County, Missouri, 1859," 272*n7;* C. F. Jackson to O[bediah]. B. Pearson, Esq., June 1, 1855, Arrow Rock Tavern Board Papers, 1826–1913, Mss. 3087: Correspondence, folder 1, SHSM; William B. Napton to C. F. Jackson, October 3, 1857, Miscellaneous Manuscripts, Mss. 1879, SHSM; *Missouri Statesman,* November 16, 9, 1855; *Glasgow Weekly Times,* June 26, 1856; Parrish, *David Rice Atchison,* 141; McCandless, *History of Missouri,* 234; *Jefferson Inquirer,* June 21, 1856 (quote).

His censure would be brief, however, for the maturation of the Kansas issue revived Jackson's political fortunes. By 1856, public sentiment in Missouri had turned so strongly against Free-Soilers that Democrats regained outright control of the General Assembly, spurred by the increasing hostility toward the newly formed Republican party and its initial challenge for the presidency. The Republican presence charged the state's political atmosphere as never before; offspring of the Kansas controversy, the party and its platform opposed slavery in the territories, thus making it an immediately recognizable foe. With John C. Frémont—Benton's son-in-law—as the Republicans' first candidate and with Francis Preston Blair, Sr., among its founding ranks and son Frank Blair named to the party's first executive committee (despite maintaining his allegiance to the Democratic party for two full years), Missouri's Democrats took full advantage of the disintegration of their Whig rivals to regain the house. Internally, however, while the party remained divided along its traditional Benton/anti-Benton axis, the "Anties" saw rejuvenation as the Kansas tide turned away from the proslavery forces. Jackson, the indefatigable freedom fighter, now reemerged for many partisan Democrats as a viable leader of their faction, and at the Anties' convention (each faction nominated its own slate of candidates and delegates to the national nominating convention at separate meetings in the respective chambers of the statehouse) he received election as party chairman. Frank Blair, charged in this conservative renascence as a "black Republican" and fearful of the imminent ascendance of the Anties, predicted that "they will inaugurate in Missouri the same reign of terror which exists in Kansas."[9]

Still, Jackson's image yet proved too controversial for his faction—or his district's voters—to support his candidacy for elected office. In 1856, he ran unsuccessfully to fill the vacant seat in the General Assembly. He would, however, receive his faction's largesse. The first act of the General Assembly, now Democrat-controlled, was to appoint Jackson as the state's first bank commissioner. No sinecure, this was a paid position with an annual salary of five thousand dollars that would require Jackson's banking expertise as well as his political savvy. Even the *Missouri Statesman,* no friend of Jackson's, remarked that "politically, we are free to say that he is the best qualified man of his party for the post to which he has been elected." Jackson would countersign and register every note delivered to a state bank for circulation, keep the plates or dies for the printing of state notes, and regulate distribution of those notes only to those banks that had enough specie to back them. Moreover, Jackson's responsibilities as commissioner would include examining the books of the various banks, comparing the notes on hand and in circulation with the capital each of the banks had in reserve, and annually

9. Parrish, *Frank Blair,* 60–62, 63 (quote); McCandless, *History of Missouri,* 267–68.

reporting the condition of them—along with quarterly statements from the banks themselves—to the governor. With an office in St. Louis and a room at its posh Barnum's Hotel, Jackson spent the next three years largely away from his Saline County home, either in St. Louis or traveling around the state, an imposition he found not altogether unpleasant.[10]

Yet such an appointment did not satisfy Jackson's rekindled political ambitions, if ever they had cooled, particularly once the bitter disappointment following the Lecompton Constitution in Kansas prompted many Missourians to turn to Jackson as their standard-bearer. Indeed, the state's governor during the commencement of the Kansas crisis, Sterling Price, once a Central Clique stalwart, had proved largely ineffective by attempting to moderate the state's ruptured leadership. Yet Price's barren single term from 1853 to 1857 as the state's potentate stemmed most clearly from his unwillingness to pander to the angry proslavery electorate who looked to him as leader and who grew in number and strength as the violence on the western border reached its apex. Supportive of slavery (as governor he had attended the Lexington Convention), Price as a moderate Democrat nonetheless expressed disdain for Atchison and his rabid followers who disrupted the party as well as the state and threatened the Union. Indeed, Robert M. Stewart, the northerner who had moved to St. Joseph, took care not to make the same mistake. Elected almost exclusively by proslavery votes (the new litmus in the state's political world, supplanting party and intraparty alignments that had ruled Missouri's politics for three decades) in a contested special 1857 election, Stewart stood up strongly for slavery and states' rights in his inaugural address. "The executive and the General Assembly of this State," he trumpeted, "have declared the sentiments of the people with reference to different attempts at federal usurpation and aggressive sectional agitation. . . . They are loyal to their own institutions; and . . . they suffer no interference with them by others."[11]

10. Secretary of State Election Returns (Congressmen, Officials), 1856, Capitol Fire Documents, 1806–1957, microfilm reel CFD-186, folders 16377–84, MSA; *Missouri Statesman*, March 13, 1857 (quote); Burks, "Thunder on the Right," 326–27; *Missouri House Journal*, 19th General Assembly, 1st Sess., 1857–1858, 5–6; Bill from A. W. Sproule and Co. to C. F. Jackson, June 16, 1857, John S. Sappington Papers, Mss. 1027, box 3, folders 66, 68, SHSM; Bill from John Brook to C. F. Jackson, June 16, 1857, and bills from Barnum's Hotel to C. F. Jackson, June 16, September 1, 1857, February 14, 1858, both in ibid., box 3, folder 68, SHSM.

11. Shalhope, *Sterling Price*, 100–132; *Glasgow Weekly Times*, October 29, 1857 (quote). Trusten Polk, an ardent proslavery, anti-Benton candidate from St. Louis, won election as governor in 1856. In January 1857, Polk received election to the U.S. Senate to fill the vacated seat of Henry S. Geyer. Polk's "promotion" after only days in office drew widespread criticism both in the state and within the Democratic ranks, largely for its apparent cronyism and because it revealed Polk as an opportunist. Justice William B.

The 1858 midterm election only confirmed Missouri's transition toward a more extreme proslavery political stance, nowhere more evident than in the state's traditional free-soil locus: St. Louis. In Benton's fief and in the very year of Old Bullion's death (the emotion of which easily might have prompted his legions to resurrect his legacy with a strong turnout), "Free Democrats" Frank Blair and Gratz Brown both lost their reelection bids, Blair for Congress and Brown for a fourth term in the Missouri house, amid charges of fraud. The clear victors were so-called National Democrats, those who opposed Benton and free territories in the West; Blair and other Bentonites received taunts of being "Black Republicans." St. Louis County alone sent twelve to the Missouri house when just two years earlier all of their representatives had been Bentonites. The rest of the state witnessed even more dramatic support for the Ultras, as they were called, largely as protection against the Republican threat. In all, seventy-four Democrats won seats in the house, while in the senate the party ruled over its opposition, twenty-four seats to nine. At separate conventions held at Georgetown and Fayette each had approved resolutions that supported their party as the lone palisade against the Black Republican onslaught and which endorsed the entire Missouri delegation in Congress "save and except F. P. Blair, Jr., of St. Louis, who has proven recreant to this State." The author of both of these sets of resolutions was Claib Jackson, whose political stock had risen rapidly in the volatile and vengeful sectional melée.[12]

By 1860, Jackson had received solicitations to return to public life from many Missouri sectors and, sensing the shifting political winds, he announced to a close group of supporters in the fall of 1859 that he intended to run for governor. Rumors had circulated for more than a year that Jackson would seek the governorship; in late August of 1858, at an Arrow Rock barbecue "to exult over the downfall of Blair and his satellites," Jackson was the keynote speaker, leaving all in attendance secure in the assumption that he was contemplating a canvass. The following October, he was conspicuously

---

Napton referred to it as "a gross outrage upon public opinion and upon party policy. . . . He is no politician—knows nothing of the true principles of our government which he never studied—but is merely a democrat from association, education and habit." Polk served one six-year term as U.S. senator, then served as one of Missouri's senators in the Confederate Congress. See Parrish, Jones, and Christensen, *Missouri*, 137–38; Napton Diary, folder 3, 209–10.

12. Peterson, *Freedom and Franchise*, 83–85; Parrish, *Frank Blair*, 72–73; Smith, *Blair Family in Politics*, 429–30, 439–41; *Marshall Democrat*, April 30, 1858 (quotes); McCandless, *History of Missouri*, 286; Shalhope, *Sterling Price*, 135–37. Shalhope misidentifies the Fayette resolutions' author as Sterling Price; the wording of the Georgetown resolutions, introduced by Jackson, are virtually identical to those of Fayette's resolutions down to the specific condemnation of Blair. In 1860, the U.S. House voted not to seat Richard Barrett and awarded the seat to Blair.

present at the Alton, Illinois, senatorial debate between incumbent Stephen Douglas and candidate Abraham Lincoln—the last of seven—recognizing its national implications and the political opportunity that his presence offered. In the summer of 1859, the *Liberty Tribune* accused him of making "fourth of July speeches" in preparation for a campaign. Robert Stewart, though ardently proslavery, remained mute on the threats of secession now emanating from the cotton states and, exacerbated by his northern birth, he now appeared unreliable to many of those newly found southerners in the party. One supporter wrote to Jackson from Canton that "Judge Clark and myself had a conversation on the subject of who should be our next Governor and we agreed that you were the man we needed. I have conversed with others enough to believe that you can get the voice of this corner of the vineyard." Even Clique member John J. Lowry—who had turned away from Jackson with the rest of the state—now counseled Jackson on his best tack for election, thus welcoming him back into the fold.[13]

Yet Claib Jackson did not enjoy the complete support of his party, much less the Ultras. The controversy that had thrown Jackson abruptly from office five years earlier haunted him still. Benjamin F. Massey, learning of Jackson's intended run for governor, commented to one of the faction's elders that despite "a very general desire to unite the old democratic party[,] Jackson's warmest friends fear this could not be done with him. Were it not for this feeling I think he would be nominated. . . . Amongst other things Jackson has too much record, and though it is a record I could in the main approve, yet it is full of occurrences that will lose him votes, in every division of the whole state, without at the same time getting him one Single vote." The *Jefferson Inquirer* saw in his call for unified party support for his candidacy no *"meaner, lower,* or more *bare faced* piece of shameless brazen faced impudence." Massey, among others, felt that Jackson's penchant for cronyism made him an unattractive gubernatorial aspirant: "The impression now is that he is completely sold to the Bank influence. And if he could be nominated at all for Gov, it would be by that influence. I am sorry, very sorry, to have to talk this way about Jackson." Another detractor was more blunt: "C. F. Jackson has dabbled with the Banks till he has made a fortune and till the bank paper has fell to 1 & 1½ per cent discount." Yet even Massey,

---

13. *Marshall Democrat,* September 3, 1858 (first quote); Grissom, "Personal Rec ollections," 507; Robert W. Johannsen, ed., *The Lincoln-Douglas Debates,* 286; *Liberty Tribune,* August 5, 1859 (second quote); William H. Lyon, "Claiborne Fox Jackson and the Secession Crisis in Missouri," 424; P. Carr to C. F. Jackson, January 15, 1859, John S. Sappington Papers, Mss. 1027, box 3, folder 95, SHSM; C. F. Jackson to John Brown, Esq., July 5, 1858, ibid., box 3, folder 68, SHSM; James Ellison to C. F. Jackson, January 24, 1860, ibid., box 3, folder 70, SHSM (third quote); J. J. Lowry to C. F. Jackson, September 11, 1857, ibid., box 3, folder 67, SHSM.

along with others in the party both in Missouri and in Congress, realized that the climate now made Jackson perhaps the strongest contender for the state's highest elected office.[14]

The party nominating convention that met in April in Jefferson City was a stormy affair, not only because of the controversy surrounding Jackson's candidacy for the gubernatorial nomination but also as a result of the imminent candidacy of Democrat Stephen A. Douglas for president. Clearly, though the Ultras had gained sway, the party was anything but harmonious. Discord erupted immediately upon Jackson's relinquishment of the chair's gavel, as the convention knew he would soon be nominated for governor; the fiery debate over a temporary chairman forecast the tenor of the entire four-day meeting. A Douglas/anti-Douglas schism rived the delegates largely along the traditional Benton/anti-Benton fault line; the subsequent temporary chairmen (Sterling Price replaced Jackson's initial replacement, Robert Aycock, when the furor threatened his already poor health) each proved unable to control the raucous confusion and violent invective that rocked the legislative chamber in which the convention sat. The crescendo surrounding the nomination of delegates to the national convention dwarfed the nominations for governor. Through the tumult, Jackson received the party's nomination for governor over Waldo P. Johnson, his leading opponent, on the fourth ballot. His support had come largely from the party's uninstructed delegates, representing virtually half of the convention, who carried his nomination. Despite his relatively concordant nomination and despite the fact that the proslavery faction had carried every contest in the convention, from nominations of candidates (including the lieutenant governor, Thomas Caute Reynolds, no relation to the former governor and an ardent southern rights candidate) to dictating the platform, the discordant convention indicated clearly that Jackson had no party mandate.[15]

Jackson felt this weight during his summer campaign. Regarded widely as the standard-bearer of the Ultras, Jackson received ardent support from that faction's constituents. One wrote to him from Independence that his recent nomination was "evidence that the cause of Southern rights, for which you

14. Ben Hughes to C. F. Jackson, January 6, April 4, 1860, both in John S. Sappington Papers, Mss. 1027, box 3, folder 70, SHSM; B. F. Massey to J. F. Snyder, July 9, December 18, 1859, John F. Snyder Collection, box 1, MHS (first quote), *Jefferson Inquirer,* June 30, 1860 (second quote); Massey to Snyder, March 12, 1860, John F. Snyder Collection, box 2, MHS (third quote); John S. Phelps to Snyder, January 29, 1860, ibid., box 2, MHS; W. P. Johnson to Snyder, December 29, 1859, ibid., box 1, MHS; B. F. Walker to Snyder, March 7, 1860, ibid., box 2, MHS (fourth quote).

15. *Daily Missouri Democrat,* April 11–13, 1860; *Daily Missouri Republican,* April 10–13, 1860; Shalhope, *Sterling Price,* 138–41; Smith, *Blair Family in Politics,* 495; John F. Snyder, "The Democratic State Convention of Missouri in 1860," 112–22; Lyon, "Jackson and the Secession Crisis," 424–25.

have zealously contended, is in the ascendant in our own great state; and I feel a perfect assurance that in your election we will blot out the base insinuation that Missouri is preparing to desert her Southern Sisters, and show farther that we desire hereafter not to be controlled by 'Northern Men, with Southern principles.' " Yet Jackson also now carried the standard of the entire Missouri Democracy, and sought to harmonize the competing factions, an already difficult task that national events soon rendered nearly insuperable. The national political edifice crumbled during the spring, with four candidates vying for election—two from the Democratic party. The sectional debate had torn the party of Jackson asunder, and two candidates—Stephen Douglas and John C. Breckinridge—represented northern and southern wings of the party, respectively, in the national contest. A third candidate, Tennessean John Bell, represented the Constitutional Union party, an alignment of old-line southern Whigs and nativist "Know-Nothings," its platform an assuagement of the nation's cleavage over slavery by appealing to those Union-loving border residents. The final candidate, Illinoisan Abraham Lincoln, a northwesterner, led the antislavery Republicans in their party's second campaign. The slate approximated separate races in each section of the nation. As Jackson began campaigning in May 1860, he found his own base of support eroding as the national political structure splintered. After conferring with William B. Napton and other close advisers, he determined to maintain a noncommital campaign, endorsing neither Douglas, the party's "regular" nominee, nor Breckinridge, the southern rights candidate (and Jackson's private favorite) in hopes of attaining party unity in the maelstrom of popular politics.[16]

Jackson made his canvass in the southwestern portion of the state, a region normally all but ignored by Missouri politicians. The decision was not so quixotic; southwestern Missouri was the home ground of Waldo P. Johnson, who carried twice as many instructed delegates to the recent convention as any of the other candidates and among whose bitter supporters Jackson now sought votes. He set a grueling schedule, speaking in twenty-four different towns in twenty-six days during which he covered more than six hundred miles by horse and carriage—including more than forty miles on two separate days—over terrain that progressed from rolling prairie to rugged Ozark plateau to flinty pine and cedar woodlands. Starting in Independence, Jackson spoke almost exclusively in small towns such as Granby, Ozark, Hartville, Houston, Waynesville, Linn Creek, Tuscumbia, Bolivar, Lebanon, and California, as well as in the region's largest town, Springfield. Touted

16. Samuel Ralston to C. F. Jackson, April 24, 1860, John S. Sappington Papers, Mss. 1027, box 3, folder 71, SHSM (quote); Lyon, "Jackson and the Secession Crisis," 426–27; Parrish, *History of Missouri*, 1–2.

as "the most thorough canvass ever made in the S. W. & embraces many counties never before visited by a candidate," Jackson omitted only those county seats judged either too distant for a day's travel or whose counties lacked sufficient population to make the trip worthwhile.[17]

The pace was exhausting enough, but an unexpected and unprecedented opponent made the trip even more draining. Beginning in Springfield at the end of the campaign's second week, a conservative local judge and farmer, Sample Orr, attended Jackson's rallies and at the conclusion of his speeches often mounted the platform and spoke against many of Jackson's nebulous stances, such as state railroad subsidies and banking policies. That Waldo Johnson had come out for Jackson only made Orr's offensive more unexpected and infuriating. An angry Jackson refused Orr's request to become part of the canvass, prompting the independent candidate to dog Jackson for the remainder of the circuit, even following him to the Boon's Lick. Orr's quick wit and provocative appearances made him a popular grassroots candidate. Already unclear as to whether he had locked up the support of the southwest, Jackson soon found that any hope of remaining neutral quickly diminished when two powerful groups of St. Louisans pressured him to announce. One group represented Nicholas Paschall, editor of the influential *Missouri Republican* (the state's largest newspaper), and they met Jackson in the town of California, his last campaign stop on his southwestern circuit, and threatened to withdraw support if he did not support Douglas. The other was a group of proslavery Democratic officeholders who wrote to the nominee and instructed him that unless he came out strongly for Breckinridge, they "shall feel it to be our duty to nominate a Standard bearer who will emphatically firmly and decidedly represent the principles of the old line democracy of the State." Jackson felt the snare tightening and resolved to announce himself at his scheduled appearance in Fayette on the last day of June.[18]

Jackson's understanding of his home state's political geography ultimately

17. C. F. Jackson's Campaign Schedule, undated [1860], John S. Sappington Papers, Mss. 1027, box 1, folder 7, SHSM (quotes); *Daily Missouri Republican*, May 28, 1860; Lyon, "Jackson and the Secession Crisis," 425–428; B. F. Massey to J. F. Snyder, March 12, 1860, John F. Snyder Collection, box 2, MHS; Morrow, "Ozark/Ozarks," 4–10.

18. Lyon, "Jackson and the Secession Crisis," 428; William E. Parrish, *Turbulent Partnership: Missouri and the Union 1861–1865*, 4–5; Parrish, *History of Missouri*, 2, 8; *Jefferson Inquirer*, July 7, 14, 21, 1860; *Missouri Statesman*, June 29, July 13, 1860; C. F. Jackson to George Taylor, July 28, 1860, George R. Taylor Collection, MHS; C. J. Corwin to J. F. Snyder, July 8, 1860, John F. Snyder Collection, box 2, MHS; John Loughborough, James B. Bowlin et al. to C. F. Jackson, June 27, 1860, Sappington Family Papers, box 6, MHS (quote). The others who signed the document were Hancock Jackson, Isaac H. Sturgeon, Daniel H. Donovan, Oscar W. Collet, Thomas L. Snead, Edward Longuemore, Colton Greene, Charles L. Rogers, Edward Haven, Jr., and James M. Loughborough.

made his decision on who he would support. His chief adviser, Napton, had schooled him well on the state's changed landscape during Jackson's time away from elective politics; proslavery Democrats now divided the state along the sectional lines that divided the nation. Napton drew the lines clearly in a candid, informed letter to Jackson:

> The northern tier of counties through which the Hannibal & St. J[oseph] road runs, after great accessions from northern emigration, is expected to cast their lot with the Emancipationists. But all recent developments of sentiment in this quarter indicate a very different state of public sentiment—there counties, especially the Eastern end of the tier, seem to be sound & firm & during the seven years war with Benton, our principal & most reliable strength lay in this quarter. The South West is expected to join in this crusade—simply because she supported Benton & has few slaves—but the South West is filled up with Tennesseans & Kentuckians, & although non slaveholders, I anticipate but little danger from them. The North West is also looked to—& I confess indications there are unfavorable. Their population is chiefly from Indiana, Ohio & Illinois—& they cannot be trusted—still, as long as the river counties maintain a firm posture, even with St. Louis & the North West to contend against, we may consider ourselves safe.[19]

Believing the largest portion of the state to be secure for the Ultras, Jackson determined that his best hope for the election would come from its center of population: St. Louis. Boasting nearly 160,000 free residents—a full 15 percent of the state's free population—Jackson could not simply ignore this massive constituency which, like most of Missouri, scrutinized candidates in the enormous tension surrounding the upcoming elections. Jackson gambled that his reputation would sustain the majority of conservative Democrats no matter which national candidate he supported. The St. Louis voters, long resistant to out-state candidates, especially those from the central river counties and particularly one recognized as an anti-Benton, proslavery Ultra, now would need assurances that Jackson intended a course of moderation if elected to the state's highest office in the light of secession flashes rumbling from the cotton states. Indeed, Jackson determined to align with Douglas, but in order to maintain the angry rural vote he would maintain a clear delineation that he was, above all party affiliation, staunchly proslavery and unwaveringly states' rights.[20]

Rumors of Jackson's impending decision circulated even before he made his official announcement, largely because the choice would not affect him alone, but also the others on the Democratic slate. Preparatory to what he

19. William B. Napton to C. F. Jackson, October 3, 1857, Miscellaneous Manuscripts, Mss. 1879, SHSM; Parrish, *History of Missouri*, 7–8.
20. Wade, *Slavery in the Cities,* 327; Parrish, *History of Missouri*, 6–7; Lyon, "Jackson and the Secession Crisis," 428–29.

knew would be the most important speech of his campaign, Jackson spoke at rallies in Fayette and Boonville, vilifying those who deviated, however slightly, from the proslavery platform as "Black Republican[s] of the blackest hue" and further accusing them of opposing the fugitive slave law. At Fayette, Jackson and Reynolds announced their choice: they would support Stephen Douglas as the Democratic nominee for president. As a stunned audience in his long-time hometown listened, Jackson argued somewhat weakly that despite his support for squatter sovereignty in the territories—including his having turned against the Lecompton Constitution, ending proslavery hopes in Kansas—Douglas's stance against abolitionism made the party safe in his hands if elected president. Yet Jackson attempted to appease those Ultras in the crowd by tempering his stance on the Illinoisan who was now so controversial in Missouri by claiming that his personal choice was for Breckinridge, but in pursuit of party unity he would support the "regular" candidate. Jackson—since Atchison's retirement the bellwether of Missouri's radical proslavery element—had resumed his role as political chameleon and assumed the color—however temporarily—of the state's moderates.[21]

Unfortunately, Jackson's transparent effort to smooth his announcement for Douglas only served to confuse many out-state Ultras. "How it is possible for men who sustained the Jackson resolutions to go for Douglas, is strange to me," speculated Benjamin F. Massey just before the Fayette meeting, "there is not a Douglas democrat in the state that I know of that occupied Douglas's position." Similarly, former aspirant Waldo Johnson reacted from Warrensburg: "Rumor says here that Jackson & Reynolds are out for Douglass [*sic*] but I won[']t believe." Newspapers across the state abandoned Jackson's candidacy; the *Jefferson Inquirer* declared him ineligible for election for having taken up residence temporarily in Kansas, thus violating the four-year residency rule. Hastily called county meetings throughout Missouri denounced him. Mosby M. Parsons condemned him as a turncoat, claiming that "we should not let the Epithet of 'Bolter,' so fluent in Claib Jacksons mouth, have any terms for us. He is the supporter of a sectional candidate opposed to the principles of our platform and in so doing he bolts our principles, our promise to support him is now void for a failure of Consideration We are no longer bound by it—but our duty to our party and

21. Abiel Leonard to C. F. Jackson, June 29, 1860, Abiel Leonard Papers, Mss. 1013, box 12 (uncombined), folder 404, SHSM; Jackson to Leonard, July 1, 1860, ibid., box 12 (uncombined), folder 405, SHSM (quote); Lyon, "Jackson and the Secession Crisis," 429–30; *Daily Missouri Republican*, July 11, 1860. In his 1962 dissertation on Jackson, Walter M. Burks claims that Jackson's stand for Douglas represented his true political convictions, arguing against the prevailing historical opinion that Jackson's stance was disingenuous, designed to win the election. Of the extant evidence, none substantiates Burks's contention.

its principles demands that we should discard him without hesitation." Upon verification of the announcement days later, Massey—soon to win election as secretary of state—could contain neither his confusion nor his anger:

> [T]he Devil has broken out in another quarter. Jackson and Reynolds spoke at Fayette on Saturday the 30th inst. and both came out Strong for Douglas. Isn't that a stunner? . . . I tell you sir, I am absolutely bewildered. Men are acting so entirely contrary to the course of their whole past lives, as to confound me. . . . When I can not be of any service in Sustaining the rights of the south any longer in Mo. I will go where I can be. And I hope these tender footed, mouthy pro slavery men in Mo., who surrender at the time their services are most needed, will live to see the day when every big buck negro in the state will have the right to range himself along side of them, their full equal in every political right, and the political right being secured the social equality will soon follow as a matter of course. And I believe they are pursuing such a course, that if this does not overtake them, it will most certainly come upon their children.[22]

Jackson's Fayette speech brought his southwest canvass to a ringing close. Confidants suggested that he lie low until the election, a practical strategy in the minefield that would be Missouri during the next month. Indeed, a week after the controversial Fayette announcement, Reynolds addressed a letter to Jackson at Arrow Rock advising him after a canvass of the western counties that "the prevalent feeling seems to be in favour of uniting in our August elections & leaving the presidential question for discussion afterwards. . . . We cannot be expected to pursue a course which may defeat *us* while it elects *them*. Such 'heads I win, tails you lose' kind of a policy will not do, and the State ticket should *stand* or *fall* together." Jackson appears to have disagreed, for he continued to speak, but he made only limited appearances and remained on the familiar ground of the Boon's Lick. His speeches, as the campaign correspondent for the *Jefferson Inquirer* related, "dealt largely, in glittering generalities," avoiding as much as possible any public statement that opponents might use against him, leading the correspondent to question, if venomously, "Whether the snake that made the track, Was going South or coming back."[23]

More important, the position that Jackson and Reynolds assumed caused Missouri's gubernatorial race to mirror the national fracture; two candidates immediately entered the race, both of whom represented factions of

22. Waldo P. Johnson to J. F. Snyder, July 5, 1860 (second quote); B. F. Massey to Snyder, June 26, 1860 (third quote), July 4, 1860 (fifth quote), and M. M. Parsons to Snyder, July 8, 1860 (fourth quote), all in John F. Snyder Collection, box 2, MHS; *Jefferson Inquirer,* July 21, 1860; Lyon, "Jackson and the Secession Crisis," 429–30; *Daily Missouri Republican,* July 11, 1860.

23. Thomas Caute Reynolds to C. F. Jackson, July 9, 1860, Thomas C. Reynolds Papers, MHS (first quote); *Jefferson Inquirer,* July 7 (second and third quotes), 23, 1860.

the Democratic party that were outraged by Jackson's alignment. While Jackson represented the "regular" Democrats, conservative Breckinridge Democrats—true to their word, and with Mosby Parsons at their helm—quickly renounced him as their candidate and from St. Louis named Hancock L. Jackson, former governor, as their choice. An ephemeral coalition of moderate Benton Democrats, unmoored Whigs, former Know-Nothings, and even some Republicans rewarded Sample Orr's initiative by nominating him in Jefferson City as the "Opposition" or Constitutional Union candidate. James B. Gardenhire of Cole County was the Republican nominee. As the last-minute candidates scrambled to gain support in the short month before the August 6 election, Jackson traveled to St. Louis after news reached him of the widespread furor and met with Hancock Jackson in hopes of heading off a split in the party. One observer related that "Hancock told him how he could do it—by backing square out. Claib admitted that he had committed a great blunder; though he would make a public statement that he was mistaken in saying that Douglas was the *regular* nominee. . . . I believe they will both be beaten—Claib. and Reynolds. . . . We have plenty of time to *beat* traitors. Jackson and Reynolds are badly scared."[24]

The election proved tight, and tensions ran high on election day and for days after until state officials released the final results. Jackson had won by 7,863 votes, carrying just under 47 percent of the 158,579 popular votes cast; Sample Orr finished second with just over 42 percent of those votes, while the remaining candidates, Hancock Jackson and James Gardenhire, together carried just 11 percent of the vote. The new governor-elect drew support relatively evenly from the various sections of the state; he carried seventy counties while receiving respectable ballots in all of the remaining thirty-five counties. In the slaveholding Boon's Lick counties, Jackson drew a mixed response, splitting them relatively evenly with Orr. In St. Louis, the state's only Republican stronghold, Jackson ran a strong second, presumably because of his support for Douglas, thus validating his strategy of announcing for him. As important to him, the state election saw a raft of Breckenridge Democrats elected to the General Assembly, having claimed 15 of 33 seats in the senate and 47 of 132 seats in the house. Almost with a wink and a nod, Claib Jackson managed to be everything to nearly everyone.[25]

24. Lyon, "Jackson and the Secession Crisis," 430; Snyder, "Democratic State Convention," 124; Parrish, *Frank Blair,* 85–86; *Missouri Statesman,* August 3, 1860; George R. Taylor to C. F. Jackson, July 27, 1860, and Jackson to Taylor, July 28, 1860, both in George R. Taylor Collection, MHS; C. J. Corwin to J. F. Snyder, July 24, 1860, John F. Snyder Collection, box 2, MHS (quote).

25. C. J. Corwin to J. F. Snyder, August 8, 1860, E. L. Edwards to Snyder, August 11, 1860, both in John F. Snyder Collection, box 2, MHS; Lyon, "Jackson and the Secession Crisis," 430–31; *Jefferson Inquirer,* September 15, 1860; *Missouri Statesman,*

With a three-month wait between the state election and the national election, many moderate Missourians became edgy about whether the governor-elect's unconventional stance on the presidency was genuine. That Breckenridge Democrats had done so well in the legislative contests was an obvious source of concern for those within and without the party who recognized well the dire implications of the November election. Many recalled Sample Orr's haunting campaign prediction that should Jackson be elected "you must prepare to withdraw from the Union, shoulder your muskets, resist the Federal Government, and march to victory over your brothers and friends in your sister States." Despite his claim to support Douglas, speculation that Jackson was in reality a secessionist grew rampant after he attended a Breckenridge convention in Jefferson City in late September, though he did not go so far as to publicly declare for his Kentucky kinsman. His presence caused Douglas Democrats such as Sterling Price, chairman of the party's state central committee, to move to force the governor-elect into line by issuing a card in the St. Louis newspapers calling upon him to answer whether he would continue to support the party's regular nominee. Tactfully laid, Price's gauntlet was nonetheless unmistakable. Forced to respond, Jackson maintained his evasion, restating his enigmatic stance in a speech in Boonville whereby in effect he supported both Breckenridge and Douglas as candidates for the presidency.[26]

In November, Missouri proved Douglas's only victory, the only state in the entire Union he carried in full in the calamitous election. Many Missourians, like the residents of the other border slave states, saw the candidacy of Breckenridge (virtually all of his votes came from sparsely populated counties in the south-central portion of the state) as being as sectional as that of Lincoln (nearly all of whose votes in Missouri came from Germans in St. Louis and its environs) and rejected both "Union splitters and rail splitters" at the polls. Compromise candidates Bell and Douglas garnered nine-tenths of the state's votes and more than seven of every ten of the Boon's Lickers' ballots; as important, Douglas prevailed over Bell in the region by the narrowest of margins, and not one of the state's largest slaveholding counties gave their votes to Breckenridge. Despite the inroads of the Breckinridge Democrats

September 7, 1860; Hurt, *Agriculture and Slavery in Little Dixie*, 296–99; Walter H. Ryle, *Missouri: Union or Secession*, 160; Shalhope, *Sterling Price*, 142; Official Vote of the State, 1860, William C. Breckenridge Papers, Mss. 1036, microfilm reel 2, folder 11, 94–95, SHSM; Secretary of State Election Returns, 1860, Capitol Fire Documents, 1806–1957, microfilm reel CFD-187, folders 16418–25, MSA; Sceva B. Laughlin, "Missouri Politics during the Civil War," 423–24.

26. *Daily Missouri Republican,* September 25, October 5, 1860; *Missouri Statesman,* July 13, 1860 (quote); Lyon, "Jackson and the Secession Crisis," 430–31; Shalhope, *Sterling Price,* 142–46.

in the state legislature, moderates—Douglas Democrats and Constitutional Unionists—outnumbered them ninety to sixty-two. Even in St. Louis, the state's Republican stronghold, Douglas ran a strong second to Lincoln while Breckenridge polled only 544 votes. Missourians called for, above all else, temperance on the now-related national issues of slavery and secession.[27]

Jackson could not have misinterpreted the state's election results, particularly those in the Boon's Lick. While Missourians evinced a sympathy for the South and its rights, even portraying themselves to northerners or antislavery adherents as being southerners themselves, they did so only in the context of the slaveholding imperative. Jackson, as a resident of the region, recognized well the centrality of slavery in the results of the state election. Libertarian Missourians yet equated the property rights of slaveholders with the federal government's protection of them, so much so that Abiel Leonard claimed from Fayette that "Howard County is true to the Union. Our slaveholders think it is the sure bulwark of our slave property." Indeed, Kansas had been lost, but not through the fault of the governmental system; rather, the fault lay with Yankee usurpation of democracy. Missourians, closest to the territorial West, held that the states could yet correct the imbalance by invoking, rather than abandoning, the national democracy. Douglas had championed individual rights—even to the extent of opposing Kansas's corrupted attempt to gain entrance as a slave state—and Missourians rewarded him for it with their vote. So long as democracy, however imperfect, prevailed in the Union and so long as the federal government protected liberty by upholding individual rights—including that of slaveholding where it existed—Missourians would remain loyal. Yet, as the success of the Breckenridge Democrats in the legislative races indicated, their fidelity was now decidedly uneasy.[28]

Yet another sound emanated from Missourians' call for moderation, one that Jackson clearly heard. That clarion was one of noninterference. That Missouri was the source, whether immediately or originally, of the era's most celebrated court case—the controversial Dred Scott decision, in which the U.S. Supreme Court ruled that a Missouri slave was not entitled to his freedom for having lived in both a free state and in the portion of the Louisiana Territory determined as forever free by the Missouri Compromise—could not have been lost on the state's residents. Yet the case itself caused little stir, either as sustained and reversed respectively by the circuit and state supreme courts (for the latter, Jackson's patron William B. Napton wrote the court

27. Hurt, *Agriculture and Slavery in Little Dixie*, 297–98 (quotes); Daniel W. Crofts, *Reluctant Confederates: Upper South Unionists in the Secession Crisis*, 76–79; Peterson, *Freedom and Franchise*, 99; William Roed, "Secessionist Strength in Missouri," 416–17. Douglas also split New Jersey's electoral vote.

28. Roed, "Secessionist Strength in Missouri," 297–98 (quote); Crofts, *Reluctant Confederates*, 104–22; Ryle, *Missouri*, 160–62, 166.

opinion) in St. Louis or as struck down again on appeal in Washington. Yet it was Chief Justice Roger Taney's 1857 opinion that property restrictions were protected by the Fifth Amendment, and thus he declared the Missouri Compromise unconstitutional. The implications were clear to Missourians in that the ruling challenged federal proscriptions of individual rights. Admittedly, Missourians embraced a paradox, one that mirrored their perceived place within and without the Union; they used a federal court ruling to challenge federal authority in the states, at once accepting and rejecting the federal imperative. Opposing secession was only part of Missourians' intermezzo; the calumny of governmental intervention was the other, as one Unionist Missourian demonstrated when he wrote that "whilst the destiny of Mo. is my destiny, so long as I am one of her citizens; Yet whilst there is a possibility of her maintaining her position as one of the Sovereign states of this Union, I shall as ever be found battling in my humble way to Secure a *continued* and *perpetual* Existence of her present relations to our once happy government." The words of one Waverly resident reflect the qualified loyalty even more clearly. Supporting secession, he claimed, was "to advocate treason, insubordination, reckless disregard for law [and would bring] bloodshed, devastation and ultimate subjugation of our country by foreign powers." For this individual, with the West as his country, the foreign powers were the North and the federal government.[29]

Clearly, Jackson's election and the family's subsequent move proved a source of great anxiety for the entire family, especially Eliza. Just before the election, daughter Luda wrote to her mother from Hannibal that "you are very anxious about the election I know. I hear such a variety of opinions on the subject that I am perfectly disgusted with politics. I think Pa has been shamefully treated myself," while stepson Erasmus Pearson wrote to her from Louisiana, Missouri, soon after the election, congratulating her "on Pa's election to the office of Governor of Mo, and that too by such a large Majority as is indicated by the returns thus far. Your fears are now dissipated, that it is a Matter settled." In his preparations for his tenure as governor in Jefferson City, Jackson, on the day before he moved to the governor's mansion, entered into a contract with his youngest son, Claib, Jr., to manage the farm and his bondpeople in his absence. For the four years he would presumably be away, Claib, Jr., would receive one-half the proceeds of the farm operations—"by which is meant, one half of the grain, Hemp &c grown on the farm, one half of the increase in the Stock of all Kinds on the farm and one half the increase of the Servants on the farm"—while taking

29. Fehrenbacher, *Slavery, Law, and Politics: The Dred Scott Case in Historical Perspective*, 121–50; Crofts, *Reluctant Confederates*, 130–42; Ryle, *Missouri*, 71–72, 155; Hurt, *Agriculture and Slavery in Little Dixie*, 298–99 (second quote), 300 (third quote).

responsibility for half of the expenses. Jackson and his son would in effect be equal partners, though the property (with the exception of that produced under the namesake's management) would remain in the hands of the father. Jackson continued to keep his share of the Sappington pill business. By the last of December, the Jacksons had taken up decidedly inelegant residence in the state capital.[30]

Jackson had no time to savor any temporal pleasures of the sum of his life's work in the ramshackle governor's residence on the Missouri River's south bluff. The month of December had witnessed a culmination of another more paramount process, one that witnessed the nation being torn apart. Within weeks of Abraham Lincoln's election to the presidency, and ten days before the Missouri General Assembly convened, South Carolina exercised what it considered its ultimate state's right—to withdraw from the union of states. Six other cotton states were currently holding elections for delegates to conventions that would deliberate similar responses. As the tocsin of dissolution hung heavily over the nation, an anxious crowd—including a joint session of the legislature—assembled in the house chambers of the Missouri statehouse on the cold evening of January 3, 1861, to listen to the outgoing governor's farewell address. More specifically, they came to hear the state's new chief executive speak to the latest and most portentous of the nation's political crises. The lawmakers in the audience came to size up Missouri's controversial fourteenth governor, who once had so bitterly divided them and who now postured himself between the state's latest factional incarnations—ones he had helped originally to create.[31]

The two governors' speeches could hardly have been more different in tone. Stewart hit all the appropriate chords for one assailed as a closeted abolitionist by those who had long supported the man to whom he would soon offer his gavel. Indeed, he may well have been speaking directly to his successor. He spoke bitterly of the Republicans, condemning them as the enemies of peace and tranquility in the nation, and enjoined the state's residents to avoid the passions that were moving the cotton states toward secession, a right he denied. "Missouri, will stand by her lot and hold to the Union as long as it is worth the effort to preserve it," the outgoing governor declared. "She cannot be frightened from her propriety by the past

30. Luda [Louisa] J. Lamb to Eliza W. Jackson, July 30, 1860 (first quote), and E. D. Pearson to Eliza W. Jackson, August 9, 1860 (second quote), and Contract between C. F. Jackson and his Son C. F. Jackson, Jr., December 28, 1860 (third quote), all in John S. Sappington Papers, Mss. 1027, box 3, folder 71, SHSM; Last Will and Testament of Claiborne Fox Jackson, 1862, Will Book B, Saline County [Missouri], 138–40, microfilm reel C11591, MSA.

31. Giffin, *First Ladies of Missouri*, frontispiece-1, 76–77; William C. Davis, *"A Government of Our Own": The Making of the Confederacy*, 9; Parrish, *History of Missouri*, 1.

unfriendly legislation of the North, nor be dragooned into secession by the extreme South. . . . She is able to take care of herself, and will be neither forced nor flattered, driven or coaxed, into a course of action that must end in her destruction."[32]

Ascending the podium, Jackson—now sporting a beard to enhance his authority—offered the audience a startlingly different message, one that he had gleaned from the words of those moderate constituents who harbored little want for war, but even less for interdiction. "The South," he argued clearly, "are not the aggressors. They only ask to be let alone. If some have regarded their action as hasty, has not the occasion been extraordinary? . . . If South Carolina has acted hastily, let not her error lead to the more fatal one—an attempt at coercion. . . . We hear it suggested in some quarters that the Union is to be maintained by the sword. . . . The project of maintaining the Federal Government by force may lead to consolidation or despotism, but not to Union. . . . That stands upon the basis of justice and equality, and its existence cannot be prolonged by coercion." His passion up, Jackson drove home his point with force, tying the elements of identity that by 1861 had come to define being southern with a now passionate opposition to federal authority, and linking Missouri to that identity:

> The first drop of blood shed in a war of aggression upon a sovereign State will arouse a spirit which must result in the overthrow of our entire Federal system, and which this generation will never see quelled. . . . The destiny of the slave-holding States of this Union is one and the same. So long as a State continues to maintain slavery within her limits, it is impossible to separate her fate from that of her sister States who have the same social organization. . . . The identity, rather than the similarity, of their domestic institutions; their political principles and party usages; their common origins, pursuits, tastes, manners, and customs; their territorial contiguity and commercial relations—all contribute to bind them together in one sisterhood. And Missouri will in my opinion best consult her own interests, and the interests of the whole country, by a timely declaration of her determination to stand by her sister slave-holding States, in whose wrongs she participates, and with whose institutions and people she sympathizes.[33]

Jackson's words served as far more than mere inflamed rhetoric; he had completed for Missourians the cant of southernness. The faith blended traditional ties of culture, heritage, and economic pursuits with the overarching

32. Buel Leopard and Floyd Shoemaker, eds., *The Messages and Proclamations of the Governors of the State of Missouri*, vol. 3, 333 (quote); Nagel, *Missouri*, 128; Snead, *The Fight for Missouri*, 13–17.

33. Paintings in the Arrow Rock Tavern, National Society of Colonial Dames in the State of Missouri Papers, 1968–1974, Mss. 3584, folder 1, SHSM; *Missouri Statesman*, January 18, 1861 (quotes); Snead, *The Fight for Missouri*, 17–25; Parrish, *Turbulent Partnership*, 6–7; Lyon, "Jackson and the Secession Crisis," 431–32.

ligature of slavery, knotted now by an entrenched commitment to "resist to the death" (in Jackson's earlier words) any threat to individual rights posed by an oppressive federal government. As Jackson echoed Calhoun's argument that "the object of constitutional guaranties is to protect the rights of minorities; and it is to such guaranties, and not to legislative compromises, that the South must look for protection and security," he provided for Missourians more than a tautology that Missouri *"stand by the South."* Indeed, Jackson now told his fellow countrymen in this life crisis of the Union that Missouri *was* the South.[34]

Jackson's speech met with thunderous applause. A day later, his supporters in the legislature demonstrated that they had heard well the new governor's words. His address had called for a convention to determine Missouri's future standing in the union of states as well as asking for legislation to strengthen the state militia. At once prodding and flattering the representatives by reminding them that "it may require some degree of moral courage on the part of many members . . . to cast any vote . . . best calculated to remove the burthens which now rest upon all of us," Jackson saw the legislature take up his challenge by initiating bills that would ultimately honor both of his requests. The state's lawmakers saw that the question of Union was now paramount and acted promptly, goaded in part by a well-publicized call to arms Jackson had made days before his recent speeches to them. "Let us exhaust all the means in our power to maintain our rights in the Union," Jackson had written boldly just prior to his departure for Jefferson City, "let us preserve the government if possibly in our power; but if after having tried all the remedies within our grasp, if these should fail—as I fear they will—then I say let us dissolve the connection and maintain the rights which belong to us AT ALL HAZARDS AND TO THE LAST EXTREMITY. . . . Let there be no threats, no bravado, no gasconading, but firmly and determinedly let us take our position in the right and stand by it to the last." Within ten days, the legislature had set February 18, 1861, as the date for electing delegates to a convention that would "consider the then existing relations between the government of the United States, the people and governments of the different States, and the government and people of the State of Missouri; and to adopt such measures for vindicating the sovereignty of the State and the protection of its institutions, as shall appear to them to be demanded."[35]

34. *Missouri Statesman,* June 8, 1849 (first quote), January 18, 1861 (second quote); Joseph A. Igel, Jr., "A Rhetorical Evaluation of Claiborne Fox Jackson's Speeches on Slavery and States' Rights: 1847–1861," 25–27.

35. James Peckham, *General Nathaniel Lyon and Missouri in 1861,* 22; Draft of C. F. Jackson's Inaugural Address to the General Assembly of Missouri, undated [30 December 1860], John S. Sappington Papers, Mss. 1027, box 1, folder 7, SHSM (first quote); *Daily Missouri Republican,* April 30, 1861 (second quote); Lyon, "Jackson and

The date proved prophetic. On that afternoon in Montgomery, Alabama, the new Confederate States of America inaugurated its first president, Jefferson Davis, on the portico of the Alabama statehouse. In the days surrounding the Missouri General Assembly's authorization of the election, the American house of cards fell as the cotton states—Mississippi, Florida, Alabama, Georgia, Louisiana, and Texas—withdrew in sequence from the Union. Jackson had recommended that state delegates be present at the gathering, but the legislature instead sent a five-member delegation to a Virginia-initiated peace conference in Washington. The days leading to the state convention elections were highly charged; Abiel Leonard predicted that "if Missouri is forced out of the Union you & I & every other man who has any thing—land or slaves are ruined—I have made up my mind to that & therefore mean to meet the issue with all the zeal & resolution that the conviction generates . . . to be active & fearless." The legislature's adoption of a resolution against coercion, claiming that in that event Missouri would join with "their Southern brethren to resist the invaders at all hazards," caused many to fear that covert secessionists would soon carry the convention election. Aikman Welch, a member of the legislature, warned that "these disunion and secession gentlemen when they appear before the people will 'sing hosannas to the Union,' and loud as any, but I hope the people every where, will put the question to each of them directly 'Will you, for any cause which yet exists, vote for an ordinance of secession.' "[36]

As Missourians faced the grim realization that the nation as they once knew it existed no longer, the candidates who sought election to the upcoming convention elections framed the mood of the state with their self-applied labels. In this most exigent canvass, candidates identified themselves not along party lines but as supporting one of three general principles regarding Missouri's future relation to the union of states. The most conservative were the Unconditional Unionists, largely Republicans, who declared for the maintenance of the Union regardless of circumstance. Their leader was Frank Blair, recently seated in the U.S. House after recognition of his charges of fraud in the 1858 election, whose brother, Montgomery, would soon sit

---

the Secession Crisis," 433; Sara Lee Sale, "Governor Claiborne Fox Jackson and His Role in the Secession Movement in Missouri," 13–15; Parrish, *Turbulent Partnership,* 7–8; *Jefferson Inquirer,* January 5, 1861 (third quote). The General Assembly stipulated that any vote by the convention that should change the existing relationship with the federal government would require ratification by the state's voters.

36. Charles P. Roland, *The Confederacy,* 24–25; Abiel Leonard to James S. Rollins, January 17, 1861, James S. Rollins Papers, Mss. 1026, box 3, folder 72, SHSM (first quote); *Missouri House Journal,* 21st General Assembly, 1st Sess., 1861, 87–88 (second quote); Aikman Welch to Abiel Leonard, January 22, 1861, Abiel Leonard Papers, Mss. 1013, box 12 (uncombined), folder 412, SHSM (third quote).

in Lincoln's cabinet. At the other extreme were the States' Rights, or Anti-Submission, candidates, who maintained that they would vote for secession if elected to the convention. By far the most numerous were the Conditional Unionists, moderates who advocated Missouri's continuance in the Union but only so long as the federal government did not interfere with states' rights to determine its own course by way of coercion. In meetings, rallies, editorials, and speeches throughout the state, each sought to cast Missouri's die on the momentous question of Union or disunion.[37]

In the weeks prior to the election, Jackson was active—politically and otherwise—in preparing for the possibility of Missouri's secession. One member of the legislature related that Jackson "was assiduous in his endeavors to defeat the insertion [into the Convention Bill] of a clause submitting the action of the convention to the people, in case they should pass any ordinance changing the relations of Missouri to the Federal Government. . . . Gov. Jackson declared, after we had succeeded in affixing that provision to the bill, that 'it wasn't worth a damn.'" On January 18, Jackson received a commissioner from Mississippi, conspicuously attending his address to the legislature on that evening and cascading him publicly among the Jefferson City politicos. Yet his exertions proved more martial. Upon Jackson's instructions, on January 8 his lieutenant governor, Thomas Caute Reynolds, one of the staunchest Anti-Submissionists among the state's leaders, held a mass proslavery meeting in St. Louis that resulted in the organization of a paramilitary group who called themselves "Minute Men" and who "pledged Missouri to a hearty co-operation with our sister States, in such measures as shall be deemed necessary for our mutual protection against the encroachment of Northern fanaticism and the coercion of the Federal Government." A week later Jackson requisitioned the state's quota of arms from the Ordnance Bureau in Washington—including some 410 muskets, 302 rifles, 40 cavalry sabers, and 160 sets of infantry and cavalry accouterments—and requested a gun carriage for a six-pound cannon, stating that "I have several very good guns, that I can mount by having a proper carriage as a model." Jackson's queries about armaments were much more than incumbent; by the last week of January, Jackson was attempting to secure the arms at the St. Louis Arsenal, the largest federal arsenal in the slave states, with 60,000 muskets, 90,000 pounds of powder, 1.5 million ball cartridges, and 40 field pieces, as well as the machinery to manufacture arms and ammunition. He had sent an emissary, Daniel M. Frost, a state senator, West Point graduate, and commander of the state militia (and who had recently been the nominal leader of the

37. Parrish, *History of Missouri*, 6–7; Parrish, *Turbulent Partnership*, 8–9; Snead, *The Fight for Missouri*, 53–59; Sale, "Jackson and the Secession Movement," 16–18; Shalhope, *Sterling Price*, 148–51.

previous fall's "Southwest Expedition," in which 600 militia from St. Louis campaigned on the Kansas border against "Jayhawkers" and now remained), to meet on January 24 with the arsenal's commander, William H. Bell, and convinced the North Carolinian not to resist any attempt by the governor to claim the arsenal in the event of the state's secession.[38]

Whatever plans Jackson might have laid to initiate secession in the state took a dramatic turn on the day of the convention election. In a remarkably peaceful vote, Unionism prevailed over disunion with thunderous resonance. Of 140,000 votes cast, Unionists—whether Conditional or Unconditional, and they received nearly equal votes—polled nearly 110,000, or just less than eight in every ten. So sure were Missouri's voters of their desire to preserve their connection to the federal union that not one avowed secessionist candidate received election to the convention among the ninety-nine delegates so elected, though in several counties the margin was but razor-thin. Yet neither did Missourians reward those known to be Republicans; only four were elected, and all from St. Louis. "The result was a surprise to every one, and a bitter disappointment to the South," recalled Thomas L. Snead, editor of the proslavery *St. Louis Bulletin.* "Senators and Representatives, who had up to that time been clamorous for arming the State, announced that they interpreted the late vote as declaring that the people of Missouri were overwhelmingly opposed to the enactment of any warlike measures, and that consequently they would themselves vote against these bills." An angry St. Louis commission merchant, L. B. Harwood, predicted that "the Convention . . . I think will do nothing, I think their attachment to the union is so great they are willing to sacrafice [*sic*] Right,—Principle, and every thing else for the sake of the name." The secessionists' emotion perhaps offers the best litmus of the clarity of the verdict; Missouri had yet showed unequivocally for the Union. Within a month, the convention would hold to its bargain; when its members calmly voted 98–1 in favor of a resolution declaring that "no adequate cause [existed] to impel Missouri to dissolve her

38. Aikman Welch to Abiel Leonard, January 22, 1861, Abiel Leonard Papers, Mss. 1013, box 12 (uncombined), folder 412, SHSM (first quote); Sale, "Jackson and the Secession Movement," 16 (second quote); C. F. Jackson to Col. H. K. Craig, January 16, 1861, Claiborne Fox Jackson Letter, Ms. 1788, SHSM (third quote); Requisition for Ordinance [*sic*] and Ordinance [*sic*] Stores . . . for the year 1861, undated [1861], Record Group 3: Governor's Papers: Claiborne Fox Jackson, General Correspondence 1861, box 1, folder 1, MSA; Edward C. Smith, *The Borderland in the Civil War,* 116, 122, 127; Basil W. Duke, *Reminiscences of General Basil W. Duke, C.S.A.,* 37; D. M. Frost to C. F. Jackson, January 24, 1861, in Robert J. Rombauer, *The Union Cause in St. Louis in 1861,* 142–43; Miller, "Daniel Marsh Frost," 382–83; Phillip T. Tucker, " 'Ho, For Kansas': The Southwest Expedition of 1860," 22–36; John S. Bowen to Claiborne Fox Jackson, March 10, 1861, Missouri Volunteer Militia Papers, 1860–1865, Duke.

connections with the Federal Union," they became the only state convention that voted not to sever its ties to that union.[39]

Yet neither did the convention declare that the federal government held sovereignty over Missouri, especially in regard to its rights of property. The Committee on Federal Relations approved the Crittenden Compromise, recently rejected by Congress, which called for constitutional protections of slavery where it existed and reaffirmed Missouri's devotion to "the institutions of our country." Moreover, the convention approved an amendment to its report that the president withdraw federal troops from "the forts within the borders of the seceding States where there is danger of collision between the State and Federal troops," a clear message to the administration that coercive measures ran counter to state sovereignty. With twenty-three votes in favor, the convention managed to defeat a second amendment that pledged Missouri "to take a firm and decided stand in favor of her sister slave States" in the event that the national government refused to negotiate with the Confederacy or should the other border states secede. Finally, the convention punctuated its stand for state autonomy by receiving a representative from Georgia, who "invited the State of Missouri to unite with the Southern states in forming a Southern Confederacy." Indeed, buttresses adorned— and supported—Missouri's seemingly steadfast edifice of Union.[40]

The historian James McPherson has written that Missouri's stand for state autonomy was tantamount to secession. To border state residents, whether in Missouri or Kentucky, nothing could have been farther from the truth. Viewing with resolute seriousness their status as border states, residents believed themselves both geographically and ideologically between the polar extremes of northern abolitionism and southern secessionism and thus they would serve naturally as moderators of the gathering storm. A Harvard student wrote to a friend at home in Kentucky, "The fact is, Kentucky & the other border states are the main pillars of the union. And all things considered they are the great regulators in the present domestic quarrel.

---

39. Parrish, *History of Missouri*, 6; Parrish, *Turbulent Partnership*, 9–14; Roed, "Secessionist Strength in Missouri," 419–21; Snead, *The Fight for Missouri*, 66–67 (first quote); L. B. Harwood to W. B. Sappington, March 11, 1861, John S. Sappington Papers, Mss. 1027, box 4, folder 95, SHSM (second quote); *Proceedings of the Missouri State Convention*, 11–12 (third quote), 13–20. The convention met originally at the Cole County courthouse in Jefferson City, but because of cramped quarters and the secessionist atmosphere the delegates moved to the Mercantile Library Hall in St. Louis, reconvening on March 4, the same day that Abraham Lincoln took the presidential oath of office in Washington, D.C.

40. *Proceedings of the Missouri State Convention*, 46–49, 55–57, 58 (first quote), 237–45 (second quote, p. 237), 217–18 (third quote), 219–30; Smith, *Blair Family in Politics*, 26–29; Parrish, *Turbulent Partnership*, 10–14; Lyon, "Jackson and the Secession Crisis," 433.

You will allow me therefore to propose *thirty three times nine cheers for Old Kentucky."* A Missourian wrote just as passionately: "Father informs us that you had heard I had bolted my position as an advocate of the Union. My Answer to the report is *never, never, never.* Whilst the destiny of Mo. is my destiny, so long as I am one of her citizens; Yet whilst there is a possibility of her maintaining her position as one of the Sovereign states of this Union, I shall as ever be found battling in my humble way to Secure a *continued* and *perpetual* Existence of her present relations to our once happy government." That summer, a border state conference called together at Frankfort, Kentucky, saw only representatives from the two states in attendance. While the infant Confederate states might have held forth state sovereignty as the constitutional cornerstone of secession, border state residents believed their duty lay in defending state sovereignty only against extremism within the Union. Until the federal government attempted to make war upon a sovereign state, or to coerce one of the loyal states to make war upon the seceded states, neutrality was anything but secession.[41]

With such a mandate, only the least astute or most doctrinaire of chief executives would pursue any secessionist course that deviated from the clear will of the people of Missouri. Contrary to the claims of many who have written since, Claib Jackson was neither. A quarter century of personal struggle to achieve this office, this power—with the knowledge gained of the human caprice that drives the political realm—were not lost on Jackson, a survivor of the savagery. Having risen phoenix-like from exile only months earlier, Jackson recognized implicitly that an overt pursuit of secession, in defiance of not one but now three contrary dicta, would in all likelihood cost him not only his governorship but also all chance of the state's ultimate alliance with the Confederacy. Rashness would serve neither purpose. Yet Jackson did indeed want Missouri's secession, and being an erudite judge of public opinion, he was anything but dismayed at the expected outcome of the recent convention. In fact, if anything, he was encouraged by it, for Jackson had hatched a plan. He now intended to set a trap that, once sprung, would ensnare the federal government and propel Missouri out of the Union. Tragically, what Claib Jackson did not tell his fellow Missourians was that they would soon become the bait.[42]

41. McPherson, *Battle Cry of Freedom,* 294–95; E. A. Sophocles to H. T. Duncan, Jr., January 1, 1861, Duncan Family Papers, 71M38, UK (first quote); John A. Hockaday to James S. Rollins, May 6, 1861, James S. Rollins Papers, Mss. 1026, box 3, folder 74, SHSM (second quote); Crofts, *Reluctant Confederates,* 195–214.

42. Arguments that Jackson disregarded the decision of the state convention in pursuit of secession originated with Snead, *The Fight for Missouri,* 68–69; see also McElroy, *Struggle for Missouri,* 40; Smith, *Blair Family in Politics,* vol. 2, 29–30; Parrish, *David Rice Atchison,* 214; Peterson, *Freedom and Franchise,* 100.

10

"WALL OF FIRE"

It is a great mistake to suppose that . . . [Missouri] could at this time be classified as a Union state. It is true there was amongst them all a reverence for the Union and it was hoped that all difficulties could be amicably settled and the Union preserved without raising the question of primary allegiance to their own state. . . . [B]ut it may be confidently assumed that at least two-thirds of the voters of the state outside of St. Louis held that "if the North (meaning the Federal Government), pending the attempt to adjust matters peaceably, should make war upon any Southern state, Missouri would take up arms in its defense." This was the declaration but such is not Unionism.

JAMES O. BROADHEAD, "ST. LOUIS DURING THE WAR"

Claib Jackson was a shrewd judge of popular mood. As a career office-seeker, he had mastered the intricate steps that the minuet of politics required; he now applied the motions instinctively, sensing their effect on his partners while measuring those of his adversaries. Jackson had no intention of foisting secession upon his Missouri constituents; indeed, he recognized implicitly that he had neither mandate nor need to do so. The state convention's ringing repudiation of the issue of immediate secession echoed unmistakably over Missouri, but even more resonant was its stand against the federal government's coercion of the states. Former Governor Robert M. Stewart's appeal to Missourians to maintain the state's allegiance to the Union through "the high position of armed neutrality" in his absence now actually strengthened his successor's hand in preparing for secession. Jackson saw rightly that the actions that would prove most singular to Missouri's course would not be his; rather, they would be the federal government's.[1]

Clearly, Jackson recognized that he occupied the proverbial catbird's seat. The people of Missouri, unlike those in the seceded states, had declared themselves neither above nor below the Union, but equal in stature to it. Allegiance to their nation came only through its respect for their state, a distinction Missourians would now demand. Stewart himself had set the terms, warning of their ephemeral nature: "As matters are at present Missouri will stand by her lot, and hold to the Union as long as it is worth an effort to

1. Snead, *The Fight for Missouri,* 15–16 (quote); "The Civil War in Lexington, Missouri," unpublished manuscript, Marie Oliver Watkins Papers, Mss. 2689, folder 63, SHSM.

preserve it. . . . In the mean time Missouri will hold herself in readiness, at any moment, to defend her soil from pollution and her property from plunder by fanatics and marauders, come from what quarter they may. . . . She is able to take care of herself, and will be neither forced nor flattered, driven nor coaxed, into a course of action that must end in her own destruction." Jackson now merely needed to maintain fealty to his home state in order to satisfy these conditions. Should the free states of the federal government, on the other hand, make war on the slave states in an effort to bring them back into the Union, Missouri's geographical position—being now surrounded on three sides by free states—and the river systems it controlled rendered the state a gateway through which troops would inevitably need to move in order to reach the Confederacy. In effect, coercion by way of military force was inevitable in Missouri.[2]

Jackson now needed only to prepare the state for its defense and portray himself as the state's indefatigable defender. To cultivate his public image as Missouri's sentinel, as well as to crystallize notions of Missouri's state sovereignty and potential victimization, he proclaimed his paramount devotion to his state whenever possible. On one occasion, after receiving a commissioner from Georgia, one observer recalled that "Jackson raised aloft a banner of the State, and called upon the Southern men of Missouri to rally under its folds, fearless of the gathering forces of those who were rebelling against her." The power of this "state first" image as secession corollary was both obvious and disturbing to the state's Unconditional Unionists. One such member of the state convention, St. Louis attorney James O. Broadhead, charged that "the cry of 'making war upon a sovereign state' so freely used in the convention and out of it was a subterfuge and designed to elicit and strengthen the regard and sympathy which the people had for their state as a political entity to which as such they had become attached."[3]

Alarmed by the apparent rise of antigovernment sentiment in the state, Unconditional Unionists in St. Louis actually strengthened Jackson's hand. Frank Blair began arming the city for war, enlisting thousands of Germans into Home Guard units while actively soliciting government arms and ammunition for them through his brother, Montgomery. Fearful residents, hearing the muffled tramp of boots emanating from the Turner Halls in which the Germans drilled, met publicly and passed resolutions that pledged "a hearty cooperation with our sister Southern states and such measures as shall be deemed necessary for our mutual protection, against encroachment of northern fanaticism, and the coercion of the Federal government." Blair

2. Snead, *The Fight for Missouri,* 15–16 (quote).
3. Ibid., 69 (first quote); Broadhead, "St. Louis during the War," unpublished manuscript, James O. Broadhead Papers, MHS (second quote).

soon convinced the War Department that the city's secessionist Minute Men intended to capture the undermanned arsenal and arranged the transfer of eighty U.S. Army regulars under command of Captain Nathaniel Lyon from Kansas. In Lyon, a rock-ribbed antislavery zealot, Blair found both an extremist and an ally. Together, the two men soon threw the city into a frenzy of fear so pronounced that in the March city elections Republicans suffered a complete defeat, losing control of the city government they had dominated for the past four years. Even St. Louis, the state's Unionist capital, now evinced a clear distrust of the new president it had only recently helped to elect. As one Unionist wrote, "it is impossible in my opinion to hold the people in check many days longer unless the Union men can be furnished with Some appricable [*sic*] reason for Some of the acts of the government which will Satisfy the people that it is not the intention either to attack Mo—or provoke an attack on her part to afford an excuse to whip her into submission."[4]

Many in the state's interior saw opportunity in the interregnum for an upheaval even more ominous than the nation's political fracturing. The imminent statehood of Kansas exacerbated the fear of slave escape that had surfaced in the recent territorial conflict; Missouri slaveholders now feared that their institution was threatened whether they stayed in the Union or not. One Missourian wrote to his brother in Texas

> I learned today that your state has certainly gone out and I am glad of it but as we stand on the border I think it would be our interest if we could get a compromise from the North something like Mr. Critenden [*sic*] proposes (that is, if they would grant us that "mile") to stay in the Union then we would have something to protect our slaves but if we go out we cannot remain a "slave" state nearly surrounded by free states. . . . The slave owners here are beginning to think seriously about trotting towards the gulf. Hard times and the existing difficulties will work "wonders" for the state I fear. If Texas does not suit you it will not do to return to Missouri.

The residents of Polk County feared that the "present distracted & unsettled state of the public mind" would provide incentive for slave rebellion and formed a protective organization to ensure "that no negroes (Free or Slaves)

4. Snead, *The Fight for Missouri*, 94–95; *Daily Missouri Democrat*, January 9, 1861 (first quote); Galusha Anderson, *A Border City during the Civil War*, 71; Peckham, *Lyon and Missouri*, 69–71, 93–95; Arthur Roy Kirkpatrick, "Missouri on the Eve of the Civil War," 108; Smith, *Borderland in the Civil War*, 148–49; Parrish, *Frank Blair*, 90–95; J. P. Lancaster to J. O. Broadhead, May 9, 1861, James O. Broadhead Papers, box 1, MHS (second quote). For an assessment of Lyon, see Christopher Phillips, *Damned Yankee: The Life of General Nathaniel Lyon*. The Turners, or *Turnverein*, were athletic and social clubs maintained by German immigrants in St. Louis and other American cities that proved important vehicles for martialing federal volunteers from the German community.

shall be allowed to transcend the rules of decorum" while scrutinizing any "suspected [white] person [who] holds opinions at Variance with our laws & interests, and persists in tampering, & intermedling [*sic*] with our institutions." As Missourians began to perceive plots at every turn, their commitment to the Union wavered as the days passed. Time clearly was working on the governor's side.[5]

Missouri's fraying tightrope gave way on April 15 with news that the small federal garrison holding Fort Sumter, in Charleston's harbor, had surrendered to state troops after nearly thirty-three hours of bombardment. In response, Abraham Lincoln called for seventy-five thousand volunteers for ninety days of national service to put down the rebellion in the seceded states "too powerful to be suppressed by the ordinary course of judicial proceedings." Missouri's quota, reported Secretary of War Simon Cameron to the state's governor, would be 3,123 men. Claib Jackson's response to Cameron was immediate and icily uncompromising: "Sir:—Your requisition is illegal, unconstitutional and revolutionary; in its object inhuman & diabolical. Not one man will Missouri furnish to carry on any such unholy crusade against her Southern sisters." He called for the legislature to meet in special session on May 2 to take "measures to perfect the organization and equipment of the Militia and raise the money to place the State in a proper attitude for defense." The governor had laid down Missouri's gauntlet, but it was one that most of its residents wished laid. A day earlier, Nicholas Paschall, editor of the state's largest newspaper, wrote, "We need not wait for the answer of the governor of Missouri to this demand upon the state for her quota of troops. The people are ready to respond now, and they will not contribute one company for any such purpose. They will not make war upon the South."[6]

5. Joseph M. Chrisman to Dear Sir [Lucius Washburne], January 29, 1861, Washburne Family Papers, Mss. 2971, box 1, folder 1, SHSM; Resolutions for Polk County, March 17, 1861, John F. Snyder Papers, box 2, MHS (quotes); R. J. Robertson to J. F. Snyder, May 3, 1861, ibid., box 2, MHS.

6. McPherson, *Battle Cry of Freedom*, 273–74 (first quote); James G. Randall and David Donald, *The Civil War and Reconstruction*, 176–78; Arthur Roy Kirkpatrick, "Missouri in the Early Months of the Civil War," 235; S. Cameron to Governor Jackson and others, April 15, 1861, *ORR*, ser. 3, pt. 1, 69; C. F. Jackson to Hon. Simon Cameron, April 17, 1861, Bryan Obear Collection, Mss. 1387, folder 10, SHSM (second quote, a photostat of the letter is printed in *MHR* 55 [April 1961], inside rear cover, and a printed copy of the letter is published in *ORR*, ser. 3, pt. 1, 82–83); Leopard and Shoemaker, eds., *Messages and Proclamations of the Governors of Missouri*, vol. 2, 384 (third quote); *Daily Missouri Republican*, April 27, 16, 1861 (fourth quote). Created in 1859 by the state legislature, the Volunteer Militia of Missouri was neither the county-based militia existing under the state constitution nor the militia guaranteed by the second amendment to the U.S. Constitution. The Military Bill would have reorganized this body. See William Garrett Piston and Thomas P. Sweeney, "Don't Yield an Inch!" 12–14.

And the state exploded in a frenetic series of events. Buoyed by Jackson's stinging response, proslavery partisanship gave way in many parts to open secessionism. One observer, James Peckham, recalled that in St. Louis "secession was rampant everywhere. . . . In all places the secesh were noisy and undisturbed. The enemies of the Government were rapidly providing themselves with arms and ammunition, and preparing for organization under the new military bill, which they confidently expected would speedily pass the Legislature. . . . To those not in the secret, it seemed as if secession in Missouri was an accomplished fact." On April 19, fifteen cannon reports boomed from Capitol Hill in Jefferson City in honor of Jackson's response and Virginia's secession, which had occurred on the same day. Meetings held throughout the state's interior called for the legislature to override the convention's ruling and pass an ordinance of secession, after erecting southern or secession flags. One flew superciliously above the Berthold Mansion, headquarters of the Minute Men, while others reported them displayed in Jefferson City within yards of the governor's mansion. A miniature Confederate flag protruded even from a flower pot that sat on the porch next to the governor's front door. Just days after Jackson's response, secessionists captured the three-man garrison of the federal arsenal at Liberty, robbing it of a moderate number of muskets, rifles, pistols, and sabers, as well as ammunition and three six-pound cannon. One St. Louisan wrote soberly that "there is now no union. . . . As long as there was a possibility of an amicable adjustment, I was for Union, but now that all hope is lost, and the Union is virtually disolved [*sic*]. Common sense dictates, that her interest are identified with the South." Another Missourian proclaimed, "The Secession fever is raging and if Lincoln shall not stay his hand, the devil himself cant Keep Missouri in the Union."[7]

Missouri's Unionists, too, quickly became active, perhaps more than the state's secessionists and certainly with far greater magnitude. One Unionist in the town of Louisiana claimed that a local meeting at "our city Hall was crowded to its utmost capacity, in all which Crowd, there were not more than *twelve disunionists*. I had the house *carefully counted*. . . . It is reported

7. Peckham, *Lyon and Missouri*, 56 (first quote), 64; Burks, "Thunder on the Right," 365; *Glasgow Weekly Times*, May 9, 1861, cited in Shalhope, *Sterling Price*, 154; R. J. Robertson to J. F. Snyder, May 3, 1861, and T. W. Freeman to Snyder, May 10, 1861, both in John F. Snyder Papers, box 2, MHS; Broadhead, "St. Louis during the War"; Prosecution for Treason/United States v. Tucker, undated [1861], 1–2, James O. Broadhead Papers, MHS; Kirkpatrick, "Missouri in the Early Months of the Civil War," 237; Report of Benjamin Farrar, April 21, 1861, *ORR*, ser. 1, pt. 1, 649; Michael Gillespie, "The Battle of Rock Creek," 36–37; L. B. Harwood to W. B. Sappington, March 11, 1861, John S. Sappington Papers, Mss. 1027, box 4, folder 95, SHSM (second quote); B. F. Massey to J. F. Snyder, April 29, 1861, John F. Snyder Papers, box 2, MHS (third quote).

here that the Secession Company (military) at Louisville intimated to John W Davis they intended to raise a flag on his farm—where he informed them he would certainly shoot some of them if they did—all this shows the desperate character of the material we have to deal with. They must be desperate indeed when such a man as Mr Davis is wrought up to the Shooting point." Unionist Home Guard units sprang up in towns throughout the state's interior, convinced of the governor's disloyalty, assuring one resident of Jefferson City that "the Old Fox will be well watched here. His movements are carefully guarded and will be hard of detection, but we may catch him yet." St. Louis surpassed them all in the sheer volume of mobilization. Indeed, Frank Blair returned to St. Louis on the day of Jackson's rejection of Lincoln's call, armed with a War Department authorization of five thousand stand of arms to those Republican "Wide Awakes" and German "Black Jägers" who would enlist in the federal army. With an enlistment agent in the city, John M. Schofield, whose presence Jackson had ignored, Blair and Lyon by week's end had mustered and armed more than twenty-five hundred recruits at the St. Louis Arsenal, with authorization for as many as ten thousand. That such action was unconstitutional (Congress alone had authority to create federal volunteers, who were neither state militia nor members of the U.S. Army) only implicated government officials from Lyon and Blair to Lincoln in a vast conspiracy against the states, as many Missourians saw the matter. Moreover, the St. Louis military leaders had managed to secret virtually the entire cache of arms and munitions at the arsenal across the river to Illinois, thus thwarting any repeat of the Liberty Arsenal predation.[8]

These Unionists had reason for such vigilance, for Jackson had stepped up his efforts to prepare the state for a second effort at secession. On the day of Lincoln's call for troops, he received a letter from Frost in St. Louis who apprised him of the strengthening of the arsenal's defenses. Claiming that "if Lyon is allowed to go on, it will be but a short time before he will have this town and the commerce of the Mississippi at his mercy," Frost suggested that the governor send an emissary to the Confederacy to obtain mortars and siege artillery for an attack upon the arsenal in the event that the state seceded—a step that Jackson claimed already to have taken. Finally, Frost suggested that Jackson order the commander of the militia in the St. Louis district to form a camp of instruction near the city and authorize him to muster militia companies into the service of the state. Jackson recognized that until the General Assembly passed the military bill that he had requested in his

8. P. Draper to J. O. Broadhead, April 26, 1861 (first quote), Allen P. Richardson to Broadhead, April 30, 1861 (second quote), and Broadhead, "St. Louis during the War" (third and fourth quotes), all in James O. Broadhead Papers, box 1, MHS; Phillips, *Damned Yankee*, 159–67.

inaugural address, he had no authority to call out the state militia. He did have the power to order militia commanders to assemble their men for "training" at "convenient" locations throughout the state, and therefore he instructed Frost to establish a camp at St. Louis on May 3. Jackson remained cautious in wielding his public authority, knowing that the best chance for Missouri's secession lay in his maintaining the role of steward rather than assuming that of provocateur. Virtually every newspaper editor in the state, including the influential *Missouri Republican* and *Missouri Statesman,* agreed with him; the *Statesman* was satisfied enough by Jackson's "PEACE POLICY" to publicly declare the governor *"against secession."*[9]

However politic Jackson's public actions might have appeared to Missourians, his private intentions now moved him toward more overt maneuvering for the state's secession. Requesting artillery from Confederate President Jefferson Davis, to "batter down [the] walls, and drive out our enemies [from] The Arsenal at St Louis, now under the command of an Abolition officer, [which] it is feared will be greatly in our way in the event of active hostilities being Commenced against the Confederate States," Jackson wrote buoyantly that "Missouri has been exceedingly slow and tardy in her movements hitherto, but I am not without hope that she will promptly take her stand with her Southern sister States." Yet upon learning that he would soon receive artillery from the captured arsenal at Baton Rouge and that Davis "look[ed] anxiously and hopefully for the day when the star of Missouri shall be added to the constellation of the Confederate States of America," Jackson could but reluctantly delay the Confederate president's request for a regiment for service, claiming that "we are using every means to arm our people and, until we are better prepared, must move cautiously." Eleven days earlier, on April 19, Jackson wrote to David Walker, president of the Arkansas convention, that, impelled by Lincoln's call for troops, Missouri would soon determine to leave the Union, admitting to him

> I have been, from the beginning, in favor of prompt action on the part of the southern states, but a majority of the people of Missouri, up to the present time, have differed with me. What their future action may be, no man, with certainty, can predict or foretell, but my present impression is—judging from the indications hourly occurring—that Mo will be ready for secession in less

9. Broadhead, "St. Louis during the War"; Draft of the 1858 Militia Bill, Missouri Militia Collection, MHS; McElroy, *Struggle for Missouri,* 62–63; Snead, *The Fight for Missouri,* 148–49; Phillips, *Damned Yankee,* 176; *Daily Missouri Republican,* April 27, 1861 (first quote); *Missouri Statesman,* May 3, 1861 (second, third, and fourth quotes). On April 17, Jackson sent Basil W. Duke and Colton Greene, both ardent secessionists, to Montgomery, Alabama, to meet with Confederate President Jefferson Davis to procure artillery for the Missouri militia. See C. F. Jackson to Jefferson Davis, April 17, 1861, Jefferson Davis Letters, box 1, Duke; Duke, *Reminiscences,* 44–50.

than thirty days; *and will secede,* if Arkansas will only get out of the way and give her a free passage. Missouri and Arkansas have been called upon by an abolition President for troops to whip their southern brethren and friends into the support of a miserable, Black Republican, fanatical administration; and the question is, shall they assist in this hellish work, or, like true and noble states stand by their friends, and perish with them, if need be, in the sustainment of their common rights? Whatever may have been our prior differences, it seems to me, that the time has come, when all true southern men should be united as a band of brothers against the common enemy. Public sentiment here is rapidly leading to this point. A few days more will determine all.[10]

Indeed, Jackson's intent to use "armed neutrality" as a strategy for secession became well known among those who favored Missouri's scission. Benjamin F. Massey, elected with Jackson as the new secretary of state, soon intimated to John F. Snyder, a Bolivar Democratic scion, that the governor's

10. C. F. Jackson to Jefferson Davis, April 17, 1861, Jefferson Davis Letters, box 1, Duke (first and second quotes); Jefferson Davis to C. F. Jackson, April 23, 1861, in Rombauer, *Union Cause in St. Louis,* 212–13 (third quote); Jackson to Davis, April 28, 1861, ORR, ser. 1, pt. 1, 689 (fourth quote); C. F. Jackson to Hon. David Walker, April 19, 1861, Governor's Papers: Claiborne Fox Jackson, General Correspondence, 1861, box 1, folder 3, MSA (fifth quote). Another letter purported then and since as being Jackson's, dated April 28, 1861, and addressed to Joseph W. Tucker, a native South Carolinian, lawyer, and editor of St. Louis's *Missouri State Journal,* makes similar yet more implicatory statements regarding Jackson's stance on Missouri's secession. Used widely by historians, including myself in an earlier study of Nathaniel Lyon and Missouri's crisis of Union, the letter includes the following statement: "I do not think Missouri should secede today or tomorrow but I do think it good policy that I should *publicly so declare.* I want a little time to arm the state and I am assuming every responsibility to do it with all possible dispatch. . . . [Missouri] ought to have gone out last winter when she could have seized the public arms and public property & defended herself. This she has failed to do & must now wait a little while. . . . Who does not know that every sympathy of my heart is with the South?" The letter, which federal troops on Lyon's orders reportedly seized on July 12, 1861, in a search of Tucker's office, resulted in the editor's arrest and subsequent prosecution for treason prior to his flight from St. Louis to Neosho, then ultimately to the Confederate states, where he published the *State Journal*'s successor, the *Missouri Army* (later the *Jackson* [Miss.] *Argus and Crisis)* from late 1861 to 1863. A close analysis of the handwriting of the letter suggests that Jackson may well not have written it. A comparison of the original letter, located in the James O. Broadhead Papers at the Missouri Historical Society, with other extant samples of Jackson's handwriting (especially his inaugural speech, located in the John S. Sappington Papers at the State Historical Society of Missouri, the lengthiest sample of Jackson's writing) reveals inconsistencies in a number of key letters as well as the overall form and spatial dimensions of the chirography itself. Nothing indicates that Jackson dictated the letter to an amanuensis; indeed, the letter begins with the phrase, "I write this letter in confidence . . ." The events surrounding the "discovery" of the letter lend further doubt to the letter's authorship. Tucker's strident opposition to the extremism of Unconditional Unionists in St. Louis resulted in harsh editorials in his *State Journal,* targeting Blair and Lyon. On July 12, Lyon ordered his adjutant general in St. Louis, Chester Harding, to arrest Tucker and suppress his paper. The city's Committee of Safety,

plan now drew strength from the highest circle of Missouri's officeholders. "Secession is tremendously popular," wrote the buoyant state officer,

> the great difficulty now is to Keep secession back awhile. Almost literally we have nothing for our people to defend themselves with. We want them to have a chance to make and save a bully big crop. . . . We will have but little difficulty, if any about money, but the arms and ammunition is the devil. If we know where to get them, there would be great difficulty in getting them here, but in a few months they must be provided if we have to make them ourselves. . . . Price will call the convention shortly. He says he Know[s] they would pass an ordinance of secession in a day, and but for that it would be called forthwith, the idea is now not whether we will secede, but the only question is when and this will depend on the headway we may make in arming and equiping [*sic*].

Three days later, Massey wrote again, now employing an even more cognitive tone, claiming, "We are here, entirely satisfied an ordinance would be sustained now by the people by a very large majority. A united north is fast making a united south. . . . We are doing something even in advance of the action of the legislature toward getting arms and ammunition, though I can not tell you exactly what it is. . . . There is also something going on about guns &c, . . . [I] am thus content to leave the execution to those whose special duty it is."[11]

Clearly, Jackson was privy to these secessionist impulses and machinations. As the months had passed, the governor came to recognize the volatility of the situation in St. Louis as well as the fact that Lyon and Blair were zealots (they had managed to remove from command the moderate commander of the army's Department of the West, William S. Harney). Jackson now moved

---

a powerful coterie of politicians who served as a Unionist military junto in the city, replaced Asa S. Jones, the government attorney, with one of their members, lawyer James O. Broadhead, as supervisor of the search of Tucker's office. Deputy U.S. Marshal Ephraim H. Tunnicliff, a native of Buffalo, New York, claimed to have discovered the letter in Tucker's desk and which, in the words of Unionist observer James Peckham, "more than any other document then in loyal hands justified the policy of Lyon." Once publicized, the letter went far to delegitimize Jackson's authority as governor. Much of the substance of Tucker's subsequent arraignment, with Broadhead as prosecutor, centered around the verification of Jackson's handwriting in an attempt to substantiate his authorship of the letter, to which the various witnesses offered decidedly mixed responses. Given the analysis and the contemporary controversy surrounding the letter's veracity, I have chosen not to use it as evidence of Jackson's secessionist impulses, which his unpublicized—and thus unpoliticized—letter to Walker reflects amply. See Peckham, *Lyon and Missouri*, 158–59, 286–87, 301; William F. Swindler, "The Southern Press in Missouri, 1861–1864," 399; Shalhope, *Sterling Price*, 233, 236–37; Broadhead, "St. Louis during the War"; Prosecution for Treason/United States v. Tucker, undated [1861], 1–2, James O. Broadhead Papers, MHS; *Missouri Statesman*, August 2, 1861.

11. B. F. Massey to J. F. Snyder, April 26 (first quote), 29 (second quote), 1861, both in John F. Snyder Papers, box 2, MHS.

to provoke them into initiating an incident that would accelerate events in his favor. On May 3, the day after the legislature met in special session, the governor issued a message that again requested the reorganization of Missouri's militia in order to provide fully for the state's defense, which, in light of the well-publicized mobilization occurring in St. Louis, seemed imminent. Jackson appears to have tipped his hand, at least for one Jefferson City resident, who wrote on that day that he would "Leave this afternoon for Saint Louis, *fleeing from the wrath to come.*" Two days later, legislators again took up debate on the bill as militia units from all over the state converged on their various district encampments, a measure prescribed by the 1858 Militia Act and carried on every year since. On May 6, Frost established his district camp of instruction at wooded Lindell's Grove, on the far western edge of St. Louis; appropriately, he named it Camp Jackson.[12]

As if scripted, Missouri's world turned upside down within four days of the militia's encamping. On May 10, Lyon and Blair marched some 6,500 troops from the St. Louis Arsenal to Camp Jackson, forcing the surrender of those 669 militia (of 891 in camp) who had not managed to escape the converging federal columns. Prompted by reports that the Confederate cannon from Baton Rouge, poorly disguised in boxes marked as marble, had arrived at night by steamer and that they, along with those cannon held by the state and shipped to Frost "for repairs," were secreted to the camp, as well as by reports that had Jefferson City awash in troops, powder, and arms—including the cannon taken from the Liberty Arsenal—Lyon had ordered a preemptory strike. His force captured the militia, many of whom were clearly secessionist, naming their company streets "Beauregard" and "Davis" for the Confederate general and president and displaying secession flags; one even wrote the night before to his brother in Natchez, Mississippi, on Confederate stationery—a letter that was never delivered for federal troops captured it the next day—that "we shall conquer for the Southern Confederacy and Jef Davis *Dam* Lincoln and the Stars and Stripes. we are for the south." Then, in a grandiose display of might, Lyon marched the prisoners under guard, through hostile throngs that now packed the city streets for nearly the entire six miles from the camp to the arsenal. The humiliating procession soon erupted in violence; in response to a small fracas near the center of the column, the barely trained Home Guard units opened fire on the crowd, resulting in twenty-eight deaths and as many as seventy-five injuries. For the next days rioting tore

12. Phillips, *Damned Yankee*, 159–65; James W. Covington, "The Camp Jackson Affair, 1861," 201–3; Anderson, *Border City during the Civil War*, 88–89; Parrish, *Frank Blair*, 99–101; W. Turner to anonymous [D. R. Atchison], May 3, 1861, David Rice Atchison Papers, Mss. 71, folder 10, SHSM (quote); Parrish, *History of Missouri*, 12–13; Draft of the Militia Bill, 1858, Missouri Militia Collection, MHS.

through St. Louis's normally quiet brick streets; thousands fled the "Black Dutch" government troops who, as many frightened residents believed, were "shooting women and children in cold blood."[13]

The "*coup de tat* at St. Louis," as one Missourian referred to the Camp Jackson affair, was not only the watershed of Missouri's southern odyssey but also might well have been the single most catalytic event in the state's history. Termed "the greatest military blunder of the Civil War" by one contemporary—phraseology that historians have echoed since—the action galvanized Missouri's countryside, turning thousands of residents who had recently given support to the federal government into strong southern rights advocates. By representing that government as a coercive power, the military junto in St. Louis now caused shoestring Unionists to regard them—and not the Confederates—as warmongers. "Frank Blair is dictator," moaned one resident, "and if the slightest show of resistance is made we will be crushed out," while another predicted that "The rain of *perfect teror* [*sic*] *has* commenced." Even Unconditional Unionists now found their allegiance tested, if not ended, in the aftermath of Camp Jackson. Charles Gibson, recently arrived in the nation's capital as solicitor of the U.S. Court of Claims, heard the news over the telegraph while in Philadelphia. "The report came upon me like a bomb," Gibson moaned. "I learnt since I came here of some daring villains—abolitionists, that are as eager for Missouri to secede as Gov. Jackson is, in order that they might 'pitch in.'" Uriel Wright, a member of the convention that had voted so decisively against secession, was more declarative: "If Unionism means such atrocious deeds as I have witnessed in St. Louis," he proclaimed, "I am no longer a Union man."[14]

Within hours of the incident, news of the federal coup reached the state capital. The legislature was in special session, debating the military bill that Jackson had requested, when late in the afternoon the governor himself

13. Parrish, *Frank Blair,* 100–103; Allen P. Richardson to J. O. Broadhead, April 24 (first quote), 30 (second quote), 1861, both in James O. Broadhead Papers, box 1, MHS; Phillips, *Damned Yankee,* 181–95; Snead, *The Fight for Missouri,* 168–72; G. W. to Dear Bro, May 9, 1861, Camp Jackson Papers, MHS (third quote); Krug, ed., *Mrs. Hill's Journal,* 13–17, 18 (fourth and fifth quotes); Alice E. Cayton to Alexander Badger, May 12, 1861, Badger Papers, MHS.

14. J. B. Henderson to J. O. Broadhead, May 13, 1861, James O. Broadhead Papers, box 1, MHS (first quote); Phillips, *Damned Yankee,* 192–99; William C. Breckenridge to S. B. Laughlin, April 15, 1921, William C. Breckenridge Papers, box 2, MHS (second quote); Parrish, *Turbulent Partnership,* 24–26; Parrish, *Frank Blair,* 102; Unsigned to Dear Sister, May 20, 1861, Civil War Collection, box 1, MHS (third quote); Allen P. Richardson to J. O. Broadhead, May 11, 20 (fourth quote), 1861, both in James O. Broadhead Papers, box 1, MHS; Charles Gibson to Thomas T. Gantt, May 13, 1861, Charles Gibson Papers, MHS (fifth quote); J. Thomas Scharf, *History of St. Louis City and County,* vol. 2, 1485 (sixth quote).

rushed into the chamber, fresh from St. Louis where he probably had witnessed the repercussions of the Camp Jackson fracas, and relayed the news to several confidants. Within fifteen minutes the legislature had passed Jackson's long-debated military bill and soon adjourned. Just after midnight, summoned by the alarming peals of church bells that Jackson had ordered rung, legislators met again in emergency session amid rumors that three regiments of federal troops were heading for Jefferson City. In wild haste, the armed and anxious state legislature passed another act declaring that "the City of St. Louis has been invaded by citizens of other states, and a part of the people of said city are in a state of rebellion against the laws of the state," and granting the governor sweeping military powers "to take such measures as in his judgment he may deem necessary or proper to repel such invasion or put down such rebellion." Anxious legislators—including the governor—sent their families from Jefferson City in anticipation of a federal advance. Within a week, the legislature had given Jackson authorization to take possession of the state's railroads and telegraph lines "whenever in his opinion the security and welfare of the State may require it" and requested that Jackson mobilize the state militia. Missouri careened toward yet another conflict; a war within a war.[15]

Jackson's gambit had worked, for virtually all of the state's newspapers condemned the camp's capture. The governor quickly sought to capitalize on the emotion surrounding Missouri's apparent atavism. Within minutes of passage of the legislature's late-night defense act, Jackson dispatched squads from the newly reorganized state militia (now called, fittingly, the Missouri State Guard, and soon to number as many as two thousand, though poorly if at all armed) in Jefferson City to guard and if necessary to burn the railroad bridges spanning the Gasconade (the replacement for the bridge on which he had nearly lost his life) and Osage Rivers. He ordered the state's powder stores dispersed around the countryside and to militia commanders throughout the state, removed the state treasury funds, and appointed Sterling Price—whom Jackson had once considered a "submissionist" for his conservative leadership of the secession convention but who now, in the aftershock of Camp Jackson, had cast his lot with the governor—as commander of the State Guard. Price, the former brigadier general in the

15. Snead, *The Fight for Missouri,* 172–74; *Daily Missouri Democrat,* May 13, 1861, quoted in Peckham, *Lyon and Missouri,* 169–76, also 165–67; Bill, Barnum's Hotel [St. Louis] to C. F. Jackson, May 13, 1861, John S. Sappington Papers, Mss. 1027, box 3, folder 71, SHSM; Kirkpatrick, "Missouri in the Early Months of the Civil War," 240; Jackson to Elixa Jackson, June 3, 1861, in Park and Morrow, *Women of the Mansion,* 132; *Laws of the State of Missouri, 1861,* 48 (first quote); Act to Authorize Governor to Seize railroads and telegraph lines, May 13, 1861, EG Box 30, Huntington (second quote); Parrish, *Turbulent Partnership,* 24; Parrish, *History of Missouri,* 14–17.

Mexican War and governor, was one of the most popular men in the state, and his appointment would offer legitimacy to both the State Guard and Jackson's effort to mobilize the state. Jackson addressed the troops more than once, assuring them that they were enlisted only to defend the capital of their homeland against foreign invaders while conveniently ignoring their secessionist flags fluttering in the streets before his home.[16]

Jackson now found many sympathetic ears. When Price ordered out the state militia in all sectors, thousands flocked in patriotic rage to recruiting stations throughout Missouri seeking to liberate their homeland from "Goths and Vandels [*sic*]" who they now saw as the vanguard of federal coercion. "Missouri is my country," one State Guard officer boasted, and its defense was to him the "holy cause of liberty." "The time has arrived," proclaimed former St. Louis Mayor William Carr Lane, "when every patriot ought to show his hand, acting in stern and harmonious action, until the iron heel of the despot shall be removed from the neck of Missouri," while another resident seethed, "My blood boils in my veins when I think of the position of Missouri—held in the Union at the point of Dutchmen's bayonets—I feel outraged . . . but the sullen submission of downtrodden men will be avenged the more terribly in the days of their uprising—may I live to see that day." Yet another was more somber. "Deadly collisions have taken place between the citizens of the state and the so-called Federal troops . . . resulting in an antagonism of feeling which will take many long years to remove. . . . I entertain no hope for a better result: I fear that the disaffected will never return to their allegiance to the government." He might well have been right; one militia enlistee at Jefferson City proclaimed that "they are ordered here to defend the Capitol, and they firmly believe that the Government is the worst of enemies, intending to invade unlawfully the Soil of Missouri."[17]

---

16. Burks, "Thunder on the Right," 383; Allen P. Richardson to J. O. Broadhead, May 11, 24, 1861, and Prosecution for Treason/United States v. Tucker, undated [1861], 1–2, both in James O. Broadhead Papers, box 1, MHS; R. W. Settle and M. L. Settle, "Empire on Wheels," unpublished manuscript, p. 3, Marie Oliver Watkins Papers, Mss 2689, folder 63, SHSM; C. F. Jackson to George R. Taylor, May 14, 1861, George R. Taylor Collection, MHS; Jackson to J. F. Snyder, May 20, 1860, John F. Snyder Collection, box 2, MHS; Snead, *The Fight for Missouri,* 173–74, 180–81; Peckham, *Lyon and Missouri,* 167–68; Thomas C. Reynolds to C. F. Jackson, April 5, 1861, Thomas C. Reynolds Papers, MHS (quote); Shalhope, *Sterling Price,* 158–59; Albert Castel, *General Sterling Price and the Civil War in the West,* 14; Phillips, *Damned Yankee,* 243; Parrish, *History of Missouri,* 17.

17. J. D. and B. P. McKown to Son, May 29, 1861, John D. McKown Papers, Mss. 2335, SHSM (first quote); John T. Hughes to R. H. Miller, August 29, 1861, in "Letter from Col. John T. Hughes," *Liberty Tribune,* September 13, 1861 (second and third quotes); "Reminiscences of Patrick Ahern," undated, Mrs. Jesse P. Henry Papers, MHS; William Carr Lane to Sterling Price, June 3, 1861, William Carr Lane Papers, box 8, MHS (fourth quote); D. C. Hunter to John F. Snyder, May 24, 1861, John F. Snyder Papers,

Despite the windfall change of mood, Jackson did not move recklessly, though pressured to push for secession. Though no federal troops moved from St. Louis toward Jefferson City, the jittery militia had fired the Osage River bridge, partially destroying it. Jackson ordered the bridge rebuilt the following day. Moreover, he learned that federal authorities had restored William Harney to command in St. Louis and the conservative old general had arrived in the city in time to witness the rioting. To Jackson's surprise, Harney not only condoned Lyon's controversial actions but issued a proclamation that condemned the military bill as "an indirect secession ordinance [that] cannot and ought not to be upheld or regarded by the good citizens of Missouri." Recognizing that Harney's turnabout now threatened to temper the inflamed mood of the state's residents, he dispatched Price to St. Louis to meet with the federal department commander, a move that confirmed the suspicions of the frustrated lieutenant governor, Thomas Caute Reynolds, that Jackson's conservatism stemmed from his fear of federal military intervention. Convinced that the governor's delaying tactic would cost the state the chance for secession, Reynolds traveled alone and uninstructed to the Confederate capital to appeal for troops. Price worked out an agreement with Harney on May 21 that maintained the fragile balance between state and federal authorities in the state. So long as the state government kept order in Missouri, federal troops would not intervene militarily in its affairs and then only in cooperation with the state troops, "the united forces of both governments are pledged to the maintenance of the peace of the State, and the defense of the rights and the property of all persons without distinction of party." Harney, in effect, had pledged the federal government's own neutrality in Missouri.[18]

box 2, MHS; Unsigned to Dear Sister, May 20, 1861 (fifth quote) and H. S. Turner to Dear General, July 15, 1861 (sixth quote), both in Civil War Collection, box 1, MHS; A. P. Richardson to J. O. Broadhead, May 20, 1861, James O. Broadhead Papers, box 1, MHS (seventh quote).

18. Memoirs of M. Jeff Thompson, Meriwether Jeff Thompson Papers, Mss. 1030, folder 2, 13–14, 17–19; Parrish, *History of Missouri*, 16, 20; Kirkpatrick, "Missouri in the Early Months of the Civil War," 258–61; Robert E. Miller, " 'One of the Ruling Class'—Thomas Caute Reynolds: Second Confederate Governor of Missouri," 425–34; C. F. Jackson to George R. Taylor, May 14, 1861, George R. Taylor Collection, MHS; A. P. Richardson to J. O. Broadhead, May 20, 1861, James O. Broadhead Papers, box 1, MHS; Sterling Price and William S. Harney to the People of the State of Missouri, May 21, 1861, *ORR*, ser. 1, pt. 3, 374–75 (quote); Gerald Cannon, "The Harney-Price Agreement," 42. Jackson sent a personal emissary, Edward C. Cabell, to Richmond to confer with Davis on Missouri's behalf. Reynolds apparently was so disgusted by Jackson's apparent conciliation that he briefly considered returning to Missouri and assuming the governorship if Jackson abided by the terms of the Harney-Price agreement. Reynolds never regained the esteem he once held for Jackson; his diary rarely and only obliquely mentions the governor. See also Reynolds, "General Sterling Price and the Confederacy,"

While eliciting generally favorable responses from Missouri's moderates, the Harney-Price agreement—published in the newspapers—drew censure from the extremists on both sides. M. Jeff Thompson, a former mayor of St. Joseph and member of the state convention who had helped to prepare the military bill and who now advocated secession, ignored Jackson's earlier admonitions against leaving the state to solicit aid from the Confederate government. Seeing the governor before he left, he left his "temporising [*sic*] and vacillating" friend with bitter parting words: "Governor, before I leave, I wish to tell you the two qualities of a soldier, one he must have, but he needs both: one of them is Common Sense and the other is Courage—, and By God! you have NEITHER." Unconditional Unionists decried the agreement with equal vehemence, but for different reasons. "Our friends here and the friends of the Government were very much dissatisfied with the terms of the arrangement," wrote U.S. District Attorney James O. Broadhead, "in as much as it seemed to leave that protection in the hands of the very power by which it was imperiled." Many other such Unionists—including Nathaniel Lyon—"regarded [the agreement] only as a trick of the secession Governor, to gain time, get arms and prepare again for war." Seeking "a resignation of Jackson & Co—nothing else will give peace to the State and nothing less will save Jackson's neck from the halter," Broadhead obtained from Attorney General Edward Bates "a warrant out for Jackson for Treason—but it will not be served yet—perhaps not at all—if he makes a proper settlement." Just a week later, an aide of Frank Blair's served Harney with orders relieving him of command for a second time. As Lyon assumed command in the interim, radicalism would now move federal authority in Missouri. The effects would be both immediate and catastrophic.[19]

For Jackson, the renascence of "Lyon the murderer" (as one newspaper referred to him) was likely not unwelcome; he recognized that another event such as Camp Jackson would propel the state into secession. Calmly, he wrote

unpublished manuscript, 18–44, and Reynolds to Jefferson Davis, January 20, November 13, 1880, all in Thomas C. Reynolds Papers, MHS; Diary of Thomas C. Reynolds, 1862–1866, Thomas Caute Reynolds Papers, microfilm, LC.

19. Memoirs of M. Jeff Thompson, Meriwether Jeff Thompson Papers, Mss. 1030, folder 2, 19, SHSM (first and second quotes); Donal J. Stanton, Goodwin F. Berquist, and Paul C. Bowers, eds., *The Civil War Reminiscences of General M. Jeff Thompson,* 11–16, 46–50; J. O. Broadhead to Montgomery Blair, May 22, 1861 (third quote) and J. O. Broadhead to Edwin Draper, May 21, 1861 (fourth quote), both in James O. Broadhead Papers, box 1, MHS; Nathaniel Lyon to Miner Knowlton, May 26, 1861, quoted in Ashbel Woodward, *Life of Nathaniel Lyon,* 260–61 (fifth quote); Phillips, *Damned Yankee,* 206–9; Parrish, *Frank Blair,* 104–7. M. Jeff Thompson claims in his memoirs to have begun his advocacy of secession once the state convention had established the imprimatur of the Unconditional Unionists and removed the meeting from Jefferson City to St. Louis.

Eliza, at home at Fox Castle, on June 3, "Since the removal of Gen. Harney it is thought that Lyon will commence vigorous operations in the state to subdue the people of the state. I very much fear he will do it, but if he does, I shall resist him with all the power I can call to my aid. It is my duty to remain at my post, and I shall do so let what may come." Despite such bravado, many of the state's moderates feared the effects of just such a fiasco and several managed to convince the reluctant Jackson to contact the federal commander for a meeting. The request became public enough for one politico to reprove the State Guard leader for the "most ill advised proposition. . . . Let the abolitionist chief communicate with *you.*" Fearing arrest, Jackson gained from Lyon the promise of free passage to and from St. Louis, and with Price and an aide traveled on June 10 by train, arriving that evening at the sumptuous Planters' House, next to the courthouse.[20]

The next morning, after some disagreement as to the place of the meeting, Lyon and Blair, accompanied by an aide, met with the state leaders in the governor's suite. Unlike Price's interview with Harney, this meeting was anything but cordial. For the first half hour, Jackson and Price spoke conciliatively, proposing strict neutrality and offering such concessions as the disbanding of the State Guard and discontinuance of further militia musters in return for the same for the Home Guard now under federal arms. Quickly, Lyon came to dominate the meeting, refusing to concede any point on federal authority, rejecting the state leaders' calumet. After four heated hours, Lyon declared bluntly, "Better, sir, far better that the blood of every man, woman, and child within the limits of the State should flow, than that she should defy the federal government. *This means war.*" Turning on his heels, Lyon strode briskly out of the room, leaving the remaining five men in stunned silence. Missouri's nightmare—and its final metastasis—could now begin.[21]

Neither Claib Jackson nor Sterling Price could have predicted Lyon's peremptory declaration of war. Yet clearly they understood its implications in the fullest sense. Hastening back to Jefferson City, taking care to destroy the Gasconade River bridge and cut the telegraph wires in the event that Lyon would send troops, the governor had his aide, Thomas L. Snead, prepare a

---

20. Parrish, *Frank Blair,* 107–8; Peckham, *Lyon and Missouri,* 159 (first quote); C. F. Jackson to Eliza Jackson, June 3, 1861, in Park and Morrow, *Women of the Mansion,* 132 (second quote); William Carr Lane to Sterling Price, June 3, 1861, William Carr Lane Papers, box 8, MHS (third quote); Phillips, *Damned Yankee,* 211–14.

21. Parrish, *Frank Blair,* 107–8; Phillips, *Damned Yankee,* 211–14; *Daily Missouri Democrat,* July 2, 1861, and Snead, *The Fight for Missouri,* 199–200 (quote); Peckham, *Lyon and Missouri,* 247–48. While Thomas Snead's 1886 account of Lyon's dramatic peroration ("I would see you, and you, and you, and you, and you, and every man, woman, and child in the State, dead and buried") has more verve, the more contemporary account, published three weeks later in the *Daily Missouri Democrat,* is likely the more accurate rendition.

proclamation for public release under Jackson's name the following day. Now presented with the opportunity to bring to fruition his passive-aggressive strategy for Missouri's secession, Jackson used the proclamation to reiterate the theme that he was confident would sound most clearly among the state's residents: that the federal government was the aggressor bent upon peaceable Missouri's coercion. "A series of unprovoked and unparalleled outrages have been inflicted upon the peace and dignity of this Commonwealth," the alarming message began, "and upon the rights and liberties of its people, by wicked and unprincipled men, professing to act under the authority of the United States Government." At every opportunity, Jackson wove a rich tapestry of oppression, selecting strands resonant among freedom-loving Missourians. "The solemn enactments of your Legislature have been nullified; . . . your commerce with your sister States has been suspended; . . . peaceful citizens have been imprisoned without warrant of law; unoffending and defenseless men, women, and children have been ruthlessly shot down and murdered; and other unbearable indignities have been heaped upon your State and yourselves."[22]

The proclamation further condemned Lyon and Blair for their "utter contempt" of the Harney-Price agreement and offered a rendition of the Planters' House conference that charged "it was the intention of the administration to take military occupation, under these pretexts, of the whole State, and to reduce it, as avowed by General Lyon himself, to the 'exact condition of Maryland.' "[23] Reminding the state's residents again, if disingenuously, that "Missouri is still one of the United States; that the Executive Department of the State government does not arrogate to itself the power to disturb that relation," Jackson's message also averred the state's power to call "a convention; which will, at the proper time, express your sovereign will." This said, Jackson's opus concluded with a call to arms, both literal and figurative. In the literal sense, the governor called for fifty thousand militia volunteers "for the protection of the lives, liberty, and property of the citizens of this State." Figuratively, however, Jackson's statement offered the dénouement of Missouri's identity, a logical progression from the clarion of his inaugural address, a call to arms for Missourians to become southerners in the fullest sense. Beyond mere abstraction—the disavowal of

22. Governor's Proclamation, June 12, 1861, Claiborne Fox Jackson File, Mss. 2447, folder 1, SHSM (quotes); *Boonville Observer Extra*, June 12, 1861; Peckham, *Lyon and Missouri*, 249–52; Snead, *The Fight for Missouri*, 200–206. Citations from the subsequent paragraph are from the same.

23. Because of the strategic importance of Maryland to the national capital, Lincoln suspended the writ of habeas corpus there, declared martial law, and federal troops quickly took control of transportation lines and began suppressing secessionists. The Maryland legislature declared for neutrality. See McPherson, *Battle Cry of Freedom*, 284–90.

federal imperative, whether constitutional or congressional, in the question of slavery—Missourians now should effect the southern apotheosis by the forcible expulsion of federal authority, disavowing its right (as Lyon had claimed it) to rule over their state and over themselves. "Fellow citizens," it exhorted,

> All our efforts toward conciliation have failed. We can hope nothing from the justice or moderation of the agents of the Federal Government in this State. They are energetically hastening the execution of their bloody and revolutionary schemes for the inauguration of civil war in your midst; for the military occupation of your State by armed bands of lawless invaders; for the overthrow of your State government; and for the subversion of those liberties which that Government has always sought to protect; and they intend to exert their whole power to subjugate you, if possible, to the military despotism which has usurped the powers of the Federal Government. . . . [Y]ou are under no obligation whatever to obey the *unconstitutional* edicts of the military despotism which has enthroned itself in Washington, not to submit to the infamous and degrading sway of its wicked minions in this State. . . . Rise, then, and drive out ignominiously the invaders who have dared to desecrate the soil which your labors have made fruitful, and which is consecrated by your homes.

Jackson's passionate message resounded in many Missourians' ears, spurring some to action. On the day of the proclamation, one resident of Bloomfield, on Crowley's Ridge overlooking the state's table-flat Bootheel, wrote angrily to his Republican brother in Indiana that

> More rapidly and irresistably [*sic*] is the accursed, villainous, oppressive, tyrannical, disloyal despotic Lincoln dynasty alienating my feelings from the Country I once loved, . . . that love of American Liberty, equal rights, and self government has called upon me to cut loose from oppression and through [*sic*] of[f] the shackles which enslaves and trammels me and my posterity. . . . I will be in the Struggle for Liberty, let me not meet any of my Kindred there. I love the sunny south, the land of the free and the home of the brave. . . . A government derives its just power from the consent of the governed, & Missourians say they will not suffer coercion or invasion. Our state tried to make peace while there was a hope but, your party would not. Missouri, I tell you is gone, driven out by the Military despotism which now spreads her dark mouth over us, and I do assure you that if Missouri does not through [*sic*] off the shackles, I will secede.

M. Jeff Thompson remembered similarly: "every Southern man in the State, from the Iowa line to Arkansas was picking his flint, cleaning his gun, and sharpening his knife to be ready for the coming storm. . . . [S]hall we yield to this blind and wicked fanaticism? Shall we bend our necks, while this car of Juggernaut crushes our lives and our liberties? Or shall we, like men, who know our just rights & dare maintain them, stand up against this traiterous [*sic*] crusade, and drive back the invading horde . . . ?" Though neither man owned slaves, both would soon serve in the Missouri State Guard.[24]

For the second time in his public life (the first having been the so-called "Jackson Resolutions"), Claib Jackson's name appeared on a document another had written, articulating inclusion by principle with a region of which Missouri was not a part. And for the second time, Jackson's public words triggered his banishment from public office, this time by force. Within hours of reception of the publication of Jackson's proclamation, Lyon embarked with two thousand men on a military expedition toward Jefferson City, traveling up the Missouri River by boat rather than by rail, as Jackson had expected. Simultaneously, another five-hundred-man force moved from St. Louis by rail toward Rolla, a pincer campaign intent upon catching the governor and any State Guard troops that might serve him between the two forces. Jackson learned of the expedition's departure on June 13 and had little time to prepare. Having had the state powder and stores removed to the more defensible town of Boonville (a largely German, Unionist populace in Jefferson City now rendered it unattractive in light of the approach of German federals) when he had learned of Harney's second removal, Jackson hastily wired supporters and militia commanders around the state of the latest events, ordering them to move with all haste to Boonville (where his old nemesis, General John B. Clark, commanded a contingent of the State Guard) while he prepared to evacuate the capital. Jackson and his staff frantically gathered the state papers, appropriated much of the currency and treasury records and the state seal (one resident later recalled incorrectly that the governor pitched it down a well), ordered the destruction of three railroad bridges west of Jefferson City so as to impede pursuit, and with other state officials embarked on the steamer *White Cloud*, leaving the capital late on the same evening. The legally elected state government was now fugitive.[25]

24. V. W. Hale to C. S. Ellis, June 12, 1861, V. W. Hale Personal File, Mss. SC669, IndHS (first quote); Memoirs of M. Jeff Thompson, 18–19, and Address to the Citizens of Missouri, undated, both in Meriwether Jeff Thompson Papers, Mss. 1030, folder 2, SHSM (second quote); Stanton, Berquist, and Bowers, eds., *Reminiscences of M. Jeff Thompson,* 14. Hale served as an officer in the 2nd Cavalry, Missouri State Guard, while Thompson became a brigadier general.

25. Telegrams, C. F. Jackson to J. F. Snyder, June 13, 1861 [two mismarked as July 13], John F. Snyder Collection, box 2, MHS; Albert Cotsworth to Kate Draper, October 8, 1934, Draper-McClurg Family Papers, Mss. 3069, folder 80, microfilm reel 4, SHSM; George R. Taylor to Col. Ward, August 3, 1861, George R. Taylor Collection, MHS; Snead, *The Fight for Missouri,* 206–9; Phillips, *Damned Yankee,* 215–18; Arthur Roy Kirkpatrick, "The Admission of Missouri to the Confederacy," 368. Other state officials (other than Price) who left with Jackson were: B. F. Massey, secretary of state; Alfred W. Morrison, state treasurer; William S. Mosely, state auditor; John F. Huston, register of lands. Legislators included senators Warwick Hough, Thomas J. Churchill, James H. McBride, and Robert Y. L. Peyton, and representatives Aaron H. Conrow, Thomas W.

Two days later, Lyon's troops occupied the Missouri capital. While squads of federals searched the Capitol and state buildings, some of these troops looted the abandoned governor's mansion: one newspaper correspondent reported that "Sofas were overturned, carpets torn up and littered with letters and public documents. Tables, chairs, damask curtains, cigar-boxes, champaign-bottles, ink-stands, books, private letters, and family knick-knacks were scattered everywhere in chaotic confusion." The federal comman-der remained only overnight, leaving behind a small garrison (some of whom boarded in the abandoned governor's mansion) and pressing on for Boonville. The federal troops debarked eight miles east of the town and climbed the river road up the bluffs toward the State Guard camp nearby, where the governor's two youngest sons, Will and Claib, Jr., served in the militia ranks. Of the thousands of troops Lyon had expected to find in camp, only a few hundred had actually arrived, confident but ill-armed with squirrel rifles and shotguns to combat federal muskets.[26]

Learning of the federal approach on the night of June 16, a panicky Jack-son ordered his nephew, John S. Marmaduke, a recent West Point graduate who now commanded the largest contingent of guardsmen, to prepare to meet the federal host. The next day, after just twenty minutes, Lyon's troops routed the outnumbered State Guard, sixty of whom surrendered while the rest fled toward town with the federal troops advancing steadily upon them. Lyon quickly captured the abandoned State Guard camp, including two pieces of artillery as well as stores and equipment, and occupied Boonville that afternoon. A despondent Jackson sent word to Price—who had gone on to Lexington to assume command of troops there upon hearing rumors that a Kansas host was preparing to enter the state—to join his forces southwest of Boonville. He then sent his disgraced state defenders in headlong flight toward the southwestern portion of the state, unaware that yet another fed-eral host was moving to intercept them. In a buggy he had recently charged to the people of Missouri, Jackson headed to his Arrow Rock home, where he hastily gathered his personal papers and some belongings in preparation for an inevitable search of his home, apprised Eliza of his intentions, and left the farm and slaves in her care. He then rode off, meeting up with the state troops at Syracuse.[27]

Freeman, and Thomas A. Harris. See Sale, "Jackson and the Secession Movement," 43–44; *Jefferson Inquirer,* June 16, 1861.

26. McElroy, *Struggle for Missouri,* 123–25; *Daily Missouri Democrat,* June 17, 1861, in Peckham, *Lyon and Missouri,* 260–63; Thomas W. Knox, *Camp-Fire and Cotton Field: Southern Adventure in Time of War,* 40–42, quoted in Parrish, *History of Missouri,* 24 (quote).

27. Nathaniel Lyon to George B. McClellan, June 30, 1861, *ORR,* ser. 3, pt. 1, 12–14; Paul Rorvig, "A Significant Skirmish: The Battle of Boonville," 127–48; Knox,

Jackson's dejected troops trudged southward, leaving behind an unde-termined number of recruits from northern Missouri who had been unable to reach Boonville before Lyon's preemptive strike. After pausing briefly at Warsaw (where Jackson sent Price southward to assist other emissaries in the enlistment of aid from Arkansas Confederates), the State Guard forces converged near Lamar. The column of nearly four thousand—half of whom were unarmed—quickly moved southward through steady rains that now impeded their progress. The weather actually proved a blessing for it delayed Lyon's pursuing troops even more than it did the governors' forces. Lyon had remained at Boonville for nearly two weeks to gather supplies, horses, and wagons for his campaign which, because of his hasty departure from St. Louis and his choice of a river expedition, he lacked. By the time he ordered his troops out of camp, the federal commander contended with flooded rather than merely rising rivers, worse than Jackson's men had faced in the past few days. At Lamar, David Rice Atchison joined the governor's staff as principal aide, boosting the troops'—and the governor's—morale, and Jackson used the time to thoroughly organize his command.[28]

Striking out at daybreak on July 5 (two days after Lyon left Boonville), Jackson's Missouri State Guard columns approached Carthage when they encountered the southwest force of Lyon's expedition under the command of Franz Sigel. After a sharp fight, the armed State Guard troops—who outnumbered Sigel's men four to one—had nearly surrounded the federals before they retired from the field. Jackson's force pushed on toward Neosho and the next day met up with Sterling Price, who had ridden ahead to meet with Confederates in Arkansas in hopes of encouraging them to enter the state. Unsuccessful in this effort, the three men determined that Jackson and Atchison could now best serve their state by diplomacy. After assisting Price in encamping the state troops at Cowskin Prairie, in McDonald County, the governor, a small cadre of aides (including Jackson's son, Will), and the former senator left the state on July 12, traveling south through Arkansas's Boston Mountains toward Little Rock. Low on capital, Jackson borrowed money from sympathetic Fort Smith residents before reaching Little Rock on the July 19 forenoon. The state governor, Henry Rector, received the two men at the state capital, and that evening, though weary, Jackson addressed

Camp-Fire and Cotton Field, 43–44; Shalhope, *Sterling Price,* 166–67; Snead, *The Fight for Missouri,* 212–16; Kirkpatrick, "Admission of Missouri to the Confederacy," 366; Park and Morrow, *Women of the Mansion,* 132–33; *Missouri Statesman,* June 28, 1861.

28. Sterling Price to Jefferson Davis, November 10, 1861, *ORR,* ser. 1, pt. 3, 734–36; Snead, *The Fight for Missouri,* 216–22, 230–32; Kirkpatrick, "Missouri in the Early Months of the Civil War," 259–61. Much later, Price estimated wishfully that between five and ten thousand recruits remained in northern Missouri.

an enthusiastic audience. Next morning, he and Atchison pushed on toward Memphis.[29]

On July 22, the same day that Jackson reached Memphis and convinced the Confederate commander there, Leonidas Polk, to send troops into southeast Missouri, the Missouri state convention met again in emergency session at the Capitol in Jefferson City. The commitment to conciliation that had pervaded the initial convention was not so evident in this subsequent meeting; the atmosphere was fractious and contentious nearly from the outset. Unionists quickly sought to declare vacant the "expatriated" executive branch, which had committed treason for defying federal forces, and moved to fill those state offices now open, including those in the General Assembly. For days, a defiant, prosouthern faction of approximately twenty-five members (largely from the river counties and southeastern Missouri) parried with constitutional arguments that delayed the Unconditional Unionists's efforts to delegitimize the elected government. In the end, their efforts failed to persuade the seventy-five member convention, which voted to amend the state constitution in order to replace the exiled state officials, and abrogated the Military Act that the legislature had recently passed in fear of duress. The convention then seated Hamilton R. Gamble as provisional governor, Willard P. Hall as lieutenant governor, and Mordecai Oliver as secretary of state. All three men—two Virginians and a Kentuckian, respectively—were staunch Unionists. This administration would maintain steadfast support for the federal government for the duration of the war. If anything at all, Jackson was now Missouri's "Governor in the saddle." Some residents found his mysterious absence anything but comforting; Mary Rollins wrote her husband, James, a congressman in Washington, "I fear we are to have trouble in Missouri yet no one seems to know where Claib Jackson is but the idea seems to be that he will return, and give us battle before long."[30]

Although Jackson had determined originally to accompany Confederate

29. Snead, *The Fight for Missouri,* 216–22, 230–32; Kirkpatrick, "Missouri in the Early Months of the Civil War," 259–61; Military Order [General Order No. 16] of C. F. Jackson, July 4, 1861, EG Box 30, Huntington, also in *ORR,* ser. 1, pt. 8, 705; David C. Hinze and Karen Farnham, *The Battle of Carthage: Border War in Southwest Missouri, July 5, 1861,* 223–25 and passim; Parrish, *David Rice Atchison,* 215–16; *Missouri Statesman,* August 9, 1861; Samuel Boyd to W. B. Sappington, December 6, 1867, John S. Sappington Papers, Mss. 1027, box 3, folder 74, SHSM; *Arkansas Gazette,* July 20, 1861.

30. Parrish, *Turbulent Partnership,* 35–36 (first quote), 37–47; Peckham, *Lyon and Missouri,* 286; *Proceedings of the Missouri State Convention,* 5–18; C. F. Jackson to George B. Hunt, August 1, 1861, Civil War Collection, MHS (second quote); Mary Rollins to James S. Rollins, July 8, 1861, James S. Rollins Papers, Mss. 1026, box 3, folder 75, SHSM (third quote). The quote "Governor in the saddle" was written in pencil at the bottom of the letter from Jackson to Hunt, but not in Jackson's handwriting. The term

General Gideon Pillow's "Army of Liberation" into Missouri's Bootheel, at Atchison's bidding he opted to press on to Richmond to meet with Jefferson Davis. Word had reached him that the Confederate president had lost confidence in his devotion to the southern cause as a result of his cautious actions following the Camp Jackson fiasco, a notion likely hastened by Thomas Reynolds's recent visit (though Reynolds had lobbied strongly for Confederate intervention). Indeed, on June 5 Davis had written to Jackson denying him military or financial assistance until the state convention took the step of voting for secession. Weighing the obvious risk of abandoning his state—and thus any chance he, as chief executive, might have had to shape events by returning to Missouri with Confederate forces—at this critical juncture, Jackson opted to attempt to close the widening breach between his and the Confederacy's administrations. The Missourians arrived in Richmond on July 26 and that evening Jackson offered an enthusiastic address to a large crowd gathered before the Spotswood Hotel, promising to drive the "Yankee invaders" from Missouri upon his return and gaining for him from a newspaper reporter the sobriquet, "the Game Cock Governor." For the next two days, Jackson and Atchison met with Davis and the two men's resolve (along with Atchison's good relationship with Davis) appears to have softened the rigid president's stance on the exiled Missouri governor. Davis promised Jackson financial assistance as soon as Missouri had seceded and once the Confederate Congress could appropriate it. Relieved, on July 31, the pair boarded a train bound for Memphis.[31]

Jackson did not tarry in Memphis; he moved on immediately to New Madrid, in the cotton-rich Bootheel, where the lieutenant governor had already accompanied the Confederate host encamped there. After conferring with Reynolds and Atchison on the Confederate president's terms, Jackson issued a "Proclamation of Independence" (which Reynolds wrote) declaring Missouri an independent and sovereign state, an act he argued was constitutional based upon the federal violation of Missouri's "general, great and essential principles of liberty and free government," and upon the powers afforded him by the Military Act. The message had no authority; the men

---

has taken on wider usage as a derisive epithet characterizing Jackson's futile efforts to maintain authority while in exile.

31. Jefferson Davis to C. F. Jackson, June 5, 1861, *ORR*, ser. 1, pt. 53, 707; Snead, *The Fight for Missouri*, 231–34; Reynolds, "General Price and the Confederacy," 47; T. C. Reynolds to Jefferson Davis, November 13, 1880, Thomas C. Reynolds Papers, MHS; Parrish, *David Rice Atchison*, 216–17; Shalhope, *Sterling Price*, 167–70; Arthur Roy Kirkpatrick, "Missouri's Secessionist Government, 1861–1865," 127–37; Kirkpatrick, "Missouri in the Early Months of the Civil War," 259–66; *Missouri Statesman*, August 2, 16, 1861; *Daily Richmond* [Virginia] *Enquirer,* July 27, 29, 1861, quoted in Kirkpatrick, "Admission of Missouri to the Confederacy," 369–70 (quotes). Pillow's force of six thousand men occupied New Madrid on July 28, 1861.

designed it largely to placate Confederate officials and to sound the call that Missouri's fugitive government had returned to the state with the liberating Confederate force, hopeful that it would spur recruitment to the State Guard. Upon learning of the Confederate Congress's appropriation of one million dollars for Missouri troops, an exultant and appreciative Jackson promptly sent a copy of the proclamation—along with a request for the appointment of a major general west of the Mississippi—on to the administration in Richmond. After ordering the State Guard in the area to work in concert with Pillow's command, Jackson and Atchison boarded a steamer and returned to Memphis to confer with Polk on coordinating the Missouri campaign.[32]

Within days, Jackson learned of Price's and Ben McCulloch's defeat of Lyon at Wilson's Creek, near Springfield, on August 10. With the governor in Memphis, and despite the refusal of the Arkansas commander to cooperate further with Missouri troops (whom he considered "undisciplined and led by men who are mere politicians"), Price advanced north to reclaim his state from federal clutches and to reestablish the authority of its elected government. Moreover, Price intended to move to the Missouri River counties, where he could resume State Guard recruitment in its most fertile source and also interrupt federal control of the river. Jackson hastened to Springfield, accompanied by an escort of 150 armed Tennesseans recruited for the journey, leaving Reynolds to attend to "all such matters as he may judge to require immediate action of the executive of the State without the delay necessary to receive my orders." Arriving there on September 7, he found himself too late to meet Price, who had left more than a week earlier. Undaunted, Jackson and his "body guard" pushed on, catching up with the State Guard at Warrensburg, where he made a "violent secession speech" to a large, enthusiastic crowd, "assur[ing] them they had but to make an effort for their righteous cause and that they must triumph over Lincoln's cowardly hirelings." He then rode ahead with a large cavalry escort to Lexington, where he intended to set up his capital, and met in the local Masonic college with other exiled legislators who had accompanied Price's troops. Upon the approach of a three-thousand-man federal force, Jackson urged Price—now commanding some fifteen thousand troops—to move forward and engage the federals, who now fortified the Masonic college. Jackson watched as Price's troops besieged the federal command, using wetted hemp bales as shields as the lines slowly closed on the garrison; on September 21, after three

32. *Missouri Statesman*, August 23, 1861; Memorandum, June 2, 1886, Thomas C. Reynolds Papers, MHS; Leopard and Shoemaker, *Messages and Proclamations of the Governors of Missouri*, vol. 3, 389–90 (quote), 391–93; Parrish, *History of Missouri*, 33–34; Kirkpatrick, "Admission of Missouri to the Confederacy," 371–72; C. F. Jackson to E. C. Cabell, August 8, 1861, *ORR*, ser. 1, pt. 3, 639; M. Jeff Thompson to W. J. Hardee, August 7, 1861, ibid., ser. 1, pt. 3, 633.

days of fighting under a hot autumn sun, the federal commander, James A. Mulligan, surrendered his hungry and thirsty troops. After the battle, Jackson briefly addressed the sullen federal troops before paroling them.[33]

Jackson's jubilation at his apparent liberation of Missouri was short-lived. The army remained at Lexington for ten days, gaining several thousand more recruits, but without support from Confederate troops in distant Arkansas or the Bootheel, Price soon found himself unable to contend with the forty thousand federal troops under John C. Frémont now approaching him, threatening to cut off any retreat to the south. Despite the disappointing decision to withdraw, Jackson used the brief victory to mold public opinion toward immediate secession. Jackson had Atchison confiscate the printing press and equipment of the *Platte City Argus,* with which he issued a proclamation that called the General Assembly to meet at Neosho on October 21 to effect "an immediate and unconditional connection with the Southern Government." Having sent Reynolds, Cabell, and Thomas Snead separately to Richmond to hasten the Confederate Congress's authorization of Missouri's admission to the Confederate States, Jackson knew from his meetings with Davis that any such authorization would occur only "upon the condition that the [Confederate constitution] shall be adopted and ratified by the properly and legally constituted authorities of said State." Jackson now needed officially to call the state's governing body together to effect secession. Appropriating more than thirty-seven thousand dollars from local banks, Price again turned the State Guard southward on the last day of September while Jackson traveled eastward under escort to Arrow Rock, gathering up Eliza and their nearby children, including his stepchildren, sons- and daughters-in-law, grandchildren, and many slaves, who loaded their personal belongings, household furniture, and farm implements onto carriages and farm wagons. The solemn caravan creaked south, abandoning Fox Castle and passing the Marmaduke farm, which stood in silent testimony to the symbolism of the act; despite a lifetime of ambition, Jackson had never truly become master of his or any world.[34]

33. B. McCulloch to W. J. Hardee, August 24, 1861, *ORR*, ser. 1, pt. 3, 672 (first quote); McCulloch to J. P. Benjamin, December 22, 1861, ibid., ser. 1, pt. 3, 743–49; Proclamation of Sterling Price, August 20, 1861, ibid., ser. 1, pt. 53, 730; C. F. Jackson to Thomas C. Reynolds, August 6, 1861, EG Box 30, Huntington (second quote); *Missouri Statesman*, August 9 (third quote), September 13, 20, 1861 (fourth and fifth quotes); Kirkpatrick, "Admission of Missouri to the Confederacy," 375–77; McElroy, *Struggle for Missouri*, 175–76; James A. Mulligan, "The Siege of Lexington, Mo.," 307–13; *Harper's Weekly*, October 19, 1861.

34. Swindler, "Southern Press in Missouri," 399; Kirkpatrick, "Admission of Missouri to the Confederacy," 377–79; "An Act to aid the State of Missouri," August 20, 1861, *ORR*, ser. 4, pt. 1, 576–77 (first quote); C. F. Jackson to Jefferson Davis, August 13, 1861, ibid., ser. 1, 53, 725; Jackson to Davis, October 21, 1861, ibid., ser. 1, pt. 3,

Indeed, in his absence from the state, Missouri's Unionists had done much to delegitimize Jackson's governorship. Publication of his private letter to David Walker of the Arkansas Convention, as well as a letter of dubious validity addressed to Joseph W. Tucker, editor of the pro-Confederate *Missouri State Bulletin,* and dated four days prior to the meeting of the convention in which Jackson reputedly admitted arming the state in active preparation for secession, went far to undermine any claims he might have had to his defense of the state's stand for neutrality. Former governor Robert M. Stewart published a public appeal upon learning of Jackson's and Price's foray to Lexington, warning Missourians, "If the man, whom you have repudiated as Governor for his treasonable acts, is allowed to resume his seat, and you are brought within the reach of his power, your homes and lives will not be worth an hours purchase. His chosen free-booting General offers you protection. It is such protection as the Vulture gives the lamb! If you wish to have your towns and cities given up to sack and slaughter, your homes robbed and ravished, your fields desolated, and your property plundered by these soldiers of fortune, then open wide your doors and welcome the invaders to their bloody feast." The *Missouri Statesman* charged baldly that Jackson held "deliberate purpose to precipitate the State out of the Union," claiming that the letters they published "prove conclusively that he is the wrong man, in the wrong place, at the wrong time." The influential paper then condemned Jackson for duplicity and laid the blame for the state's war firmly in his lap, accusing him of "secretly concocting plans to precipitate the State into a revolution, and into the bosom of the Southern Confederacy." Others throughout the state agreed with the charge; upon hearing that the state's Democrats sought to put Jackson on their gubernatorial ticket in the upcoming November elections (the provisional government had granted itself authority only until the state could hold a regular election), the editor of the *Bethany Union* growled, "We think they can consistently run no one else, and no one else would be more easy to defeat. We want a chance to vote against the traitor, to redeem ourselves, we voted for him once."[35]

718; Jackson to Davis, November 5, 1861, ibid., ser. 1, 53, 754–55 (second quote); Ben McCulloch to J. P. Benjamin, October 14, 1861, ibid., ser. 1, pt. 3, 718–19; Mulligan, "Siege of Lexington," 313; Park and Morrow, *Women of the Mansion,* 126–28; Parrish, *Turbulent Partnership,* 34–35. The offensive and defensive alliance between Missouri and the Confederacy, though officially dated August 20, 1861, occurred on October 31, 1861. Rather than return from Richmond to Missouri to assist Jackson, whom he no longer respected, in December of 1861 Thomas Reynolds traveled to South Carolina, where he spent the entire next year.

35. Appeal to the People of Missouri, 1861, A. W. Reese, Recollections of the Civil War, 1870, Mss. 3627, microfilm reel 1, vol. 1, 723–24, SHSM (first quote); *Missouri Statesman,* August 2 (second, third, and fourth quotes), 16, 1861 (fourth quote). For

Within days of the Boonville debacle, Jackson's name was mere memory for many Missourians. St. Louisan Gerard B. Allen intoned that "A few crazy men, with Governor Jackson at their head, may have dreamed of secession, but they had neither men, money, or the necessary implements of war, for such a Quixotic enterprise," while a resident of St. Charles predicted that "unless Jackson should be very fortunate in his undertakings all will be glad of having got rid of him." George Caleb Bingham was more blunt: "Poor Claib and poor Price! their career began in honor, but prosecuted in hypocracy [*sic*], has at length terminated in infamy."[36]

Jackson was present in Neosho when the remnant of the Twenty-first General Assembly met, under protection of Price's army, at the Newton County courthouse. The body had nowhere near a quorum—nineteen senators and sixty-eight representatives (one contemporary source reported that only two persons were present on October 21)—and the governor spent the entire first week securing enough members to put together an ordinance of secession. Jackson probably was able to do so only by appointing proxies for those legislators who did not follow him to Neosho. Regardless, the governor provided the rump legislature with a set of instructions, beginning with a secession ordinance. By the end of the first business day, October 28, both houses of the assembly had passed the brief measure, which declared passionately that Missouri "does again take its place as a free and independent Republic" because a "despotic and arbitrary" federal government

> has wantonly violated the compact originally made between said Government and the state of Missouri, by invading with hostile armies the soil of the State, attacking and making prisoners the militia whilst legally assembled under the state laws, forcibly occupying the state capital and attempting through the instrumentality of domestic traitors to usurp the state government, seizing and destroying private property, and murdering with fiendish malignity peaceable citizens, men, women and children, together with acts of atrocity indicating a deep settled hostility towards the people of Missouri and their institutions.[37]

---

a discussion of the content of the Tucker letter and the controversy surrounding it, see note 10 in this chapter.

36. Gerard B. Allen to James S. Rollins, July 26, 1861, James S. Rollins Papers, Mss. 1026, box 3, folder 76, SHSM (first quote); A. Shekel to Rollins, June 28, 1861, ibid., box 3, folder 75, SHSM (second quote); George C. Bingham to Rollins, June 29, 1861, ibid., box 3, folder 75, SHSM (third quote).

37. Parrish, *David Rice Atchison*, 219–20; Kirkpatrick, "Admission of Missouri to the Confederacy," 379–85; *Journal of the Senate of the Rebel Legislature*, 3–4, 7–9, 12–13, 19, 34–38, 40–41; An Act declaring the political ties heretofore existing between the State of Missouri and the United States of America, dissolved, October 28, 1861, Missouri Confederate Archives, 1861, Mss. 2722, folder 1, SHSM (quotes). The question of quorum in this "rebel legislature" has long been a source of controversy; no journal of the house of representatives exists, and the Senate Journal contains no roll call or statements

Moreover, the assembly took the extraordinary step of electing senators and representatives to the Confederate Congress—an act Jackson acceded to only because of the current exigencies but not before declaring it the "most extraordinary bill in the history of legislation" that would "place the state in a false and ludicrous position before the world"—after which the assembly adjourned and removed with Price's army south to more distant Cassville. There, Jackson signed the secession ordinance and excitedly sent copies on to the Confederate administration, explaining that the extraordinary conditions in Missouri prevented a ratification referendum, but that he was certain that four-fifths of the voters "desire an immediate and unconditional connection with the Southern Government, and I pray that soon it may be consummated."[38]

The consummation was not long in coming. On November 28, the Confederate Congress admitted Missouri as a full and equal member, and the same day President Davis proclaimed Missouri the twelfth Confederate state. Learning of the act from Reynolds the next day in Memphis, Jackson exclaimed, "God be praised. This is the happiest moment of my life." Columbia's *Missouri Statesman* saw the matter differently. "The people of Missouri for three weeks past," its editor spat, "have been in Dixie's happy land, without knowing it. . . . But what a mockery is this. Here we have a Governor secretly assembling the Legislature in an obscure and distant corner of the State, a hundred and fifty miles from the seat of government, and packing it with such members, and such only, as would answer the treasonable purposes of Gov. Jackson."[39]

Missouri now had two governments claiming sovereignty within the state, while yet another two governments claimed the state's fealty outside its borders. The tangle of authority manifested itself most clearly among the state's pro-Confederate leadership. Though claiming themselves a member of the Confederacy, in reality Missouri's southern leaders behaved as if they considered the state an independent republic. This independence

---

on the quorum. The collection catalogued as Missouri Confederate Archives, 1861, Mss. 2722, 2 folders, SHSM, provides names for some of those present, but contains no complete list.

38. C. F. Jackson to the Speaker of the House of Representatives, November 8, 1861, Missouri Confederate Archives, 1861, Mss. 2722, folder 1, SHSM (first and second quotes); Jackson to Jefferson Davis, November 5, 1861, *ORR*, ser. 1, 53, 754–55 (third quote).

39. An Act admitting Missouri to the Confederacy, November 28, 1861, ibid., ser. 1, 53, 758; Jackson to Thomas C. Reynolds, November 29, 1861, EG Box 30, Huntington (first quote); *Missouri Statesman*, November 22, 1861 (second quote). Those senators and representatives named to the Confederate Congress were: John B. Clark and Robert L. Y. Peyton, senators; William M. Cooke, Thomas A. Harris, Casper W. Bell, Aaron H. Conrow, George G. Vest, Thomas W. Freeman, and John Hyer, representatives.

revealed itself no more clearly than when Price determined to move again into middle Missouri in November. Price had requested military assistance from several authorities, including Jefferson Davis, who responded that until Missouri tendered her troops—Price's State Guard—for Confederate service, the Confederacy could send no troops into the state. While Price attempted to shame Boon's Lick recruits into state service, Jackson belatedly attempted to solicit Bootheel volunteers for Confederate service. The farce of neutrality now expunged, Jackson's régime found its very existence clinging precariously to the viability of the state's military forces. With federal forces in firm possession of the state's capital, its largest city, and its river, rail, and communications networks, any claim of the exiled government's viability as the campaigning season closed was at best dubious. The legislature, rather than remain unprotected or follow Price northward, adopted a resolution to adjourn and reconvene in March 1862, at New Madrid, where the proximity of Confederates at nearby Columbus, Kentucky, would presumably shield it from federal advances. In December, Jackson, too, traveled northward to meet with Price at Richmond, Missouri, then hastened to New Madrid, where he soon boarded a steamer for New Orleans. There, Jackson spent a winter of discontent, wrestling with the Davis administration over Missouri's place—and its responsibilities—within the Confederacy as well as obtaining arms, equipment, and funds for those Missouri soldiers without.[40]

While Jackson pushed relentlessly for Missouri's Confederate inclusion, he drew some comfort from the knowledge that his family was out of harm's way. When he and Atchison left Little Rock for Richmond, he sent his son, Will, and son-in-law, Charles L. Lamb, to northern Texas, where they purchased land in Eliza's name in Red River County. The pair returned to Arkansas and retrieved the remainder of the Jackson refugees, then led them back to a small, "dismal" farm amid cane breaks, pine forests, and cotton

40. Shalhope, *Sterling Price*, 184–92; Leopard and Shoemaker, *Messages and Proclamations of the Governors of Missouri*, vol. 3, 395–400; C. F. Jackson to Jefferson Davis, December 29, 1861, Arrow Rock Tavern Board, Papers, 1826–1913, Mss. 3087: Correspondence, folder 1, SHSM (quote); Jefferson Davis to C. F. Jackson, December 30, 1861, January 8, 1861, ORR, ser. 1, pt. 8, 717, 733; Jackson to Davis, December 30, 1861, ibid., ser. 1, pt. 8, 724–25; Jackson to Sterling Price, December 30, 1861, ibid., ser. 1, pt. 8, 725–26; Sterling Price, General Order #11, Headquarters Missouri State Guard, December 2, 1861, ibid., ser. 1, 53, 758; M. Jeff Thompson to Jackson, December 8, 1861, ibid., ser. 1, pt. 8, 704–5; Thompson to Price, January 1, 1862, ibid., ser. 1, pt. 8, 727–28; Burks, "Thunder on the Right," 433–36; Jackson to Thomas C. Reynolds, November 29, 1861, EG Box 30, Huntington. The conflict over sovereignty (encapsulated in the well-known incongruence between Sterling Price and Ben McCulloch) led Jefferson Davis to appoint Earl Van Dorn, rather than Price, as commander for the Trans-Mississippi as he had no prior connection with Missouri or its troops. See various letters in ORR, ser. 1, pt. 3, 718, 722, 731–38, and ser. 1, pt. 8, 736–37, 744–47.

fields. Sheltered by Indian country to the immediate north, the north Texas frontier proved a haven for a number of Missouri political refugees, including Atchison, who settled during the war years in nearby Grayson County. In order to supplement the farm's meager income, reports had the Jackson clan operating a sawmill in nearby Clarkesville, the county seat. The family suffered badly from recurrent bouts with ague, the malarial fevers Eliza's father had grown wealthy in fighting. Jackson himself, however, spent no time at the farmstead, its central home place surrounded by smaller cabins and shanties for family members and slaves. He had little time for family after leaving New Orleans in January 1862, for the Confederacy's newest star—always dim—appeared doomed to eclipse.[41]

Throughout the fall, Jackson had struggled with the Davis administration to name a commander for the trans-Mississippi theater of operations, separate from the Western Department. Price and others pressured him that the appointment go to a native of the Far West; indeed, Price was adamant that he was the only man "fit for the place." Jackson might well have felt obliged to intervene on Price's behalf. Without rank in the Confederate army, yet with troops under his immediate command authorized to enlist in Confederate service, Price's appointment would smooth the halting transition of Missouri into full Confederate inclusion. Yet Jackson, "acknowledg[ing that] there is a mystery about this whole affair," recognized that Davis was reluctant to appoint Price, whether from the embarrassment of the open feud with McCulloch or from a long-standing friction between Price and Davis held over from the Mexican War. The exiled governor, struggling to regain his state, held back from full support for Price's case, holding above all else that the appointment should go to a man who would give a high priority to Missouri's liberation.[42]

Jackson now made every effort to regain Missouri. In Memphis, en route to New Orleans, he had conferred with Albert Sidney Johnston, then commanding the entire Western Department, hoping to convince him to

41. C. L. Lamb to W. B. Sappington, March 24, 1869, John S. Sappington Papers, Mss. 1027, box 3, folder 76, SHSM; Park and Morrow, *Women of the Mansion*, 127–28; Parrish, *David Rice Atchison*, 220–21; *Missouri Statesman*, October 24, 1862; Burks, "Thunder on the Right," 440–41; M. Jeff Thompson to C. F. Jackson, January 16, 1862, *ORR*, ser. 1, pt. 8, 735–36.

42. C. F. Jackson to Jefferson Davis, October 12, 1861, *ORR*, ser. 1, pt. 3, 718 (first quote); Jackson to Sterling Price, December 30, 1861, ibid., ser. 1, pt. 8, 725–26 (second quote); E. C. Cabell to Davis, August 16, 1861, ibid., ser. 1, pt. 3, 652–53; Shalhope, *Sterling Price*, 191–96. Price and McCulloch quarreled at the outset of the Wilson's Creek campaign, largely over McCulloch's perception of the Missouri State Guard as an untrained rabble and Price's steadfast inclusion of these forces in the ensuing campaign. The battle itself widened the breach, with McCulloch afterwards refusing to cooperate in battle with the Missourians and their commander. Phillips, *Damned Yankee*, 241–44.

invade Missouri, but without success. Now, in February, Union successes in Tennessee drew troops from the region. By all appearances the Confederacy would abandon Missouri. Jackson then conferred with the newly appointed commander of troops in Arkansas, Earl Van Dorn, at Des Arc on the White River, and found the Mississippian enthusiastic for resuming war in Missouri. Learning that federal troops under Samuel Curtis had driven Price from Missouri, and that the legislature could not meet as scheduled in New Madrid because of yet another federal advance, Jackson convinced Van Dorn to join with Price's retreating force and with nearly sixteen thousand troops marched to strike Curtis's ten thousand men in northwestern Arkansas. Writing "I shall go to the Army," Jackson accompanied the southern host's advance through frigid weather and a week later witnessed their dismal defeat at the battle at Pea Ridge and the subsequent retreat, first to Des Arc and then across the Mississippi to Memphis. Aside from small cavalry raids, Confederate troops would not again enter Missouri for more than two years.[43]

Claiborne Jackson would not live to see that day. He traveled briefly to Marshall, Texas, in late July to meet with the governors of Arkansas, Texas, and Louisiana and to discuss the Davis administration's seeming lack of concern with the trans-Mississippi Confederate states (the group made several requests of Davis for competent military leadership, supplies, and funds for the payment of troops, the latter of which was of enough concern for Jackson to authorize the printing of Missouri scrip, considered virtually worthless, thus staining the former banker's fiduciary record in his last effort). To keep up morale, the governors published a statement (with Jackson's name at the head) which claimed that they "have every assurance that the President has neither forgotten nor abandoned us, and are well satisfied that in a short time the proper steps will be taken by him for fully protecting the integrity of our soil, where it has not yet been polluted, and for driving the enemy back from amongst us, by interposing a stubborn resistance to his further advance at every point. . . . It is for liberty and life we fight!" Two months later, Jackson was in Little Rock establishing recruiting camps in northern Arkansas and southern Missouri. As Waldo P. Johnson, his former political rival now in Confederate service, recalled, Jackson took great care to "[turn] over to General Holmes all the State property at this place, embracing a large amount of clothing and other army stores: also all now in Mississippi. The Governor also made an order turning over all the State guards now

43. Shalhope, *Sterling Price*, 191–96; Jackson to M. M. Parsons, March 1, 1862, EG Box 30, Huntington (quote); McPherson, *Battle Cry of Freedom*, 404–5; Parrish, *History of Missouri*, 46–48; Shalhope, *Sterling Price*, 198–207; M. Jeff Thompson to Jackson, March 3, 1862, *ORR*, ser. 1, pt. 8, 765. For a thorough examination of the battle of Pea Ridge, or Elkhorn Tavern, see William L. Shea and Earl J. Hess, *Pea Ridge*.

in Missouri to the Confederate States, requiring them to report to me, withdrawing from all persons all power to recruit in future for the Missouri State Guard." The act was far more than mere completion of the tortuous path to binding Missouri militarily to the Confederacy; Jackson knew that he was dying.[44]

Jackson suffered from a stomach cancer that had withered his vigorous physique and tuberculosis, both of which limited what strength he could muster to continue the fatiguing schedule that in all likelihood had accelerated these debilitating diseases. In the next month, wracked with pain, the exiled governor managed to travel by ambulance between Little Rock and Camden, making several public addresses urging financial support from Arkansans for the Missouri military campaigns that he knew offered his only chance of returning to his home state and reclaiming the dominion he believed he still possessed. Yet his health worsened appreciably, indicated no more starkly than by Jackson's virtual disappearance from the public record. By late November, as Jackson battled pneumonia brought on in part by the laudanum he took to ease his intense pain, his physicians sent word to his family in Texas to hasten to his simple room at Pulaski House, the boardinghouse that stood across the river from the Arkansas capital. Only Eliza and son-in-law John S. Pearson managed to arrive at his bedside in the first days of December, as winter's damp chill settled over the Arkansas hills. On December 7, a day after preparing a brief will, Claib Jackson died in a laudanum haze, a stranger in a strange land, much like the Confederate state of Missouri itself.[45]

44. Jefferson Davis to F. R. Lubbock, C. F. Jackson, T. O. Moore, and H. M. Rector, September 12, 1862, *ORR*, ser. 1, pt. 8, 879–80; Address to the Citizens and Soldiers of the States of Missouri, Arkansas, Louisiana and Texas, July 28, 1862, M. J. Solomons Scrapbook, 1861–1863, 483, Duke (first quote); *Missouri Statesman*, March 7, May 16, 1861; Missouri State Notes, January 1, 1862, M. Jeff Thompson Papers, Mss. 1030, folder 1, SHSM; Waldo P. Johnson to Sterling Price, September 15, 1862, *ORR*, ser. 1, pt. 8, 880 (second quote); Parrish, *History of Missouri*, 48–49; Burks, "Thunder on the Right," 442–44.

45. Parrish, *History of Missouri*, 48–49; Burks, "Thunder on the Right," 442–44; Park and Morrow, *Women of the Mansion*, 129; Last Will and Testament of Claiborne Fox Jackson, December 6, 1862, microfilm reel C11591, Will Book B, Saline County [Missouri], 138–40, MSA; *Arkansas Patriot*, December 11, 1862; *Columbia Missouri-Herald*, September 18, 1903.

EPILOGUE

AVATAR

FOUR YEARS OF fighting for the preservation of their world and their heritage, four years of measuring themselves against the Yankee in the intimate and searching contact of battle, had left these Southerners far more self-conscious than they had been before, far more aware of their differences and of the line which divided what was Southern from what was not. And upon that line all their intensified patriotism and love, all their high pride in the knowledge that they had fought a good fight and had yielded only to irresistible force, was concentrated, to issue in a determination, immensely more potent than in the past, to hold fast to their own, to maintain their divergences, to remain what they had been and were. . . . And of these phrases the great master key was in every case the adjective Southern.

WILBUR J. CASH, *THE MIND OF THE SOUTH*

The tragedy enacted on Missouri's wide stage in no way ended with Claiborne Jackson's death. If anything, it merely closed one middle scene. The *Missouri Statesman* saw fit to include a brief notice of the death of the "fugitive governor" at the bottom of the second page, fourth column, of its January 9, 1863, edition; the *Jefferson City People's Tribune* mentioned Jackson's death only on July 3, 1867. Indeed, by the time of Jackson's demise, the bitter plot of Missouri's epic had begun to unfold, whether for the Jackson family or for the state itself, far eclipsing Claib Jackson's supporting role in the drama.[1]

The war years witnessed a rapid and nearly complete fall of the Jackson house. Strangely, its collapse had started on an auspicious note. In the spring of 1861, after celebrating the marriage of their youngest daughter, Ann Eliza, to John A. Perkins, a Virginia-born schoolteacher living in Saline County, as well as their youngest son, Claib, Jr., to the daughter of a Georgetown, Missouri, grocer, the family quickly paid the war's heavy toll. Their sons Will, fresh from law school at the University of Virginia (likely on alumnus William B. Napton's recommendation) and Claib, Jr., then twenty-one, quickly went into the State Guard, both receiving commissions as officers from their father. In the fall of 1861, after Price's advance and retreat from Lexington, both William P. and Wade M. Jackson, the exiled governor's surviving brothers,

1. *Missouri Statesman*, January 9, 1863 (quote); *Jefferson City People's Tribune*, July 3, 1867.

274

suffered arrest by Union forces in Howard County for refusing to take the test oath and aiding and abetting the enemy. Because of their relationship to the rebel governor, William was confined to a military prison in St. Louis while Wade was banished from the state until the summer of 1863. So powerful was the association of Jackson with the partisan warfare only beginning in Missouri that the local newspapers proclaimed one of the state's most notorious guerrillas, Jim Jackson, to be the exiled governor's son, a guilt by association stemming solely from their last names. In retaliation, after serving as his father's aide, Will returned to Missouri during the summer of 1862 as a recruiting officer for the Confederate army, basing himself in Saline County and canvassing the Boon's Lick and northern Missouri for volunteers. He also engaged in "bushwhacking . . . prov[ing] a great annoyance to the militia and Yankees in that section," as one comrade related to his dying father. He then returned to service in Arkansas and Mississippi. Returning to a ransacked family farm immediately after the war, Will found himself confined in a Boonville jail already in the summer of 1865, charged with robbery and murder for an incident in Glasgow, as the gaping wounds that the war had opened remained fresh. The following spring, the Howard County sheriff sold the farm of his uncle, William, for nonpayment of taxes.[2]

Arrest and harassment were merely prefatory to the greater Jackson family tragedy. Claiborne Jackson's death proved only the first of several that visited themselves upon the fractured immediate family during the war. A grieving Eliza remained in Little Rock for many months after her husband's demise, and her presence did not escape the notice of Missouri's new Confederate governor, Thomas Caute Reynolds, who returned from South Carolina to assume the office upon news of Jackson's rapid decline. Reynolds hastened first to Richmond to confer with Confederate officials, then issued a proclamation assuming power as the legally authorized governor of Missouri before leaving for Arkansas. He set up temporary headquarters in Camden, where he found many of the state records from Jackson's administration. Learning

2. Eighth U.S. Census, 1860, Population Schedule, Pettis and Saline Counties [Missouri], NA; *Missouri Statesman,* August 6, 1880, June 10, 1863; William S. Jackson file, United Daughters of the Confederacy, Missouri Records, Mss. 3188, folder 150, SHSM; George E. Leighton to William H. Seward, March 3, 1862, *ORR,* ser. 2, pt. 2, 251; Report of William Jones, March 8, 1864, ibid., ser. 2, pt. 7, 244; *Columbia Missouri-Herald,* September 18, 1903 (quote); *Glasgow Weekly Times,* November 2, 1866; Fellman, *Inside War,* 231–33. Thomas Jackson, the other Howard County sibling, died on August 31, 1852. See *Missouri Statesman,* September 10, 1852. Arrested by Colonel Alexander F. Denny of Glasgow, William S. Jackson was released on two thousand dollars bond. I have been unable to determine the outcome of the case against him. The U.D.C. records indicate only that he was "harassed by civil authorities." See Brownlee, *Gray Ghosts of the Confederacy,* 215, 239–40.

of Eliza's residence at Little Rock, he sent Colonel R. M. Stith to collect "all the funds, papers, transportation or stock that belonged to the State of Mo." from the former governor's widow. A distressed Eliza, "ignorant in business matters, [and] much at a loss how to act," as she claimed to her son in a poignant letter, responded to Stith's demand, "I had no funds in my possession except some silver coin, about the amt. of your Pa's salary which had been reserved for that purpose. He said it was what your Pa had a right to do and was all right." A shaken Eliza, claiming that she "never felt the necessity of having one of my sons with me as I do now," quickly returned to the family's rude homestead in Texas. Within a year, in March 1864, her youngest son, Claib, Jr., was dead, killed in action near Laredo, a corner of the Confederacy even darker than Missouri's, and buried in an unmarked grave. Four months later, on July 5, Eliza died suddenly as well, the victim of malarial fevers her father had spent a lifetime curing; she, too, like her husband and son, was buried in foreign clay.[3]

Thomas Reynolds continued his predecessor's attempts to secure Confederate intervention on Missouri's behalf. Concerned that the military leaders did not recognize his authority as governor, Reynolds nonetheless established his capital at Little Rock and began active communications with Sterling Price, an ally, as well as General Theophilus Holmes, commander of the District of Missouri and Arkansas, and General Edmund Kirby Smith, the new commander of the Trans-Mississippi Department. As had Jackson, Reynolds began active cooperation with the other regional Confederate governors (especially after the fall of Vicksburg, which isolated the Trans-Mississippi) and served as chair of a Committee of Public Safety at a conference at Marshall, Texas, in August 1863. The Confederate evacuation of Little Rock forced Reynolds to relocate his capital, first to Shreveport, then ultimately to Marshall, the center of operations for the Trans-Mississippi Department and where he rented the home of a Texas supreme court justice for his executive building. By the fall of 1864, Reynolds's exertions had secured approval for a foray into Missouri, a massive cavalry raid that Price, at Reynolds's behest, would lead. A wistful Reynolds had become convinced that the conservatives of Missouri, along with those in Kentucky, would soon unite with the disaffected "Copperheads" of the Old Northwest to reestablish the traditional western state alliance that would support, if not

3. *Missouri Statesman*, June 30, August 11, 1865; Kirkpatrick, "Missouri's Confederate Capital," 45; Eliza W. Jackson to My Dear Son, May 23, 1863, in Park and Morrow, *Women of the Mansion*, 129–30 (quotes), also 126; Giffin, *First Ladies of Missouri*, 80–82; Burks, "Thunder on the Right," 346–47*n81;* Santos Benavides to John S. Ford, March 19, 1864, *ORR*, ser. 1, pt. 34, 647–48; B. P. Gallaway, ed., *The Dark Corner of the Confederacy: Accounts of Civil War Texas as Told by Contemporaries*, 169.

join outright, the Confederacy. An invasion of Confederate troops would impel this restoration.[4]

Price's raid, conducted during October and November 1864, proved a failure of monumental proportions. With its primary goals being the capture of St. Louis, the reestablishment of Missouri's elected government— Reynolds accompanied the troops—and the rallying of Confederate Missourians to the flag and to the Cause (as many as a hundred thousand stood waiting, by one wishful estimate), the raid failed to achieve any of its objectives. The twelve thousand horsemen (four thousand of whom were unarmed, a recurrent problem with the Missouri troops) soon proved to be looters and deserters rather than redeemers, and their languid pace, despite being mounted, allowed federal troops in St. Louis and Kansas to turn back Price's Missourians from their intended approach to St. Louis and to harass his columns continually as they moved westward through the Boon's Lick. After a pitched battle at Westport, the largest battle fought west of the Mississippi, Price's men withdrew south along the Kansas-Missouri border into Indian Territory and eventually to Texas. An incensed Governor Reynolds recognized immediately that the conduct of Price and his men had turned most of the Missouri populace firmly against him and the state's Confederates and ended any chance for Reynolds's restoration. He criticized Price bitterly, calling his raid a "disgracefully managed expedition," and published a lengthy diatribe in a Texas newspaper as well as writing Confederate officials, urging them to remove Price from active service. Price's acrid response captured the complete marginalization of Missouri's exiled government as the exchange turned nearly absurd: the former governor Price, now a Confederate, dismissed Reynolds, the legal successor to the most recently elected governor—both Confederates—as "one . . . who pretends to be, and styles himself in it, the Governor of the State of Missouri." Reynolds's icy rejoinder completed the symbolic devolution of Missouri's Confederate odyssey. Addressing Price's derogation of his political authority, an indignant Reynolds fumed, "The Federals take the same view of my position; but he [Price] has the distinction of being the first man in our lines to publish his concurrence with them in it."[5]

4. Thomas C. Reynolds to S[terling]. Price, December 4, 1863, and June 2, 1864, *ORR,* ser. 1, pt. 8, 918 and 998; Reynolds to Price, October 2, 1864, ibid., ser. 1, pt. 41/3, 976–77; Price to Reynolds, July 22, 1864, *ORR,* ser. 1, pt. 41/3, 1020; Price to Reynolds, November 2, 1863, and June 9, 1864, ibid., ser. 1, pt. 8, 905–8 and 999–1000; Kirkpatrick, "Missouri's Secessionist Government," 45–50; Shalhope, *Sterling Price,* 215, 231, 242–48.

5. Thomas C. Reynolds to E. Kirby Smith, November 19, 1864, quoted in Shalhope, *Sterling Price,* 275 (first quote), also 256–80; Stephen B. Oates, *Confederate Cavalry West of the River,* 113–54; Castel, *General Sterling Price,* 196–255; Christopher Phillips,

Reynolds's quest for legitimacy within the Confederacy, however successful within or without Missouri, served only as a maudlin adjunct to the true civil war in the state, one that operated, like the state itself, on the margin of the military conflict. While as many as thirty thousand Missourians fought in uniform for the Confederacy—one-fourth of its eligible men—thousands more fought as guerrillas, subjecting Union soldiers and civilians in virtually all sections of the state to more than three years of rampant bushwhacking, sniping, hit-and-run raiding, arson, and murder. These partisans' numbers represented but a fraction of those who served in the Confederate army, but their influence on the state's populace far surpassed any mustered by Missourians in gray. One need only look at the index of civilian arrests made by the federal army during the war, housed at the National Archives, and see the overwhelming preponderance of those arrests made in Missouri, as compared with all other states, to understand the severity of its war within a war. By one estimate, nearly twenty-seven thousand Missouri citizens lost their lives at the hands of these partisan raiders, whose ubiquity has prompted historian James M. McPherson's claim that "More than any other state, Missouri suffered the horrors of internecine warfare and the resulting hatreds which persisted for decades after Appomattox."[6]

The final clause of McPherson's insightful conclusion proves telling. For many Missourians, the bitterness and lingering hatred associated with the experience of war derived not from the violent activities of pro-Confederate guerrillas, but from the repressive measures that state and federal officials initiated to contain the widespread terrorism. The old state convention, made up of Unionists and dominated by Unconditional Unionists, quickly instituted the "test oath," administered to civil officials forswearing their giving aid or comfort to Confederates or pro-Confederate partisans. Offered as an amnesty provision to those in the State Guard who had followed Jackson

---

"Price's Missouri Raid," in Richard N. Current, ed., *Encyclopedia of the Confederacy*, vol. 3, 1252–55; Kirkpatrick, "Missouri's Confederate Capital," 50, 51–52 (second quote, p. 51); Reynolds to Price, October 2, 10, 1864, *ORR*, ser. 1, pt. 41/3, 976–77 and 1000–1001. Reynolds published his condemnation of Price in the Marshall *Texas Republican*, December 17, 1864. The proceedings of the court martial that Price insisted upon convened in Shreveport on March 8, 1865, to vindicate his leadership of the campaign in Missouri are in *ORR*, ser. 1, pt. 41, 701–29.

6. Nagel, *Missouri*, 129, 133–35; Index of Names, 1859–1865, Registers of the Records of the Proceedings of the U.S. Army General Courts-Martial, 1809–1890, Record Group 153: Records of the Office of the Judge Advocate General (Army), M1105, microfilm reels 2–3, NA; William E. Parrish, "Missouri," in Current, *Encyclopedia of the Confederacy*, vol. 3, 1055; Mark E. Neely, Jr., *The Fate of Liberty: Abraham Lincoln and Civil Liberties*, 44; Richard S. Brownlee, *Gray Ghosts of the Confederacy: Guerilla Warfare in the West, 1861–1865*, 110–57; McPherson, *Battle Cry of Freedom*, 292 (quote), 783–88. For the most comprehensive study of Missouri's guerrilla war, see Fellman, *Inside War*.

and Price and now wished to return to the state, the test oath was transformed in 1862 when federal department commander Henry W. Halleck and district commander John M. Schofield extended the requirement to all persons suspected of disloyalty. They did so to avoid reparations for the cost of caring for Unionist refugees whom Confederate sympathizers had driven from their homes, as well as for compensation for loyalists' property damaged by partisans. Federal policy called for immediate execution of guerrillas captured while destroying property, and for trial by military commission for those suspected of being partisans, with death being the mandatory penalty. In response to William Quantrill's August 21, 1863, raid on Lawrence, Kansas, a foray that resulted in 183 civilian murders, the greatest such atrocity of the brutal war, Brigadier General Thomas E. Ewing, Union commander of the western district of Missouri, issued General Order No. 11, which forced the near depopulation of four entire Missouri counties. Nearly ten thousand residents were thus banished from their homes—so many of which were destroyed by Charles R. Jennison's Kansas "Jayhawker" cavalry that the area soon became known as the "Burnt District"—for the duration of the war unless they took the test oath. Few did.[7]

As indicated by the infamous Order No. 11, the federal government met Missouri's proliferation of partisan warfare with equal severity. The historian Mark Neely has written that Missouri's civil war achieved the "matchless reputation as the scene of cruel guerrilla warfare and desperate military repression." The imposition of martial law, a legal phenomenon distinct from the suspension of the writ of habeas corpus, occurred in Missouri earlier than in any other state. Federal provost marshals and troops, aided by thousands of Missouri State Militia (M.S.M.) and Enrolled Missouri Militia (E.M.M.), who as adjuncts to federal authorities provided the largest portion of troops in the state, strictly regulated movement, trade, published material, and even recreational activities. Rather than restraining the U.S. Army from violations of civil liberties, the military commissions that operated in the state actually supported the military authority that wielded enormous discretionary power. Together, for nearly four years they deprived Missouri's civilian populace of individual rights they would otherwise have enjoyed in the absence of federal troops. Indeed, Neely has concluded, "More such arrests occurred in Missouri than in any other state by far." His evidence, which he admits is "fragmentary," speaks volumes; the 4,770 "political prisoners" interred in St. Louis's Gratiot Street prison alone represented one of every one hundred male Missourians; this figure does not include the thousands of civilians

---

7. Neely, *The Fate of Liberty*, 46–48; Parrish, *History of Missouri*, 44–45, 51–53, 99–101; Fellman, *Inside War*, 95–97; Brownlee, *Gray Ghosts of the Confederacy*, 122–25, 126–27 (quote).

arrested and confined in dozens of military prisons throughout the state (nor does it include the thousands of Missouri soldiers held as Confederate prisoners of war). By his own estimation, the potential number of civilian prisoners held in Missouri might well have been "staggering."[8]

Any illusion of federal conciliation disappeared almost immediately. In July 1861, Brigadier General John Pope, commander of the District of North Missouri, levied fines against all residents within a five-mile radius of any damaged railroad lines unless they could prove conclusively that they had resisted the saboteurs. In one motion, Pope had effectively inverted the hallmark of American jurisprudence. The inversion spread with the assessments throughout the state, with "assessment boards" in every county compiling lists of disloyal residents—including some of those who had taken the oath—along with their property value and estimated resources, to calculate fines and reparations for the ravages of guerrilla warfare. In January 1863, General John McNeil ordered three hundred thousand dollars collected in the District of North Missouri; only widows and children with property of less than five thousand dollars would be exempt "unless they have given aid and comfort to the guerrillas." Those who refused such levies had their property confiscated. Moreover, the local provost marshals often required bonds for good behavior from those judged as being "secesh"; in the Liberty district alone, provost marshals required 612 persons to post bond in 1862, which ranged from one thousand to ten thousand dollars each and totaled $840,000. The provost in Palmyra reported taking in as much as $1 million in the same year.[9]

The widespread misemployment of the federal policies for suppression of civil unrest might well have provided the choicest grist for the long-lasting bitterness among Missourians. In their capacity as law enforcers, the Union state militia and their commanders often settled old personal scores against proslavery neighbors or flaunted their position of power by its very use with federal imprimatur. George Caleb Bingham, who was an officer in the M. S. M. before becoming state treasurer, made clear his intent for hard-handedness in 1861 when he declared, "The neutrality policy which our friends have been generally urging has never struck me as being manly or patriotic. To pronounce Secession treason in one breath, and in the next to declare neutrality between the traitors and the Constituted authorities who are endeavoring to maintain the government, seems to me to be twin brother

8. Neely, *The Fate of Liberty*, 44–45 (first quote, p. 44), 46 (remaining quotes); Fellman, *Inside War*, 33–34. Neely's work is the only one to have offered quantified calculations of civilian arrests in Civil War Missouri.

9. Mark Grimsley, *The Hard Hand of War: Union Military Policy toward Southern Civilians, 1861–1865*, 38; Brownlee, *Gray Ghosts of the Confederacy*, 164–67; Parrish, *History of Missouri*, 67.

to the treason. . . . The fact is Governments are for purposes of Coercion alone, those who are willing to do right need no laws to impel them to the performance of duty." Routinely, provost marshals and militia commanders made arbitrary arrests of civilians—especially those who had not taken the oath—infuriating the civilian populace.[10]

Despite recognizing the inexactness of designations of loyalty and disloyalty, Union officials routinely depended on local Unionists for their designations of local residents that were themselves implicitly political and often personal. The state militia soon became both extension and enforcer of the barometer of loyalty; in July 1862, all able-bodied white males between the ages of eighteen and forty-five were required to take the oath and enroll for militia duty or be placed on the local assessment list as disloyal. The widespread harassment, including confiscation of property and banishment, that Union troops and state militia engaged in drove thousands of residents from their homes. Undisciplined troops only compounded the misery of many rural Missourians, especially those who lived on the border with Kansas, where Jayhawkers' retribution for the long border conflict devolved into freebooting and outright terrorism of residents whom the Kansans viewed uniformly as traitorous. These Kansans initiated a scorched-earth policy years before commanders in the East employed such extremism. One Jackson County resident calculated his losses from six raids of his farm between January 1861 and August 1863 at just over forty-one hundred dollars— 84 percent of which occurred on one raid in the latter month when Union troops destroyed his house, barn, carriage, wagon, kitchen, and smokehouse. Such treatment of civilians occurred throughout the state.[11]

Federal policy and its enforcement, arbitrary and not, moved far beyond mere harassment. As early as August 1861, John C. Frémont, then the western department's commander, set down capital parameters when he proclaimed, "All persons who shall be taken with arms in their hands within these lines shall be tried by court-martial, and if found guilty will be shot." Though Lincoln modified the order so that none could be executed without his consent, Missourians were shocked. The following May, district commander John M. Schofield reiterated the intent of federals to mete out harsh retribution for the mounting guerrilla war by proclaiming, "The time has passed when insurrection and rebellion in Missouri can cloak itself under

10. Fellman, *Inside War,* 32–37, 44–52; Parrish, *History of Missouri,* 52–56; Parrish, *Turbulent Partnership,* 85–86; G. C. Bingham to James S. Rollins, May 16, 1861, James S. Rollins Papers, Mss. 1026, box 3, folder 74, SHSM (quote).

11. Parrish, *History of Missouri,* 66–70; McPherson, *Battle Cry of Freedom,* 784–85; Grimsley, *Hard Hand of War,* 190–204. Grimsley argues rightly that much of the "hard war" activities of the Union Army originated with the troops themselves, rather than being derived from military policy.

the guise of honorable warfare," and ordered his men to shoot on site any person "caught in arms." Federal authorities made good their commanders' orders and regularly executed captured guerrillas, especially after Quantrill's raid on Lawrence, Kansas, when a virtual manhunt occurred and hundreds of suspected partisans received summary execution. Perhaps the best known of Missouri's countless atrocities occurred in October 1862, when ten suspected partisans held in local prisons were shot in a public spectacle at Palmyra in retaliation for the disappearance of a local Unionist. The incident has since borne the epithet, the "Palmyra Massacre."[12]

Such actions brought no reproof from the president, though they drew sharp reprisals from the state's military leaders, one of whom—M. Jeff Thompson—threatened to "hang, draw and quarter a minion of said Abraham Lincoln" for every "citizen soldier" so executed. To punctuate, the passionate Thompson vowed that if the federal commander did not withdraw his intention, "I will retaliate ten-fold, so help me God." While St. Joseph's former mayor did his best to make his boast more than idle, thousands of Missourians magnified his modest calculation exponentially in their initiation of violence against federal and state forces—as well as Unionist civilians—in their midst. Yet most commenced their subversive activities only after federal policy included the emancipation of slaves.[13]

As with the other eventual federal objectives adopted during the course of the conflict, the wartime liberation of bondpeople had its genesis in Missouri. This occurred despite widespread disavowals. As early as May 1861, conservative St. Louis Unionist Thomas T. Gantt wrote to then-department commander William S. Harney of a conversation with a Greene County resident, who "asked me whether I supposed it was the intention of the United States Government to interfere with the institution of negro slavery in Missouri or any Slave State, or impair the security of that description of property." "Of course," Gantt averred, "my answer was most unqualifiedly, and almost indignantly in the negative. I told him that . . . I felt certain that the force of the United States, would, if necessary, be exerted for the protection of this, as well as any other kind of property." Yet Gantt, noticeably

---

12. Fellman, *Inside War,* 66 (first quote); Parrish, *History of Missouri,* 52–53 (second and third quotes, p. 52); William E. Parrish, " 'The Palmyra Massacre': A Tragedy of Guerrilla Warfare," 263–67; Parrish, Jones, and Christensen, *Missouri,* 175–78; Grimsley, *Hard Hand of War,* 23–39; Brownlee, *Gray Ghosts of the Confederacy,* 88–89, 90–91 (fourth quote, p. 90). Grimsley's otherwise fine work offers a contradictory argument for a conciliatory federal policy in Missouri, despite the restrictive actions of such federal military leaders as Lyon, Pope, Frémont, Halleck, Samuel Curtis, and John McNeil, the latter of whom ordered the "Palmyra Massacre."

13. M. Jeff Thompson to Whom it May Concern, September 2, 1861, *ORR,* ser. 2, pt. 1, 181 (first and second quotes); Neely, *Fate of Liberty,* 36.

anxious, saw fit to query the department commander, himself a slaveholding Tennessean, whether he had answered correctly. Harney responded that he would have answered the same, but noted, "I am not a little astonished that such a question could be seriously put. . . . I should as soon expect to hear that the orders of the Government were directed towards the overthrow of any other kind of property as of this in negro slaves." Just as Harney's naïveté cost him his command, so did slaveholders such as Gantt—convinced that their loyalty to the Union would forestall either such abomination—watch with horror as the ousted department commander's rhetorical negation became prophesy.[14]

Ironically, when Harney's successor issued his August 30, 1861, proclamation, it received national notoriety not so much for its death sentence for guerrillas, but for its authorization of emancipation in Missouri, the aspect of the edict to which Lincoln most objected. While Lincoln's rebuke of the Pathfinder might have cheered Missouri's slaveholders, however temporarily, it did little other than hasten Frémont's removal from command. Already in the summer of 1861, as Lyon chased Jackson and Price toward Arkansas, Kansas Jayhawkers such as James Montgomery and Charles Jennison were leading military forays into western Missouri, confiscating the property of rebel sympathizers, including slaves, with the intent of using them as soldiers. At the same time, Illinois troops in northeastern Missouri were doing similarly. By January 1862, the First Kansas Colored Infantry regiment had received its commission, the first black regiment of the war. That summer, senator and quasi-general James H. Lane was openly enlisting emancipated Missouri slaves into federal service, interpreting liberally Congress's authorization to Lincoln "to employ as many persons of African descent as he may deem necessary and proper for the suppression of this rebellion" and even more liberally his own recruiting instructions. Lane boasted that he had enlisted two full black regiments of "Zouaves d'Afrique" before the president had finished drafting his own emancipation proclamation. They had fought against white Missourians before any others took the field. By the end of 1863, more than eighty-three hundred black Missourians—nearly two-fifths of its black men of military age—had joined the federal army.[15]

14. Thomas T. Gantt to William S. Harney, May 14, 1861 (first and second quotes), and Harney to Gantt, May 14, 1861 (third quote), both in Ira Berlin et al., eds., *Freedom: A Documentary History of Emancipation, 1861–1867,* ser. 1, vol. 1, 413–14.

15. Parrish, *History of Missouri,* 99–101; H. S. Lipscomb to W. S. Harney, August 9, 1861, in Berlin et al., eds., *Freedom,* ser. 1, vol. 1, 414–15; Fellman, *Inside War,* 66; Albert Castel, *A Frontier State at War: Kansas, 1861–1865,* 90–91 (first quote), 92–94; C. P. Buckingham to James H. Lane, July 22, 1862, *ORR,* ser. 3, pt. 2, 959; Lane to Edwin M. Stanton, August 5, 1862, ibid., 294–95, 312–14; Stanton to Lane, August 23, 1862, ibid., 444–45; Shelby Foote, *The Civil War—A Narrative: Fort Sumter to*

The issue of emancipation and the federal army's role in the process opened new fissures in Missouri's fractured political landscape. While loyal Missouri slaveholders initially sat on their hands when federal troops confiscated the property of disloyal residents, including slaves, they grew increasingly uncomfortable with the U.S. Army's penchant for employing fugitive slaves in their midst. When, in March 1862, Congress prohibited Union soldiers from returning fugitive slaves to their masters, encouraging antislavery officers and soldiers to protect slaves from their pursuers, Missouri's slave owners saw the presence of the federal army (as well as the avowed antislavery persuasion of virtually all of its commanders, beginning with Frémont) as a harbinger of widespread emancipation. Gen. Samuel R. Curtis, who took command in Missouri in the fall of 1862, only confirmed such suspicions when he instructed provost marshals to grant certificates of freedom to all slaves entitled to freedom under the Second Confiscation Act. Union officers offered emancipation to slaves who had escaped from disloyal masters, a phenomenon that quickly provided slaves with incentive for flight regardless of their masters' political conviction. In fact, slaves who escaped to Union lines frequently portrayed their masters as disloyal, causing many slave owners considerable trouble with local assessment boards as well as costing them the chance to retrieve their bondpeople if they were not inclined to take the oath.[16]

Despite Missouri's exclusion from Lincoln's Emancipation Proclamation, enlistment of black troops signaled the disintegration of slavery in Missouri, an inevitability not lost on the state's slaveholders. One angry Missourian condemned the enlistment as a "d-mb-d abolition Scheme to steal negroes," while another from Franklin County, more circumspect, decried enlistment as "Evil by civil process." The latter, "a loyal man faithful to the Union and the constitution of the U. States," who, as of June 1863, retained a portion of his slaves, went on to plead with the president that "I wish my rights to be protected in an open & substantial manner, that the people may see that there is property in being a loyal man, extending even to the protection of his property. I wish it to be effectual[.]" The Union men of Lexington were more direct: "The President's Proclamation of 1st Jany '63 does not embrace Missouri. Why should the radicals enforce it here—at the point of the bayonet? This is grievous, a crying evil and calls loudly for redress—. . . We ask a repeal of this abolition order; this military license to steal our negroes." Neither redress nor repeal would come, though a gradual abolition

Perryville, 558 (second quote); Dudley T. Cornish, *The Sable Arm: Negro Troops in the Union Army, 1861–1865*, 59, 66, 78; Berlin et al., eds., *Freedom*, ser. 1, vol. 2, 557.

16. Berlin, et al., eds., *Freedom*, ser. 1, vol. 1, 399–404; ser. 1, vol. 2, 553–58; Parrish, *History of Missouri*, 87–97.

plan proposed by the moderate provisional governor, Hamilton R. Gamble, passed in the summer of 1863. When in 1864 Missouri's Radical Unionists gained control of the state leadership (aided by the disfranchisement of those who would not take the test oath), and dominated the state convention that met in January 1865, the fate of this slaveholders' once-democracy was set. On January 11, Governor Thomas C. Fletcher signed the immediate emancipation act that the convention had passed with only four dissenting votes and which overturned an 1863 state enactment that set the date of universal emancipation for July 4, 1870.[17]

Rather than accept the inevitability of black liberation, many white Missourians resisted the revolutionary social change with fear and anger. "Our wives and daughters are panic stricken," wrote one Lafayette County resident, "and a reign of terror as black as hell itself envelops our county." Many who had once believed that their state's stand for the Union would protect the peculiar institution within its borders now unleashed their fury by joining in the partisan warfare that exploded with the coming of emancipation. The provost marshal at Lexington had captured the contagion of Missourians' bitterness over emancipation when he wrote in August 1863, "The Negro in this County is the all 'inspiring theme' with many of the people. It is not the 'Rebellion, the Bushwhackers or the Rebel Sympathisers['] in Mo. but the Negro is the source of all our trouble, and the great question that divides the people Hundreds of men who were it not for the negro would be union men are now very doubtful. Many of them make the preservation of the institution of slavery a 'condition predicent' [*sic*] to the Union thereby effectually identifying their interests with the rebellion." Indeed, one researcher has found that guerrillas in western Missouri were the sons of farmers who were twice or three times more likely to have owned property—including slaves—than the average Missourian, an indication of the centrality of slavery in the conflict as a whole. Perhaps more important, Union troops and loyalist citizens were not their only target; former and current slaves bore the brunt of this reign of terror. One such bushwhacker claimed that he had been "instigated by the late slave owners to hang and shoot every negro he can find absent from the old plantation." This extension of violence to black and Unionist Missourians reflects more than a broadening of the war's scope; symbolically, rural Missourians had linked slavery's death with

---

17. W. A. Pollion to Dr. Martine, December 28, 1863, in Berlin et al., eds., *Freedom*, ser. 1, vol. 1, 476–79 (first quote); Charles Jones to His Excellency Abraham Lincoln, March 24, 1863, in ibid., 450–53 (second and third quotes); John F. Ryland et al. to His Excellency Governor Gamble, June 4, 1863, in ibid., 457–58 (fourth quote); Parrish, *History of Missouri*, 102–18; Parrish, "Reconstruction Politics in Missouri," 1–8; William E. Parrish, *Missouri under Radical Rule, 1865–1870*, 3–4, 14–19.

the tyranny of the federal government and lashed out at the progenitor and the progeny. Statutory emancipation did little to stem either the violence or the resultant resentment. As a Union general commanding the Boon's Lick region wrote from his vantage in March 1865: "Slavery dies hard. I hear its expiring agonies and witness its contortions in death in every quarter of my district. In Boone, Howard, Randolph, and Callaway the emancipation ordinance has caused disruption of society equal to anything I saw in Arkansas or Mississippi in the year 1863."[18]

Slavery indeed died hard in Missouri, but not simply because of the loss of property or even because of the specter of black freedom. In the minds of many white Missourians, black liberation and emancipation served as the symbolic culmination of a two-decade-long crusade by an increasingly despotic federal government to strip the state's citizens of their individual rights. Though Radicals in the state had effected slavery's constitutional death, many slaveholders—galvanized by the unholy trinity of confiscation, enlistment, and emancipation—saw them and the provisional government as little more than agents of an abolitionist government in Washington. The 1865 state constitution, enacted by Radicals, included such proscriptions as the ironclad oath for voting, officeholding, jurors, lawyers, preachers, teachers, and corporation officials and trustees, as well as ousting all of the state judiciary, from the supreme court to the local level, replacing them with Radical appointments. In November of 1865, William B. Napton, one of those justices removed by the "Ousting Ordinance" for refusing to take the oath, railed against the

> reign of radical absolutism [that] promises to be indefinitely protracted. . . . The whole machinery of government is in the hands of the Radical party, and although destitute of any talented leaders, they have so completely taken possession of all the avenues of power that without some revolutionary effort all attempts to dislodge them will be fruitless. . . . Constitutional liberty, such as we once thought to be indispensible to American life, has ceased to be regarded as among the practicable desiderata of citizenship. We resemble the French after the Revolution and its attendants and consequents had worried them for twenty or thirty years, and would hail with satisfaction the absolutism of some respectable leader—but none such seems destined to appear here for many years to come and the hydra headed monster yet has sway—King Numbers—that is, at the north, where all the real power of the government is

18. Fellman, *Inside War*, 70 (first quote); H. B. Johnson to General, August 14, 1863, in Berlin et al., eds., *Freedom*, ser. 1, vol. 2, 577–78 (second quote), 558–61, 562 (third quote); Don Bowen, "Guerrilla Warfare in Western Missouri, 1862–1865: Historical Extensions of the Relative Deprivation Hypothesis," 30–51; Michael Fellman, "Emancipation in Missouri," 50–56; Clinton B. Fisk to James E. Yeatman, March 25, 1865, *ORR*, ser. 1, pt. 48, 1257 (fourth quote).

now fixed and fixed forever. The South and West are mere outlying provinces, governed directly and indirectly at Washington.[19]

Missouri's version of the nation's "Negro question" would cast even longer shadows, fracturing the morass that was the state's postwar politics almost beyond that of Benton's day. While the harsh Radical state constitution (the state's politicos in 1866 abandoned any pretense of party designations, a long legacy in Missouri, in favor of ideological labels) had forced fissures in the faction's granite, outright ruptures occurred once its "Charcoal" leaders moved beyond emancipation and began the call for "freedom and franchise," meaning black suffrage, leading many to assume they stood for complete citizenship for the state's freedpeople. "Claybank" conservatives, grown solid with federal violation of the state's neutrality and wartime interdiction, now found strength from crossover former Radicals (and wartime Republicans) such as Frank Blair who supported the Thirteenth Amendment but stridently opposed the Fourteenth. Once Lincoln's stalwart in the state, Blair now condemned Missouri's Radicals for building a faction based upon the "malignant passions . . . [of] exasperation, retaliation, and revenge." The 1868 elections proved the Radicals' zenith; their hold on Missouri politics was tenuous—even in the state's cities—as Conservatives rallied to the defense of the beleaguered president, Andrew Johnson, who took his case against the Radical Republican Congress's amendment for black equality to the people. Self-styled "Liberal Republicans" first challenged the Radical "Jacobins" for factional dominance, then bolted in 1870, eliminating any chance for unified opposition necessary to hold off the growing Conservative ranks. By 1872, the Liberal movement in Missouri had collapsed completely; Conservative ascendance beckoned.[20]

19. Parrish, Jones, and Christensen, *Missouri,* 191 (first quote); Napton Diary, folder 4, 316–17, MHS (second quote); Parrish, *Frank Blair,* 232–33. Napton took the oath in 1865 and eventually regained his seat, but only with the following attachment: "I take this oath, with the accompanying declaration, that I am not to be understood as denying or disavowing any opinions or sympathies expressed or entertained, in reference to the past action of the federal or state governments, which opinions and sympathies I do not regard as having anything to do with one's allegiance or loyalty, and I protest against the validity of all that part of the oath which related to *past acts* as conflicting with the Constitution of the United States and the fundamental principles of all our state governments." See Napton Diary, folder 4, 318, MHS; Parrish, *Missouri under Radical Rule,* 59–61.

20. C. Vann Woodward, *Reunion and Reaction: The Compromise of 1877 and the End of Reconstruction,* 245; H. B. Johnson to General, August 14, 1863, in Berlin et al., eds., *Freedom,* ser. 1, vol. 2, 577–78 (first quote); Parrish, *History of Missouri,* 93 (second and fourth quotes), 234–57, 258–59 (sixth quote, p. 258); Peterson, *Freedom and Franchise,* 130–34 (third quote, p. 130), 135–44 (seventh quote, p. 135), 226–31; *Appendix to the Congressional Globe,* 38th Cong., 1st Sess., 48–49 (fifth quote); Parrish, *Frank Blair,* 231–45; Parrish, *Missouri under Radical Rule,* 288–326.

While power, as ever, proved the ultimate source of the state's political maelstrom, Missourians' new mantra of white supremacy merely reshaped what was once a commitment to the state's social good, slavery. In the 1870s and 1880s, Missourians completed an ideological transformation that now spanned three decades, to which Claib Jackson had given his life initiating and shepherding. Not so much a "redemption"—the term former slave-state residents forced to suffer Reconstruction measures used to describe their Democratic restoration—as a reformation, the Missouri populace now created a worldview in which race, region, and above all wartime allegiance defined their sense of identity. As early as 1870, St. Louis minister William M. Leftwich charged angrily in his *Martyrdom in Missouri,* a "true history of the war," that because of the federal government's "recklessness of life and wantonness of destruction, and in all its most shameless, and revolting, and nameless crimes perpetrated upon the unoffending, the innocent and the helpless, the non-combatant population of Missouri has suffered more than any other class of people in any State." His message reached Missourians, deepening their psychological reformation of the recent conflict. Union general, Liberal Republican, and German outsider Carl Schurz's meteoric appearance on the state's splintered political stage only hastened this Conservative purgation, one that Missouri bushwhacker Jim Jackson (widely linked to Claib Jackson) had forecast, if inelegantly, just after the state's vote for emancipation as the war hastened to its bitter close. "[I]f you dont make dam negroes leve there ride away," he scrawled to a farmer in Ralls County, " i will hadn [hang] the last negro on the plase and you will fair wors for we cant stand the dutch and negroes both." Though Jackson ultimately received the same summary justice that he offered Missouri's freedpeople, his spirit—as well as his prophecy—would haunt Missouri's postwar world.[21]

THROUGH THE HOT summer of 1875, yet another state constitutional convention met in Jefferson City, this time to "wipe from the statute books that 'sum of all villianies' the Draconian Code, which for studied malignity and concentrated malice has no parallel in the history of the human race," as one St. Louis Democrat vowed. The composition of the sixty-eight-

21. W[illiam] M. Leftwich, *Martyrdom in Missouri: A History of Religious Proscription, the Seizure of Churches, and the Persecution of Ministers of the Gospel, in the State of Missouri during the Late Civil War, and under the "Test Oath" of the New Constitution,* 131–32 (first and second quotes); Fellman, "Emancipation in Missouri," 50 (third quote); Parrish, *History of Missouri,* 248–50; Parrish, *Missouri under Radical Rule,* 228–33, 250–67, 340n3. Jim Jackson and one of his men were captured in Pike County while trying to leave Missouri in June 1865. Despite having received parole under President Johnson's amnesty, he was executed after a hasty trial for robbery and murder. See *Missouri Statesman,* June 23, 29, 1865.

man body told its own story. All but eight were Conservative Democrats, rendering inert the handful of Republicans. Three-fourths of the group had been born in what were then slave states, twenty-four in Kentucky alone. More than half of those present had either served—whether militarily or civilly—or supported the Confederacy. The chairman was Waldo P. Johnson, who had lost his seat in the U.S. Senate in 1862 for joining the Confederacy after Jayhawker senator James H. Lane had destroyed his home in Osceola the previous fall. Johnson had served first in the Confederate army as a lieutenant colonel under Sterling Price, then as senator from Missouri in the Confederate Congress. The group quickly overturned the proscriptive provisions of the 1865 Radical constitution and then passed measures making it difficult for any government, whether federal or state, to restrict its citizens' individual rights, including the privilege of suspending the writ of habeas corpus, tightening definitions of treasonable activity, and prohibiting the state government from confiscating the property of those so convicted. Missouri's conservative reformation was complete.[22]

Neither the new Missouri constitution nor the parity enjoyed by former rebels in the convention's delegation was an aberration. The conservative renaissance had stirred a phoenix, one that now spread wings broader and fuller than those of its previous, feeble incarnation. Out of the anger and betrayal of the wartime experience, a Confederate memory was emerging, signaled initially by the welcome, even celebration, of former Confederates returning to Missouri. In the war's immediate aftermath, a host of the state's Confederate leaders—including Generals Sterling Price, Jo Shelby, and Daniel M. Frost, as well as quasi-Governor Thomas Caute Reynolds and Senator (both Confederate and Union) and former Governor Trusten Polk, had left the country for Mexico, where under French aegis they sought to replicate the ruling race of southern planters of which they were never a part. Most were back in the state within a few years, along with former Senator David Rice Atchison, engaging in business, farming, or practicing law. In 1875, former Confederate President Jefferson Davis toured the state, receiving in Atchison's estimation a "cordial reception everywhere in Missouri . . . ; the homage paid him is to virtue and great principles; he is the representative of the lost cause and all that it involved."[23]

22. *Jefferson City People's Tribune,* November 23, 1870, quoted in Peterson, *Freedom and Franchise,* 189; Lawrence O. Christensen and Gary R. Kremer, *A History of Missouri—Volume IV: 1875–1919,* 1–3; Parrish, *History of Missouri,* 43*n*, 48, 290–92; Jay Monaghan, *Civil War on the Western Border, 1854–1865,* 196.

23. Shalhope, *Sterling Price,* 281–89; Carl Coke Rister, "Carlota: A Confederate Colony in Mexico," 33–50; Robert E. Miller, "Daniel Marsh Frost, C.S.A.," 394–97; Parrish, *David Rice Atchison,* 222–24 (quote); William E. Parrish, "Jefferson Davis Comes to Missouri," 344–56.

Inverting Carl von Clausewitz's famous dictum, Missourians in the 1870s employed politics as another means to achieve war goals. M. Jeff Thompson, immortalized as the Confederacy's "Swamp Fox" in this southern creationism, reflected this recognition of the restorative power of politics when he wrote to controversial Louisville editor George D. Prentice in 1867, "I am compelled to obey the laws, and being an elector simply gives me an opportunity to make the laws more favorable—then will confidence be restored, and plenty abound once more." While most Radicals quickly retired to political obscurity, retaining strength in but a few Missouri counties, former Confederates swept into state offices, including Thomas Caute Reynolds, who served in the state legislature. In 1875, the Missouri legislature elected Francis M. Cockrell, a former Confederate general, to replace the despised Carl Schurz in the U.S. Senate. Four years later, George G. Vest, who had represented the state in both houses of the Confederate Congress, joined him there. Cockrell served three decades in the Senate; Vest stayed nearly a quarter century. The delineations of state politics based upon former wartime allegiances—and, more important, the power of the former Confederates on the political landscape—caused Thomas Reynolds to write to Jefferson Davis in 1880 of "my experience among some Missouri politicians of their inclination to 'remember to forget' matters which may affect their present aspirations." The political reversions had become so pronounced by 1883 that the editor of the *St. Joseph Herald* remarked, "Ever since the Democrats have been in power in the State there has been a division of offices by common consent between what is known as the Union element and the Confederate element. . . . Next year [Jo] Shelby proposes that the Confederates shall also have the Governorship, and is therefore committed to Gen. Marmaduke." The rebel Shelby got his wish; in 1884, less than two decades after the war's conclusion, John Sappington Marmaduke, the former Confederate general, son of the state's former governor and nephew of its celebrated rebel governor, assumed the reins of power. His inauguration completed the Sappington-Marmaduke-Jackson triumvirate as it signaled a Confederate apotheosis.[24]

Or very nearly so. Missourians quickly broadened their Confederate ascendance from the political realm to the psychological. As early as 1870, Missouri communities began constructing Confederate memorials to their Lost Cause

---

24. Kirkpatrick, "Missouri's Confederate Capital," 52–53; Monaghan, *Civil War on the Western Border,* 185 (first quote); M. Jeff Thompson to George D. Prentice, June 16, 1867, Meriwether Jeff Thompson Papers, Mss. 1030, folder 1, SHSM (second quote); Thomas C. Reynolds to Jefferson Davis, November 13, 1880, Thomas C. Reynolds Papers, MHS (third quote); Parrish, *Missouri under Radical Rule,* 324–25; Christensen and Kremer, *History of Missouri,* 16–17 (fourth quote).

and their fallen loved ones. Organizations such as the United Daughters of the Confederacy and Sons of Confederate Veterans, soon demigods in the politics of memory, erected these monuments in Kansas City, St. Louis, Jefferson City, Springfield, and St. Joseph, as well as in small towns such as Lone Jack, Independence, Keytesville, Warrensburg, Liberty, and Lexington. In Higginsville, former Confederates such as Daniel M. Frost plied the state and private benefactors to establish a Confederate Veterans Home, as well as an accompanying Veterans Cemetery. Such memorials served not just to honor the valiant dead but also as counterweight to charges of these soldiers' unpatriotic and traitorous behavior. Indeed, Missourians—like their counterparts in other border states—sought to preserve the memory of those who sacrificed their lives repelling federal invaders from their loyal states. One can see such defiance nowhere better than in Palmyra, where a granite obelisk on the courthouse lawn stood silent vigil, a reminder of the atrocity the community had suffered at the hands of federal troops.[25]

Such construction was more than physical. The act of memorialization bound Missourians with the other Confederate states, not only in the replication of such activities, as was occurring throughout the South, but also by entwining their shared experience of war. Yet Missouri's version of the conflict was different than that of most of the Confederate states, thus the prism of its residents' memory tilted slightly. Without the large pool of army veterans around which to rally, as well as a dearth of traditional military engagements and battle sites to commemorate, Missourians celebrated the state's singular paramilitary past, one that conjured, in one historian's words, "the legend of the noble guerrilla." As the historian David Thelen has written so well of this syndrome in Missouri:

> There are times and places where defenders of traditional values have felt so desperate in the face of onrushing change that they have placed their hope for deliverance not in traditional leaders, such as priests and politicians, but in men who fearlessly attacked the symbols of the new order while upholding the old. Regarded as criminals by the promoters of change and their law, these social bandits were nurtured and shielded by people who shared their values. Since the bandits seemed capable of striking at will and made their victims look ridiculous and ineffectual, their supporters made them into the object of heroic legends that confirmed the power of tradition.[26]

25. Foster, *Ghosts of the Confederacy,* 127–44; Ralph W. Widener, *Confederate Monuments: Enduring Symbols of the South and the War Between the States,* 132–36; Stephen Davis, "Empty Eyes, Marble Hands: The Confederate Monument and the South," 2–8, 16–19; Miller, "Daniel Marsh Frost," 398. My thanks to Professor Fitz Brundage for pointing me to sources on Confederate monuments.

26. Fellman, *Inside War,* 247–63 (first quote, p. 247); Thelen, *Paths of Resistance,* 70–71 (second quote, p. 70).

More than any other state, Missouri became synonymous with partisan raids and raiders, an image that began before the war's end and which it carried far beyond the immediate region. So prevalent was this perception that Senator Carl Schurz complained about being taunted in his brief stint in Washington of representing "the Robber State." The mystique of these "social bandits"—born in wartime and in many cases perpetuated by their postwar careers as bank and train robbers—far eclipsed the populace's recognition of their murderous deeds during and after the war. Bill Anderson, the Younger brothers (Cole, Bob, John, and James), William Quantrill, Frank James and, above all others, his brother Jesse James, became in the public's eyes Robin Hoods—men of honor who had defended their homes, their women's virtue, and their neighbors' liberty from undemocratic invaders—for their valiant resistance to federal tyranny and, for some, their heroic deliverance from postwar symbols of the new order, namely railroads and banks. The image was clearly popular among Missourians soon after the war; one wartime guerrilla, Samuel Hildebrand, published his autobiography in 1870 under his self-styled cognomen, "the unconquerable Rob Roy of America."[27]

The Confederate mystique, once established, capped a process that had spanned decades. Yet Missouri's transformation was not yet complete, for it gradually assumed a shape that Missourians had until the postwar years limited to the political realm. Residents of this former slave state now articulated a southern identity—itself a political entity in that it derived from Missourians' frustration with government—that transcended the immediate celebration of a Confederate heritage or even a Lost Cause. Perhaps the most lasting symbol of Missouri's Confederate heritage—and which at the same time served as a bridge to the adoption of southern identity in at least one portion of the state—was the adoption of the term "Little Dixie" as a moniker for the Boon's Lick, the former slaveholding center of the state. Unknown before and during the war itself, the origin of "Little Dixie" approximated former Confederate John Sappington Marmaduke's ascendance to governor. A Kansas City newspaperman in 1941 traced the term to the congressional candidacy of John B. Hale, who popularized it as a description for the central river counties while campaigning in the Second Congressional District in 1887. In a speech at Paris, Hale reputedly referred to the solid Democratic counties as the "Little Dixie of Missouri Democracy," regaling its residents for their solid allegiance to the party that spanned the nineteenth and much of the twentieth centuries. One study found that all but two of the traditional

27. Thelen, *Paths of Resistance*, 70–77 (first and second quotes, p. 70); Fellman, *Inside War*, 247–63; Nagel, *Missouri*, 133–35; Christensen and Kremer, *History of Missouri*, 16; Hildebrand, *Autobiography*.

Boon's Lick counties voted solidly Democratic between 1872 and 1952. Today's visitors will see road signs and billboards delineating Little Dixie as they speed through the area on Interstate 70; indeed, in 1957 the state officially designated a wildlife area in the region by the same name. The common sobriquet reflects more than past and current voting trends; it stands as a distorted symbol of what Missourians believed they were culturally, yet never were, and what they were never politically, yet would not now believe.[28]

For Missourians, southern identity grew from anger, resentment, and from a sense of betrayal at the hands of the federal government they had long distrusted, but to which many maintained steadfast allegiance until despots' heels trod on their once-democratic shore. In that sense, then, southern identity for Missourians was western identity once removed, a commitment to liberty sown in the endless, beckoning soil of the great West, nurtured by the proliferation of slavery and its attendant societal benefits, steeped by the growing free-soil movement and the northern invasion of the West, hardened by the crime that abolitionist Yankees (with federal imprimatur) committed in Kansas, and cemented by the war that the federal government and antislavery warriors brought into their midst despite their continued, if compromised, loyalty to that government and the Union itself. Missouri's southern identity, then, was in essence born of an ideology of defiance, itself the product of a political process through which the federal government forced integration at the point of a bayonet. Indeed, in one of his short stories—and after an admittedly brief personal introduction to the state's war—Missouri's most famous nineteenth-century observer, Samuel Clemens, recounted his understanding of the "natural" transition of the state's rural populace to the intrusion of war, as well as his own construction of regional identity in 1885, from something western to something southern:

> Out West there was a good deal of confusion in men's minds during the first months of the great trouble—a good deal of unsettledness, of leaning first this way, then that, then the other way. It was hard for us to get our bearings. . . . Our State was invaded by the Union forces. . . . There were scores of little camps scattered over Missouri . . . composed of young men who had been born and reared to a sturdy independence, and who did not know what it meant to be ordered around by Tom, Dick, and Harry, whom they had known familiarly all their lives, in the village or on the farm. . . . [T]his same thing was happening all over the South.

28. *Kansas City Times,* December 5, 1941, cited in Daniel Joseph Conoyer, "Missouri's Little Dixie: A Geographical Delineation," 1–3, 224–314 passim; Crisler, "Missouri's Little Dixie," 130–39; John H. Fenton, *Politics in the Border States,* 156–57; Albert E. Twombly, *Little Dixie,* passim. Conoyer concludes after but a two-week field observation that little remained in "Little Dixie" in 1971 of what he assumed was a once-southern cultural heritage. He delimited the region with such evidence as surnames, speech patterns, food preferences, farm acreage, and agricultural products.

Though no allegory, the story offers its readers a clear metaphor. In Clemens's own mind, and in the space of but one of Mark Twain's paragraphs, war had transformed what was once the West into the South.[29]

Couched in the defense of liberty, the lodestar for this passage from western to southern identity was the assault upon and ultimate destruction of slavery. While the war indeed accomplished that fact, its legacy claimed far more. The historian William Barney has written that "the greatest irony of the war" was the fact that "the North won the battles but the South dictated the peace terms." In Missouri, as in other former slave states, peace would come only with redemption, or as the historian Michael Fellman has written similarly and appropriately of the state's postwar epiphany, "On the symbolic front, the southern cause was less clearly the loser." While the former seceded states undertook the process of constructing "the frontier the Yankee created," many displaced Missourians—marginalized in the North, the South, and now even the West—forged a new place in the grim new world. Those who had once conflated liberty, democracy, and slavery now linked themselves and their future to the past of a free and brave yet wronged slaveholding nation whose cause, though defeated, had been just. As yet another historian has written of the embittered historical consciousness of postwar southerners as a whole, Missourians invoked "a consciousness of change, of suspension between two worlds, a double focus looking both backward and forward." Yet the North's denial of their middle heritage caused Missourians to take one last mythological leap; rather than admit their western paradise lost, Missourians denied that it had ever existed, and thus that they had ever been part of it. Almost as northerners had expected, even decreed, these rebels had become southerners. As late as 1998, at least one nondenominational church in the Missouri Ozarks has emblazoned on its crest the battle flag of the Confederacy.[30]

For a time, it appeared that Claiborne Jackson would hold no place in the new order. Only in the fall of 1871 did Jackson family members exhume their parents' remains from their separate resting places in Arkansas

29. Eugen Weber, *Peasants into Frenchmen: The Modernization of Rural France, 1870–1914,* 485–96; Mark Twain, "The Private History of a Campaign that Failed," *Century Magazine* (1885), in Lawrence Teacher, ed., *The Unabridged Mark Twain,* vol. 1, 1193, 1202 (quotes).

30. William L. Barney, *Flawed Victory: A New Perspective on the Civil War,* 194 (first quote); Fellman, *Inside War,* 247 (second quote); Cash, *Mind of the South,* 105 (third quote); John Shelton Reed, *Southerners: The Social Psychology of Sectionalism,* 21–26 and passim; George B. Tindall, "Mythology: A New Frontier in Southern History," in Frank E. Vandiver, ed., *The Idea of the South: Pursuit of a Central Theme,* 12 (fourth quote); *Kansas City Star,* April 3, 1998.

and Texas and have them returned to Missouri. They interred them in the Sappington cemetery on the estate of William S. Jackson, once an outlaw, now the clerk of the Saline County Court. His father's home, Fox Castle, no longer stood sentry over the quiet family cemetery; it had burned to the ground the previous April. The tragedy was symbolic; unable to pay the $5,089.20 in back taxes he owed on the land, Will would soon relinquish the estate to his uncle, William B. Sappington, who lived in "damned fool" splendor (as his father once had said) a half mile away and who held the land in a deed of trust. In a cemetery without his name and in soil that was only briefly his, Claib Jackson was again mere vassal of the Sappington fief. In memorial, the Jackson heirs erected a stately, twin-pillared monument, made in Boonville, over their parents' shared grave, inscribing it with the biblical "Gather my Saints together unto me." Derived from the Bible's fiftieth psalm, the completed verse proclaimed righteousness for those who covenanted with God through sacrifice, and retribution for the wicked.[31]

The epitaph offered more than simple memorial for a fallen combatant; it prophesied a resurrection writ large. Missouri's saints were indeed gathering, canonizing in dim memory an unlikely martyr once they had adopted their newfound southern identity. In 1926, three score years after the end of the war, the *Columbia Missourian* proclaimed hopefully that among the Confederate images to be carved into the granite face of Georgia's Stone Mountain, the zenith of Lost Cause memorials in the New South, would be that of Claiborne Fox Jackson. This paladin of southern courage, the elected governor of a neutral slave state who suffered exile in resisting the Yankee invasion and death in leading his state into the Confederacy and thus into the South, would serve a permanent symbol of resistance and sacrifice to all who sought the new southern mythology. Had this latest personification of

31. E. D. Pearson to W. B. Sappington, January 10, 1872, John S. Sappington Papers, Mss. 1027, box 3, folder 79, SHSM; *Jefferson City People's Tribune,* February 7, 1872; William S. Jackson file, United Daughters of the Confederacy, Missouri Records, Mss. 3188, folder 150, SHSM (first quote); *Missouri Statesman,* April 21, 1871; August 6, 1880 (second quote); J. C. Sappington to Charles Van Ravenswaay, January 20, 1937, and Conversation with the McMahan sisters of Arrow Rock, November 16, 1937, both in Charles Van Ravenswaay Collection, Mss. 2668, folder 7, SHSM; William S. Jackson to W. B. Sappington, February 16, 1873, John S. Sappington Papers, Mss. 1027, box 3, folder 81, SHSM; Inventory of Estate of William S. Jackson, August 4, 1880, and Lucy V. Jackson to Probate Court, May 1883, both in Saline County Probate Records, Case no. CE-1217, microfilm reel C8245, MSA. After Will Jackson's death his widow, Lucy, with permission of the property's owner, William B. Sappington, erected a small log cabin on the former Sappington/Jackson estate near the cemetery and named it "Fox Castle." The cabin, used largely as a summer dwelling, has incorrectly been cited as having been erected by Eliza Jackson, Claiborne's widow.

the "Eternal Claib" come to pass, it would well have been the first accurate depiction of the opaque figure once known widely as "the Fox." Only in defiant, mythical relief would either this man of the West or his worlds—the one in which he lived and the one he left behind—carve a place in the South.[32]

32. *Columbia Missourian*, February 10, 1926; Gaston, *New South Creed*, 244–46 and passim.

BIBLIOGRAPHY

PRIMARY SOURCES

Manuscript Collections

Duke University, Special Collections, William R. Perkins Library, Durham, North Carolina
    Jefferson Davis Letters
    Missouri Volunteer Militia Papers, 1860–1865
    M. J. Solomons Scrapbook, 1861–1863
Henry E. Huntington Library and Art Gallery, San Marino, California
    EG Box 30
Indiana Historical Society Library, Indianapolis
    John Dowling Papers, Mss. M87
    V. W. Hale Personal File, Mss. SC669
Kansas State Historical Society, Topeka
    Packard Family Collection
Kentucky Department of Libraries and Archives, Frankfort
    Fleming County [Kentucky] Tax Assessment Books, 1822, 1824–1829, 1831, 1833–1834, 1837–1841, microfilm reel 007970
    Fleming County [Kentucky] Will Books, General Index, 1798–1962, microfilm reel 344037
    Mason County [Kentucky] Tax Assessment Books, 1790–1797, 1799–1809, microfilm reel 008140
Library of Congress, Washington, D.C.
    Thomas Caute Reynolds Papers. 1 microfilm reel.
Missouri Historical Society, St. Louis, Missouri
    Alphabetical Files, Glascock Family
    Badger Collection
    Banking and Currency
    Bates Family Papers
    Blow Family Papers
    James O. Broadhead Papers
    Broadsides-Horses
    Camp Jackson Papers
    Circulars
    Civil War Collection
    Samuel B. Gardner Diary

Charles Gibson Papers
Julius J. Goldberg Collection
Willard P. Hall Papers
Mrs. Jesse P. Henry Papers
Howard County Papers
William Carr Lane Papers
Mesker Collection
Missouri Militia Collection
William B. Napton Papers
Thomas Reynolds Papers
Thomas C. Reynolds Papers
St. Louis History Papers
Saline County Papers
Sappington Family Papers
Sibley Papers
General George R. Smith Papers
John F. Snyder Collection
Sublette Papers
George R. Taylor Collection
Missouri State Archives, Jefferson City, Missouri
Capitol Fire Documents, 1806–1957, Capitol Fire Documents, 1806–
1957, 92 vols., 242 microfilm reels [microfilm reels CFD-118, 183–
87]
Circuit Court Cases, Howard and Saline Counties
Deed Records, Saline County, Missouri, microfilm reels C6227–36;
Howard County, Missouri, microfilm reels C2786–95
Governors' Papers, Record Group 3: John C. Edwards Papers, Claiborne
Fox Jackson Papers, Hancock Jackson Papers, Sterling Price Papers,
Thomas Reynolds Papers
Howard County [Missouri] Tax Lists, vols. 1–2 (1816–1841), microfilm
reel S244
Saline County [Missouri] Marriages, vol. A (1835–1851), microfilm reel
C6266
Saline County [Missouri] Wills, Book B, microfilm reel C11591
National Archives, Washington, D.C., and Kansas City, Missouri
Second U.S. Census, 1800, Population Schedule, Fleming County, Ken-
tucky
Third U.S. Census, 1810, Population Schedule, Fleming County, Ken-
tucky
Fourth U.S. Census, 1820, Population Schedule, Fleming County, Ken-
tucky; Davidson County, Tennessee
Fifth U.S. Census, 1830, Population Schedule, Fleming County, Ken-

tucky; Boone, Callaway, Chariton, Clay, Cooper, Howard, Lafayette, and Saline Counties, Missouri

Sixth U.S. Census, 1840, Population Schedule, Boone, Callaway, Chariton, Clay, Cooper, Howard, Lafayette, and Saline Counties, Missouri

Seventh U.S. Census, 1850, Agriculture Schedule, Howard County, Missouri; Population Schedule, Boone, Callaway, Chariton, Clay, Cooper, Howard, Lafayette, Platte, and Saline Counties, Missouri; Slave Schedule, Howard, Platte, St. Louis, and Saline Counties, Missouri

Eighth U.S. Census, 1860, Agricultural Schedule, Saline County, Missouri; Population Schedule, Clinton, Howard, Marion, and Pettis Counties, Missouri; Slave Schedule, Clinton, Howard, St. Louis, and Saline Counties, Missouri

Index, Record Group 153: Records of the Office of the Judge Advocate General (Army), Register of the Records of the Proceedings of the U.S. Army General Courts-Martial, 1809–1890, M1105, 8 microfilm reels.

University of Kentucky, Special Collections and Archives, Margaret I. King Library, Lexington, Kentucky

Cooper-Phillips Family Papers, Mss. 66M37

Hathaway Papers, microfilm file M-20

University of Missouri, Western Historical Manuscripts Collection, Joint Collection—State Historical Society of Missouri/University of Missouri, Ellis Library, Columbia

Lisbon Applegate Collection, Mss. 996

Arrow Rock Tavern Board Papers, 1826–1913, Mss. 3087

David Rice Atchison Papers, Mss. 71

Bingham Family Papers, Mss. 998

William Bishop Papers, Mss. 3894

William C. Boon Letter, Mss. 2209

William C. Breckenridge Papers, Mss. 1036. 2 microfilm reels.

Bernard F. Dickmann Papers, Mss. 3403

Charles D. Drake Autobiography, Mss. 1003

Draper-McClurg Family Papers, Mss. 3069

John Allen Gano Family Papers, Mss. 65

Sarah Guitar Papers, Mss. 3563

Isaac Hockaday Letters, Mss. 2728

Ira B. Hyde Papers, Mss. 2406

Claiborne Fox Jackson File, Mss. 2447

Claiborne Fox Jackson Letters, Mss. 1789–1789

Lucy Wortham James Collection, Mss. 1

Lilian Kingsbury Collection, Mss. 3724

Abiel Leonard Collection, Mss. 1013

John D. McKown Papers, Mss. 2335

Meredith Miles Marmaduke Papers, Mss. 1021

Miscellaneous Manuscripts, Mss. 1879

Missouri Confederate Archives, 1861, Mss. 2722

Missouri/Ste. Genevieve Archives, Mss. 3636

Bryan Obear Collection, Mss. 1387

William M. Paxton Papers, Mss. 1025

George Pohlman Collection, Mss. 3476

A. W. Reese, Recollections of the Civil War, 1870, Mss. 3627. 2 microfilm reels.

Herbert F. Rice Papers, Mss. 2903

James S. Rollins Papers, Mss. 1026

John Sappington Collection, Mss. 1036

John S. Sappington Papers, Mss. 1027

John Sappington Family Papers, Mss. 2889

William B. Sappington Papers, Mss. 1421

"Sketch of the Life of Dr. John Gano Bryan, 1788–1860," Mss. 2919

Frederick Starr, Jr., Papers, Mss. 2073

Meriwether Jeff Thompson Papers, Mss. 1030

U. D. C. Missouri Records, Mss. 3188

Charles Van Ravenswaay Collection, Mss. 2668

Washburne Family Papers, Mss. 2971

Marie Oliver Watkins Papers, Mss. 2689

Roy D. Williams Papers, Mss. 3769

Printed Government Documents

Appendix to the Congressional Globe. Thirty-third Congress, First Session. Washington, D.C.: Office of the Globe, 1855.

Appendix to the Congressional Globe. Thirty-fourth Congress, First Session. Washington, D.C.: Office of the Globe, 1856.

Appendix to the Congressional Globe. Thirty-eighth Congress, First Session. Washington, D.C.: Office of the Globe, 1860.

Census for 1820. Washington, D.C.: Gales and Seaton, 1821.

Compendium of the Enumeration of the Inhabitants and Statistics of the United States in 1840. Washington, D.C.: Thomas Allen, 1841.

DeBow, J. D. B., ed. *The Seventh Census of the United States: 1850.* Washington, D.C.: Robert Armstrong, Public Printer, 1853.

Fifth Census; or, Enumeration of the Inhabitants of the United States—1830. Washington, D.C.: Duff Green, 1832.

Journal of the House of Representatives of the State of Missouri, Sixth General Assembly, First Session, 1836–1837. Jefferson City: James Lusk, 1837.

Journal of the House of Representatives of the State of Missouri, Eleventh General Assembly, First Session, 1841–1842. Jefferson City: James Lusk, 1842.

Journal of the House of Representatives of the State of Missouri, Twelfth General Assembly, First Session, 1842–1843. Jefferson City: James Lusk, 1843.

Journal of the House of Representatives of the State of Missouri, Fifteenth General Assembly, First Session, 1848–1849. Jefferson City: James Lusk, State Printer, 1849.

Journal of the House of Representatives of the State of Missouri, Nineteenth General Assembly, First Session, 1857–1858. Jefferson City: State Printer, 1858.

Journal of the House of Representatives of the State of Missouri, Twenty-first General Assembly, First Session, 1860–1861. Jefferson City: State Printer, 1861.

Journal of the Senate, Extra Session of the Rebel Legislature, called Together by a Proclamation of C. F. Jackson, Begun and Held at the Town of Neosho, Newton County, Missouri on the Twenty-first Day of October, Eighteen Hundred and Sixty-One. Jefferson City: Emory S. Foster, 1865–1866.

Journal of the Senate of the State of Missouri, Sixth General Assembly, First Session, 1836–1837. Jefferson City: James Lusk, 1837.

Journal of the Senate of the State of Missouri, Fifteenth General Assembly, First Session, 1848–1849. Jefferson City: James Lusk, State Printer, 1849.

Kennedy, Joseph C. G. *Agriculture of the United States in 1860; Compiled from the Original Returns of the Eighth Census.* Washington, D.C.: Government Printing Office, 1864.

———. *Population of the United States in 1860; Compiled from the Original Returns of the Eighth Census.* Washington, D.C.: Government Printing Office, 1864.

Laws of the State of Missouri, Sixth General Assembly, 1836–1837. Jefferson City: James Lusk, 1837.

Laws of the State of Missouri, Fifteenth General Assembly, 1848–1849. Jefferson City: James Lusk, State Printer, 1849.

Laws of the State of Missouri, Passed at the Called Session of the Twenty-first General Assembly, Begun and Held at the City of Jefferson, on Thursday, May 2, 1861. Jefferson City: J. P. Ament, 1861.

Proceedings of the Missouri State Convention, Held at Jefferson City and St. Louis, March, 1861–June, 1863. St. Louis: George Knapp and Co., 1861–1863.

The War of the Rebellion: A Compilation of the Official Records of the Union and Confederate Armies. 4 ser., 128 vols. Washington, D.C., 1881–1901.

Newspapers and Periodicals
Arkansas Gazette [Little Rock]
Arkansas Patriot [Little Rock]
Boon's Lick Times [Fayette]

Boonville Observer Extra
Columbia Missouri-Herald
Columbia Missourian
Columbia Patriot
Daily Missouri Democrat [St. Louis]
Daily Missouri Republican [St. Louis]
De Bow's Review [New Orleans]
Glasgow Weekly Times
Harper's Weekly [New York]
Jefferson City Metropolitan
Jefferson City People's Tribune
Jefferson Inquirer [Jefferson City]
Liberty Tribune
Marshall Democrat
Missouri Democrat [Fayette]
Missouri Gazette [St. Louis]
Missouri Intelligencer [Franklin]
Missouri Intelligencer and Boon's Lick Advertiser [Fayette]
Missouri Register
Missouri Reporter
Missouri Statesman [Columbia]
Saint Louis Daily Union
Squatter Sovereign [Atchison, Kans.]

Printed Primary Materials

Atwater, Caleb. *The Writings of Caleb Atwater.* Columbus, Ohio: by the author, 1833.

Babcock, Rufus, ed. *Forty Years of Pioneer Life: Memoir of John Mason Peck, D. D.* Philadelphia, 1864.

Barteis, Carolyn M., ed. *Howard County Marriages 1816–1834.* By the editor, 1987.

Basler, Roy F., ed. *The Collected Works of Abraham Lincoln.* 9 vols. Springfield, Ill.: The Abraham Lincoln Association, 1953; repr., New Brunswick, N.J.: Rutgers University Press, 1988.

Bassett, John Spencer, ed. *Correspondence of Andrew Jackson.* 7 vols. Washington, D.C.: Carnegie Institution of Washington, 1926–1935.

Berlin, Ira, Barbara J. Fields, Thavolia Glymph, Stephen F. Miller, Joseph P. Reidy, Leslie S. Rowland, and Julie Saville, eds. *Freedom: A Documentary History of Emancipation, 1861–1867.* Cambridge and New York: Cambridge University Press, 1982–1993.

Boggs, Karen C., and Louise M. Coutts, eds. *Howard County* [Missouri] *Cemetery Records.* By the authors, n.d.

Chester, Greville John. *Transatlantic Sketches in the West Indies, South America, Canada and the United States.* London: Smith, Elder and Co., 1869.

Clark, Thomas D., ed. *Historical Maps of Kentucky.* Lexington: University Press of Kentucky, 1979.

————. *The Voice of the Frontier: John Bradford's Notes on Kentucky.* Lexington: University Press of Kentucky, 1993.

Crallé, R. K., ed. *The Works of John C. Calhoun.* 2 vols. New York: D. Appleton, 1854.

Darby, John F. *Personal Recollections of Many Prominent People Whom I Have Known, and of Events—Especially of Those Relating to the History of St. Louis—During the First Half of the Present Century.* St. Louis: G. I. Jones and Co., 1880.

"David Rice Atchison Letter." *Missouri Historical Review* 31 (July 1937): 443–44.

Document Containing Correspondence, Orders, &c. in relation to the disturbance with the Mormons . . . . Fayette, Mo.: Boon's Lick Times, 1841.

Drake, Daniel. *Pioneer Life in Kentucky, 1785–1800.* New York: Henry Schuman, 1948.

Duke, Basil W. *Reminiscences of General Basil W. Duke, C.S.A.* Garden City, N.Y.: Doubleday, Page and Co., 1911.

Ellsberry, Elizabeth Prather, ed. *Cemetery Records of Saline County, Missouri.* Marshall, Mo.: Marshall Chapter, Daughters of the American Revolution, 1965.

Flint, Timothy. *Recollections of the Last Ten Years.* Boston: Cummings, Hilliard, 1826.

Gallaway, B. P., ed. *The Dark Corner of the Confederacy: Accounts of Civil War Texas as Told by Contemporaries.* Dubuque, Iowa: William C. Brown, Publishers, 1968.

Gott, John K., ed. *Fauquier County, Virginia, Marriage Bonds: 1759–1854, and Marriage Returns, 1785–1848.* Bowie, Md.: Heritage Books, Inc., 1991.

Gray, Gertrude E., ed. *Virginia Northern Neck Land Grants.* 4 vols. Baltimore: Genealogical Publishing Company, Inc., 1993.

Greene, John P. *Facts Relative to the Expulsion of the Mormons or Latter Day Saints, from the State of Missouri, under the "Exterminating Order."* Cincinnati: R. P. Brooks, 1839.

Gregg, Kate L., ed. *The Road to Santa Fe: The Journal and Diaries of George Champlin Sibley and others, pertaining to the surveying and marking of a road from the Missouri frontier to the settlements of New Mexico, 1825–1827.* Albuquerque: University of New Mexico Press, 1952.

Grissom, Daniel M. "Personal Recollections of Distinguished Missourians: Claiborne F. Jackson." *Missouri Historical Review* 20 (July 1926): 504–8.

Gwathmey, John H., ed. *Historical Register of Virginians in the Revolution: Soldiers—Sailors—Marines, 1775–1783.* Baltimore: Genealogical Publishing Company, Inc., 1979.

Heinemann, Charles B., ed. *"First Census" of Kentucky 1790.* Washington, D.C.: Gaius Marcus Brumbaugh, 1940; repr., Baltimore: Genealogical Publishing Co, 1993.

Hildebrand, Samuel S. *Autobiography of Samuel S. Hildebrand: the renowned Missouri "bushwacker" and unconquerable Rob Roy of America: being his complete confession, recently made to the writers / and carefully compiled by James W. Evans and A. Wendell Keith; together with all the facts connected with his early history.* Jefferson City: State Times Book and Job Printing House, 1870; repr., Woodbridge, Conn.: Research Publications, 1985.

History of Howard and Chariton Counties, Missouri, Written and Compiled from the Most Official Authentic and Private Sources, Including a History of Its Townships, Towns and Villages. St. Louis: National Historical Company, 1883.

History of Saline County, Missouri, Carefully Written and Compiled from the Most Authentic Official and Private Sources, Including a History of its Townships, Cities, Towns and Villages. St. Louis: Missouri Historical Company, 1881.

Hulbert, Archer B., ed. *Southwest on the Turquoise Trail; The First Diaries on the Road to Santa Fe.* Denver: Overland to the Pacific Series, 1933.

Johnson, Robert Underwood, and Howard L. Conard, eds. *Battles and Leaders of the Civil War.* 4 vols. New York: Thomas Yoseloff, 1956.

Johnson, Samuel. *The Works of Samuel Johnson, Ltd.* 12 vols. London: J. Haddon, 1820; repr., New York: AMS Press, 1970.

Jones, John Beauchamp. *The Western Merchant, A Narrative Containing useful instruction for the Western man of business who makes his purchases in the east; also, Information for the eastern man whose customers are in the west; Likewise, Hints for those who design emigrating to the west. Deduced from actual experience by Luke Shortfield.* Philadelphia: Gregg, Elliot and Company, 1849.

King, Edward. "The Great South. Some Notes on Missouri: The Heart of the Republic." *Scribner's Monthly* 8 (July 1874): 264–69.

King, J. Estelle Stewart, ed. *Abstracts of Wills, Administrations, and Marriages of Fauquier County, Virginia, 1759–1800.* Baltimore: Genealogical Publishing Company, Inc., 1986.

Knox, Thomas W. *Camp-Fire and Cotton Field: Southern Adventure in Time of War.* Philadelphia: Jones Brothers and Co., 1865.

Krug, Mark M., ed. *Mrs. Hill's Journal: Civil War Reminiscences, By Sarah Jane Full Hill.* Chicago: R. R. Donnelly and Sons Co., 1980.

Leftwich, W[illiam]. M. *Martyrdom in Missouri: A History of Religious Proscription, the Seizure of Churches, and the Persecution of Ministers of the Gospel, in the State of Missouri during the Late Civil War, and under the "Test Oath" of the New Constitution*. St. Louis: S. W. Book and Publishing Co., 1870.

Leopard, Buel, and Floyd Shoemaker, eds. *The Messages and Proclamations of the Governors of the State of Missouri*. 4 vols. Columbia: State Historical Society of Missouri, 1922.

"A Memorandum of M. Austin's Journey from the Lead Mines in the County of Wythe in the State of Virginia to the Lead Mines in the Province of Louisiana West of the Mississippi, 1796–1797." *American Historical Review* 5 (1899–1900): 525–26.

Mulligan, James A. "The Siege of Lexington, Mo." In *Battles and Leaders of the Civil War,* edited by Robert Underwood Johnson and Howard L. Conard. Vol. 1. New York: Thomas Yoseloff, 1956.

Napton, William B. *Past and Present of Saline County, Missouri*. Indianapolis: B. F. Bowen, 1910.

Office of the Mayor. *A Plea to the Constitutional Convention of Missouri for Enlargement of Boundaries of the City of St. Louis*. St. Louis: City Printing Office, 1844.

Peterson, Merrill D., ed. *The Portable Thomas Jefferson*. New York: Viking Penguin, Inc., 1975.

Quisenberry, Anderson Chenault. *Kentucky in the War of 1812*. Baltimore: Genealogical Publishing Co., 1969.

Reports of Cases Argued and Determined in the Supreme Court of the State of Missouri. St. Louis: Gilbert Book Co., 1883.

Robertson, James Rood, ed. *Petitions of the Early Inhabitants of Kentucky to the General Assembly of Virginia 1769 to 1792*. Louisville: John P. Morton and Co., 1914; repr., New York: Arno Press, 1971.

Rowan, Steven C., and James Neal Primm, eds. *Germans for a Free Missouri: Translations from the St. Louis Radical Press, 1857–1862*. Columbia: University of Missouri Press, 1983.

Sampson, F. A., ed. "The Journals of Capt. Thomas [William] Becknell from Boone's Lick to Santa Fe and from Santa Cruz to Green River." *Missouri Historical Review* 4 (January 1910): 65–84.

———, ed. "Journal of M. M. Marmaduke of a Trip from Franklin, Missouri to Santa Fe, New Mexico in 1824." *Missouri Historical Review* 6 (October 1911): [1–14].

Scharf, J. Thomas. *History of St. Louis City and County*. Philadelphia: Louis H. Everts and Co., 1883.

Stanton, Donald J., Goodwin F. Berquist, and Paul C. Bowers, eds. *The*

Civil War Reminiscences of General M. Jeff Thompson. Dayton, Ohio: Morningside House, Inc., 1988.

Talley, William M., ed. *Talley's Kentucky Papers.* Fort Worth, Texas: Arrow Printing Co., 1966.

Teacher, Lawrence, ed. *The Unabridged Mark Twain.* 2 vols. Philadelphia: Running Press, 1976, 1979.

Tinling, Marion, and Godfrey Davies, eds. *The Western Country in 1793: Reports on Kentucky and Virginia by Harry Toulmin.* San Marino, Calif.: Henry E. Huntington Library, 1948.

Tocqueville, Alexis de. *Democracy in America.* Edited by Phillips Bradley. 2 vols. New York: A. A. Knopf, 1948; repr., 1997.

Troen, Selwyn K., and Glen E. Holt, eds. *St. Louis.* New York and London: New Viewpoints, 1977.

Western Americana: Frontier History of the Trans-Mississippi West 1550–1900. New Haven, Conn.: Research Publications, Inc., 1975.

White, Virgil D., ed. *Index to Revolutionary War Service Records.* 2 vols. Waynesboro, Tenn.: National Historical Publishing Company, 1995.

———. *Index to War of 1812 Pension Files.* 4 vols. Waynesboro, Tenn.: National Historical Publishing Company, 1989.

Williamson, Hugh P. "William B. Napton: Man of Two Worlds." *Missouri Bar Journal* 15 (March 1944): 208–12.

Wilson, Samuel M., ed. *Catalogue of Revolutionary Soldiers and Sailors of the Commonwealth of Virginia to whom Land Bounty Warrants were Granted by Virginia for Military Services in the War of Independence.* Baltimore: Genealogical Publishing Company, Inc., 1967.

Yantis, Netti Schreiner, and Florene Speakman Love, eds. *The 1787 Census of Virginia.* 3 vols. Springfield, Va.: Genealogical Books in Print, 1987.

Young, Chester Raymond, ed. *Westward into Kentucky: The Narrative of Daniel Trabue.* Lexington: University Press of Kentucky, 1981.

Young, Florence Nelson, and Virgil D. Young, eds. *Fleming County, Kentucky, Deed Books A–G—Abstracts 1797–1818.* 2 vols. Denver: Western Heraldry Organization, 1974.

SECONDARY SOURCES

Theses, Dissertations, and Unpublished Papers and Manuscripts

Arnold, Thomas Clay. "Rethinking Moral Economy and Political Science." Paper delivered at the Annual Conference of the Northeastern Political Science Association, Boston, Mass., November 1998.

Bellamy, Donnie D. "Slavery, Emancipation, and Racism in Missouri, 1850–1865." Ph.D. diss., University of Missouri–Columbia, 1970.

Bierbaum, Milton E. "The Rhetoric of Union or Disunion in Missouri, 1844–1861." Ph.D. diss., University of Missouri–Columbia, 1965.

Bradford, Priscilla. "The Missouri Constitutional Controversy of 1845." Master's thesis, University of Missouri–Columbia, 1936.

Burks, Walter Morrow. "Missouri Medicine Man." Master's thesis, University of Kansas City, 1958.

———. "Thunder on the Right." Ph.D. diss., University of Kansas City, 1962.

Conoyer, Daniel Joseph. "Missouri's Little Dixie: A Geographical Delineation." Ph.D. diss., Saint Louis University, 1973.

Craig, Douglas L. "An Examination of the Reasons for Missouri's Decision Not to Secede in 1860." Master's thesis, University of Missouri–Kansas City, 1969.

Igel, Joseph A., Jr. "A Rhetorical Evaluation of Claiborne Fox Jackson's Speeches on Slavery and States' Rights: 1847–1861." Master's thesis, Southwest Missouri State University, 1984.

Riley, Eula Gladys. "John Sappington, Doctor and Philanthropist." Master's thesis, University of Missouri–Columbia, 1942.

Sale, Sara Lee. "Governor Claiborne Fox Jackson and His Role in the Secession Movement in Missouri." Master's thesis, Central Missouri State University, 1979.

West, Alma Merle. "The Earlier Political Career of Claiborne Fox Jackson, 1836–1851." Master's thesis, University of Missouri–Columbia, 1941.

Williams, Lyle Keith. "Joseph Jackson (1705–1774) or Bedford and Goochland Counties, Virginia, and Descendants." By the author, 1991, Kentucky Genealogical Room, KDLA.

Wurthman, Leonard B., Jr. "Frank Blair of Missouri: Jacksonian Orator of the Civil War Era." Ph.D. diss., University of Missouri–Columbia, 1969.

Reference Works

Biographical Dictionary of the American Congress, 1774–1961. Washington, D.C.: Government Printing Office, 1961.

Current, Richard N., ed. *Encyclopedia of the Confederacy.* 4 vols. New York: Simon and Schuster, 1993.

Johnson, Allen, and Dumas Malone, eds. *The Dictionary of American Biography.* 20 vols. New York: Charles Scribner's Sons, 1937–1943.

Johnson, Samuel. *The Works of Samuel Johnson, Ll.D.* 11 vols. Oxford and London: Talboys and Wheeler; repr., New York: AMS Press, 1970.

Kleber, John E., ed. *The Kentucky Encyclopedia.* Lexington: University Press of Kentucky, 1992.

Lamar, Howard R., ed. *The New Encyclopedia of the American West.* New Haven: Yale University Press, 1998.

Slater, Joseph, ed. *The Collected Works of Ralph Waldo Emerson.* 6 vols. Cambridge, Mass., and London: Belknap Press, 1983.

Warner, Ezra J. *Generals in Blue: Lives of the Union Commanders.* Baton Rouge: Louisiana State University Press, 1964.

————. *Generals in Gray: Lives of the Confederate Commanders.* Baton Rouge: Louisiana State University Press, 1959.

Articles

Adams, Donald R., Jr. "Prices and Wages in Maryland, 1750–1850." *Journal of Economic History* 46 (September 1986): 625–45.

Adler, Jeffrey S. "Yankee Colonizers and the Making of Antebellum St. Louis." *Gateway Heritage* 12 (winter 1992): 4–21.

Ashton, John. "History of Hogs and Pork Production in Missouri." *Monthly Bulletin of Missouri State Board of Agriculture* 21 (January 1923): 1–75.

Blum, Virgil C. "The Political and Military Activities of the German Element in St. Louis, 1859–1861." *Missouri Historical Review* 42 (January 1948): 103–29.

Bowen, Don. "Guerrilla Warfare in Western Missouri, 1862–1865: Historical Extensions of the Relative Deprivation Hypothesis." *Comparative Studies in Society and History* 19 (July 1977): 30–51.

Breen, Timothy H. "The Culture of Agriculture: The Symbolic World of the Tidewater Planter, 1760–1790." In *Saints and Revolutionaries: Essays on Early American History,* edited by David D. Hall, John M. Murrin, and Thad W. Tate. New York: W. W. Norton, 1984.

Cannon, Gerald. "The Harney-Price Agreement." *Civil War Times Illustrated* 23 (December 1984): 40–45.

Cecil-Fronsman, Bill. " 'Death to All Yankees and Traitors in Kansas': The *Squatter Sovereign* and the Defense of Slavery in Kansas." *Kansas History* 16 (spring 1993): 22–33.

Chambers, William Nisbet. "Pistols and Politics: Incidents in the Career of Thomas Hart Benton, 1816–1818." *Bulletin of the Missouri Historical Society* 5 (October 1948): 5–17.

Covington, James W. "The Camp Jackson Affair, 1861." *Missouri Historical Review* 55 (April 1961): 197–212.

Cox, Isaac J. "Opening the Santa Fe Trail." *Missouri Historical Review* 25 (spring 1930): 30–66.

Craik, Elmer LeRoy. "Southern Interest in Territorial Kansas, 1854–1858." *Kansas Historical Collections* 15 (1919–1921): 376–95.

Crisler, Robert M. "Missouri's Little Dixie." *Missouri Historical Review* 42 (January 1948): 130–39.

————. "Republican Areas in Missouri." *Missouri Historical Review* 42 (July 1948): 299–309.

Culmer, Frederic A. "Abiel Leonard." *Missouri Historical Review* 28 (October 1933): 17–37.

———. "Selling Mules down South in 1835." *Missouri Historical Review* 24 (July 1930): 537–49.

Davis, David Brion. "Some Themes of Counter-Subversion: An Analysis of Anti-Masonic, Anti-Catholic, and Anti-Mormon Literature." *Mississippi Valley Historical Review* 47 (September 1960): 205–24.

Davis, Stephen. "Empty Eyes, Marble Hands: The Confederate Monument and the South." *Journal of Popular Culture* 16 (winter 1982): 2–19.

DeArmond, Fred. "Reconstruction in Missouri." *Missouri Historical Review* 41 (April 1967): 365–71.

Duffy, John. "Medical Practice in the Ante Bellum South." *Journal of Southern History* 25 (February 1959): 53–72.

Dyer, Thomas G. " 'A Most Unexampled Exhibition of Madness and Brutality': Judge Lynch in Saline County, Missouri, 1859." *Missouri Historical Review* 89 (April and July 1995): 269–89, 367–83.

Eaton, Miles W. "The Development and Later Decline of the Hemp Industry in Missouri." *Missouri Historical Review* 43 (July 1949): 344–59.

Fellman, Michael. "Emancipation in Missouri." *Missouri Historical Review* 83 (October 1988): 36–56.

Geertz, Clifford. "Thick Description: Toward an Interpretive Theory of Culture." In *The Interpretation of Cultures: Selected Essays.* New York: Basic Books, 1975.

Gerlach, Russell L. "Population Origins in Rural Missouri." *Missouri Historical Review* 71 (October 1976): 5–15.

Gienapp, William E. "The Crime against Sumner: The Caning of Charles Sumner and the Rise of the Republican Party." *Civil War History* 25 (September 1979): 218–45.

Giffin, Jerena East. *First Ladies of Missouri: Their Homes and Their Families.* By the author, 1970.

Gillespie, Michael. "The Battle of Rock Creek." *Civil War Times Illustrated* 30 (March/April 1991): 35–41.

Gorn, Elliot. "Gouge and Bite, Pull Hair and Scratch: The Significance of Fighting in the Southern Backcountry." *American Historical Review* 90 (February 1985): 18–32.

Hadlock, Milo S. "Jackson Chronology" and "Our Early Virginia Ancestor." In *Joseph Jackson (1705–1774) of Bedford and Goochland Counties, Virginia, and Descendants by Lyle Keith Williams.* By the author, 1991.

———. "Our Early Virginia Ancestor." In *Joseph Jackson (1705–1774) of Bedford and Goochland Counties, Virginia, and Descendants by Lyle Keith Williams.* By the author, 1991.

Hall, Thomas B. "John Sappington, M.D.—1776–1856." *Missouri Historical Review* 24 (January 1930): 177–99.

Harvey, Charles M. "Missouri from 1849 to 1861." *Missouri Historical Review* 2 (October 1907): 23–40.

Henretta, James A. "Families and Farms: *Mentalité* in Pre-Industrial America." *William and Mary Quarterly,* 3rd ser., 35 (January 1978): 3–32.

Isaac, Rhys. "Evangelical Revolt: The Nature of the Baptists' Challenge to the Traditional Order in Virginia, 1765–1775." *William and Mary Quarterly,* 3rd ser., 31 (July 1974): 345–68.

Kirkpatrick, Arthur Roy. "The Admission of Missouri to the Confederacy." *Missouri Historical Review* 55 (July 1961): 366–86.

———. "Missouri in the Early Months of the Civil War." *Missouri Historical Review* 55 (April 1961): 235–66.

———. "Missouri on the Eve of the Civil War." *Missouri Historical Review* 55 (January 1961): 99–108.

———. "Missouri's Secessionist Government, 1861–1865." *Missouri Historical Review* 45 (January 1951): 124–37.

Klein, Rachel L. "Frontier Planters and the American Revolution: The South Carolina Backcountry, 1775–1782." In *An Uncivil War: The Southern Backcountry during the American Revolution,* edited by Ronald Hoffman, Thad W. Tate, and Peter J. Albert. Charlottesville: University Press of Virginia, 1985.

Kohl, Martha. "Enforcing a Vision of Community: The Role of the Test Oath in Missouri's Reconstruction." *Civil War History* 40 (December 1994): 292–307.

Lamar, Howard R. "From Bondage to Contract: Ethnic Labor in the American West, 1600–1890." In *The Countryside in the Age of Capitalist Transformation,* edited by Steven Hahn and Jonathan Prude. Chapel Hill: University of North Carolina Press, 1985.

Land, Aubrey C. "Economic Base and Social Structure: The Northern Chesapeake in the Eighteenth Century." *Journal of Economic History* 25 (1965): 639–54.

Laughlin, Sceva B. "Missouri Politics during the Civil War." *Missouri Historical Review* 23 (April and July 1929): 400–426, 583–618; 24 (October 1929 and January 1930): 87–113, 261–84.

Lyon, William H. "Claiborne Fox Jackson and the Secession Crisis in Missouri." *Missouri Historical Review* 58 (July 1964): 422–41.

McCandless, Perry G. "The Rise of Thomas Hart Benton in Missouri Politics." *Missouri Historical Review* 50 (October 1955): 16–29.

McClure, Charles H. "Early Opposition to Thomas Hart Benton." *Missouri Historical Review* 10 (1915): 151–96.

Malin, James C. "The Proslavery Background of the Kansas Struggle." *Mississippi Valley Historical Review* 10 (December 1923): 285–305.

Merkel, Benjamin. "The Abolition Aspects of Missouri's Antislavery Controversy 1819–1865." *Missouri Historical Review* 44 (April 1950): 232–53.

———. "The Slavery Issue and the Political Decline of Thomas Hart Benton, 1846–1856." *Missouri Historical Review* 38 (July 1944): 388–407.

Miller, Robert E. "Daniel Marsh Frost, C.S.A." *Missouri Historical Review* 85 (July 1991): 381–401.

———. " 'One of the Ruling Class'—Thomas Caute Reynolds: Second Confederate Governor of Missouri." *Missouri Historical Review* 80 (July 1986): 422–48.

———. "Proud Confederate: Thomas Lowndes Snead of Missouri." *Missouri Historical Review* 79 (January 1985): 167–91.

Morrow, Lynn. "Dr. John Sappington: Southern Patriarch in the New West." *Missouri Historical Review* 90 (October 1995): 38–60.

———. "Ozark/Ozarks: Establishing a Regional Term." *White River Valley Historical Quarterly* 36 (fall 1996): 4–11.

Nichols, Roy F. "The Kansas-Nebraska Act: A Century of Historiography." *Mississippi Valley Historical Review* 43 (September 1956): 201–12.

Owsley, Frank L. "The Pattern of Migration and Settlement on the Southern Frontier." *Journal of Southern History* 11 (May 1945): 147–76.

Parrish, William E. "Fremont in Missouri." *Civil War Times Illustrated* 17 (April 1978): 4–10, 40–45.

———. "Jefferson Davis Comes to Missouri." *Missouri Historical Review* 57 (July 1963): 344–56.

———. " 'The Palmyra Massacre': A Tragedy of Guerrilla Warfare." *Journal of Confederate History* 1 (fall 1988): 259–72.

———. "Reconstruction Politics in Missouri." In *Radicalism, Racism, and Party Realignment: The Border States during Reconstruction,* edited by Richard O. Curry. Baltimore: Johns Hopkins University Press, 1969.

Piston, William Garrett, and Thomas P. Sweeney. "Don't Yield an Inch!" *North and South* 2 (June 1999): 10–26.

Renner, G. K. "The Mule in Missouri Agriculture, 1821–1950." *Missouri Historical Review* 74 (January 1980): 433–57.

Rister, Carl Coke. "Carlota: A Confederate Colony in Mexico." *Journal of Southern History* 11 (February 1945): 33–50.

Roed, William. "Secessionist Strength in Missouri." *Missouri Historical Review* 72 (July 1978): 412–23.

Rorvig, Paul. "A Significant Skirmish: The Battle of Boonville." *Missouri Historical Review* 86 (January 1992): 127–48.

Ryle, Walter H. "Slavery and Party Realignment in Missouri in the State Election of 1856." *Missouri Historical Review* 39 (April 1945): 320–32.

Schauinger, J. Herman, ed. "The Letters of Godlove S. Orth: Hoosier Whig." *Indiana Magazine of History* 39 (December 1943): 360–400.

Schwartz, Theodore. "Cultural Totemism: Ethnic Identity, Primitive and Modern." In *Ethnic Identity: Cultural Continuities and Change,* edited by George A. DeVos and Lola Romanucci-Ross. Palo Alto, Calif.: Mayfield, 1975.

Shoemaker, Floyd C. "Missouri's Proslavery Fight for Kansas, 1854–1855." *Missouri Historical Review* 48 (April 1954 and July 1954): 221–36, 325–40; 49 (October 1954): 41–54.

Snyder, John F. "The Democratic State Convention of Missouri in 1860." *Missouri Historical Review* 2 (January 1908): 112–22.

Strickland, John Scott. "Traditional Culture and Moral Economy: Social and Economic Change in the South Carolina Low Country, 1865–1910." In *The Countryside in the Age of Capitalist Transformation,* edited by Steven Hahn and Jonathan Prude. Chapel Hill: University of North Carolina Press, 1985.

Strickland, W. A., Jr. "Quinine Pills Manufactured on the Missouri Frontier, 1832–1862." *Pharmacy in History* 25 (1983): 54–68.

Swindler, William F. "The Southern Press in Missouri, 1861–1864." *Missouri Historical Review* 35 (April 1941): 373–99.

Tasher, Lucy Lucile. "The *Missouri Democrat* and the Civil War." *Missouri Historical Review* 31 (July 1937): 402–19.

Thompson, E. P. "The Moral Economy of the English Crowd in the Eighteenth Century." *Past and Present* 50 (1971): 76–136.

Tindall, George B. "Mythology: A New Frontier in Southern History." In *The Idea of the South: Pursuit of a Central Theme,* edited by Frank E. Vandiver. Chicago: University of Chicago Press, 1964.

Tucker, Phillip T. " 'Ho, for Kansas': The Southwest Expedition of 1860." *Missouri Historical Review* 86 (October 1991): 22–36.

Turner, Frederick Jackson. "The Significance of the Frontier in American History." *Annual Reports of the American Historical Association* (1893): 199–227.

Viles, Jonas. "Old Franklin: A Frontier Town of the Twenties." *Mississippi Valley Historical Review* 9 (March 1923): 269–82.

Welch, Donald H. "Travel by Stage on the Boonslick Road." *Missouri Historical Review* 54 (July 1960): 330–36.

Williams, D. Alan. "The Small Farmer in Eighteenth-Century Virginia Politics." *Agricultural History* 43 (1969): 91–105.

Wurthman, Leonard B., Jr. "Frank Blair: Lincoln's Congressional Spokesman." *Missouri Historical Review* 64 (April 1970): 263–88.

Books

Ackerknecht, Edwin H. *Malaria in the Upper Mississippi Valley, 1760–1900.* Baltimore: Johns Hopkins University Press, 1945; repr., New York: Arno Press, 1977.

Adamson, Hans Christian. *Rebellion in Missouri, 1861: Nathaniel Lyon and His Army of the West.* Philadelphia and New York: Chilton Co., 1961.

Adler, Jeffrey S. *Yankee Merchants and the Making of the Urban West: The Rise and Fall of Antebellum St. Louis.* Cambridge and New York: Cambridge University Press, 1991.

Anderson, Galusha. *A Border City during the Civil War.* Boston: Little, Brown, and Company, 1908.

Aron, Stephen. *How the West Was Lost: The Transformation of Kentucky from Daniel Boone to Henry Clay.* Baltimore: Johns Hopkins University Press, 1996.

Atherton, Lewis E. *The Frontier Merchant in Mid-America.* Columbia: University of Missouri Press, 1971.

Ayers, Edward L. *Vengeance and Justice: Crime and Punishment in the 19th-Century American South.* New York: Oxford University Press, 1984.

Bailyn, Bernard. *The Origins of American Politics.* New York: Knopf, 1968.

Baker, O. E., ed. *Atlas of American Agriculture.* Washington, D.C.: Government Printing Office, 1936.

Barney, William L. *Flawed Victory: A New Perspective on the Civil War.* New York: Praeger, 1975.

———. *The Road to Secession: A New Perspective on the Old South.* New York: Praeger, 1972.

Beeman, Richard R. *The Evolution of the Southern Backcountry: A Case Study of Lunenburg County, Virginia, 1746–1832.* Philadelphia: University of Pennsylvania Press, 1984.

Bell, Daniel, ed. *The Radical Right.* Garden City, N.Y.: Doubleday and Co., 1964.

Benson, Lee. *The Concept of Jacksonian Democracy: New York as a Test Case.* Princeton, N.J.: Princeton University Press, 1961.

Berlin, Ira. *Many Thousands Gone: The First Two Centuries of Slavery in North America.* Cambridge, Mass.: Belknap Press of Harvard University Press, 1998.

———. *Slaves without Masters: The Free Negro in the Antebellum South.* New York: Pantheon Books, 1974; repr., New York: Oxford University Press, 1981.

Berry, Thomas S. *Western Prices before 1861: A Study of the Cincinnati Market.* Cambridge, Mass.: Harvard University Press, 1943.

Berwanger, Eugene H. *The Frontier against Slavery: Western Anti-Negro Prejudice and the Slavery Extension Controversy.* Urbana: University of Illinois Press, 1967.

Billington, Ray Allen. *The Far Western Frontier, 1830–1860.* New York: Harper and Row, 1956.

———. *The Protestant Crusade.* New York: MacMillan, 1938; repr., Chicago: Quadrangle Books, 1964.

Bladen, Wilford A., and Gyula Pauer. *Geography of Kentucky: A Topical-Regional Overview.* Dubuque, Iowa: Kendall/Hunt Publishing Company, 1984.

Breen, T[imothy] H. *Tobacco Culture: The Mentality of the Great Tidewater Planters on the Eve of Revolution.* Princeton, N.J.: Princeton University Press, 1985.

Brown, Richard D. *Modernization: The Transformation of American Life, 1600–1865.* Prospect Heights, Ill.: Waveland Press, Inc., 1976.

Brownlee, Richard S. *Gray Ghosts of the Confederacy: Guerrilla Warfare in the West, 1861–1865.* Baton Rouge: Louisiana State University Press, 1958.

Cable, John Ray. *The Bank of the State of Missouri.* New York: Longmans, Green, and Co., 1923.

Cain, Marvin R. *Lincoln's Attorney General: Edward Bates of Missouri.* Columbia: University of Missouri Press, 1965.

Carr, Lois Green, Russell R. Menard, and Lorena S. Walsh. *Robert Cole's World: Agriculture and Society in Early Maryland.* Chapel Hill: University of North Carolina Press, 1991.

Cash, Wilbur J. *The Mind of the South.* New York: Alfred A. Knopf, 1941.

Cashin, Joan E. *A Family Venture: Men and Women on the Southern Frontier.* New York: Oxford University Press, 1991; repr., Baltimore: Johns Hopkins University Press, 1994.

Cassity, Michael. *Defending a Way of Life: An American Community in the Nineteenth Century.* Albany: State University of New York Press, 1989.

Castel, Albert. *A Frontier State at War: Kansas, 1861–1865.* Ithaca, N.Y.: Cornell University Press, 1959; repr., Lawrence: Kansas Heritage Press, 1992.

———. *General Sterling Price and the Civil War in the West.* Baton Rouge: Louisiana State University Press, 1968.

Chambers, William Nisbet. *Old Bullion Benton: Senator from the New West.* Boston: Little, Brown and Company, 1956.

Channing, Steven A. *Kentucky: A Bicentennial History.* New York: W. W. Norton and Company, 1977.

Christensen, Lawrence O., and Gary R. Kremer. *A History of Missouri: Volume IV—1875 to 1919.* Columbia: University of Missouri Press, 1997.

Clark, Thomas D. *Frontier America: The Story of the Westward Movement.* New York: Charles Scribner's Sons, 1959.

———. *The Kentucky.* New York and Toronto: Rinehart and Company, 1942.

———. *Kentucky: A Students' Guide to Localized History.* New York: Teachers College Press [Columbia University], 1965.

Clark, Thomas D., and John D. W. Guice. *Frontiers in Conflict: The Old Southwest, 1795–1830.* Albuquerque: University of New Mexico Press, 1989.

Cohen, Anthony P. *The Symbolic Construction of Community.* London and New York: Routledge, 1985.

Cooper, William J., Jr. *Liberty and Slavery: Southern Politics to 1860.* New York: Alfred A. Knopf, 1983.

———. *The South and the Politics of Slavery.* Baton Rouge: Louisiana State University Press, 1978.

Cornish, Dudley T. *The Sable Arm: Negro Troops in the Union Army, 1861–1865.* Ithaca, N.Y.: Cornell University Press, 1956.

Coulter, E. Merton. *The Civil War and Readjustment in Kentucky.* Chapel Hill: University of North Carolina Press, 1926; repr., Gloucester, Mass.: Peter Smith, 1966.

Crofts, Daniel W. *Reluctant Confederates: Upper South Unionists in the Secession Crisis.* Chapel Hill: University of North Carolina Press, 1989.

Curry, Richard O., ed. *Radicalism, Racism, and Party Realignment: The Border States during Reconstruction.* Baltimore: Johns Hopkins University Press, 1969.

Daniels, Jonathan. *The Devil's Backbone: The Story of the Natchez Trace.* New York: McGraw-Hill, 1962; repr., Gretna, La.: Pelican Publishing Co., 1992.

Davis, David Brion. *Slavery and Human Progress.* New York: Oxford University Press, 1984.

Davis, William C. *"A Government of Our Own": The Making of the Confederacy.* New York: Free Press, 1994.

———. *Breckenridge: Statesman Soldier Symbol.* Baton Rouge: Louisiana State University Press, 1974.

DeVos, George A., and Lola Romanucci-Ross, eds. *Ethnic Identity: Cultural Continuities and Change.* Palo Alto, Calif.: Mayfield, 1975.

Dillon, Merton L. *The Abolitionists: The Growth of a Dissenting Minority.* DeKalb: Northern Illinois University Press, 1974; repr., New York: W. W. Norton, 1979.

Douglas, Mary, and Baron Isherwood. *The World of Goods.* New York: Basic Books, 1979.

Etcheson, Nicole. *The Emerging Midwest: Upland Southerners and the Political Culture of the Old Northwest, 1787–1861*. Bloomington: Indiana University Press, 1996.

Evans-Pritchard, E. E. *The Nuer: The Political Institutions of a Nilotic People*. Oxford, England: Clarendon Press, 1940.

Faragher, John Mack. *Daniel Boone: The Life and Legend of an American Pioneer*. New York: Henry Holt and Company, 1992.

———. *Sugar Creek: Life on the Illinois Frontier*. New Haven: Yale University Press, 1986.

Federal Writers' Project. *Kentucky: A Guide to the Bluegrass State*. New York: Harcourt, Brace and Co., 1939.

———. *Missouri: A Guide to the "Show Me" State*. New York: Duell, Sloan and Pearce, 1941; repr., University Press of Kansas, 1986.

———. *Virginia: A Guide to the Old Dominion*. New York: Oxford University Press, 1940.

Fehrenbacher, Don E. *Slavery, Law, and Politics: The Dred Scott Case in Historical Perspective*. New York: Oxford University Press, 1978.

———. *The South and the Sectional Crisis*. Baton Rouge: Louisiana State University Press, 1980.

Fellman, Michael. *Inside War: The Guerrilla Conflict in Missouri during the American Civil War*. New York: Oxford University Press, 1989.

Fenton, John H. *Politics in the Border States*. New Orleans: Hauser Press, 1957.

Filler, Louis. *The Crusade against Slavery, 1830–1860*. New York: Harper and Brothers, 1960.

Fogel, Robert W. *Without Consent or Contract: The Rise and Fall of American Slavery*. New York: W. W. Norton, 1989.

Foley, William E. *The Genesis of Missouri: From Wilderness Outpost to Statehood*. Columbia: University of Missouri Press, 1989.

———. *A History of Missouri: Volume I—1673–1820*. Columbia: University of Missouri Press, 1971.

Foner, Eric. *Free Soil, Free Labor, Free Men: The Ideology of the Republican Party before the Civil War*. New York: Oxford University Press, 1970.

Foote, Shelby. *The Civil War—A Narrative: Fort Sumter to Perryville*. New York: Random House, 1958; repr., New York: Vintage, 1986.

Ford, Lacy K. *The Roots of Southern Radicalism: The South Carolina Upcountry, 1800–1865*. New York: Oxford University Press, 1988.

Foster, Gaines M. *Ghosts of the Confederacy: Defeat, the Lost Cause, and the Emergence of the New South, 1865 to 1913*. New York: Oxford University Press, 1987.

Freehling, William W. *Prelude to Civil War: The Nullification Controversy in South Carolina, 1816–1836*. New York: Harper and Row, 1965.

———. *The Road to Disunion: Secessionists at Bay.* New York: Oxford University Press, 1990.

Gaston, Paul M. *The New South Creed: A Study in Southern Mythmaking.* New York: Alfred A. Knopf, 1970.

Genovese, Eugene D. *The Southern Tradition: The Achievement and Limitations of an American Conservatism.* Cambridge, Mass.: Harvard University Press, 1994.

Glaab, Charles N., and A. Theodore Brown. *A History of Urban America.* New York: Macmillan Company, 1967.

Gray, Lewis C. *History of Agriculture in the Southern United States to 1860.* Washington, D.C.: Carnegie Institution of Washington, 1932; repr., Gloucester, Mass.: Peter Smith, 1958.

Greene, Jack P. *Peripheries and Center: Constitutional Development in the Extended Polities of the British Empire and the United States, 1607–1788.* Athens: University of Georgia Press, 1986.

Grimsley, Mark. *The Hard Hand of War: Union Military Policy toward Southern Civilians, 1861–1865.* Cambridge and New York: Cambridge University Press, 1995.

Hahn, Steven, and Jonathan Prude, eds. *The Countryside in the Age of Capitalist Transformation.* Chapel Hill: University of North Carolina Press, 1985.

Harris, N. Dwight. *The History of Negro Servitude in Illinois and the Slavery Agitation in That State.* Chicago: A. C. McClurg and Co., 1904.

Hinze, David C., and Karen Farnham. *The Battle of Carthage: Border War in Southwest Missouri, July 5, 1861.* Campbell, Calif.: Savas Publishing Co., 1997.

Hoffman, Ronald, Thad W. Tate, and Peter J. Albert, eds. *An Uncivil War: The Southern Backcountry during the American Revolution.* Charlottesville: University Press of Virginia, 1985.

Hofstadter, Richard. *The American Political Tradition and the Men Who Made It.* New York: Alfred A. Knopf, 1948; repr., Vintage Books, 1959.

Horsman, Reginald. *Race and Manifest Destiny: The Origins of American Racial Anglo-Saxonism.* Cambridge, Mass.: Harvard University Press, 1981.

Howard, Robert P. *Illinois: A History of the Prairie State.* Grand Rapids, Mich.: William B. Eerdmans Publishing Co., 1972.

Howe, Daniel Ward. *The Political Culture of the American Whigs.* Chicago: University of Chicago Press, 1980.

Hunt, Charles B. *Physiography of the United States.* San Francisco and London: W. H. Freeman and Company, 1967.

Hurt, R. Douglas. *Agriculture and Slavery in Missouri's Little Dixie.* Columbia: University of Missouri Press, 1992.

Ireland, Robert M. *The County Courts in Antebellum Kentucky.* Lexington: University Press of Kentucky, 1972.

Isaac, Rhys. *The Transformation of Virginia, 1740–1790.* Chapel Hill: University of North Carolina Press, 1982.

James, Marquis. *Andrew Jackson: Portrait of President.* Indianapolis and New York: Bobbs-Merrill Company, 1937.

Jenkins, William S. *Pro-Slavery Thought in the Old South.* Chapel Hill: University of North Carolina Press, 1935; repr., Gloucester, Mass.: Peter Smith, 1960.

Jennings, Thelma. *The Nashville Convention: Southern Movement for Unity, 1848–1851.* Memphis, Tenn.: Memphis State University Press, 1980.

Johannsen, Robert W., ed. *The Lincoln-Douglas Debates.* New York: Oxford University Press, 1965.

———. *To the Halls of the Montezumas: The Mexican War in the American Imagination.* New York: Oxford University Press, 1985.

Kendall, Paul Murray. *The Art of Biography.* New York: W. W. Norton, 1965.

Klotter, James C. *The Breckinridges of Kentucky.* Lexington: University Press of Kentucky, 1986.

Kulikoff, Allan. *The Agrarian Origins of American Capitalism.* Charlottesville: University Press of Virginia, 1992.

———. *Tobacco and Slaves: The Development of Southern Cultures in the Chesapeake, 1680–1800.* Chapel Hill: University of North Carolina Press, 1986.

LeSueur, Stephen C. *The 1838 Mormon War in Missouri.* Columbia: University of Missouri Press, 1990.

Levine, Lawrence W. *Black Culture and Black Consciousness: Afro-American Folk Thought from Slavery to Freedom.* New York: Oxford University Press, 1977.

Limerick, Patricia Nelson. *The Legacy of Conquest: The Unbroken Past of the American West.* New York and London: W. W. Norton, 1987.

Lucas, Marion B. *A History of Blacks in Kentucky—Volume 1: From Slavery to Segregation, 1760–1891.* Frankfort: Kentucky Historical Society, 1992.

McCandless, Perry. *A History of Missouri: Volume II—1820–1860.* Columbia: University of Missouri Press, 1972.

McCardell, John. *The Idea of a Southern Nation: Southern Nationalists and Southern Nationalism, 1830–1860.* New York: W. W. Norton, 1979.

McClure, Charles H. *Opposition in Missouri to Thomas Hart Benton.* Nashville, Tenn.: George Peabody College for Teachers, 1927.

McCormick, Richard P. *The Second American Party System: Party Formation in the Jacksonian Era.* Chapel Hill: University of North Carolina Press, 1966.

McCurry, Stephanie. *Masters of Small Worlds: Yeoman Households, Gender*

Relations, and the Political Culture of the Antebellum South Carolina Low Country. New York and Oxford: Oxford University Press, 1995.

McDougle, Ivan E. *Slavery in Kentucky, 1792–1865.* Lancaster, Pa.: Press of the New Era Printing Co., 1918.

McElroy, John. *The Struggle for Missouri.* Washington, D.C.: National Tribune Company, 1909.

McLaughlin, Andrew C. *Lewis Cass.* Boston: Houghton Mifflin, 1899; repr., New York and London: Chelsea House, 1980.

McPherson, James M. *Battle Cry of Freedom: The Civil War Era.* New York: Oxford University Press, 1988.

Meigs, William M. *The Life of Thomas Hart Benton.* Philadelphia and London: J. B. Lippincott Company, 1904; repr., New York: DaCapo Press, 1970.

Mering, John Volmer. *The Whig Party in Missouri.* Columbia: University of Missouri Press, 1967.

Meyer, Duane. *The Heritage of Missouri—A History.* St. Louis: State Publishing Co., 1963.

Meyers, Marvin. *The Jacksonian Persuasion: Politics and Belief.* Stanford, Calif.: Stanford University Press, 1957.

Middlekauff, Robert. *The Glorious Cause: The American Revolution, 1763–1789.* New York and Oxford: Oxford University Press, 1982.

Monaghan, Jay. *Civil War on the Western Border, 1854–1865.* Boston: Little, Brown, 1955; repr., Lincoln: University of Nebraska Press, 1984.

Moore, Arthur K. *The Frontier Mind: A Cultural Analysis of the Kentucky Frontiersmen.* Lexington: University of Kentucky Press, 1957.

Moore, John Hebron. *The Emergence of the Cotton Kingdom in the Old Southwest: Mississippi, 1770–1860.* Baton Rouge: Louisiana State University Press, 1988.

Morgan, Edmund S. *Inventing the People: The Rise of Popular Sovereignty in England and America.* New York: W. W. Norton, 1988.

Morris, Christopher. *Becoming Southern: The Evolution of a Way of Life, Warren County and Vicksburg, Mississippi, 1770–1860.* New York and Oxford: Oxford University Press, 1995.

Morrison, Michael A. *Slavery and the American West: The Eclipse of Manifest Destiny and the Coming of the Civil War.* Chapel Hill: University of North Carolina Press, 1997.

Nagel, Paul C. *Missouri: A Bicentennial History.* New York: W. W. Norton and Co., 1977.

Neely, Mark E., Jr. *The Fate of Liberty: Abraham Lincoln and Civil Liberties.* New York: Oxford University Press, 1991.

Nissenbaum, Stephen. *The Battle for Christmas.* New York: Alfred A. Knopf, 1996.

North, Douglass C. *The Economic Growth of the United States, 1790–1860.* New York: Prentice Hall, 1961; repr., New York: W. W. Norton, 1966.

Oakes, James. *Slavery and Freedom: An Interpretation of the Old South.* New York: Alfred A. Knopf, 1990.

———. *The Ruling Race: A History of American Slaveholders.* New York: Alfred A. Knopf, 1982.

Oates, Stephen B. *Confederate Cavalry West of the River.* Austin: University of Texas Press, 1961.

Ohnuki-Tierney, Emiko. *Rice as Self.* Princeton, N.J.: Princeton University Press, 1993.

Park, Eleanora G., and Kate S. Morrow. *Women of the Mansion: Missouri, 1821–1936.* Jefferson City, Mo.: Midland Printing Company, 1936.

Parrish, William E. *David Rice Atchison of Missouri—Border Politician.* Columbia: University of Missouri Press, 1961.

———. *Frank Blair: Lincoln's Conservative.* Columbia: University of Missouri Press, 1998.

———. *A History of Missouri: Volume III—1860–1875.* Columbia: University of Missouri Press, 1973.

———. *Missouri under Radical Rule, 1865–1870.* Columbia: University of Missouri Press, 1965.

———. *Turbulent Partnership: Missouri and the Union 1861–1865.* Columbia: University of Missouri Press, 1963.

Parrish, William E., Charles T. Jones, Jr., and Lawrence O. Christensen. *Missouri: The Heart of the Nation.* Arlington Heights, Ill.: Harlan Davidson, 1993.

Peckham, James. *General Nathaniel Lyon and Missouri in 1861.* New York: American News Company, 1866.

Peterson, Merrill D. *Thomas Jefferson and the New Nation.* London and New York: Oxford University Press, 1970.

Peterson, Norma L. *Freedom and Franchise: The Political Career of B. Gratz Brown.* Columbia: University of Missouri Press, 1965.

Phillips, Christopher. *Damned Yankee: The Life of General Nathaniel Lyon.* Columbia: University of Missouri Press, 1990.

———. *Freedom's Port: The African American Community of Baltimore, 1790–1860.* Urbana: University of Illinois Press, 1997.

Phillips, Ulrich B. *Life and Labor in the Old South.* Boston and Toronto: Little, Brown and Co., 1929; repr., 1963.

Potter, David M. *The Impending Crisis, 1848–1861.* New York: Harper and Row, 1976.

Power, Richard Pyle. *Planting Corn Belt Culture: The Impress of the Upland Southerner and Yankee in the Old Northwest.* Indianapolis: Indiana Historical Society, 1953.

Primm, James Neal. *Lion of the Valley: St. Louis, Missouri.* Boulder, Colo.: Pruett Publishing Co., 1981.

Prouse, Marcia Joy, ed. *Arrow Rock: 20th-Century Frontier Town.* Columbia: University of Missouri School of Journalism, 1981.

Rainey, Thomas Claiborne. *Along the Old Trail.* Marshall, Mo.: Daughters of the American Revolution, 1914.

Ramsay, Meredith. *Community, Culture, and Economic Development: The Social Roots of Local Action.* Albany: State University of New York Press, 1996.

Randall, James G., and David Donald. *The Civil War and Reconstruction.* Lexington, Mass.: D. C. Heath and Co., 1969.

Rawley, James A. *Race and Politics: "Bleeding Kansas" and the Coming of the Civil War.* Philadelphia: J. B. Lippincott, 1969; repr., Lincoln: University of Nebraska Press, 1979.

Reed, John Shelton. *Southerners: The Social Psychology of Sectionalism.* Chapel Hill: University of North Carolina Press, 1983.

Risjord, Norman K. *The Old Republicans: Southern Conservatism in the Age of Jefferson.* New York: Columbia University Press, 1965.

Rohrbough, Malcolm J. *The Trans-Appalachian Frontier: People, Societies, and Institutions, 1775–1850.* New York: Oxford University Press, 1978; repr., Belmont, Calif.: Wadsworth Publishing Company, 1990.

Roland, Charles P. *The Confederacy.* Chicago: University of Chicago Press, 1960.

Rombauer, Robert J. *The Union Cause in St. Louis in 1861.* St. Louis: Nixon-Jones Printing Co., 1909.

Ryle, Walter H. *Missouri: Union or Secession.* Nashville, Tenn.: George Peabody College for Teachers, 1931.

Saxton, Alexander. *The Rise and Fall of the White Republic: Class Politics and Mass Culture in Nineteenth Century America.* London and New York: Verso, 1990.

Schlesinger, Arthur M., Jr. *The Age of Jackson.* Boston and Toronto: Little, Brown and Co., 1945.

Scott, James C. *The Moral Economy of the Peasant.* New Haven: Yale University Press, 1976.

SenGupta, Gunja. *For God and Mammon: Evangelicals and Entrepreneurs, Masters and Slaves in Territorial Kansas, 1854–1860.* Athens: University of Georgia Press, 1996.

Shalhope, Robert E. *John Taylor of Caroline: Pastoral Republican.* Columbia: University of South Carolina Press, 1980.

———. *Sterling Price: Portrait of a Southerner.* Columbia: University of Missouri Press, 1971.

Shea, William L., and Earl J. Hess. *Pea Ridge: Civil War Campaign in the West*. Chapel Hill: University of North Carolina Press, 1995.

Sheehan, Bernard. *Savagism and Civility: Indians and Englishmen in Colonial Virginia*. Cambridge and New York: Cambridge University Press, 1980.

Smith, Edward C. *The Borderland in the Civil War*. New York: Macmillan, 1927.

Smith, Elbert B. *Magnificent Missourian: The Life of Thomas Hart Benton*. Philadelphia: J. B. Lippincott, 1958.

Smith, William E. *The Francis Preston Blair Family in Politics*. 2 vols. New York: Macmillan Co., 1933; repr., New York: Da Capo Press, 1969.

Snead, Thomas L. *The Fight for Missouri from the Election of Lincoln to the Death of Lyon*. New York: Charles Scribner's Sons, 1886.

Stewart, James Brewer. *Holy Warriors: The Abolitionists and American Slavery*. New York: Hill and Wang, 1976.

Summers, Mark W. *The Plundering Generation: Corruption and the Crisis of the Union, 1849–1861*. New York: Oxford University Press, 1987.

Swierenga, Robert. *Pioneers and Profits: Land Speculation on the Iowa Frontier*. Ames: Iowa State University Press, 1965.

Switzler, William F. *Illustrated History of Missouri from 1541 to 1877*. 5 vols. St. Louis: C. R. Barns, 1879.

Thelen, David. *Paths of Resistance: Tradition and Dignity in Industrializing Missouri*. New York and Oxford: Oxford University Press, 1986.

Tise, Larry E. *Pro-Slavery: A History of the Defense of Slavery in America, 1701–1840*. Athens: University of Georgia Press, 1987.

Trexler, Harrison A. *Slavery in Missouri 1804–1865*. Baltimore: Johns Hopkins Press, 1914.

Twombly, Albert E. *Little Dixie*. Columbia: University of Missouri Press, 1955.

VanDeusen, Glyndon G. *The Jacksonian Era: 1828–1848*. New York: Harper and Row, 1959.

Vandiver, Frank E., ed. *The Idea of the South: Pursuit of a Central Theme*. Chicago: University of Chicago Press, 1964.

Wade, Richard C. *Slavery in the Cities: The South, 1820–1860*. New York: Oxford University Press, 1964.

———. *The Urban Frontier: Pioneer Life in Early Pittsburgh, Cincinnati, Lexington, Louisville, and St. Louis*. Chicago: University of Chicago Press, 1964.

Walton, John. *Western Times and Water Wars: State, Culture, and Rebellion in California*. Berkeley: University of California Press, 1992.

Walzer, Michael. *Spheres of Justice: A Defense of Pluralism and Equality*. New York: Basic Books, Inc., 1983.

Ward, John William. *Andrew Jackson—Symbol for an Age*. New York: Oxford University Press, 1953; repr., 1980.

Webb, Walter Prescott. *The Great Frontier*. Boston: Houghton Mifflin, 1952.

———. *The Great Plains*. Boston: Ginn and Company, 1931; repr., New York: Grosset and Dunlap, 1957.

Weber, Eugen. *Peasants into Frenchmen: The Modernization of Rural France, 1870–1914*. Stanford, Calif.: Stanford University Press, 1976.

Widener, Ralph W. *Confederate Monuments: Enduring Symbols of the South and the War Between the States*. Washington, D.C.: Andromeda Associates, 1982.

Wilson, Clyde N. *Carolina Cavalier: The Life and Mind of James Johnston Pettigrew*. Athens: University of Georgia Press, 1990.

Woodward, Ashbel. *Life of General Nathaniel Lyon*. Hartford, Conn.: Case, Lockwood and Co., 1862.

Woodward, C. Vann. *The Burden of Southern History*. Baton Rouge: Louisiana State University, 1960; repr., New York: Mentor Books, 1969.

———. *Reunion and Reaction: The Compromise of 1877 and the End of Reconstruction*. Boston: Little, Brown and Co., 1951.

Wooster, Ralph A. *The People in Power: Courthouse and Statehouse in the Lower South, 1850–1860*. Knoxville: University of Tennessee Press, 1969.

———. *Politicians, Planters and Plain Folk: Courthouse and Statehouse in the Upper South, 1850–1860*. Knoxville: University of Tennessee Press, 1969.

Wright, Louis B. *Culture on the Moving Frontier*. Bloomington: Indiana University Press, 1955; repr., New York: Harper and Row, 1961.

Wrobel, David M. *The End of American Exceptionalism: Frontier Anxiety from the Old West to the New Deal*. Lawrence: University Press of Kansas, 1993.

Wyatt-Brown, Bertram. *Southern Honor: Ethics and Behavior in the Old South*. New York: Oxford University Press, 1982.

———. *Yankee Saints and Southern Sinners*. Baton Rouge: Louisiana State University Press, 1985.

Wyman, Mark. *Immigrants in the Valley: Irish, Germans, and Americans in the Upper Mississippi Country, 1830–1860*. Chicago: Nelson-Hall, 1984.

ACKNOWLEDGMENTS

I am a debtor. Writing books makes unavoidable this not unpleasant fact. In this case at least, and despite Thomas Jefferson's admonitions, debt does not rob one of his or her liberty. Rather, by incurring these particular debts, I have been afforded freedoms upon which I could not hope to place value, despite the restrictions that such writing demands. As I undertook them cheerfully, so do I repay them, if impecuniously.

Missouri researchers are blessed with three of the finest repositories I have run across in numerous excursions throughout the country, whether its holdings or the efficiency of its administration. Dr. James Goodrich at the State Historical Society of Missouri made available a research grant from the Richard L. Brownlee Fund, which was instrumental in my spending large blocks of time in Columbia. Diane Ayotte and the staff of the Western Historical Manuscripts Collection—an adjunct to the State Historical Society—offered cheerful assistance despite endless requests. While there, I became acquainted with Dennis Boman, an indefatigable researcher, who assisted me by generously providing primary source documents from his dissertation research on Abiel Leonard. Lynn Morrow, Joan Kiso, and Shelly Crouteau at the Missouri State Archives went well beyond the call of duty to supply me with materials, even mailing them to me after frantic phoned or e-mailed requests. The staff of the Missouri Historical Society suffered similarly, whether for manuscripts or photographs, with equal good humor. Clearly, the Missouri repositories have adopted the best of the state's Kentucky heritage, for I found in Missouri's mother state an equally pleasant and fruitful research experience. Jim Holmberg of the Filson Club and Trace Kirkwood (formerly of that fine institution) offered expertise and friendship, and I have spent many comfortable nights at Trace and Dana's Shelbyville manor. Lynn Hollingsworth of the Kentucky Historical Society and Claire McCann and William Marshall of Special Collections, Margaret I. King Library, at the University of Kentucky afforded more than their share of assistance in not one, but two projects. John Brenner of the University of Missouri Press provided expert copyediting, saving me from even more glaring errors than I might have made.

Institutionally, I have been fortunate to have many who offered assistance and support of many stripes at three different universities. At Emporia State University, Phil Kelly, chair of the Division of Social Sciences, and Lendley

Black, dean of Liberal Arts and Sciences, offered research funds with which I acquired photocopied materials as well as their unstinting support for my writing efforts and for high educational standards. Similarly, the Committee for Faculty Research and Creativity awarded me a summer stipend with which I traveled widely to gather materials. At Emporia State, my once-colleagues and yet-friends—Clay and Kim Arnold, Greg and Petra Schneider, Pat and Yvonne O'Brien, Phil and Linda Kelly, and Charlie and Diane Brown—provided a safe harbor for the discussion of creative endeavors, whether in the office or at their homes. At John Carroll University, Jim Krukones, chair of the Department of History, offered travel funds, while Matt Berg, David Robson, and Bob Kolesar offered collegiality and friendship during my visiting stint there. At the University of Cincinnati, my newest colleagues—Wayne Durrill, Barbara Ramusack, Elizabeth Frierson, Sigrun Haude, Ann Twinam, Roger Daniels, John Alexander, Zane Miller, Linda Przybyszewski, Willard Sunderland, Hilda Smith, and Mona Siegel, among others—have welcomed me warmly and made easy what could have been a difficult transition; several have offered close reading and trenchant criticisms of my work. I will be the better for being around them. Outside my own various institutions, I have received helpful criticisms from a number of other academics and professionals as well, all of whom read various drafts of the manuscript or presentations from it, including William Garrett Piston, Lynn Morrow, William Foley, Christopher Waldrep, Jason Pendleton, Gregory Schneider, and Clay Arnold.

One of the great pleasures of doing work on Missouri is the great friends I have made in the state, who inevitably made my lengthy stays too brief. Denny Davis opened the Jackson home north of Fayette and gave me a guided tour as well as a primer on small-town newspaper life. Mark Corriston of the National Archives, Kansas City branch, assisted me with several rounds of census research and offered ineffable good cheer whenever and wherever we met. Lynn and Kris Morrow, Ken Winn, Gary Kremer, John Bradbury, Jim McGhee, Jim and Sue Denny, and Bill and Nancy Piston made memorable my time in the Boon's Lick and the Ozarks. Similarly, scholars and friends throughout the country sustained me professionally and personally through the preparation of the book, including Jim McPherson, Emory Thomas, Bill McFeely, Kirk Willis, Bud Bartley, Ben and Neva Wall, Mark Plummer, Russ Duncan, Fitz Brundage, Ishmael Kimbrough, Ed and Jo Mitchell, Milton and Cindy Nesbitt, Tommy and Mandy Mitchell, Jason and Jodi Pendleton, and Lynn and Kris Morrow (the best innkeepers in the Boon's Lick).

Finally, I reserve my greatest gratitude for several individuals. Beverly Jarrett, director of the University of Missouri Press, along with Clair Willcox, the acquisitions editor, and Bill Foley, editor of the Missouri Biography

Series, allowed me the latitude to write the book as I saw fit, believing in my approach and inspiring confidence. Bill Parrish read and critiqued every chapter as I finished them (the second time he has done so for a book of mine) and generously and expertly guided me through the thicket that was nineteenth-century Missouri politics. Having known Bill for more than a decade now, I did not become fully aware of the great wealth he has provided to our understanding of the Missouri past until writing this book. For that alone, he warrants a place in the book's dedication; his friendship deserves far more. Finally, my wife, Jill, offers quiet acceptance of the numerous interruptions in our life occasioned by my other passion. No explanation of her place in the dedication is necessary.

INDEX

Page entries in **boldface** refer to illustrations